THE SCYTHIAN EMPIRE

OTHER PRINCETON UNIVERSITY PRESS BOOKS BY CHRISTOPHER I. BECKWITH

The Tibetan Empire in Central Asia

Empires of the Silk Road

Warriors of the Cloisters

Greek Buddha

The Scythian Empire

CENTRAL EURASIA AND THE BIRTH OF THE CLASSICAL AGE FROM PERSIA TO CHINA

CHRISTOPHER I. BECKWITH

PRINCETON UNIVERSITY PRESS
PRINCETON & OXFORD

Published by Princeton University Press
41 William Street, Princeton, New Jersey 08540
99 Banbury Road, Oxford OX2 6JX

press.princeton.edu

First paperback printing, 2024
Paperback ISBN 9780691240558

British Library Cataloging-in-Publication Data is available

The Library of Congress has cataloged the cloth edition as follows:

Names: Beckwith, Christopher I., 1945– author.
Title: The Scythian empire : Central Eurasia and the birth of the classical age from Persia to China / Christopher I. Beckwith.
Description: Princeton : Princeton University Press, [2022] | Includes bibliographical references and index.
Identifiers: LCCN 2022006736 (print) | LCCN 2022006737 (ebook) | ISBN 9780691240534 (hardback) | ISBN 9780691240541 (ebook)
Subjects: LCSH: Scythians—History. | Nomads—Asia, Central—History. | Civilization, Ancient. | Asia, Central—Civilization. | BISAC: HISTORY / Ancient / General | HISTORY / Russia & the Former Soviet Union
Classification: LCC DK34.S4 B43 2022 (print) | LCC DK34.S4 (ebook) | DDC 939/.51—dc23/eng/20220601
LC record available at https://lccn.loc.gov/2022006736
LC ebook record available at https://lccn.loc.gov/2022006737

Editorial: Rob Tempio and Chloe Coy
Production Editorial: Mark Bellis
Jacket/Cover Design: Katie Osborne
Production: Erin Suydam
Publicity: Alyssa Sanford and Carmen Jimenez

Jacket/Cover Credit: isolated vector illustration. Running Scythian warrior with bow and arrow. Ancient Greek decor. Black and white silhouette by Olena / Adobe Stock

This book has been composed in Arno Pro

Printed in the United States of America

CONTENTS

ILLUSTRATIONS

DIAGRAMS & TABLES

PREFACE

This book is about the earliest historical Central Eurasian steppe people, the Scythians, including their Scythian-speaking relatives the Cimmerians, both in Central Eurasia and among the ancient Persians and others in the West as well as among the Chinese and others in the East.

The Scythian Empire covered a vast territory and the ruling Scythians interacted with subject peoples in much the same way in each place, so the Scythian heritage lived on in regions far from each other which long remained out of direct contact with the rest of the world. It is thus perhaps no one's fault that the connections among them have been so completely overlooked. I have aimed to rectify the situation and show what the Scythians accomplished. While working on the book I discovered many other notable, even exciting, things that have also been widely missed. Sometimes previous writers already touched on them, but their findings have been lost in a sea of scholarship from one or another perspective, while other things seem not to have been noticed at all by anyone before.

Partly because of the vicissitudes of history, in which earlier periods are less well supported by good data than more recent periods, shifts in scholarly interests have occurred over time and space. Work on the Scythians, the Medes, and the first (Achaemenid) Persian Empire, as well as the first (Ch'in) Chinese Empire, among other related topics, is thus extremely spotty. The Scythians are today almost exclusively the province of archaeology and art, along with some historical anthropology and sociology. Much of the writing on them is quite negative in tone. The Scythians are roundly condemned, often in terms that are unacceptable today for a living people, and the idea that the Scythians actually established anything resembling an empire is beyond imagining for most writers. Many have argued that the (Scytho-)Mede Empire is a fiction. The Ch'in Empire remains one of the least studied and least understood topics in Chinese history. And the Achaemenid Persian Empire is a major topic for several fields, but much of what has been written even recently about its foundations is based more on traditional beliefs than on good data and analysis.

In addition, the topics and associated data that archaeologists, historians, Iranicists, and Sinologists think are important have received quite a lot of attention, while those that they consider unimportant have languished, or they have been completely ignored, so that these topics are not much more advanced than they were half a century or more ago. This is especially true of almost anything related to the languages. Although there are linguists and other scholars who specialize in Iranic languages, linguistics as a whole is little known (and mostly avoided) by historians today. However, a great deal is actually known, or knowable, about the Scythian language, so we have more good hard data for Scythian history than it seems anyone ever suspected—more than enough to show that they founded the first true empire, and the biggest one for over a millennium, which stayed united for as long as most of the later and better known steppe empires.

Some Scythian-related topics have already been examined by many scholars, and are certainly interesting and important, and even well known. But I do not work in the biobibliographical approach and leave most such topics to others who are interested. Instead, I have chosen to focus on misunderstood or neglected topics, and especially fully unnoticed ones, which are therefore new, regarding the early Scythians and the Classical West Scythians, Scytho-Medes, and East Scythians (Hsiung-nu) and their relations with their neighbors the Greeks, Assyrians, Persians, Chinese, and so on. This history is connected to the later history of Central Eurasia and its relations with the peripheral peoples of Eurasia, on which my own previous publications largely focus.

Because of problems with the kinds of data and scholarship available, the many questions that need to be answered, my own limitations, and production issues, this book is organized in a somewhat novel fashion, with the most crucial notes retained as footnotes, and further details or lengthier discussion given in endnotes. The chapters are mainly topical, so the narrative threads in them sometimes overlap.

In addition, although I have been generously given extra time to write, the times themselves changed drastically during the writing, above all from a terrible pandemic. Because it restricted me and many other fortunate ones to home, I was often forced to make do with sources already available to me, preventing me from consulting many good studies new and old. That made the book more of a challenge than I expected when I began the imperial-sized task of writing it many years ago. It has also taken longer to finish. I hope my loyal readers find it worth the wait.

ACKNOWLEDGEMENTS

I would like to thank Michael McRobbie, President of Indiana University from 2007 to 2021, who very kindly granted me a research leave so that I could work full time on this book and a partly related book on Imperial Aramaic. In addition, I would like to thank then Provost Lauren Robel and Vice-Provost Liza Pavalko, Dean Lee Feinstein and Executive Associate Dean Nicholas Cullather of the Hamilton Lugar School of Global and International Studies, and Jamsheed Choksy, then Chair of the Department of Central Eurasian Studies, all of whom supported me for this leave. I am also indebted to our departmental secretary, April Younger, for help with many things; to the Indiana University Library, especially the Inter-Library Loan staff; and to Amy Van Pelt, Kristina McReynolds, and the other staff of Hamilton Lugar School Support Services for expert assistance with research funding and the acquisition of research materials.

I would also like to thank everyone who carefully read the manuscript during its long gestation and offered comments and corrections that have much improved the final product, in particular Jason Browning, Yanxiao He, Andrew Shimunek, Chen Wu, and the anonymous peer reviewers.

For assistance with various problems I am indebted to Brian Baumann, Matthew R. Christ, Yanxiao He, György Kara,† Fu Ma, William Nienhauser, Andrew Shimunek, Nicholas Sims-Williams, Matthew W. Stolper, Nicholas Vogt, Michael L. Walter, and Chen Wu, and for valuable discussions, Nicola Di Cosmo, Yanxiao He, and Timothy Taylor, among many others.

I am grateful to Leonard Van der Kuijp for inviting me to give the 2016 Richard N. Frye Memorial Lecture at Harvard University, entitled

"The Scythians, the Medes, and Cyrus the Great", on April 18, 2016. It is the first major step I took toward the writing of this book, and is ultimately behind Chapters 2 and 3.

The gist of most of the Prologue was first presented in a lecture entitled "The Scythians and the Persian Empire at the Onset of the Classical Age", given at Indiana University on September 19, 2019.

Chapter 4 derives in part from a long article, "The Earliest Chinese Words for 'the Chinese': The Phonology, Meaning, and Origin of the Epithet *Ḥarya ~ Ārya* in East Asia", published in 2016 in *Journal Asiatique*. I would like to thank the editors for their kind permission to reuse some of it. The full article contains texts and much other material that is not included here.

What became parts of Chapters 5 and 6 were presented in a lecture entitled "The Language of Zoroaster in the Scythian and Persian Empires", given at Indiana University on March 4, 2020.

The genesis of Chapter 7 was in an article, "On the Ethnolinguistic Identity of the Hsiung-nu", published in 2018, and a lecture entitled "The Scythian Language of the Hsiung-Nu in Mongolia and North China" given at the Oriental Library (Toyo Bunko) in Tokyo, June 9, 2019. I would like to thank Hiroaki Endo and Yoshio Saito for their kind invitation, and as always, Tatsuo Nakami for his generous hospitality.

The kernel of Chapter 8 was presented in a lecture entitled "The Three Ecbatanas and the Silk Road" in the second Indiana University–Peking University Workshop, "The Silk Road: Between Central Eurasia and China", in Bloomington, March 23–24, 2018.

Much of the Epilogue grew out of a lecture entitled "Scythian Philosophy: Or, Was There a Classical Age of Eurasia after All?" given at Indiana University on March 4, 2020, and again, slightly revised, as "Scythian Philosophy and the Classical Age", given online at Università degli Studi di Napoli "L'Orientale" on October 7, 2020. I would like to thank Jamsheed Choksy, Tommaso Trevisano, and Andrew Shimunek for help with the organization of these lectures.

I am greatly indebted to Fereydoun Rostam and Keyvan Mahmoudi of the University of Tehran for their beautiful, easy-to-use "Kakoulookiam" font for Old Persian cuneiform, which they have posted for free on the internet. It is a valuable contribution to Old Persian studies.

Among the sources used for the illustrations, I would particularly like to thank Jona Lendering, whose Livius.org website has made available much informed material on the ancient empires and their cultural artifacts; Karen Radner of Ludwig-Maximilians-Universität München; Anastasia Mikliaeva of the Hermitage; Robbie Siegel of Art Resource, Inc.; and Anthony Deprez, of The Avantiques Collection, for their efficient, friendly help with my permission requests.

In view of the heavy use I have made of sources available on the internet during the pandemic, I would like to express my gratitude to all of the individuals and institutions who have generously made them freely accessible to the public. Without this tremendous help my book would be very much poorer.

I especially would like to thank my editor, Rob Tempio, and production editor, Mark Bellis, and all the staff at Princeton University Press for their kind support, and for the beautiful finished volume. Above all, I thank my wife Inna, and Natasha and Laura, for giving me extra time to work on this book.

TERMINOLOGY

EURASIA is a geographical term. It means "the continent of *Europe-and-Asia*", that is, one large unbroken stretch of land, like *Africa, South America, North America, Australia,* and *Antarctica*. The word *Eurasia* thus does not refer to some vague sub-region between Europe and Asia (and the word *Eurasian* does *not* refer to a mixture of Europeans and Asians). Eurasia means the whole Eurasian continent, from the Atlantic Ocean to the Pacific Ocean, from the Arctic Ocean to the Indian Ocean. As far as physical geography is concerned, "Europe" is not actually a continent at all, nor is "Asia". They are both parts of one and the same physical continent, *Eurasia,* one entire continent that includes all of Europe and all of Asia.

CENTRAL EURASIA is the huge world region surrounded by Europe on the west, the Near East on the southwest, South Asia and Southeast Asia on the south, East Asia in the east, and the Arctic in the north. From earliest Antiquity down to early Modern times, Central Eurasia had a complex mixture of animal husbandry, agriculture, and urban cultures dominated by steppe zone animal herders and great Central Asian cities. Today 'Central Eurasia' still exists, but unlike '(Western) Europe', '(East) Asia', etc., schoolchildren are not taught about it, and most scholars seem not to have learned anything about the region. Central Eurasia today includes independent Mongolia, Kazakhstan, Kyrgyzstan, Tajikistan, Uzbekistan, Turkmenistan, and Afghanistan, as well as autonomous East Turkistan ("Xinjiang"), Tibet, Inner Mongolia, Kalmykia, Ossetia, Tatarstan, Bashkortistan, Sakha ("Yakutia"), and other realms and peoples, such as the far-ranging Evenki, all with their own fascinating languages and cultures, most of which are seriously endangered today.

CENTRAL ASIA is the partly urbanized, largely agricultural region in the southern center of Central Eurasia. It includes what is now northeastern Iran, almost all of Afghanistan, Turkmenistan, Uzbekistan, Tajikistan, and the Tarim Basin region of East Turkistan (now Chinese *Xinjiang* 'New Territory'). Most of Central Asia is very dry and depends on irrigation to be habitable. It is under much stress today because of human-caused climatic change.

The SILK ROAD is a modern romantic term for the premodern lands in between the civilization of East Asia and the civilization of Europe. Some reference is made to the existence of cities in Central Asia along the way, so as a result, the term has been used to refer to urbanized Central Asia *without mentioning it*. Other than for the romance (which I cheerfully approve of), the term is imprecise and best avoided.[1]

MEDIA is the name of a specific geographical region in Antiquity. In the earliest records it was extremely fragmented, with dozens of independent chiefdoms and many different languages, mostly non-Indo-European. The people of Media at that time are referred to as *Medians* in this book. During the period of Scythian rule, the Medians shifted linguistically and culturally to Scythian and thus became a united people. The traditional term for their Scythian dialect is *Median*. The sources do not distinguish between the early and later people of Media, calling them all *Mādā* or the equivalent, i.e., 'Medes', but in this book I usually refer to the new people, after their Scythian creolization and unification, as *Scytho-Medes*. I have attempted to make the distinction as clear as possible.

EARLY ZOROASTRIANISM is the term used in this book specifically for the system of thought presented in the Old Avestan collection of *Gāthās* 'Hymns' or 'Songs' of Zoroaster, as well as in the inscriptions of Darius I 'the Great', whose Behistun Inscription (dated ca. 519 BC) is the earliest actually attested source on any variety of Zoroastrianism.

1. See Endnote 1.

I follow Mary Boyce in taking the *Gāthās* to formally include only the parts in verse, thus excluding the *Yasna Haptaŋhāiti*,[2] which is written in Old Avestan, but in prose, not verse. It is now often included among the *Gāthās*, but besides being in prose it includes much distinctive later content that should not be projected back onto the system in the *Gāthās*. Early Zoroastrianism is to be distinguished from the religious system that evidently preceded it, Early Mazdaism, as well as from all later forms of Zoroastrianism.

IRANIC vs. IRANIAN: See Transcriptions and Conventions.

2. Boyce (2011).

TRANSCRIPTIONS & CONVENTIONS

Old Iranic

I generally follow contemporary Iranists' rendering of Old Iranic languages, with a few important exceptions explained in the footnotes and endnotes. When I have quoted other scholars verbatim I have retained their transcriptions unchanged, or have noted any changes I have made. Because both scholars and laymen now regularly confuse the terms *Iranian* and *Iranic*, with often disastrous results, I use the term *Iranian* only to refer to the modern country called Iran, its inhabitants, culture, and so on. By contrast, essentially following the usage of John Perry,[1] I use the term *Iranic* for the language family that includes Avestan, Median (Scytho-Median), Persian, Scythian, Sogdian, Old Khotanese, Ossetian, Pashto, and other related languages ancient and modern, previously called "Iranian".

Semitic

For Assyrian and Babylonian Akkadian I follow the system of the *Chicago Assyrian Dictionary* (*CAD*). For Imperial (Biblical) Aramaic I follow the transcription system used in my introductory Aramaic grammar.[2]

Chinese

It is still traditional in works on *premodern* Chinese culture to transcribe all Chinese characters as they are read (i.e., pronounced) today in Modern Standard Chinese (MSC), or Standard Mandarin. That is because

1. Perry (1998).
2. Beckwith (forthcoming-a).

the reconstruction of earlier periods of Chinese is still primitive at best and most reconstructions are controversial. I follow traditional practice and mainly use the "modified Wade-Giles" transcription for Mandarin, because it is the most accurate and helpful for historical purposes and is still widely used by scholars of premodern China.

Important Chinese items are first presented in the format: Wade-Giles transcription | Chinese character(s) | (Pinyin transcription in parentheses).

I have thus also often provided Pinyin system transcriptions for Mandarin for the sake of readers who have learned that system. However, it is crucial for readers to know that Pinyin values of the transcriptional Latin letters often have little or even nothing to do with the traditional value of those letters in most European languages. They do not correspond well even to the pronunciation of modern Mandarin and certainly cannot be taken to represent any premodern pronunciation of Chinese, except sometimes by accident. Pinyin spellings of Mandarin can thus be very misleading for a book on Classical Antiquity. The Wade-Giles system is much more accurate not only for Mandarin but even for historical work. Nevertheless, conversion tables can easily be found online and in many standard reference works for Chinese studies.

For *attested* Middle Chinese (MChi)—i.e., medieval forms recorded in foreign segmental ("alphabetic") writing systems—each is cited in the transcription system used for the language in which the form is recorded. *Traditionally reconstructed* (or HSR)[3] Middle Chinese forms are marked with an open star (☆), and are cited from major reference works of that tradition, given in abbreviation in each instance. Where no reference is given, the reconstruction is my own, using loanword data, data from attested transcriptions, and internal reconstructions (including HSR).

For Old Chinese (OChi), reconstructed forms—marked with an asterisk (*)—are cited based on my own strictly linguistic approach (i.e., chiefly using foreign transcriptions and loanwords) presented in many publications,[4] or on major traditional HSR method studies. In the

3. Historic Sinological Reconstruction. See Endnote 2.

4. Most recently in Beckwith and Kiyose (2018).

few instances where I give a completely new reconstruction, the relevant source materials are cited and discussed.

Other Languages

The traditional standard systems used by most scholars are followed, including the Hepburn system (ヘボン式) for Japanese, and the McCune-Reischauer system (매큔-라이샤워 표기법) for Korean. There is no standard scientific transcription system for Old Tibetan, so I use a conservative system that is still used by many scholars, and is followed in many of my publications involving Tibetan.[5]

The few linguistic terms that may be unfamiliar are defined, with examples, in the Index.

5. For example, in Beckwith (2006).

SOURCES & CITATIONS

GREEK sources are cited according to traditional Classicist practice. If quoted, the texts are mostly taken from the digital versions of published editions available on the Perseus Digital Library website edited by Gregory R. Crane of Tufts University, which is cited in the text or notes simply as "Perseus". Translations from Perseus are given as "from Perseus" plus the translator's surname, e.g., for the Perseus translation of Herodotus, which is by A. D. Godley (1920), the reference is "from Perseus, tr. Godley". The full references are available on the Perseus site. For other published texts and translations, standard references are given. If otherwise unnoted, the translations are my own.

OLD PERSIAN sources are cited according to the standard practice among Iranists. Because most readers do not know the system, the codes used for cited inscriptions are given in the main Abbreviations list. In all cases the texts have been taken from the exact transliterations provided in the edition of Schmitt (2009), which have enabled me to set the passages in Old Persian cuneiform script as well as Romanized transcription. Translators are cited; otherwise the transcriptions and translations are my own.

CHINESE sources are cited in standard Sinological fashion. Texts have mostly been quoted from the Chinese Text Project (CTP), and so cited; other sources are cited in full. Translators are cited; otherwise the translations are my own.

IN GENERAL, quotations taken from secondary sources—mainly works by other scholars—are cited verbatim as given in the quoting source; if modified by me, that fact is noted. Most "second-hand" quotations have been checked against the original, but unfortunately, due to pandemic-induced restrictions, in some cases it was not possible to check the originals to ensure that the secondary source copied them correctly. Also, the inaccessibility of my own library and the Indiana University library down to shortly before the manuscript was finished meant it was not possible to check recent editions of source texts I could not find online.

ABBREVIATIONS & SYMBOLS

Akk.	Akkadian
A_2Sa	Inscription of Artaxerxes II at Susa 'a'
Ave.	Avestan
Bar.	Bartholomae (1904)
BC	Years Before the Common era (BCE)
BHS	*Biblia Hebraica Stuttgartensia*
C	consonant
ca.	circa
CAD	*Chicago Assyrian Dictionary* (Oppenheim et al.)
CAL	*Comprehensive Aramaic Lexicon* (Kaufman et al.)
CE	Years of the Common Era (AD)
cf.	*confer* 'compare'
CJK	Common Japanese-Koguryoic
CTP	Chinese Text Project
DB	Darius' Behistun Inscription main text
DBa	Darius' Behistun Inscription 'a'
dial.	dialect
DNa	Darius' Naqš-i Rustam Tomb Inscription 'a'
DPd	Darius' Persepolis Inscription 'd'
DSe	Darius' Susa Inscription 'e'
DZc	Darius' Suez Inscription 'c'

e.g.	*exempli gratia* 'for example'
EScy	East Scythian
ɣ	symbol for the sound 'gh', the voiced equivalent of 'kh' or [χ] in the name "Ba*ch*"
Gharib	*Sogdian Dictionary* (Gharib 1995)
HSR	Historic Sinological Reconstruction (the traditional Chinese reconstruction system)
id.	*idem* 'the same (as the preceding one)'
i.e.	*id est* 'that is' or 'in other words, . . .'
JDB	*Jidaibetsu kokugo daijiten, jōdaihen* (Omodaka et al. 1967)
k.	king
Kar.	Karlgren (1957)
lit.	literally
LOC	Late Old Chinese
LSJ	Liddell, Scott, Jones, *Greek-English Lexicon*
MChi	Middle Chinese
MPer	Middle Persian
MSC	Modern Standard Chinese (Mandarin) in Pinyin spelling
n.	name
ŋ	symbol for the velar nasal, the sound *ng* in English "thi*ng*", "so*ng*", etc.
NPer	New Persian
OAkk	Old Akkadian
OAve	Old Avestan
OChi	Old Chinese
OCS	Old Church Slavonic
OInd	Old Indic
OJpn	Old Japanese
OPer	Old Persian

OTDO	Old Tibetan Documents Online
OTib	Old Tibetan
p.c.	personal communication
PIE	Proto-Indo-European
PJpn	Proto-Japanese
Pul.	Pulleyblank (1991a)
q.v.	*quod vide* '(on/for) which, see . . .'
r.	reign, reigned
Rus.	Russian
Sch.	Schmitt (2014)
Scy.	Scythian
Sog.	Sogdian
Sta.	Starostin (1989)
Tak.	Takata (1988)
Tav.	Tavernier (2007)
tr.	translated by
V	vowel
w	western
WScy	West Scythian
χ	symbol for the *unvoiced* sound 'kh' in Greek, written 'ch' in Latin and in German (e.g., "Ba*ch*")
XPf	Xerxes' Persepolis Inscription 'f'
XPh	Xerxes' Persepolis Inscription 'h' (the "*Daiva* Inscription")
Y.	Yasna
YAve	Young Avestan

*	Marks any normal linguistic reconstruction
☆	Marks a traditional (HSR-type) Middle Chinese reconstruction[1]
$<$	Marks direction of internal derivation *from*, e.g.: $x < y$ ("x *derives from* y")
$>$	Marks direction of internal derivation *to*, e.g.: $y > x$ ("y *becomes* x")
←	Marks direction of loaning *from*, e.g.: English *sashimi* ← Japanese *sashimi*
→	Marks direction of loaning *to*, e.g.: English *baby carrot* → Japanese *bebīkyarotto*
δ	symbol for the sound '*th*' in English *th*e, *th*at, fa*th*er, ei*th*er, etc.
θ	symbol for the sound '*th*' in English *th*ink, *th*ought, *th*under, e*th*er, etc.

1. See Endnote 3.

THE SCYTHIAN EMPIRE

S
C
Y
Danube R.
Borysthenes R.
Western (Pontic) Steppe
Bilsk
Tanaïs (Don) R.
Olbia
Mediterranean Sea
Black Sea
Panticapaeum
Azov Sea
North Caucasus Steppe
Itil (Volga) R.
LYDIA
CAPPADOCIA
Anatolia
Central Asia
Caucasus Mts.
URARTIA
ASSYRIA
Caspian Sea
Jaxartes R.
KHWARIZMIA
Ascalon
Jerusalem
EGYPT
JUDAH
Euphrates R.
Nile R.
Tigris R.
Agamatāna (Ecbatana)
MEDIA
HYRCANIA
Oxus R.
SOGDIANA
PARTHIA
Bactra
ELAM
HARAIVA
BACTRIA
PĀRSA
Western
GANDHĀR
ARACHOSIA
Persian Gulf
Indus R.
URARTIA
Caspian Sea
Zagros Mts.
Harrān
ASSYRIA
Nineveh
Aššur
Arrapḫa
Ragā
Agamatāna (Ecbatana)
Euphrates R.
Sūḫu
Mesopotamia
Mt. Bagastāna
MEDIA
Tigris R.
Babylon
Susa
ELAM
Pasargadae
Anšan
Persepolis
PĀRSA
Persian Gulf
0
300 miles
0
300 kilometers
N
0
800 miles
0
800 kilometers

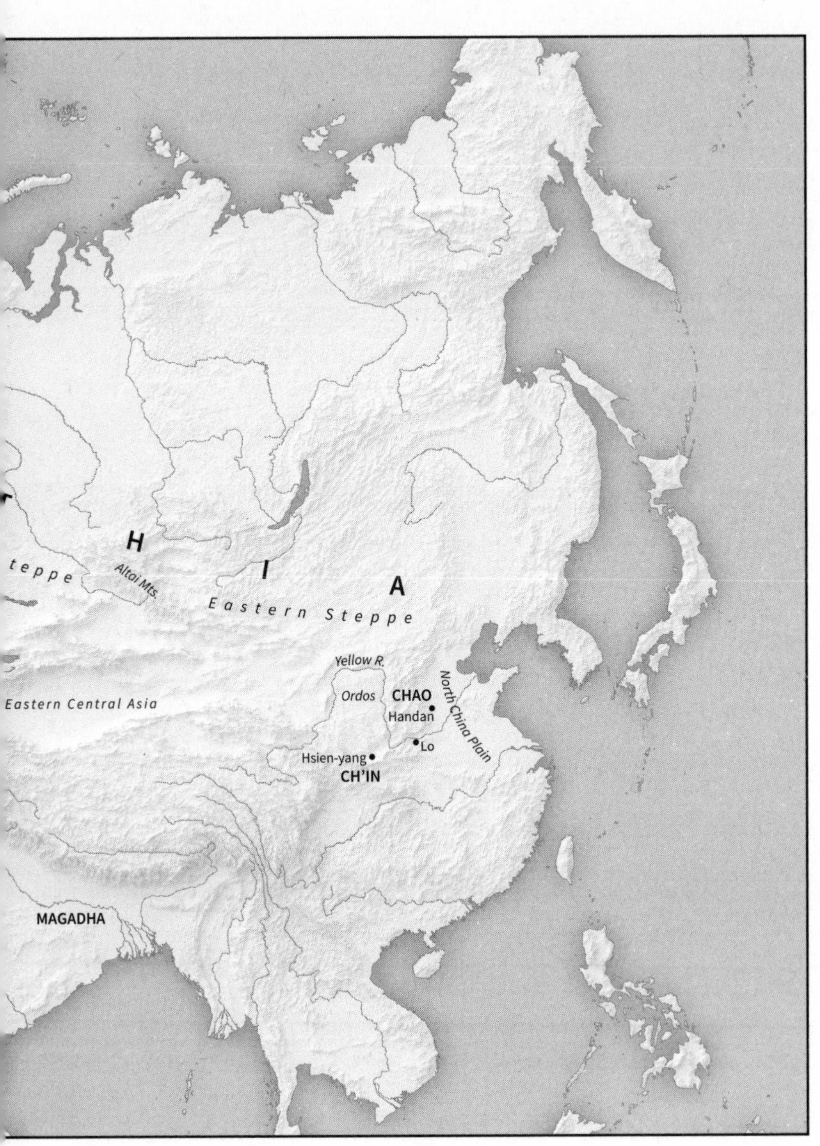
H
I
A
teppe
Altai Mts.
Eastern Steppe
Yellow R.
Ordos
CHAO
Handan
North China Plain
Lo
Hsien-yang
CH'IN
Eastern Central Asia
MAGADHA

Introduction

About 2,700 years ago, mounted Scythian warriors raced across the steppe zone of ancient Central Eurasia, southeast to the Yellow River and the region that became Chao in North China, southwest into Central Asia and Media, and west to the Danube and Central Europe. They created the world's first huge empire. Though their feat was largely duplicated by the Hun Empire of Late Antiquity,[1] the Türk[2] Empire of the Early Middle Ages, and the Mongol Empire of the Central Middle Ages, the Scythians did it first.

But did their empire last long enough to effect any changes? Did the Scythians contribute anything to world civilization beyond "better bows and arrows" and some rather spectacular gold sculptures? What about their language, religious ideas, socio-political system, and so on? Some speak as if there really was no actual historical Scythian nation at all. They speak only of *savage tribes* randomly attacking peaceful neighbors such as the Chinese and Romans, who are presented as "higher", civilized people forced to conquer the evil, *predatory barbarians* and take their land.

That is not an imaginary construct. It is the current dominant view in history writing on Central Eurasia, including on the Scythians. We

1. See Endnote 4.

2. Following convention, the spelling *Türk* is used for the early people who founded early medieval empires based in what is now Mongolia, and in particular for their ruling clan the Aršilaš 'Arya Kings' (Beckwith 2016b, q.v. Endnote 95). The generic spelling with *u* is used only in anglicized forms or for later Turkic peoples, Turkish, the Turkic languages, etc.

have long been told that we cannot expect anything good from *barbarians*, who are traditionally defined as being barely human, worthless from the beginning.[3] Herodotus, the ancient Greek 'father of history', is often quoted for negative views on the Scythians. He says of Scythian rule in Media, "the whole land was ruined because of their violence and their pride, for, besides exacting from each the tribute which was assessed, they rode about the land carrying off everyone's possessions."[4] Yet he also gives other, very different accounts of them, some quite positive. In fact, he sometimes purposely presents several views or reports on the same subject, such as his versions of the Scythian national foundation myth. However, in other cases he contradicts and even argues with "himself" on the Scythians and many other topics. That does not show that he was insane (as has actually been suggested), but that his text has been altered by later caretakers of his book, the *Histories*, who argue back and forth with each other in it about different points. Most modern scholars treat the surviving Classical text as if it was essentially perfect (other than a few minor textual errors), despite being transmitted to us by scribes for most of the last two and a half millennia, so scholars are free to pick and choose between the many contradictory passages written by "Herodotus".[5] Not surprisingly, they have mostly preferred to follow *this* "Herodotus", who says bad things about the Scythians, instead of the *other* "Herodotus" who says mainly good or at least neutral things about the Scythians.[6] Unfortunately, we do not know for certain which passages the historical person Herodotus wrote. Nevertheless, the pernicious modern view of the Scythians as evil *barbarians* is not only wrong, it is so tenacious that it has supported the

3. On the continued use of the pejorative term *barbarian* and the ideas connected to it, see Beckwith (2009: 320–362).

4. Herodotus (i 106,1), from Perseus, tr. Godley. Diakonoff (1985: 108) follows this: "The Scythians seem to have merely plundered the countries conquered by them and levied contributions, being incapable of creating a firm state order of their own."

5. The text of Herodotus contains many clearly unintended contradictions and other known errors; it is hardly perfect. Such textual problems reflect the existence of non-authorial changes. See also Endnote 5.

6. See Endnote 5.

continued misreading of Herodotus and it has prevented recognition of the Scythians' remarkably positive impact on the development of culture in much of Eurasia in Antiquity.

In fact, the Scythian Empire is one of the least known but most influential realms in all of world history. We actually have more data on it now than in the past when most educated people knew more or less who the Scythians were, but today, other than archaeologists, very few scholars work on Scythians, and no one speaks about a "Scythian Empire". Yet as shown in this book, the Scythians, alone, created an unprecedented, stable, loose-reined government structure, "the Empire", best known from its Middle East satrapy, which ruled for several centuries, mostly rather peacefully, until the conquest of Alexander the Great, who continued that same government structure.

A few earlier studies have already proposed that the Scythians had a revolutionary impact on the Ancient Near East.[7] But how, exactly, did they have such an effect on an already long civilized world region, with great peoples such as the Egyptians and Babylonians and significant innovations of their own? If the Scythians were so great, why do old maps nevertheless *not* mark the vast steppe zone from the Yellow River to the Danube, 'Here there be Scythians'? What happened to the Scythians?

And those who are interested in East Asia might ask, did they have a similar revolutionary impact on the ancient Chinese?

This book answers these questions, as well as a surprising number of unasked ones that came to light while working on the original ones, including questions about the Scythian language and Scythian philosophy.

The Scythian language is minimally attested—under that name—from the early Scythian Empire migration period down to late Antiquity, when the regional dialects finally became distinct "Middle Iranic" daughter languages and developed written forms. Nevertheless, we do have some data. Significantly for history, the *geographical distribution* of the Scythian language, as attested in inscriptions, literary texts, loanwords, and the daughter languages, constitutes invaluable "linguistic archaeological" material that reveals many things about its long-gone

7. Most clearly and openly, Vogelsang (1992).

speakers, including where, when, and how they spoke it, and in some cases, what they thought.

Studying the earliest known teachers of philosophy, who were all Scythian emigrants living outside Scythia, unexpectedly reveals the specific philosophical ideas that produced the Age of Philosophy, the hallmark of the Classical Age.

The Scythians turn out to be more fascinating, creative, and important than anyone, including this writer, ever suspected. They were unlike any other culture of Antiquity when they started out, but by the time they were done they had changed the world to be like them in many respects. It is time to rewrite the histories and revise the old maps.

The descriptions of the culture and accomplishments of the Scythians and their offspring in this book are based mostly on hard data—ancient historical records, various kinds of language material, and visual evidence, mainly sculptural—that has survived from Antiquity. It reconsiders the key participants and events in the *traditional* view of ancient history. That view has largely reversed the attested directionality of the chief innovations of the Classical Age so as to attribute them to the age-old riverine agricultural civilizations of the periphery. Reexamination of the innovations shows that they came, rather, from Central Eurasia, thanks to the Scythians.

The Prologue surveys some of these major cultural changes that took place at the end of the Archaic period and beginning of the Classical period. They are attested in different kinds of data studied by scholars of art and archaeology, history, languages and linguistics, and other fields.

Subsequent chapters discuss the historical circumstances surrounding the spread of particular Scythian cultural elements both in Central Eurasia and, especially, in peripheral regions that were for a time parts of the Scythian Empire. The best attested such region became the Scytho-Mede Empire, which was expanded by Cyrus the Great and his son Cambyses, followed by the Persian Empire of Darius the Great. It was thus, more precisely, the Scytho-Mede-Persian Empire. Virtually the same developments took place on the territory of the early Chinese-speaking peoples in the region east of the great northern bend of the Yellow River, especially the Classical state of Chao (*Zhào*), and the first

Chinese Empire founded by prince Cheng (*Zhèng*) of Chao and Ch'in (*Qín*), better known as Ch'in shih huang ti (*Qín Shǐhuángdì*) 'the First Emperor'.

Because the Scythians were the first historically known people to directly connect all of the major regions that produced Classical civilizations in Eurasia, some of the topics covered in this book have been discussed in locally focused historical studies, including monographs, collections of source material, and individual articles, altogether providing analyses of problems and extensive bibliographies. The scholarship on quite a few such topics is vast, even when the subject is limited to a lesser known disciplinary field. In such cases this writer's goal has been at most to nudge the scholarly ship a little, to move it in the right direction. However, other equally important historical topics, especially those relating to what the Scythians themselves accomplished, remain largely unstudied and unknown. They have turned out to be the most important and interesting of all, and constitute the main subject matter of this book.

The often wonderful historical, artistic, and philosophical material that has survived, in many languages, tells us much about the Scythians, who achieved truly stunning things and set in motion the dawning of the Classical Age of world civilization.

PROLOGUE

Central Eurasian Innovators

By the late 9th century BC, Central Eurasian speakers of Scythian, an Old Iranic language, developed horse riding and shooting from horseback,[1] and about a century later spread suddenly across the entire steppe zone of Eurasia,[2] establishing an enormous empire.[3] Partly because of the Scythian Empire's brief unified existence, but mainly because of lingering prejudice against pastoral peoples, the Scythians are not credited with any contributions to world civilization, with the exception of better bows and arrows.[4] Instead, Herodotus credits many revolutionary changes in Ancient Near East civilization to the Medes, mainly to their first historical king, Cyaxares. However, close examination of these changes shows the Scythians were responsible for them.

The Innovations

At the onset of the Classical Age, between the historically attested appearance of the Mede Empire and a century later Darius the Great's accession as Great King, many major changes took place in the Ancient Near East and neighboring regions, including military, political, and

1. Caspari et al. (2018); cf. Cunliffe (2020), and for riding especially Drews (2004).

2. I.e., the continent including Europe and Asia. See Terminology for a description and explanation of the terms 'Eurasia', 'Central Eurasia', 'Central Asia', and 'Silk Road', all of which have different referents and connotations.

3. See Endnote 6.

4. Diakonoff (1985: 92): "Scythian arrows and probably all archery equipment were technically and ballistically superior to those earlier used in the Near East".

religious-philosophical innovations, as well as striking changes in material culture and language.[5] Some of these innovations were noticed already by ancient Greek writers, but they were and still are usually thought to be local innovations that originated among various Near Eastern peoples, while others are said to be primordial "Iranian" cultural elements shared by all Iranic-speaking peoples. And there are still more proposals.

Yet there is no hard evidence in the Ancient Near East for the most remarkable of these particular changes, or for any antecedents of them, until shortly before the 8th to 7th centuries BC, when the Cimmerians and Scythians are first attested by name in historical records in the northern Ancient Near East—precisely the area where the innovations first appear in the same records. No one seems to have asked *why* or *how* the assemblage of changes occurred, if any of them might be related to the others, or if they might have non–Near Eastern origins. At best they are left as random, unconnected events coincidentally occurring at about the same time.

For those who would know what really happened, the questions need to be addressed. The innovations attest to the crucial, revolutionary importance of the "new" people that introduced them, a people hitherto almost completely overlooked in the history not only of the Near East but of the entire ancient world outside Central Eurasia, including China. This chapter discusses seven Scythian innovations, using remarks in Greek and Old Persian sources as points of departure. Other innovations are discussed elsewhere in this book, culminating in the Epilogue with the dazzling Scythian contribution to philosophy.

New Advanced Weapons

Herodotus (i 73) says that when the Scythians ruled Media, they taught Median boys archery. A new, *unusually short*, recurved composite bow, or "Cimmerian bow" (see Figures 1 and 5), and arrows with "Scythian" bilobate or trilobate socketed, cast-bronze arrowheads appear in the Ancient Near East beginning ca. 700 BC, exactly when the Cimmerians

5. See Endnote 7.

FIGURE 1. Western Steppe Scythian stringing the Cimmerian bow (Kul-Oba bowl).

and Scythians appear there. Archaeologists rarely agree on much, but it is accepted that these are distinctively Scythian artifacts. They are part of archaeologists' famous "Scythian Triad", a co-occurring set of crucially diagnostic elements of Scythian physical culture, including distinctive Scythian weapons and attendant gear,[6] animal-style art, and

6. The clothing and weapons of the Scythians (Sakas) in Xerxes' army are described in Herodotus (vii 64,2): Σάκαι δὲ οἱ Σκύθαι περὶ μὲν τῇσι κεφαλῇσι κυρβασίας ἐς ὀξὺ ἀπηγμένας ὀρθὰς εἶχον πεπηγυίας, ἀναξυρίδας δὲ ἐνεδεδύκεσαν, τόξα δὲ ἐπιχώρια καὶ ἐγχειρίδια, πρὸς δὲ καὶ

horse harness,[7] found at Scythian sites across Central Eurasia from the 9th century BC on.[8] However, since the arrowheads of the historical "Medes" are identical to them, are the new weapons Cimmerian, or Scythian, or even Median innovations?[9]

When the Scythians learned how to shoot from horseback, they must have soon found that the arms of the longbow made it difficult to rapidly swivel around to shoot in different directions, especially over the rear of the horse, in a "Parthian shot".[10] So a shorter bow was better, but if it were made the usual way that a longbow was made, it would be less powerful. To solve such problems they invented the short, extremely powerful recurved composite bow traditionally called the "Cimmerian bow" and introduced it when they entered the Ancient Near East, along with their improved arrowheads.

Herodotus' story also indicates that the Scythians took Median archery students hunting with them. This was not hunting for "sport", but explicitly for food, Central Eurasian style—the *grande battue* hunt,[11] which was conducted like war and provided practice for it. Naturally the

---

ἀξίνας σαγάρις εἶχον. "The Sakas—Scythians—had on their heads tall caps, upright and stiff and tapering to a point; they wore trousers, and carried their native bows and daggers, and also *sagaris* axes." From Perseus, tr. Godley. His "dagger" is the *akinakes* 'Scythian short sword'. He does not mention the omnipresent Scythian invention, the *gorytos* bow-and-arrow case (noted below), which is regularly represented in ancient artistic portrayals of Scythians. See Chapter 6 and Appendix B for these items.

7. Kuzmina (2007). For discussion and references to the literature see Taylor et al. (2020).

8. So far the earliest known kurgan (burial mound) sites to be excavated (some ongoing) are in Tuva: Arzhan 0 (Tunnug 1), dated to the 9th century BC; Arzhan 1, also dated to the 9th century; and Arzhan 2, an unlooted and therefore unusually rich site now dated to the 7th century BC. See Chugunov et al. (2010) and Caspari et al. (2018), which gives a good overview, with bibliography, of the investigated Arzhan sites (six or seven so far).

9. Diakonoff (1985: 92); see also Endnote 8.

10. Assyrian bas-reliefs portray even late Assyrian kings shooting with a longbow on horseback. The question is not if it is possible to do that or many other things on horseback, it is whether doing so is difficult or effective in the heat of battle, i.e., not while one's heroic portrait is being painted on stone for the relief sculptors to carve. Certainly one could not easily and safely twist around to perform a classic "Parthian shot" at speed, with a longbow, while galloping away from one's enemies—especially without stirrups, which were not to be invented for nearly a millennium more.

11. Allsen (2006). The term refers to the use of encircling beaters who make noise to drive the animals of a wide region to its center, where they can be easily killed.

FIGURE 2. Western Steppe Scythian scene with Cimmerian bow and *gorytos* (Kul-Oba bowl).

Scythians used their characteristic weapons at that time. Their special bows and arrows themselves[12] are regularly shown being carried on the left side in a special Scythian invention, the *gorytos* (Figure 2), a combination bow-case and quiver.

12. See Endnote 8.

FIGURE 3. Mede in *bashlyq* with *akinakes* short sword, holding *barsom* (Oxus Treasure).

FIGURE 4. Scythian *sagaris* battle-axe, detail (Greek vase).

Their other characteristic weapons are known through Greek sources and loanwords into Greek, from archaeological excavations across their entire vast territory, and from bas-reliefs at Persepolis, where Scythians and Scythianized peoples are regularly shown bearing them. They are the *akinakes* 'short sword' (Figure 3),[13] worn on the right hip, and the *sagaris* 'battle-axe' (Figure 4), both also well attested in early Far Eastern burials of Scythians. All are designed for use by cavalrymen who rode and fought before stirrups were invented. The same applies to their new, fitted clothing (Figure 5).

The usual rhetoric is that the Medes and Persians *copied* these weapons from the Scythians, but that is not correct. All evidence—including Herodotus—shows that the Medes were creolized Scythians, or

13. See Endnote 9.

FIGURE 5. Scythian archer (Greek vase).

"Scytho-Medes", so their weapons were effectively native to them. The Persians were also partly creolized in the same way, though they remained distinct in language, as well as in many other respects, including their dress and weapons, which were identical to the Elamites' at the time of Darius I. Language evidence in Chapter 5 (supported by analysis of the royal lineages of Cyrus and Darius in Chapter 4) shows that the Persians had been dominated first by the early Scythians, and then by the Scytho-Medes, before Darius took over the realm and called it a "Persian" Empire in the monumental inscriptions he erected in Elamite,

Akkadian, and his own language, Old Persian. Nevertheless, by the time of Alexander the Great the Persians dressed as Scytho-Medes and mostly used the same weapons, as shown in Greek portrayals from that time. (See Figures 7 and 13 and Appendix B.)

Feudal Hierarchical Sociopolitical Structure

Under Cyaxares (*Huvaχštra, r. ca. 620–585) and his son Astyages[14] (r. 585–550) the Mede Empire is credited with having an unprecedented political system alien to Hellenic home civilization, such that although Herodotus (i 134,3) describes it perfectly, he struggles to understand it:

> Under the rule of the Medes, one tribe would even govern another. The Medes ruled over all nations (in their realm), but (actually) they ruled the nearest people to them, and those people ruled the people next to them in turn, *in the same way that the Persians accord honor*; for the nation was organized in a series of overlordships and mandates.[15]

Herodotus thus explicitly links the Mede system to the later Persian system, about which he says:

> They honor most those who live nearest them, next those who are next nearest, and so going ever onwards they assign honor by this rule: those who dwell farthest off they hold least honorable of all; for they think they are themselves in all regards by far the best of all men, and that the rest have only a proportionate claim to merit, until those who live farthest away have least merit of all.[16]

14. Schmitt (2011b), following other Iranists and Indologists, reconstructs the name as "*Ṛšti-vaiga- 'swinging the spear, lance-hurler'," but this is problematic; see Endnotes 10 and 117.

15. Herodotus (i 134,3): ἐπὶ δὲ Μήδων ἀρχόντων καὶ ἤρχε τὰ ἔθνεα ἀλλήλων, συναπάντων μὲν Μῆδοι καὶ τῶν ἄγχιστα οἰκεόντων σφίσι, οὗτοι δὲ αὖ τῶν ὁμούρων, οἳ δὲ μάλα τῶν ἐχομένων, κατὰ τὸν αὐτὸν δὴ λόγον καὶ οἱ Πέρσαι τιμῶσι: προέβαινε γὰρ δὴ <πᾶν> τι ἔθνος ἄρχον τε καὶ ἐπιτροπεῦον. From Perseus, corrected according to the Budé edition (Legrand 1932–1954, 1: 152). The translation of the last clause is a quotation from the rendering in *LSJ* online, s.v. προβαίνω. I am indebted to Yanxiao He for his perceptive comments on this passage, and for the Budé edition text.

16. Herodotus (i 134,3), from Perseus, tr. Godley. See Endnote 10.

Xenophon adds one important comment on the feudal nature of this system that recalls the better known Western feudal system of the Middle Ages:

> In times past it was their national custom that those who held lands should furnish cavalrymen from their possessions and that these, in case of war, should also take the field.[17]

These passages have not received much attention.[18] Most historians now say that Darius took over the pre-existing empire of Cyrus the Great, a Mede-Elamite, who had founded it by conquest[19] but simply left existing realms intact, thus inventing the Persian feudal system.[20] In other words, this striking imperial structure, a complete novelty from the point of view of the Ancient Near East, was accidentally built by Cyrus. Or as Briant argues, he inherited the Elamite system: "the kingdom of Cyrus and his successors owes more to the Elamite legacy . . . than to Median borrowings" and "far from being a 'nomadic and primitive' state, the kingdom of Cyrus, based on the Elamite model, was forged with administrative devices that evoke and presage the organization seen fully in operation in Fārs [i.e., Pārsa] at the time of Darius."[21] Jacobs presents an alternative: "Sound evidence is nonetheless extant to prove that major administrative complexes in Achaemenid times originated from earlier structures: Persia herself, Babylonia, Egypt, and Lydia. Analogous conclusions about Media, Bactria, and Arachosia impose themselves. . . . those major complexes are called *Great Satrapies.* They are in part still recognizable as blocks in the Bisitun inscription, although there the central areas of the older empires and their main provinces—Lydia as well as Cappadocia, Babylonia as well as Assyria,

17. Xenophon, *Cyropaedia* viii 8,20, from Perseus, tr. Miller.

18. E.g., Briant (2002: 66) cites the Xenophon passage, but does not mention the two passages from Herodotus. See Diagram 1 below.

19. He and his son Cambyses did *expand* it by conquering realms west of Iran and adding them to the Empire.

20. See Endnote 11.

21. Briant (2002: 27); the scare quotes are his. However, none of the realms he mentions were either "nomadic" or "primitive", including those of the Medes and Persians before Cyrus.

Media as well as Armenia, and so forth—already form standard units in the imperial administration, . . . [that are] referred to as *Main Satrapies*. A third level of administrative hierarchy, the components of which are . . . called *Minor Satrapies*, is recognizable in large parts of the empire, though not everywhere."[22] Briant's section "The Structure of the Median Kingdom" is based on Herodotus but actually omits the section (Herodotus i 134) where the feudal socio-political structure of the Medes and Persians is described.[23] Others start with Darius and note that he inherited the empire of Cyrus and Cambyses, but claim he radically restructured it.[24]

However, the father of Astyages, Cyaxares, had already overthrown the mighty Assyrian Empire. (See Chapter 2.) The Mede realm taken over by Cyrus—an event also recorded in Akkadian sources—was already huge, and after his and his son Cambyses' additions it was gigantic. When Darius took it over, it was many times the greatest extent of the former Assyrian or Egyptian "empires", which were tiny by comparison. The reason the Empire could grow so large was its relatively loose, typically Central Eurasian feudal hierarchical structure, which allowed a great deal of local autonomy—"freedom"—and thus considerable flexibility. However, the reason none of its heirs, whether Cyaxares or Cyrus (with one exception) or Darius, changed it is that the Empire's political-economic-religious structure as a whole was tightly interwoven and could not be changed. This was demonstrated by the disaster resulting from the religious changes of Cyrus and Cambyses. They clearly did not understand that because local "national God" cults legitimized local national rulers, i.e., independent kings, a single unified empire required a single ruler legitimized by a single God, as in the monotheism of Darius the Great described in his Behistun and other inscriptions.

22. Jacobs (2006/2011). Synchronically his analysis is correct, but see the discussion below.

23. See Endnote 12.

24. See the discussion by Jacobs (2011), who emphasizes the fact that "the administration was structured hierarchically" and that the satrapy list "remains essentially identical from the times of Cambyses until the early years of Xerxes I", precluding any restructuring by Darius, though as noted he considers Cyrus to have founded it by incorporating conquered territories unchanged, along with their subordinate and sub-subordinate rulers.

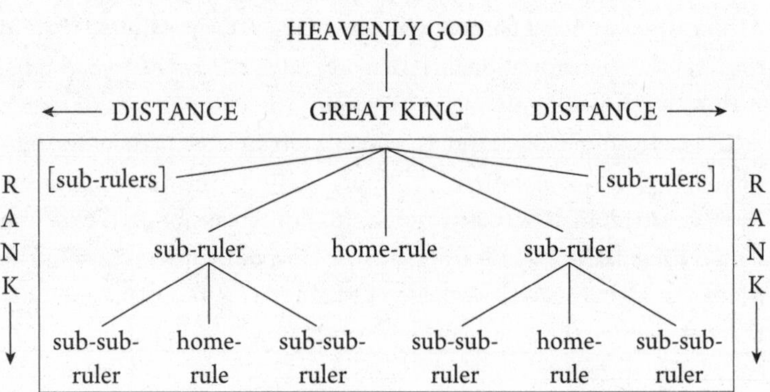

DIAGRAM 1. Scytho-Mede-Persian Imperial Feudal Hierarchy.

Herodotus's description (in i 134) of the Imperial feudal system is represented graphically in Diagram 1,[25] marking rank [his "honor"] vertically, and distance horizontally. There were three significant structural levels: Great King, satraps ("sub-kings"), and sub-satraps (or "under-satraps").

Although Jacobs too does not mention the above-quoted description by Herodotus, his summary of the attested structure of the Achaemenid Empire agrees perfectly with it: "The hierarchical structure meant that several Minor Satrapies formed a Main Satrapy, and two or more Main Satrapies a Great Satrapy. The central Minor Satrapy always gave its name to the Main Satrapy, and likewise the central Main Satrapy gave its name to the Great Satrapy. . . . The administrators of Great Satrapies were in each case newly appointed by the royal court".[26]

Could this ancient feudal system be Elamite, or Assyrian, or Urartian? Feudalism is absolutely unattested among the Elamites and other peoples of the Ancient Near East, so the answer to that question is negative. The originators must have been people from a neighboring region characterized by having a feudal political-economic structure. But people do not "borrow" or "trade" their political-economic structure and practically all the rest of their culture, including their language, from their neighbors.

25. This is exactly the Scythian system, down to details.
26. Jacobs (2006/2011).

Already Herodotus (i 134) saw that the Persians followed the earlier Mede system. Since the Medes have often been said to be "nomadic and primitive", as some still suggest, we must ask how they could develop such a sophisticated, and unprecedented, political-economic-religious system.

Here we must note that Herodotus says the Medes changed their name; originally they called themselves *Arias*, which meant 'members of the Royal clan of the Scythians.' How then did the Scythians develop the system?

At home in Central Eurasia, the Scythians were normally dispersed over a vast territory of open steppe, and moved regularly while tending their herds of horse, sheep, and cattle. In ruling their thinly spread out realm they developed a new political-economic system, feudalism.[27] It was a loose, hierarchical system in which the king ruled over several oath-bound subordinate lords who each ruled over part of the national territory and in turn ruled over several oath-bound subordinates and their sub-portions of land, all without chattel slavery.[28] This system also allowed rapid collection of an army of pastoralist warriors to repel invasions, which were a hazard of highly mobile steppe life from Scythian times on.[29]

Herodotus in addition describes the hierarchical structure of the Scythian steppe realm itself, saying it was divided into three *basileiai* (βασιλεῖαι) 'kingdoms', each subdivided into *archai* (ἀρχαί) 'realms', each of which were subdivided into *nomoi* (νομοί) 'provinces', with a *nomarch* over each of the *nomoi*.[30]

The Medes, the heirs of the Scythians, thus simply continued the Scythian imperial system, because they were Scytho-Medes. They spoke Imperial Scythian, as shown in Chapter 5, and in general followed

27. Known since the work of Vladimirtsov (1934) on medieval Mongol feudalism.

28. See Endnote 13.

29. However, despite scholarly misconceptions, the full-scale major wars with peripheral peoples began with attacks by those agricultural civilizations, whose people coveted Central Eurasians' land and wealth, as we usually know from the agricultural civilizations' own records, when they exist (Beckwith 2009).

30. Herodotus (iv 66); cf. Khazanov (2016: 180–181).

their inherited Scythian culture, which is archaeologically indistinguishable from Scythian culture.

A New Religious Philosophy

Perhaps the single most striking feature of the Empire under the Great King Darius I and his son Xerxes is their unprecedented, explicit belief in only one "Capital G" Great God, Ahura Mazdā, whom they call *Baga Văzărka* 'the (one) Great God'. He was the God who created heaven and earth—unlike the many "small g" gods or other Gods[31]—and established the one Great King, *χšāyathiya văzărka*, the King of kings *χšāyathiya χšāyathiyānām*, as ruler. It is significant that the word *văzărka*, though by form Median, is attested only in the Old Persian inscriptions, where it refers exclusively to the (one) great God (Ahura Mazdā), the (one) great King, the (one) great Earth, and the (one) great Empire.[32] Herodotus says of the Persians:

> It is not their custom to make and set up statues and temples and altars.[33] . . . But they are accustomed to mount up to the highest peaks to offer sacrifice to *Dia* ('Heavenly God'); and they call the whole circuit of the heavens *Dia*.[34]

This is radically different from Archaic Near Eastern polytheistic religion. The Great Kings Darius and Xerxes condemn the worship of other

31. I.e., those condemned by Jeremiah (10:11). The Great "God" is sometimes even given the title "God of gods", as in Daniel (2:47) אֱלָהּ אֱלָהִין (*BHS* 1386) *Ĕlāh Ĕlāhīn*, exactly parallel to the Old Persian title "King of kings" in the royal inscriptions. It has been said that the Assyrians, Urartians, etc., used this title for their kings much earlier than Darius, but none of their *gods*, however important, are ever called "god of gods". Even Ahura Mazdā, the one and only Great God, is never called 'God of gods' in Old Persian. He is sometimes called 𐎶𐎰𐎡𐏁𐎫𐏐𐎲𐎥𐎠𐎴𐎠𐎶𐏐 *maθišta bagānām* 'greatest of the gods', but the word for 'great' is the ordinary one, not 𐎺𐏀𐎼𐎣 *vazărka* 'the one Great'. The "one Great God" is unique because he created everything else, including the other gods. So *pace* Sch. 214, *maθišta* is not "praktisch Superlativ zu *vazṛka*- 'groß'."

32. See Endnote 14. On the Indicizing *ṛ* in the now popular transcription *vazṛka* see Endnote 117.

33. Herodotus (i 131,1), from Perseus, tr. Godley.

34. Herodotus (i 131,2): οἳ δὲ νομίζουσι Διὶ μὲν ἐπὶ τὰ ὑψηλότατα τῶν ὀρέων ἀναβαίνοντες θυσίας ἔρδειν, τὸν κύκλον πάντα τοῦ οὐρανοῦ Δία καλέοντες; from Perseus. *Dia* is Greek, a form of the word *Zeus*.

supramundane contenders for the unique position of Great God. They call such contenders *Daivas*, the "other Gods" condemned by Jeremiah and rejected by the Ten Commandments.[35] Darius and Xerxes say nothing negative about the many "small *g*" non-universal "gods" and spirits because they belong to an entirely different lower-order category, no doubt in a heavenly feudal hierarchy like the earthly one. Most scholars reject any possibility that Darius' monotheistic system is related to the Early Zoroastrianism of the *Gāthās*, claiming it to be an Archaic *Persian* belief inherited from the Proto-Iranians or even "Indo-Iranians".[36]

In Central Eurasia, warriors were richly rewarded by their oath-bound lord in this life and in the next life, which was believed to be like this life. The judge who would ensure all fulfilled their oaths was the one "Capital G" heavenly God, "Great God, Ahura Mazdā, who created this earth and that heaven, who created man, who created happiness for man".[37] Great God was the progenitor of the first king of the Scythians, whose lineage accordingly descended from God.[38] It was the only legitimate royal line among Central Eurasian peoples for many centuries.

One Eternal Royal Line

Cyrus II the Great, the conqueror of Babylon, was at least part Elamite. He gives his royal lineage in the *Cyrus Cylinder*, saying in Neo-Babylonian Akkadian that he is "NUMUN (*zērum*) *darium ša šarrūtim*", 'a descendant [lit., 'seed'] of an eternal royal line',[39] meaning that he is legitimate and has a divine background.[40] In the Old Persian inscriptions, Darius says he is "an Ariya and seed of an Ariya", where Old Persian *Ariya* means 'the legitimate heavenly royal line' or 'one belonging to the royal line'.[41] Is

35. Jeremiah (10:11).

36. See Endnote 15.

37. Darius the Great's Tomb Inscription "a" at Naqš-i Rustam (DNa 1–4), q.v. Endnote 78.

38. See Chapter 1. Similarly Khazanov (2016: 172).

39. *CAD* 21:95b, quoting the *Cyrus Cylinder* 5R 35:22; cf. *CAD* 3:116b, and *CAD* 21:89b: '*zēru* (*zar'u* in OAkk) s.; 1. seed (of cereals and other plants), 2. acreage, arable land, 3. semen, 4. male descendant(s)'.

40. See the discussion of the Foundation Myth of Cyrus the Great in Chapter 3.

41. See Endnote 16.

the idea Persian, then? Or, because the earlier statement of Cyrus is written in Babylonian Akkadian and agrees with similar statements by earlier Babylonian rulers—is it Babylonian?

The Scythians called the one legitimate Royal line *Ariya* ~ *Aria* ~ *Ḥarya* (these are the earliest attested spellings of the word in Old Persian cuneiform, Greek script, and Old Chinese characters respectively), all from Old Scythian *Ḥarya*.[42] The word is an adjective and is attested in many other languages which borrowed it in the very same meaning, also as an adjective, which is often used nominally in the sense 'the Royal one(s)'. Thus in addition to its main usage, referring to *people* who belonged to the lineage ('the Royal ones'), it is also used to refer to the *language* ('the Royal one') spoken by the people belonging to the lineage. Historically it is attested as being used by the Scythians to refer to their ruling clan, the "Royal Scythians" of Herodotus and the "Saka (Scythian) kings" of the Chinese histories, as well as many other rulers claiming descent from them down to the Türks and Togon at least.[43]

In his discussion of the mostly legendary early history of Media, Herodotus remarks that the earlier name of the country was *Aria*, and it was only changed later to *Media*.[44] Also, one of the two identifiable clan names in his list of the six clans of the Medes is the *Arizantoi* *Aria-zantu 'Arya-clan', the only one of the six with a transparently Iranic name.[45] In the earliest attested native Old Iranic language texts, the Old Persian inscriptions of Darius and his immediate successors, Darius says he is *Ariya Ariyačiça* 'an Ariya and seed [lineage descendant] of an Ariya', meaning 'a member of the Royal lineage and descendant of a member of the Royal lineage'.

One of the most outstanding Scythian words and expressions identified so far is thus West Scythian *Aria* ~ Old Persian *Ariya* ~ Bactrian *Aria*/*Ḥarya*, East Scythian *Ḥarya*, all forms of one word meaning 'royal

42. The Old Chinese word is recorded in an exact transcription in Old Tibetan, so I have omitted an asterisk. For detailed analysis of the word and related forms (Beckwith 2016a) see now Chapters 4 and 6.

43. See Endnote 17.

44. Herodotus (vii 62,1). His explanatory story is based on a folk etymology, but clearly attests the name. In fact, he has it backwards in a sense, since the Medians became Scythians (Arias) and thus Scytho-Medes.

45. Herodotus (i 101).

line, or royal one(s)'.[46] This word *Ḥarya*, transcribed in Old Chinese as 夏 or 華—today read *Hsia* (*Xià*) and *Hua* (*Huá*) respectively in Mandarin[47]—came to be used by Chinese speakers in the 4th century BC to refer to *themselves*, i.e., 'us, the Chinese',[48] meaning those who belonged to the legitimate ruling lineage, *Ḥarya*. Yet at the same time the expression *Ta-Hsia* 大夏 (*Dàxià*) 'Great *Ḥarya* ~ the *Ḥarya* Empire' referred to the easternmost extension of the Scythian Empire in what was then a frontier region where the steppe and the Chinese culture zone overlapped. That same term was later used to refer also to Bactria, as we learn from the account of the visit of Chang Ch'ien 張騫 (*Zhāng Qiān*) to that region in the late 2nd century BC. The Kushan king Kanishka the Great (fl. early 2nd century CE) uses *Aria* (written in Greek script) to refer to the rulers' Scythian-descended language there, which is today known as Bactrian.[49] The unique epithet of the legitimate royal lineage of the Scythians in these places is thus actually known. It is *Aria* = *Ariya* = *Ḥarya*, forms of one and the same word attested in numerous transcriptions from around Eurasia in ancient and early medieval times, all with the same specific meaning.

Functional Reorganization of the Army

Herodotus credits many revolutionary changes to King Cyaxares ([*H]uvaχštra,[50] r. ca. 620–585 BC), the first contemporaneously attested king[51] of the Medes. Among other changes he says Cyaxares "first organized the men of Asia in companies and posted each arm apart, the spearmen and archers and cavalry: before this they were all mingled together in confusion."[52] Most scholars, following Diakonoff, now claim that the Urartians and Assyrians made the innovation, followed

46. See the detailed presentation in Chapter 4.

47. See Endnote 18.

48. It often occurs with the optional Chinese collective plural marker. See further in Chapter 4.

49. On Bactrian see Sims-Williams (1988/2011, 1999–2012).

50. In Akkadian transcription, *Umakištar*; Akkadian does not have a *v*/*w* and uses *m* to transcribe it.

51. This section thus does not include the legendary *earlier* "Median" or "Mede" kings in Herodotus. They are discussed in Chapter 2.

52. Herodotus (i 103,1), from Perseus, tr. Godley.

later by the Medes.[53] But why would they, or anyone, want to make such a change?

To maximize the impact of a corps of highly trained mounted archers, the Scythians needed to separate the cavalry from the rest of the army, a move that is reflected in the ætiological story of the East Scythian (Hsiung-nu) prince *Bagatvana,[54] who is better known as *Mo-tun* in the modern Mandarin pronunciation of the Chinese characters that transcribe his name.[55] He trained his cavalry corps to shoot in unison at whatever he shot, with revolutionary effect.[56] The Medes, as archaeologists have long known, used Scythian arrows, and as Herodotus tells us they learned how to ride and shoot from the Scythians. So they had a powerful Scythian-style cavalry, the main military function of which was mounted archery. Not only to be effective, but to be able to fight as cavalry at all, meaning both together and at a gallop, it was crucial to separate the cavalry from other slower-moving, obstructing units of the army during battle. That resulted in the functional distinction of different army units described by Herodotus.

In general, scholars have followed Diakonoff.[57] However, the Cimmerians and Scythians necessarily made this particular innovation *in the Central Eurasian steppe* in order to maximize the power of their mounted cavalry archers.[58] It was only when the Cimmerians and Scythians entered Urartia, Assyria, and Media, where they used it to great effect, that it was actually introduced to the Ancient Near East.[59] Yet the Medians did not need to be "influenced" by the Urartians and Assyrians in order to acquire this innovation. The Cimmerians and Scythians dominated Media and its neighbors for at least a century in all, long enough to creolize the many unrelated and disunited peoples of Media into one

53. See Endnote 19. Cf. Chapter 2 and Endnote 74.
54. Old Iranic *Bagātvana* 'capable through God'; Tav. 140.
55. Mo-tun 冒頓. In Pinyin spelling it is *Modun*. Cf. Endnote 20.
56. For the famous story of his rise to power see Beckwith (2009: 5–6).
57. See Endnote 19.
58. See Drews (2004) on early attestations of mounted archery.
59. Cf. Endnote 21.

people, Scytho-Medes, who spoke Scythian and followed Scythian ways. The Scytho-Medes grew up as Scythians, riding Scythian style and shooting with Scythian bows and arrows—which they are documented as using, since their arrowheads cannot be distinguished from Scythian arrowheads. Media was famous in premodern times as the home of the finest horses in the Middle East. Careful study of the Akkadian sources has conclusively shown that the Scytho-Mede military, under the Medes' first fully historical king Cyaxares, almost singlehandedly overthrew the Assyrian Empire in the late 7th century, between 615 and 609 BC.[60] Thus, although Herodotus wrongly credits Cyaxares with personally innovating most of the new culture actually received from the Scythians via their rule and creolization of the Medians (a process he explicitly describes), the Chinese sources attest to the very same changes, also courtesy of the Scythians. Cyaxares thus simply *retained* the entire cultural package he inherited directly from the steppe Scythians, including the pragmatic Central Eurasian battle order.[61]

A New Type of Fitted Clothing

Herodotus says that the Persians "wear Mede clothing, considering it to be more beautiful than their own."[62] His comment is well supported by other Classical Greek sources. Aristophanes (*Wasps* 1135–1155) describes Greeks wearing fashionable new fitted garments "straight from Ecbatana", the capital of Media. A century after Herodotus, Ctesias gives a different explanation. He claims that the remarkable outfit was invented by Semiramis, a young Assyrian queen dated by Herodotus (i 185)

60. Zawadzki (1988) shows that the Babylonian scribes failed to be consistent in their attempt to distort the historical record in favor of Babylon. The records reveal that most of the campaigns were conducted by the Medes alone and the Babylonians had little to do with the overthrow of Assyria. See Chapter 2.

61. See Endnote 22.

62. Herodotus (i 135): καὶ γὰρ δὴ τὴν Μηδικὴν ἐσθῆτα νομίσαντες τῆς ἑωυτῶν εἶναι καλλίω φορέουσι; from Perseus. It is preceded by his remark (i 135), "Persians, the most of all people, accept foreign customs".

to the 8th century.[63] Ctesias says her outfit was subsequently adopted by the Medes, then by the Persians:

> She made herself an outfit which did not allow anyone to determine whether the person wearing it was a man or a woman. This clothing was suitable for traveling in the burning heat, while it protected her complexion, and as it was fluid and youthful, it let her do whatever she wanted. It was altogether so lovely that later, when the Medes reigned over Asia, they always wore the raiment of Semiramis, and after them the Persians did the same.[64]

These closely fitted garments with sleeves and trousers, and the close-fitting *bashlyq* headgear, were Scythian inventions designed for horse riding.[65] The trousers worn while actually riding were footies—one-piece pants with attached feet (like children's pajamas)—made of leather, as shown in the Persepolis bas-relief of the *Sakā Tigraχaudā* 'Pointed-cap Scythians.'[66] (See Figure 6.)

They are presenting footies and the *candys* as tribute and wear their eponymous "caps", which are simply a pointed variant of the *bashlyq*, the headgear worn by Scythians, Medes, and many others living in regions formerly ruled by the Scythians and their Scytho-Mede successors.[67] Such clothes protected the wearer from the horse's rough hair (like Western cowboys' chaps), and they also would not billow up while riding, or get caught in the bow. The *bashlyq* (which has different regional shapes) prevented the owner's long hair from doing the same thing. When not riding, they wore elegant cloth trousers and shoes. They loved intense colors, and their fabrics had beautiful patterns woven into them, as represented in Classical Greek portrayals.

63. Diakonoff (1985: 90). Herodotus was not far off, as the historical Semiramis' floruit is 811 BC.

64. Ctesias (*Persica* F1b); see Appendix B for the full Greek text and English translation, references, and further discussion.

65. For the possibly earliest preserved trousers see Beck et al. (2014).

66. The *bashlyq* is often called a "tiara" in the scholarly literature, but that name is drastically misleading, as it has nothing to do with what is *today* called a *tiara* in English.

67. Also, tomb figurines from Ch'in-Han period China show riders wearing footies of leather, for the same reason given above, and a stylized form of the *bashlyq*.

FIGURE 6. Sakā Tigrakhaudā Scythians bearing tribute of footies and *candys* (Persepolis).

After about a half century of Cimmerian and Scythian rule over Media, Urartia, Cappadocia, Parthia, and Bactria, the creolized Medes, Urartians, and others wore the same outfit and bore the same weapons seen in the dress of the nationally identified throne-bearers in the reliefs at Naqš-i Rustam (see Figure 15):[68] plain mid-calf-length tunic with round neck; belt with *akinakes* pending at an angle from the right hip and tied to that leg at the bottom edge of the tunic; trousers; shoes; *bashlyq*[69] with side pieces tied back. The outfits shown are formal *court* versions of the

68. The analysis here is based on the drawing by Walser (1966). See further in Appendix B.

69. For most of the figures the court *bashlyqs* and pointed *bashlyqs* are depicted as squashed down by the horizontal beam of the bas-relief's giant throne, but the headgear is still slightly different for each nation.

FIGURE 7. Scytho-Medes and Persians in court outfits and weapons (Persepolis).

peoples' national dress, judging by the Scytho-Medes' rounded *bashlyq*-derived headgear[70] and the Persians' upright crown-like hat (Figure 7).

They also wear shoes (see Figures 1 and 2); i.e., the trousers shown are not one-piece "footies" (see Figures 6 and 13). The Scytho-Mede outfits are identical to those of the Areian, Drangianan, and Arachosian (with the exception that these three are shown wearing heavy boots, with their trousers stuffed into the tops of the boots). The Scythians or Sakas are shown wearing the same outfit as the Scytho-Medes from the waist down; its distinctive feature is the elegant bordered mid-calf-length

70. There is a visible line showing where they are pulled back; the hanging ends are visible on the Mede.

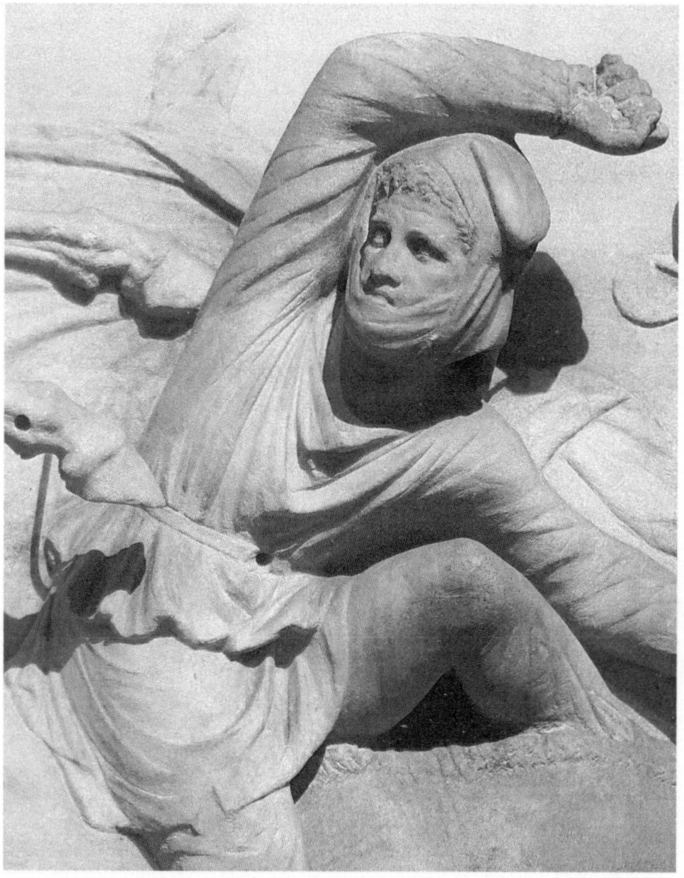

FIGURE 8. Late Achaemenid man in Mede riding dress (Alexander Sarcophagus).

tunic with crossed-over v-neck, and close-fitting trousers. (See Figure 5.) The Scythians were the fashion masters of their day.

Ctesias' story, even though it is not true, is important because it describes the *bashlyq* (see Figures 1, 8, and 15) and because it recognizes that the Scytho-Medes did not invent the outfit, which was characterized as being closely fitted to the body (as humorously presented in Aristophanes) and is usually shown in Greek art as skin-tight, though in late Achaemenid images it is shown as soft, and not tight (Figure 8).

FIGURE 9. Neo-Assyrian period Median tribute bearer to Sargon II (Dur-Šarruken).

In Antiquity and the Middle Ages, clothes usually marked national identity. The Greeks could wear foreign clothes as a fashion statement, but that worked only because people recognized them *as foreign*.[71] Thus, on earlier Assyrian bas-reliefs, the Assyrians and Medians are easily identifiable. The Medians are always bareheaded, with leggings, wearing a tunic shown as being half smooth fabric and half hairy animal skin or fur (Figure 9).

The Medians' outfit is thus completely unlike the classical Scytho-Mede costume in question here. The Assyrians wear unrelated clothes of their own (Figure 10).

No one from either people wears bashlyqs, trousers, etc. Thus the outfits of the Medians and Assyrians portrayed in the Assyrian reliefs of the late Neo-Assyrian period are unrelated to those of the Scytho-Medes and Persians in the Persepolis bas-reliefs a mere century later, and Semiramis did not invent them. Under the Achaemenids the Scytho-Medes and their former closely subordinate nations[72] wear the same court dress except for their distinctive variants of the *bashlyq* and tunic; from the waist down it is the same outfit worn by the Scythians, and the weapons are identical too (see Appendix B). Unlike the Scythians, Scytho-Medes, and former subject peoples, the Persians wear

71. Cf. Endnote 23.
72. Jacobs (2006/2011).

FIGURE 10. Neo-Assyrian period Assyrian archers of Tiglath Pileser III (Kalhu).

completely unrelated, highly distinctive Elamite robes, and bear equally distinctive Elamite weapons (Figure 11).

But two centuries later at the very end of the Achaemenid period, and in early post-Achaemenid times, the Persian clothes and weapons shown in Greek art are identical to Mede "riding dress", the outfit described by Ctesias (Figures 8 and 13).[73]

73. See Appendix B.

FIGURE 11. Medes in *candys* and Persians in Elamite outfit (Persepolis).

A New Language

The Old Persian inscriptions are full of loanwords from one or more different Old Iranic languages. Many historians today think there was no Mede Empire and the Medes are historically doubtful, but study of the inscriptions as well as study of the bas-reliefs in Persepolis—in which the Medes are omnipresent—led earlier scholars to conclude that the Medes were important, and that their language was the source of the many loanwords in Old Persian.[74] Was this "Median" therefore identical to the new language that had such a powerful impact on the Empire as a whole, including even Pārsa (Persis, now Fârs), the Persian homeland, where Persian was spoken?

The language data and ancient geographical sources show that from the Zagros Mountains of Media to the Hindu Kush Mountains on the frontiers of India, one particular language was spoken by most of the local

74. Meillet and Benveniste (1931: 7–8).

people and by the imperial administrators, but it was not Old Persian (though it was slightly influenced by that language), and it was not generic "Old Iranian" as some still say. Inscriptions, loanwords, and ancient writers confirm that one language was spoken in that region, and that it was *different* from Persian. But where did it come from, and who spoke it originally?

Because the Scythians came from the Central Eurasian steppes and settled in precisely these regions—Central Asia, Iran, and vicinity—they must be the speakers.[75] The language of the steppe Scythians has been said to represent in "*grosso modo* the stage of linguistic development of Avestan and Old Persian."[76] That is, it is an Old Iranic language of the Classical period. However, while Scythian is virtually identical to Avestan, it is sharply distinct from Old Persian, whether in vocabulary (comparing Persian—sans loanwords—to Avestan, Median, and Scythian)[77] or in full texts, as shown in Chapter 5.

One remarkable fact about Scythian is that the ruling elite of both the ancient Persians and the ancient Chinese used the Scythian loanword *Ariya* ~ *Aria* ~ *Ḥarya* 'royal, belonging to or pertaining to the legitimate royal lineage' in exactly the same way, both as an epithet for *themselves* (the rulers) and equally for their *language*. In Old Persian it is first attested in this usage in ca. 519 BC (in the Behistun Inscription), and in Chinese texts from the 4th century BC on. The word soon became the respective people's ethnonym in both places, and continues to be used in their languages as part of the native national name of Persia (*Īrān*)[78] and of China (*Hua* from Old Chinese *Ḥâryá*).[79] Adopting a loanword as one's national ethnonym is surely significant. The meaning of the word tells us that these peoples inherited the word from a ruling clan or clans who already used it for members of their legitimate ruling

75. See Terminology for *Central Eurasia* vs. *Central Asia*.

76. Schmitt (2003: 6).

77. There are many more than those already identified because some words do not have the typical "diagnostic" features of the Scythian-Median-Avestan language and are difficult or impossible to distinguish from Old Persian. See Chapters 5 and 6.

78. See Endnote 24.

79. See Endnote 25.

lineage descended from the God of Heaven. In Antiquity, in both realms, Heavenly God is said to have legitimized the Great King. The spread of this word thus makes good sense as human history.

The *Ariya* ~ *Aria* ~ *Ḥarya* 'Royal' language went with the Royal Scythians everywhere their warriors established Scythian rule and intermarried with the local women, producing creole Scythians who spoke Scythian (*Aria* 'the language of the Royals'), as Herodotus (i 73) tells us in his account of the Scythians in Media. The people of that country, he says, were previously called by everyone Ἄριοι *Arias* (Herodotus vii 62,1), 'Royals'. He also tells us that the Medes had earlier been ruled by the Scythians. The 'Royal' language of the Scythians and Scytho-Medes thus spread throughout the huge region of Southwestern Asia that the Scythians conquered and ruled in their initial expansion, and was maintained later by the Scytho-Medes' enlarged continuation of the Empire, and subsequently by the Scytho-Mede administrators of the Persian Empire.[80]

The "Median" language best known from many loanwords in the Old Persian inscriptions, and the Avestan language, which is attested in transmitted texts, are both dialects of the introduced Scythian language, as shown in Chapter 5. Another term for the language could be "Scythian-Median-Avestan", but the Mede material we have is linguistically the same as the Scythian material we have, with few exceptions, and both are the same language as Avestan, as shown in Chapter 5. No doubt one undifferentiated language, Scythian, was introduced by the Scythians during their initial expansion.

The later expansion of the Scytho-Mede Empire ruled by the Scytho-Medes of Cyaxares and his successors spread their *Imperial Scythian* culture and language even farther, so that it is attested as the physical and intellectual culture of most of the Persian Empire. This is the language noted later by Strabo (fl. 62 BC–23 CE), who says:

> The name . . . [of the geographical region] *Ariana* is extended so as to include [Parthia, Areia, Drangiana, Arachosia, and] *some part of*

80. See Endnote 26.

Persia and of Media, and [up to] the north of Bactria and Sogdiana; for these nations speak nearly the same language.[81]

In other words, they still spoke Imperial Scythian even in Strabo's day, though with more dialectal variation. Significantly, he says only *part* of Persia was Scythian-speaking.[82] That is because the Persians spoke a language, Old Persian, which was so different from Imperial Scythian that a monolingual speaker of one certainly could not understand the other, as shown in Chapter 5.[83] It is also striking that Old Iranic words which are demonstrably Old Persian both *etymologically* and *phonologically* (unlike Old Persianized loanwords) seem to appear less often as loanwords in other Ancient Near Eastern languages. In short, Imperial Scythian was the lingua franca and dominant spoken language of the Empire, not Persian. The Scythian language and its Imperial Scythian dialect and subdialects are treated in detail in Chapters 5 and 6.

Scythian culture did not spread by "influence" or "contact", not to speak of "trade" or commerce along the "Silk Road". These ideas, no matter how popular they may be, do not conform to the data. The zone of Scythian culture did not expand in any of the ways that many now think culture spreads. It spread beyond Scythia as a result of Scythian *rule* over large frontier areas at the edge of the steppe zone. That rule

81. Strabo (xv 2,8): ἐπεκτείνεται δὲ τοὔνομα τῆς Ἀριανῆς μέχρι μέρους τινὸς καὶ Περσῶν καὶ Μήδων καὶ ἔτι τῶν πρὸς ἄρκτον Βακτρίων καὶ Σογδιανῶν: εἰσὶ γάρ πως καὶ ὁμόγλωττοι παρὰ μικρόν; from Perseus, tr. Hamilton and Falconer, slightly edited. Briant (2002: 181) translates the second half: "For these speak approximately the same language, with but slight variations". By "some part of Media" not speaking the language, Strabo no doubt refers to Armenia (former Urartia) and several other countries that were counted as part of the Great Satrapy of Media. What is significant is that he *explicitly* excludes part of Media and at the same time part of Persia (Persis, Pārsa), the other part being the Persian-speaking one. The other regions named are thus known to have spoken the same language in Hellenistic times. See Endnote 27.

82. See Meillet and Benveniste (1931: 7–8) and see further in Chapter 5. Old Persian already has many Imperial Scythian loanwords in it, but Middle Persian has even more of them, including many specifically Zoroastrian words, altogether giving the language a heavy admixture of Imperial Scythian lexical material.

83. See Endnote 28.

produced creolization, both of language and of culture in general. The peoples of the new regional creolized cultures *became* Scythians, though they often succeeded in retaining their old local name and identity. The most outstanding example is the Scytho-Mede nation, the Medes, composed of the Scythianized and unified peoples of the many previously unrelated and disunited peoples living in the geographical region of "Media". The Persians, too, were first partly Scythianized by the Scythians themselves. Later, during the Persians' rule of the Empire, they indirectly helped spread Scythian culture into neighboring regions, increasing the territory where it was known and practiced, because they continued to use the Scytho-Medes as the administrators of the Empire. They clearly did this not only because the Scytho-Medes were experienced imperial administrators, but most importantly because they spoke the dominant language, Imperial Scythian—though the Scytho-Medes who ran the Imperial court must have learned enough Persian to be able to interpret as well. The Persians also retained Imperial Aramaic, a West Semitic language related to Hebrew and Arabic, as the usual *written* medium.[84] From the late Empire period on, Persian was again affected even more powerfully by Imperial Scythian, leading to the development of Middle Persian.

In short, what is now referred to as "Mede" culture or "Avestan" culture was in origin the culture of the Scythians, who had a powerful, revolutionary effect not only on Central Eurasia but on every Scythianized region across the continent of Eurasia as far as China, as will be seen.[85]

The following chapters give fuller treatment of the topics introduced in this Prologue, as well as treatment of additional key topics, some of which have long been controversial or ignored. They clarify the early history of the Scythians and their contributions which changed the world and led to the Classical Age, as shown in the Epilogue.

84. In the early Persian period under Darius the Great, Elamite was the most widely used administrative language, according to the distribution of bureaucratic documents found so far by archaeologists. However, most of the scribes have Persian names, and it is thought that Persianization of Elam was already nearly complete by that time.

85. For the distinct terms 'Eurasia' and 'Central Eurasia', which refer to different things, see Terminology.

1

The Scythians in the Central Eurasian Steppes

The Scythians, pastoral nomads of the vast steppe grasslands of Central Eurasia, were the world's first really mobile people, as remarked in both Greek and Chinese sources.[1] They developed a special culture that was remarkably coherent internally, with its key elements clearly connected to other elements. At the top of the divine-human feudal hierarchy was the categorically unique Heavenly God, who created the heavens and the earth as well as the one, semi-divine, Royal lineage. Although there were other gods (especially in frontier contact regions), they did not belong to the same category as Heavenly God, who was necessarily one. The Scythians also developed a striking National Foundation Myth, which became a sort of living epic history. These are characteristic traditional beliefs of Central Eurasian pastoral peoples throughout history from the Scythians down to early modern times.[2]

Since the Scythians believed that their rulers, whom Herodotus calls the "Royal Scythians", were descended directly from Heavenly God, that made God not only the ruler of Heaven but also the rightful head of the entire earthly feudal-hierarchical socio-political structure, from the Great King himself to his personally appointed vassals (called by Herodotus *archai*), to those below them (the *nomoi*), down to the free

1. Herodotus and Ssu-ma Ch'ien describe exactly the same culture, as many have noted.
2. Beckwith (2009: 1–3); for the Scythians, see also Khazanov (2014).

men at the very bottom. As Herodotus (iv 73) explicitly states, there was no chattel slavery among the Scythians.[3]

The Great King and his lineage are referred to in various ancient and medieval languages as *Ariya, Aria, Ḥarya,* or *Ārya,*[4] all versions of the same word meaning specifically 'of or pertaining to the one legitimate royal lineage', or 'royal' for short. In traditional Central Eurasian cultures this lineage was of great importance because, having come from God's realm its members would "return home" upon death, along with their oath-bound comitatus 'guard corps' members, who in many Central Eurasian languages are called "the Friends".[5]

The Scythian language itself was also called *Aria* ~ *Ariya* ~ *Ḥarya,* or a variant of it, meaning 'the royal one', i.e., 'the *language* of the royal ones'. As late as the Middle Ages the language of a Central Eurasian ruling people is typically so called, regardless of the linguistic relationship of the royal lineage members' actual language. That is, in the beginning the language was Scythian,[6] an Iranic language, but when later legitimate rulers no longer spoke Scythian or another Iranic language, they still referred to themselves and their language as *Aria* ~ *Ariya* ~ *Ḥarya* 'the Royal one(s)'.[7]

It was for the sake of their Friends that the *Ḥarya* ~ *Aria* rulers organized their realms to establish peace, maximize prosperity, and encourage commerce of all kinds. Each lord who had a comitatus had to support his Friends and reward them regularly with valuable treasures, especially gold. It was the symbol of Heavenly kingship, as shown by the Scythian national foundation myth recounted by Herodotus and discussed below. Gold was obtained mainly by trade, and there was

3. Other passages in Herodotus that suggest the opposite are discussed below.

4. These are the forms attested in Old Persian, Greek, Kushan, Old Chinese, Old Tibetan, and Sanskrit; there are others. In most cases I use only the three earliest attested forms, *Ariya, Aria,* and *Ḥarya,* unless it is pertinent to cite others. The word is discussed in Chapter 4, and in more detail in Beckwith (2016a).

5. Beckwith (2009: 12–28); for textual examples see Beckwith (1984a).

6. The known culture of the Cimmerians, including their language, was identical to that of the Scythians, so we may assume that they too called the language *Ḥarya* ~ *Ariya*. Cf. Endnote 29.

7. Beckwith (2016a). Some even referred to their lineage as "Saka", as in the reports given by the early Türks to the Chinese and to the Byzantine Greeks, in both cases specifically saying they were originally "*Saka(s)*", i.e., Scythian(s). Cf. Endnote 30.

indeed much trade in the region, often involving precious materials, mostly concentrated in the Scythians' urbanized centers in Central Asia, as well as in steppe zone centers such as the huge walled city of Bel'sk (or Bilsk), which has been studied by archaeologists. A smaller trading city like it, Gelonus, is described in detail by Herodotus. Many such trading centers scattered across the edge of the forest-steppe have been found by archaeologists.[8]

The Scythians (including their relatives the Cimmerians) spread across Central Eurasia from the Altai region of Western Mongolia and Tuva in approximately the late 9th to late 8th century. In the 7th century, not long after their conquest of the steppe zone and at least the northern part of Central Asia, the Scythian nation, by that name, spread into the northern Ancient Near East and also, under various names (most importantly Ta-Hsia 大夏 'great *Ḥarya*'), into regions to the north of the early Chinese.[9]

Heavenly God

Herodotus says the Scythians' God of Heaven was named *Papaeus,* i.e., 'papa, father'. That agrees semantically with the fact that "there is only one name of an Indo-European god which we know, **Diḗus *ph*$_2$*tḗr* (Sanskrit *Dyáuṣ pitā́*, Greek *Zeùs patḗr,* Latin *Iuppiter*) . . . the god of the clear skies".[10] However, *Papaeus* is clearly a Graeco-Scythian form of Greek πάππας 'papa'.[11] Herodotus also tells us that the Scythians only worshipped one god. He does not say which one, but it was clearly their Heavenly God, as in his first version of the national foundation myth, below.

He also says they had other gods, which he lists and identifies. However, most of them seem to have been "small g" gods particular to one

8. Rolle (1989); Cunliffe (2020: 133–135).

9. See Chapter 2 on the Near East, and Di Cosmo (1999: 890–892 and passim) on the Far East.

10. See Endnote 31.

11. The very well-attested Scythian word for 'father' is *pitā-* (q.v. Endnote 125 and Chapters 5 and 6). See below on the Proto-Scythian name of Heavenly God, *Tagri.

social, cultural, or physical "thing" or region, such as found among other peoples of Archaic Eurasia, where they were typically the only gods.[12] They were categorically unrelated to God, who as a perfect universal creator could only be unique.

The Hsiung-nu (Xiongnu), the best known East Scythians,[13] called Heavenly God *Täŋri (usually spelled *Tengri*), whose name is transcribed in ancient Chinese as 撐犁. These characters are read today, in modern Chinese pronunciation, as *ch'eng-li* (*chēnglí*). The Scythians' long rule in the Eastern Steppe transmitted their God and his name to the peoples over whom they ruled and their successors, including eventually the Türks. (The Old Turkic name for the God of Heaven, *Täŋri*, is thus a loanword from Scythian *Täŋri later borrowed from Turkic by the Türks' empire-founding successors, the Mongols and the Manchus.)[14] It is from Proto-Scythian *tagri.[15]

Neither the Greek nor the Chinese sources give much detail about Scythian religious beliefs, but when the Scythian imperial realm centered in the region of what is now western and northern Iran was taken over by the Scytho-Medes, and subsequently by the Persians, Scythian religious beliefs clearly went with it. The first overtly Persian ruler of the Achaemenid Empire, Darius I, followed in the footsteps of the Scytho-Mede kings (before Cyrus) who were also evidently monotheists.[16] He tells us the core belief:

> Great God is Ahuramazdā, who created this earth, who created that heaven, who created man, who created happiness for man.[17]

12. See Endnote 32.

13. Beckwith (2018). See Chapters 6 and 7.

14. See Endnote 33.

15. See Chapter 6 for detailed discussion. The same word for 'Heavenly God' is attested very clearly in West Scythian *Thagimasadas* (*Tagi-Mazda) and *Targitaos* (*Targi-tava-). Herodotus says the god Θαγιμασάδας *Thagimasadas* (Mayrhofer 2006: 12) was worshipped only by the Royal Scythians, thus telling us that he was the One Heavenly God of the One Royal (*Aria*) people. His identification as the Scythian equivalent of the Greek god Poseidon is unlikely for a steppe people.

16. See Chapter 2.

17. Naqš-i Rustam Inscription DNa 1–6. See Endnote 78 for the Old Persian text and detailed discussion.

Darius proclaims that he restored the Empire due to the help of the God of Heaven, creator of heaven and earth, whom he calls by his specifically Zoroastrian name, Ahura Mazdā 'Lord Mazdā'. The prophet Jeremiah (10:11) tells us indirectly the very same thing:

> Let the gods who did *not* make the heavens and the earth perish from the earth and from beneath these heavens![18]

For Jeremiah and the monotheizing Hebrews, as for the Imperial Medes and Persians, there was only one true apex "Capital G" God. However, the most important *functions* of Heavenly God in Scythian society, as in Scytho-Mede-Persian society and early Hebrew society, were not metaphysical but socio-political. God was the overlord of the Scythian king, who was descended from God and was put on the throne by him. As Darius says, Ahura Mazdā made him king. All this reflects the Scythian national foundation myth, which Herodotus recounts in three versions.

The West Scythian National Foundation Myth[19]

First Version

> A man whose name was Targitao- appeared in this country, which was then desolate. They say that his parents were Dia (Zeus, the sky-god) and a daughter of the (god) Borysthene- (the Dnieper River) . . . Such was Targitao-'s lineage; and he had three sons: Lipoxaï-, Arpoxaï-, and [S]colaxaï-, youngest of the three. . . . Certain implements—namely, a plough, a yoke, a battle-axe, and a bowl, all of gold—fell down from the sky into Scythia. The eldest of [the sons], seeing these, approached them meaning to take them; but the gold began to burn as he neared, and he stopped. Then the second approached, and the gold did as before. When these two had been driven back by the

18. אֱלָהַיָּא דִּי שְׁמַיָּא וְאַרְקָא לָא עֲבַדוּ יֵאבַדוּ מֵאַרְעָא וּמִן־תְּחוֹת שְׁמַיָּא אֵלֶּה (*BHS* 803).

19. I have standardized the English text throughout the translations. There is also a very brief remark in Diodorus (ii 43,3–4) that says the Scythians were descended from the union of Zeus and the half-serpentine demigoddess Echidna (Khazanov 2016: 174).

burning gold, the youngest brother approached and the burning stopped, and he took the gold to his own house. In view of this, the elder brothers agreed to give all the royal power to the youngest ([S]colaxaï-).[20]

Lipoxaï- (Scy. 'King Lipo'), it is said, was the father of the Scythian clan called Auchatae; Arpoxaï- (Scy. 'King Arpo'), the second brother, of those called Katiari and Traspians; the youngest, who was king, of those called Paralatae. All these together bear the name of Scoloti, after their king (i.e., *Skula χšaya 'King Scola' [skula], or 'King Scyth'); "Scythians" is the name given them by Greeks.[21] . . . Because of the great size of the country, the lordships that [S]colaxaï- established for his sons were three, one of which, where they keep the gold, was the greatest.[22]

20. ἄνδρα γενέσθαι πρῶτον ἐν τῇ γῇ ταύτῃ ἐούσῃ ἐρήμῳ τῳ οὔνομα εἶναι Ταργιτάον: τοῦ δὲ Ταργιτάου τούτου τοὺς τοκέας λέγουσι εἶναι, . . . Δία τε καὶ Βορυσθένεος τοῦ ποταμοῦ θυγατέρα. γένεος μὲν τοιούτου δὴ τινος γενέσθαι τὸν Ταργιτάον, τούτου δὲ γενέσθαι παῖδας τρεῖς, Λιπόξαϊν καὶ Ἀρπόξαϊν καὶ νεώτατον [Σ]κολάξαιν. ἐπὶ τούτων ἀρχόντων ἐκ τοῦ οὐρανοῦ φερομένα χρύσεα ποιήματα, ἄροτρόν τε καὶ ζυγόν καὶ σάγαριν καὶ φιάλην, πεσεῖν ἐς τὴν Σκυθικήν: καὶ τῶν ἰδόντα πρῶτον τὸν πρεσβύτατον ἆσσον ἰέναι βουλόμενον αὐτὰ λαβεῖν, τὸν δὲ χρυσόν ἐπιόντος καίεσθαι. ἀπαλλαχθέντος δὲ τούτου προσιέναι τὸν δεύτερον, καὶ τὸν αὖτις ταὐτὰ ποιέειν. τοὺς μὲν δὴ καιόμενον τὸν χρυσὸν ἀπώσασθαι, τρίτῳ δὲ τῷ νεωτάτῳ ἐπελθόντι κατασβῆναι, καί μιν ἐκεῖνον κομίσαι ἐς ἑωυτοῦ: καὶ τοὺς πρεσβυτέρους ἀδελφεοὺς πρὸς ταῦτα συγγνόντας τὴν βασιληίην πᾶσαν παραδοῦναι τῷ νεωτάτῳ. Herodotus (iv 5,1–5), from Perseus, tr. Godley, with my emendations in brackets and clarifications in parentheses. See Endnote 36 and Beckwith (2009: 377–380) on the textual error "Colaxaïs" and its emendation (which is indicated by the following paragraph of Herodotus itself). I have changed Godley's "Targitaüs" to the Greek *Targitaos*. I have also corrected his 'sword' (for σάγαρις) to 'battle-axe', and for φιάλη I have substituted 'bowl' (it meant specifically a wide, flat bowl) for his translation 'flask' (both following *LSJ*). I have also replaced Greek inflectional *-s* with a hyphen (-) in all cases in the translation of this passage.

21. ἀπὸ μὲν δὴ Λιποξάιος γεγονέναι τούτους τῶν Σκυθέων οἳ Αὐχάται γένος καλέονται, ἀπὸ δὲ τοῦ μέσου Ἀρποξάιος οἳ Κατίαροί τε καὶ Τράσπιες καλέονται, ἀπὸ δὲ τοῦ νεωτάτου αὐτῶν τοῦ βασιλέος οἳ καλέονται Παραλάται: σύμπασι δὲ εἶναι οὔνομα Σκολότους, τοῦ βασιλέος ἐπωνυμίην. Σκύθας δὲ Ἕλληνες ὠνόμασαν. Herodotus (iv 6,1–2), from Perseus, tr. Godley.

22. τῆς δὲ χώρης ἐούσης μεγάλης τριφασίας τὰς βασιληίας τοῖσι παισὶ τοῖσι ἑωυτοῦ καταστήσασθαι Κολάξαιν, καὶ τουτέων μίαν ποιῆσαι μεγίστην, ἐν τῇ τὸν χρυσὸν φυλάσσεσθαι. Herodotus (iv 7,2), from Perseus, tr. Godley. Scholars have almost universally ignored what the text actually tells us about the names of the first three Scythians. They thus follow the ancient scribal error "Colaxaïs", which has led many astray in search of nonexistent mythological ancestors of "Cola". The problem is solved by actually *reading*, in full, what the entire section of Herodotus actually tells us about this myth and its characters.

Second Version

Heracles (son of Zeus, the sky god), driving the cattle of Geryones, came to this land, which was then desolate, but is now inhabited by the Scythians.[23] . . .

He found in a cave a creature of double form that was half maiden and half serpent; above the buttocks she was a woman, below them a snake. When he saw her he was astonished, and asked her if she had seen his mares straying; she said that she had them, and would not return them to him before he had intercourse with her; Heracles did, in hope of this reward.[24] . . .

When the sons born to her were grown men, she gave them names, calling one of them Agathyrsus and the next Gelonus and the youngest Scythes; furthermore, remembering the instructions (given her by Heracles), she did as she was told. [She judged which of them should remain in that land by watching to see who could bend Heracles' bow (to string it) and wear his warbelt.][25] Two of her sons, Agathyrsus and Gelonus, were cast out by their mother and left the country, unable to fulfill the requirements set; but Scythes, the youngest, fulfilled them and so stayed in the land. From Scythes son of Heracles comes the whole line of the kings of Scythia.[26]

23. Ἡρακλέα ἐλαύνοντα τὰς Γηρυόνεω βοῦς ἀπικέσθαι ἐς γῆν ταύτην ἐοῦσαν ἐρήμην, ἥντινα νῦν Σκύθαι νέμονται. Herodotus (iv 8,1), from Perseus, tr. Godley.

24. ἐνθαῦτα δὲ αὐτὸν εὑρεῖν ἐν ἄντρῳ μιξοπάρθενον τινά, ἔχιδναν διφυέα, τῆς τὰ μὲν ἄνω ἀπὸ τῶν γλουτῶν εἶναι γυναικός, τὰ δὲ ἔνερθε ὄφιος. ἰδόντα δὲ καὶ θωμάσαντα ἐπειρέσθαι μιν εἴ κου ἴδοι ἵππους πλανωμένας: τὴν δὲ φάναι ἑωυτήν ἔχειν καὶ οὐκ ἀποδώσειν ἐκείνῳ πρὶν ἢ οἱ μιχθῇ: τό δὲ Ἡρακλέα μιχθῆναι ἐπὶ τῷ μισθῷ τούτῳ. Herodotus (iv 9,1–2), from Perseus, tr. Godley.

25. Herodotus (iv 9,5).

26. τὴν δ', ἐπεὶ οἱ γενομένους τοὺς παῖδας ἀνδρωθῆναι, τοῦτο μὲν σφι οὐνόματα θέσθαι, τῷ μὲν Ἀγάθυρσον αὐτῶν, τῷ δ' ἑπομένῳ Γελωνόν, Σκύθην δὲ τῷ νεωτάτῳ, τοῦτο δὲ τῆς ἐπιστολῆς μεμνημένην αὐτὴν ποιῆσαι τά ἐντεταλμένα. καὶ δὴ δύο μὲν οἱ τῶν παίδων, τόν τε Ἀγάθυρσον καὶ τὸν Γελωνόν, οὐκ οἵους τε γενομένους ἐξικέσθαι πρὸς τὸν προκείμενον ἄεθλον, οἴχεσθαι ἐκ τῆς χώρης ἐκβληθέντας ὑπὸ τῆς γειναμένης, τὸν δὲ νεώτατον αὐτῶν Σκύθην ἐπιτελέσαντα καταμεῖναι ἐν τῇ χωρῇ. καὶ ἀπὸ μὲν Σκύθεω τοῦ Ἡρακλέος γενέσθαι τοὺς αἰεὶ βασιλέας γινομένους Σκυθέων. Herodotus (iv 10,3) adds at the end of this version, ταῦτα δὲ Ἑλλήνων οἱ τὸν Πόντον οἰκέοντες λέγουσι. 'This is what the Greek dwellers in Pontus say.' All from Perseus, tr. Godley. Note that Scythes, the youngest, thus inherited the "home lands" of the Scythians.

Third Version

> Scyles ('Scyth') was one of the [three] sons born to Ariapeithes, king of Scythia. His mother was of Istria, not native-born (i.e., she was non-Scythian by origin), and she taught him to speak and read Greek. As time passed, Ariapeithes was treacherously killed by Spargapeithes, king of the Agathyrsi.[27] Scyles inherited the kingship and his father's wife, a Scythian woman whose name was Opoea.[28]

The third version of the foundation myth is given in Herodotus as strictly historical events belonging to the "Third Scythian Dynasty",[29] long after the putative age of the foundation stories. It is probably based on a tale attributed by Herodotus' informants to a time shortly before his visit. He begins his account with the comment, "But according to what I heard from Tymnes, the deputy for Ariapeithes, . . ."[30] The second

27. See Endnotes 34 and 138.

28. Ἀριαπείθεϊ γὰρ τῷ Σκυθέων βασιλέι γίνεται μετ' ἄλλων παίδων Σκύλης: ἐξ Ἰστριηνῆς δὲ γυναικὸς οὗτος γίνεται καὶ οὐδαμῶς ἐγχωρίης: τὸν ἡ μήτηρ αὕτη γλῶσσάν τε Ἑλλάδα καὶ γράμματα ἐδίδαξε. μετὰ δὲ χρόνῳ ὕστερον Ἀριαπείθης μὲν τελευτᾷ δόλῳ ὑπὸ Σπαργαπείθεος τοῦ Ἀγαθύρσων βασιλέος, Σκύλης δὲ τήν τε βασιληίην παρέλαβε καὶ τὴν γυναῖκα τοῦ πατρός, τῇ οὔνομα ἦν Ὀποίη: Herodotus (iv 78), from Perseus, tr. Godley. I give *Ariapeithes* for his Latinized "Ariapithes". The other two sons of Ariapeithes (besides Scyles) are Octamasadas and Oricos (a son by Opoea); cf. Mayrhofer (2006: 14). See Alekseyev (2005) for this and other Scythian royal genealogies. The story is presented as having happened at the time of Darius. Whether or not the story is historical, ancient people, like modern, often liked to give the names of ancestors and other relatives to their children. Nevertheless, all three stories in Herodotus, and the one in Justin (in Pompeius Trogus), end up with a first actual ruler *Scythes* ~ *Scyles* (i.e., *Skula*) ~ *Scolo* (i.e., Skula) 'Scythian', the latter two, with *-l-*, being versions of the early name 'Scythian' in the pronunciation of the Scythians in Herodotus' day, as he explains (Herodotus iv 6,1–2).

29. Alekseyev (2005).

30. Herodotus (iv 76, 6): ὡς δ' ἐγὼ ἤκουσα Τύμνεω τοῦ Ἀριαπείθεος ἐπιτρόπου; from Perseus, tr. Godley. The second morpheme, *-peithes*, is a Greek transcription of Scythian *pitā* 'father' in this name. It has nothing to do with the Hellenized form *-peithes* used to write Scythian *paisa* 'ornament' in the name *Spargapeithes* (for attested *Spargapises*), q.v. Endnotes 34 and 138. Cf. the name in Justin's Latin transcription *Scolopitus*, representing Scythian *Skula-pitā 'Scythian-father'; see Ivantchik (2018), whose analysis differs slightly. The text here explicitly tells us Ariapeithes is the father of the first Royal Scythian, so his name is undoubtedly *Aryā-pitā 'Aria-father', i.e., 'Father of the Royal Scythians, the Arias'. Cf. the attested Old Iranic name *Bagapitā* 'god + father' (Tav. 138: 'whose father is [a] God'). Not with Schmitt (2003, 2018) and Mayrhofer (2006).

element in *Ariapeithes* is parallel to Latin *pitus* in the name *Scolopitus* 'Scythian-father', one of the two Scythian ancestors in the Amazon foundation myth recounted by Justin.[31] In these examples the person with *-peithes* ~ *-pitus* in his name, Scythian *pitā-* 'father', is the legendary founder, either of the Scythians or of the Scythian nation of the Amazons. Among the West Scythians, the legendary founding ancestor is thus immediately below Heavenly God[32] and one level (or generation) above the first actual ruler, the eponymous first Scythian, who in all versions is the youngest of three (or in one case two) sons, and is named "Scyth": *Scythes* (Skuδa) ~ *Skola* (Skula) ~ *Scyles* (Skula), all of which names mean 'Scythian' and have been shown to be dialect forms of one and the same word, Proto-Iranic or early Scythian *Skuδa 'Scythian', likely meaning 'archer', or literally, 'shooter'.[33]

The father of the first ruler in the first version of the myth is Targitaos, who is evidently the first king, but is presented as more like the first man.[34] The key points are that his father is the God of Heaven, his mother is an Earthly divinity, and they had three sons, of whom the youngest is the eponymous first "Scythian" king.[35] In the first version of the West Scythian myth, Targitaos is explicitly said to be the *son* of Heavenly God ("Zeus"). He in turn has three sons, in all three variants from Herodotus. The first Scythian king is the youngest of the three brothers, Scytha- or Scula- (Scythian *skula* 'Scythian'), in the first version called **Scolaxai-*, with Scythian **skula-* (from early Scythian *Skuδa-*, in Greek transcription *Scythes*, i.e., *Skutha-*) 'archer, Scythian' plus **χšaya* (in Greek transcription ξαϊ- *ksai-*) 'king',[36] thus 'King Scytha', the first king of the Scythians per se (Herodotus iv 6,78). The second version is the same, with Scythes. In the third, putatively "historical" account,

31. Justinus, *Epitome of Trogus* 2.4.1. The other son's name is Plynus. Cf. the preceding Note.

32. Similarly among the Hsiung-nu, the father of Mo-tun (the empire founder) was *T'ou-man* 頭曼 *Tóumàn*, Old Chinese *Dew(ă)maɴ(ă) transcribing East Scythian *Devamana 'the God-minded one'.

33. Szemerényi (1980); not with Schmitt (2003) and Mayrhofer (2006). Cf. Chapter 6.

34. See Endnote 35.

35. One of the two formal epithets of the East Scythian (Hsiung-nu) king is 'born of Heaven and Earth'; see Chapter 7.

36. See Endnote 36 on the textual problem.

Herodotus names the father of the historical Scyles (*Skula) as *Ariapeithes*, a king whose name, *Arya-pitā 'Aria-father', identifies him as the founder of the *Aria*—Royal Scythian—lineage. In the story he is killed by King *Spargapises of the Agathyrsi (Herodotus iv 78,2),[37] so *Ariapeithes'* son Scyles <*Skula*>, whose name is the word 'Scythian', succeeds to the throne and is thus the first Scythian king both according to the national foundation myth and according to what Herodotus says is actual Scythian history.

Scythian Religious Beliefs

Herodotus says the Scythians—regularly meaning the Scythians proper, the Royal Scythians—were monotheists, as the main national foundation myth attests.[38] West Scythian *Targitaos* is the semi-divine progenitor of the Scythians in the myth, which explicitly tells how Targitaos is the *son* of Heavenly God. It is thus not surprising that the first element in his name, *targi*, corresponds exactly to the word *täŋri ("Tengri") 'Heaven' in ancient East Scythian (Hsiung-nu dialect).[39] Both clearly mean 'Heaven' or 'God of Heaven' and go back to Proto-Scythian *tagri 'Heaven (-god)'.[40] The word is attested also in the name of the Royal Scythians' proprietary god *Thagimasadas*, which consists of *Tagi (from *Tagri)[41] plus *Mazda, as discussed in Chapter 6. The East Scythian (Hsiung-nu) word for 'Heaven, Heavenly God', *Täŋri, was later spread across the steppe zone from China to Europe by the Türks. The second element in the name *Targitaos* is accepted to be the widely attested Old Iranic word *tav-* 'to be strong', *tuvāna-* 'strength', *tvan-* 'capable', etc., as in many names, so it means 'powerful by God' or 'powerful one of God' or the like. Herodotus (iv 59,1) also gives a list of other Scythian gods, some of which may be translation equivalents of Greek god names.[42]

37. See Endnote 34 on the name Spargapeithes.

38. Cf. Khazanov (2016).

39. Beckwith (2018), which is revised in this book.

40. See Chapter 6 for details.

41. See Endnote 37.

42. Cf. Mayrhofer (2006). Most of the names are difficult to identify and in general there has been too much speculation. See Endnote 32 and Chapter 6.

A strict form of monotheism—similar to the Early Zoroastrianism of Zoroaster's *Gāthās* and the inscriptions of Darius the Great—was one of the dominant beliefs among the Scythians, including one or more of Herodotus' informants, as well as the Scythians of Achaemenes, and the East Scythians (Hsiung-nu). The earliest attested Scythian 'iconoclastic' monotheists were those who sacked the great temple of Heavenly Aphrodite (Astarte) at Ascalon (now Ashkelon on the central Mediterranean coast of Israel). Herodotus (i 105) describes it in enough detail that it is clear the event took place. But it was no accidental raid. Astarte was widely equated with Anāhitā, the chief *Daiva* 'God' of the polytheistic early Iranic peoples. Worship of Anāhitā and Mithra is condemned by Zoroaster (though he does not name them), and both of these 'False Gods' (also unnamed) were anathematized by Darius the Great in the civil war that he won in 520. Only Ahura Mazdā, Heavenly God, who created Heaven and Earth, was approved for public worship, as shown in Chapter 2.

Scythian Sociopolitical Structure

According to the Scythian national foundation myth, society was ultimately headed by the one God of Heaven, followed by his son or grandson, the one Great King, who was also God's vassal. In Herodotus' description of the steppe zone north of the Black Sea, he notes that the (West) Scythian Empire, under the Royal Scythian (Great) King, was divided into three *basileiai* (βασιλεῖαι) 'kingdoms', one of which consisted of the 'home lands' directly ruled by the Great King. Each kingdom was subdivided into *archai* (ἀρχαί) 'realms', which in turn were each subdivided into *nomoi* (νομοί) 'provinces', each of which had a *nomarch* over it.[43]

The Scythian state was thus feudal-hierarchical in structure. Ideally, the king's direct vassals were the feudal lords he appointed over the different provinces of the Scythian Empire. The latter in turn had their own feudal vassal appointees, who in turn had their own vassals. This

43. Cf. Endnote 38.

was the feudal socio-political pyramid, cemented by oaths sworn by lords and vassals, a characteristic of traditional Central Eurasian societies throughout history, as first analyzed in detail for the Mongol Empire almost a century ago.[44] The Chinese sources also describe this tripartite structure for the East Scythian state of the Hsiung-nu. As discussed in Chapter 2, the Scythian Empire based in Media, which became the Scytho-Mede Empire after the revolution of Cyaxares, was organized in this way as well, and the Persian Empire, which was the continuation of the Scytho-Mede Empire, retained that same organization, though it had grown larger, with more subordinate "kingdoms" (satrapies). Just as in every human society no one is actually "free", so too in a strict feudal society no one is really free, but the people at the bottom of the pyramid *in Central Eurasia* were technically "free" men in the sense that there was no slavery per se among the Scythians, as noted above. The Greeks and Chinese, by contrast, were slaveholding societies with different socio-political structures, so they could not understand feudal-hierarchical societies, and their historians wrongly call lower-ranking members of Central Eurasian societies "slaves".[45]

The word *satrap* (a Greek loanword from Scythian *χšaθrapā-* via a well-attested Scythian dialect form with the simplified onset *s-/š-*)[46] is used mainly in non-Persian texts for the appointed vassal rulers ("subordinate kings") of the satrapies ("Lands") of the Empire under the Persians. It does occur twice in the Old Persian inscriptions in the Old Persianized form *χšaçapā*, in one case referring to the satrap of Bactria, in the other to the satrap of Arachosia.[47] Otherwise, only the Old Persian

44. Vladimirtsov (1934/1948). Feudalism is most famous in its medieval Western European variant, which was also introduced from Central Eurasia, during the great Völkerwanderung ('migration of peoples'), when Goths, Alans, Huns, Franks, and other Central Eurasians migrated into the declining Western Roman Empire.

45. The peripheral slave societies all misunderstood the Central Eurasian hierarchical socio-political structure, and misrepresent it in their historical works. See Endnote 39. For the argument that the Scythians did practice slavery see Taylor (2021) and Taylor et al. (2020). For native Central Eurasian evidence contra, see especially Endnote 101.

46. Bukharin (2013). It is however also written in Greek with the onset <ξ> *ks*, transcribing *χš*.

47. Both attested examples, *χšaçapāvā* and *χšaçapāva(n)-* (Schmitt 2014: 284) are Old Persianized versions of the original Scythian *χšaθrapā-*, q.v. Chapter 6.

term *dahyu* is used in the inscriptions. Old Persianized *χšaçapā* is a loanword from Scythian *χšaθrapa*.

The Great King and all those of his lineage called themselves, and were called, *Ḥarya* 'royal one(s), ruling one(s)', a word attested most precisely in the early Eastern Eurasian transcriptions, whereas in the west the voiced onset (initial consonant) *ḥ* [ɣ] was lost completely and the word is written *aria* (in Greek) or *ariya* (in Old Persian) for [a.rya], usually thus given as *aria* ~ *ariya* ~ *Ḥarya*[48] in this book.[49] As an epithet for the Heavenly-ordained legitimate Scythian rulers (in both West and East Scythian) and their lineage, the word continued to be used by many later Central Eurasian rulers, including the Great Kings of the Persian, Kushan (Bactrian), Koguryo, Togon (T'u-yü-hun), Türk, and Tibetan empires, among others, as well as by the Chinese, as discussed in Chapter 4.

The Scythians—at least the Royal Scythians of the West, the ones we know the most about—swore deep oaths of friendship with each other. For a Scythian, his Friend was his companion in life and after death. No Scythian would leave a battle alive if his Friend had been killed.[50] After a lord's death the surviving members of his band of Friends, his comitatus (only the inner core members if it was a large comitatus), died to accompany him to the next life. The lord was buried with great wealth so that he could continue to bestow it on his Friends, and they fought for him and feasted with him in Paradise, as in this life.[51] The great symbolic value of gold to the Scythians and later Central Eurasians[52] was thus perhaps not due so much to the fact that it was costly in this world, but rather that it symbolized the bright daylit sky, Heaven, and the next world. In effect, gold was worth even more there than here.

The comitatus institution based on friendship was the heart and soul of the Scythian socio-political-economic system. It was cemented by

48. The eastern Eurasian form is explicitly transcribed as འརྱ་ <*ḥarya*> [ɣa.rya] in Old Tibetan. See Chapter 4.

49. The word is not written "<*arya*>" in any anciently attested language.

50. See the presentation of typical Scythian beliefs and practices in Lucian's *Toxaris*.

51. Beckwith (2009: 12–23). For a survey of recent archaeological finds see Cunliffe (2020) and Caspari et al. (2018).

52. Allsen (2002). Cf. Walter (2013).

the people's belief in the God of Heaven and a reward in Paradise for the virtuous who were true and carried out their oaths. The Scythian economy, which grew wealthy from trade and taxation, seems to have been driven to a great extent by the need to acquire valuable goods that could be bestowed on the comitatus warriors, the Friends, in return for their oath to fight to the death for their lord.

The Royal Language of the Scythians

Not only were the king and his ruling lineage referred to by the epithet 'the *royal* one(s)', so too was the Scythian language. It is regularly and explicitly called *Aria* ~ *Ariya* ~ *Ḥarya*, 'the language of the royal ones',[53] those who belong to the legitimate royal lineage. The first Achaemenid Persian ruler, the Great King or King of Kings Darius I, refers to the *language* of the first Old Persian inscription, erected on Mt. Bagastāna ('God-place', now Behistun, Bisitun, Bisotun, etc.), as <Ariya> *Aria*. Scholars have attempted to interpret this as referring to the writing system, which was newly created to write it, or to the "Iranian" family of languages, but in the Rabatak Inscription of the Kushan ruler Kanishka the Great (r. ca. 127–150 CE),[54] the Great King also says he put the text αριαο <ariao>[55] 'into Aria', i.e., 'into the Royal one', referring to the Iranic language in which his inscription is written, Bactrian. At the same time the Chinese call the Bactrian-Kushan realm Ta Hsia 大夏 (*Dàxià*) 'Great Ḥarya, the Ḥarya Empire'. Because Bactrian is written in Greek script, which the Kushans inherited from their Greek predecessors in the region going back to Alexander the Great, and they originally used it to write the Greek language, *Aria* can only refer to the royal language, Bactrian, not the script.[56] The only other time the word *Ariya* (= *Aria* = *Ḥarya*) is used by Darius is when he refers to himself as *Ariya Ariyaciça* 'an *Ariya*, seed of an *Ariya*'. The phrase 'seed of an Ariya'

53. See Endnote 40.
54. Bracey (2017).
55. Sims-Williams (2004: 56).
56. See Chapter 3 for discussion of this usage of the word for other languages.

means explicitly 'a member of the royal lineage' of kings who ruled "the Empire".[57]

Who were these Ariya predecessors, of which Darius claimed to be a descendant (alongside his polytheistic relative Cyrus and his sons, whom he replaced as Great King)? They could only be the Scytho-Medes, or the Scythians themselves, who had actually created the Empire. As shown in Chapter 2, the first fully historical Scytho-Mede king, Cyaxares, was by his actions a monotheist, probably an Early Zoroastrian like Darius. The latter's father, Vištāspa, has a Scytho-Median name and was the sub-satrap over Parthia and Hyrcania (under the Great Satrapy of Media) in 522 when his son Darius ascended to the throne. Despite popular arguments that Darius was actually a usurper and a commoner, both claims are essentially impossible, as shown in Chapters 3 and 4.[58]

In short, the term *Ariya* ~ *Aria* ~ *Ḥarya* refers to the ruling lineage of the first Empire—the Scythian Empire—and to the royal language of its "Heavenly" lineage holders, the *Ariya* ~ *Aria* ~ *Ḥarya* 'royal ones', in Old Persian, Old Chinese, Sanskrit, Tokharian A, Old Turkic, Togon, Old Tibetan, and other languages.[59]

Scythian Home Life

The Scythians were on the whole healthy, long-lived people who spent their time mainly herding and caring for their domestic animals—especially horses, cattle, and sheep—and preparing dairy products from their milk; wool from their sheep, with which they made felt and wove

57. DNa, lines 13–14. See Chapter 3, Note 106 for the Old Persian text. The expression is also used in the Daiva Inscription of Xerxes (XPh). See the discussion in Chapter 2, where earlier parallels in Akkadian are quoted. Cf. Briant (2002: 181), who notes: "the term *arya* originally referred to ancestral nobility". However, despite Briant's following remark on the word Ἐνάρεες *Enarees* (Herodotus (i 105, iv 67), it certainly does not transcribe Avestan *anairya* (from a hypothetical Old Scythian *an-arya), since Herodotus makes it clear concerning the *non-masculine* characteristics of the Enarees, whose name is thus *a-narya; see Chapter 6.

58. Cf. Shahbazi (1994/2012).

59. Beckwith (2016a, 2016b); cf. Chapter 4.

fabrics; and leather from the cattle and sheep hides. Strabo (fl. 62 BC–23 CE) remarks on the late Scythian-Sarmatian people he knew:

> Now although the Nomads are warriors rather than brigands, yet they go to war only for the sake of the tributes due them; for they turn over their land to any people who wish to till it, and are satisfied if they receive in return for the land the tribute they have assessed, which is a moderate one . . . ; but if the tenants do not pay, the Nomads go to war with them . . . ; if the tributes were paid regularly, they would never resort to war.[60]

As nomadic herders, they followed a regular cycle, moving from pasture to pasture around the year at the relaxed pace of the oxen which pulled their felt houses-on-wheels. They kept house cats as pets, and no doubt as mousers.[61] Their children grew up out on the steppe, learning to take care of the animals and to process their products, and also to ride, shoot, and hunt. Ssu-ma Ch'ien describes life among the East Scythians, the *Hsiung-nu* 匈奴 (*Xiōngnú*), i.e., *Suŋlâ:[62]

> They nomadize, herding their domestic animals. The majority of their animals are horses, cattle, and sheep. . . . They move around following the water and grass. They do not have walled cities that they permanently dwell in, nor do they work at cultivating the fields, though each has his own piece of land. . . . When the boys can ride sheep, they shoot birds and mice with bow and arrow. When they are half grown they then shoot foxes and rabbits, which they eat. When they have a warrior's strength and can pull a [warrior's] bow, they all become armored cavalrymen.[63]

60. Strabo (vii 4,6), from Perseus, tr. Jones.

61. Aeschylus, *Prometheus Vinctus* 709–710. They kept donkeys too, according to the archaeology (Rolle 1989: 100–101), *pace* Herodotus. Cf. Note 65.

62. The first known Chinese contact with the Hsiung-nu took place in 318 BC (Di Cosmo 1999: 960).

63. *Shih Chi* 110: 隨畜牧而轉移。其畜之所多則馬、牛、羊，... 逐水草遷徙, 毋城郭常處耕田之業，然亦各有分地。... 兒能騎羊，引弓射鳥鼠；少長則射狐兔：用為食。士力能彎弓，盡爲甲騎。From CTP (correcting 毌 in the second to last phrase to 彎 from the *Han Shu*); similarly, Watson (1961, 2:155).

This account indirectly refers to the Scythians' great skill in metallurgy. They smelted ore and made their own armor, horse gear, arrowheads, and other metal products that they needed, and were eager to trade them (as well as their animals and animal products) for foreign goods, especially luxurious, expensive things such as gold and silk.

Despite Ssu-ma Ch'ien's comment that "they have no walled cities", echoing Herodotus' similar remark, the Greek and Chinese sources themselves describe them for us, and several rather large ones have been found archaeologically, though mainly in mixed forest-steppe or mountainous regions rather than the open steppe.[64] Moreover, at least three major cities in what became Persia and China were named, and probably founded, by the Scythians in peripheral regions (see Chapter 8). Nevertheless, the important point, as both Herodotus and Ssu-ma Ch'ien stress, is that the ruling Royal Scythian people were nomadic and did not like being cooped up in walled places of any kind. Herodotus says:

> But the Scythian race has made the cleverest discovery that we know in what is the most important of all human affairs; I do not praise the Scythians in all respects, but in this, the most important: that they have contrived that no one who attacks them can escape, and no one can catch them if they do not want to be found. For when men have no established cities or forts, but are all nomads and mounted archers, not living by tilling the soil but by raising cattle and carrying their dwellings on wagons, how can they not be invincible and unapproachable?[65]

64. Cunliffe (2020: 128–135); Taylor et al. (2020).

65. Herodotus (iv 46,2–3): τῷ δὲ Σκυθικῷ γένει ἓν μὲν τὸ μέγιστον τῶν ἀνθρωπηίων πρηγμάτων σοφώτατα πάντων ἐξεύρηται τῶν ἡμεῖς ἴδμεν, τὰ μέντοι ἄλλα οὐκ ἄγαμαι: τὸ δὲ μέγιστον οὕτω σφι ἀνεύρηται ὥστε ἀποφυγεῖν τε μηδένα ἐπελθόντα ἐπὶ σφέας, μὴ βουλομένους τε ἐξευρεθῆναι καταλαβεῖν μὴ οἷον τε εἶναι. τοῖσι γὰρ μήτε ἄστεα μήτε τείχεα ᾖ ἐκτισμένα, ἀλλὰ φερέοικοι ἐόντες πάντες ἔωσι ἱπποτοξόται, ζῶντες μὴ ἀπ᾽ ἀρότου ἀλλ᾽ ἀπὸ κτηνέων, οἰκήματα τε σφι ᾖ ἐπὶ ζευγέων, κῶς οὐκ ἂν εἴησαν οὗτοι ἄμαχοί τε καὶ ἄποροι προσμίσγειν; from Perseus, tr. Godley.

Scythian Literature

Like their Proto-Indo-European ancestors and their own descendants, including the Alans and later peoples of the steppe zone, the Scythians certainly had a rich oral epic literature, a cultural characteristic exclusive to Central Eurasian peoples and former Central Eurasian peoples down to modern times. They thus had bards who sang the great deeds of their heroes, as the earliest Central Eurasians, the Proto-Indo-Europeans, had done before them.[66] Like the Friends in the comitatus, the Scythian poets[67] were no doubt rewarded by their patrons with great wealth, following the ancient Indo-European cultural pattern that has been reconstructed by Watkins and other scholars and was traditional in societies that had an epic bard tradition:

> Reciprocal exchange relationships . . . were central to the ancient Indo-European peoples. In their societies, a gift entailed a counter-gift, and an act causing damage entailed the payment of recompense. . . . (In) the relationship obtaining between the Indo-European poet and his patron (typically a king), the poet sang the patron's fame, and in return the patron bestowed largesse on the poet. The relationship was vital to both parties: the king's livelihood depended on the poet's . . . praises (in Ireland, for example, a "king without poets" was proverbial for "nothing"), and the poet lived off the largesse bestowed by the king.[68]

In addition to their lost heroic epic poetry, the Scythians cultivated religious poetry. The *Gāthās* or 'Hymns' of the prophet Zoroaster, written in Old Avestan (an archaic dialect of Imperial Scythian), are the most

66. Beckwith (2009: 14–15). Rolle (1989) briefly discusses Scythian epic poetry performances based on archaeological findings. See also Endnote 41.

67. Unfortunately we do not have any accounts of the bards of the ancient Scythians, but we do have references to bards among the Parthians in Antiquity, and among Central Eurasians from early medieval times onward. See the preceding Note and Endnote 42.

68. Watkins (2011: 15).

famous surviving examples.[69] Other examples of verse are written in Young Avestan (the chief spoken dialect of Imperial Scythian).[70]

The bards of the Scythians' later close relatives and successors in the Western Steppe, the Alans, transmitted key motifs of Scythian epic poetry to early medieval Western Europe, where they formed the core of what became the King Arthur cycle of tales. The Alans' modern descendants, the Ossetian-Alanic people of the North Caucasus region, still preserve related heroic epic stories in their own language, a direct descendant of Scythian.[71]

69. See the edition and translation by Humbach and Ichaporia (1994).
70. For Avestan literature see Hintze (2009).
71. See Endnote 42.

2

The Scythians in Media and Central Asia

Conquest and Empire

The steppe zone is not sharply demarcated internally, so the nomadic Cimmerians and Scythians spread into frontier regions with good pasturage outside the main Central Eurasian steppe zone. In the west they reached the Zagros Mountains and vicinity, including the regions of Urartia and Mannaea, and especially Media (what is now northern and western Iran, far eastern Anatolian Turkey, and northern Iraq), where there was outstanding pasturage. In the east, they occupied the Eastern Steppe, including what is now Tuva, Mongolia, Inner Mongolia, and the region east of the great northern bend of the Yellow River, which overlapped with the northern frontier of the ancient Chinese. Horse riders are first attested there in the 8th to 7th centuries archaeologically.[1] In the south they occupied Central Asia almost to the Persian Gulf.

At least one steppe cultural characteristic—a new battle order designed for mounted archers—suddenly appears in the northern frontier zone of Urartu and Assyria in the mid-8th century. It marks the textually not yet mentioned appearance there of the Cimmerians (Gimirri), a people who were culturally Scythian.[2] The Cimmerians are first

1. Di Cosmo (1999: 912); cf. Tokhtas'ev (2012), who notes the people's specifically Scythian physical culture.

2. See also Endnotes 6 and 29.

documented in the Ancient Near East shortly after, in ca. 720–714, during the reign of Sargon II of Aššur (r. 721–705). Their physical culture is indistinguishable from that of the Scythians who followed them a few decades later.[3]

The name of the first known Cimmerian king, Teušpā (fl. 679 BC), is characteristically Scythian (*teu-* is no doubt well-attested *tava-* 'strong', and -(*a*)*spā* is the well-attested Scythian word for 'horses'). A later king, Sandakšatru (fl. 640 BC), also has a purely Scythian name, *Sandaxšaθra*.[4] The two peoples thus spoke Scythian but evidently represented different political groups, or nations, within one "Cimmerian-Scythian" culture, as many have concluded. Because they were actually one culture with a political distinction, not two *cultures*, and (based on the data) they all spoke the language we call Scythian, their culture is usually referred to in this book as "Scythian" culture. The archaeologists' "Scythian triad"—distinctive elements of the people's physical culture, namely their characteristic weapons (short sword, trilobate arrowhead, battle-axe), horse gear, and "Animal Style" art—as well as their language and unique socio-political-religious system, dominated the entire vast region from its earliest appearance onward.

Assyrian records first attest the Scythians, under that name, in the Ancient Near East in 676/675 BC. Herodotus says they came from the Sea of Azov region and went south keeping the Caucasus Mountains on their right. But having come ultimately from the area of Tuva and Western Mongolia far to the east, where Scythian physical culture is earliest attested archaeologically, they probably arrived first via Bactria, Parthia, and what is now northern Iran, thus keeping the Caucasus Mountains

3. Tokhtas'ev (2012); Diakonoff (1985). The Akkadian sources do not always distinguish between Cimmerians (Akkadian *Gimirri*) and Scythians (Akkadian *Iškuza-* ~ *Aškuza-*), often calling them all *Gimirri*.

4. The well-attested name *Teušpā* is clearly Iranic. Skjærvø (2006) says, "In 679 B.C.E. the Cimmerians under their king Teušpā invaded Assyria but were defeated by Esarhaddon. The king's name could conceivably be Iranian (e.g., *tava-spā- 'he whose power is swollen')", or perhaps *tava-aspā '(one having) powerful horses'. Akkadian Sa-an-dak-KUR-ru, transcribing (partly ideographically) *Sandaxšaθra*, is a very clear transcription, both word elements of which are well attested in Old Iranic: *sanda-* 'to effect, perform' (cf. OAve *sand-* Justi 1895: 283) + the very well known *xšaθra-* 'realm, empire', perhaps 'Empire-builder' or the like. See also Endnote 43.

on their right.[5] The Cimmerians and Scythians are well attested in Akkadian sources at that point, being involved in local wars in the Ancient Near East, either allied with the Assyrians or allied with someone else against them.

In Akkadian the Scythians are called *Iškuzai* or *Aškuzai*, close transcriptions of Old Scythian *skuδa-, which is also recorded at about the same time in Greek by Hesiod as *Scythes* *skut^{h}a- for *skuδa- 'Scythian'.[6] Not surprisingly, the Scythians' unique arrowheads have been found in the walls of cities and fortresses from this period all over the Near East as far as Egypt, whether shot by Scythians or by Scytho-Medes.[7]

The leader of the Scythians in 680/677 BC was a prince or king named *Spakaya* (in Assyrian transcription *iš-pa-ka-a-a*, representing Scythian *spakaya*),[8] who chronologically is also the first named Scythian person mentioned in any source. His name, a diminutive form of Scythian *spaka-*, identical to Scytho-Median *spaka* 'dog'[9] (q.v. Table 1), is thus 'Doggie'. Entering the frontier region of what is now northern Iran from the east, either via Parthia in Central Asia or via the passage below the Caucasus Mountains running along the west coast of the Caspian Sea, or both, the Scythians made their way west into eastern Anatolia via Media and Urartu (Armenia)—according to Herodotus, while they were pursuing their rivals the Cimmerians. However, they are now believed to have had little to do with the Cimmerians, as the latter

5. Herodotus (i 104; iv 12,3). The Scythians thus spread from the Altai Mountains in the far Eastern Steppe and spread west over the entire steppe zone, as the historically better attested Türks and Mongols did later. Cf. Endnote 44.

6. See Szemerényi (1980), the classic study. The initial *i-* or *a-* vowel is epenthetic (added by Akkadian speakers to make the cluster *sk* pronounceable for them). Ivantchik (2018) gives the Akkadian as *Áš-gu-za-a-a, Iš-ku-za(-a-a)*, representing *Ašguzai, Iškuzai*, but the first Akkadian form can be corrected to *Aškuzai* because the name also occurs in the Hebrew Bible as אַשְׁכְּנַז *Aškənaz* (Gen. 10,3 and 1 Chr. 1,6) and אַשְׁכְּנָז *Aškənāz* (Jer. 51,27), where the *n* is an ancient scribal error for *w* [w] or [u]. See Endnote 45.

7. See Endnote 46.

8. Mayrhofer (2006: 9): *Spaka-i̯a (i.e., Spakaya), noting "(Hinweis R. Schmitt)". Cf. Ivantchik (2018), who gives the dates "between 680/79 and 678/7".

9. The word *spaka* is attested in Herodotus as σπάκα *spaka*, and glossed as 'female dog' in Greek (Herodotus i 110,1) because it is the name of the hero's adoptive mother in the received text of Cyrus' national foundation myth. Cf. Endnote 47.

mainly lived further to the west in Anatolia, while the Scythians were basically centered in northwestern Media.[10] When the Scythians entered the region of Media it was extremely fragmented, with dozens of petty chieftains ruling mostly non-Indo-European-speaking peoples, as the Assyrian sources plentifully attest. There was thus no unified "Mede" realm before the Scythians, and no actual "Medes" in the ethnolinguistic sense. Media was strictly a geographical region, not an ethnolinguistic entity or a political unit.[11] It was only after the creolization of Media by the Scythians that the people there spoke the language traditionally called "Median"—a dialect of Scythian, an Old Iranic language[12]—as discussed in Chapter 5.

The Scythians fought the Cimmerians, and both fought with and against the Urartians, dominating them long enough to thoroughly Scythianize the Urartians' dress and weaponry,[13] and directly or indirectly the organization of their military, as well as other aspects of their culture.[14] All three peoples fought both for and against the Assyrians, the great power of the Ancient Near East at the time.

The Assyrians record that in about 670 the Scythian ruler known in Greek transcription as *Protothyes*, in Akkadian as *Bartatua* ~ *Partatua*, for Scythian *Părăθutava,[15] negotiated a marriage treaty with the Assyrians.[16]

10. Herodotus (iv 11,1) also gives an alternative story, which he says he thinks is more reliable than any other, namely that "the nomadic Scythians inhabiting Asia, when hard pressed in war by the Massagetae, fled across the Araxes River to the Cimmerian country": Σκύθας τοὺς νομάδας οἰκέοντας ἐν τῇ Ἀσίῃ, πολέμῳ πιεσθέντας ὑπὸ Μασσαγετέων, οἴχεσθαι διαβάντας ποταμὸν Ἀράξην ἐπὶ γῆν τὴν Κιμμερίην; from Perseus, tr. Godley. Unfortunately, there are several rivers named Araxes in ancient sources. Worse, Herodotus continues with an absurd story about the Cimmerians abandoning their supposed home region that became western Scythia of the Pontic Steppe region.

11. See Chapter 3, and on the mythology see Endnote 48.

12. Lubotsky (2002).

13. Vogelsang (1992: 175); Lubotsky (2002) dates the Urartian changes to the 7th century BC.

14. See the Prologue. In the Old Persian text of the Behistun Inscription Urarṭu is always called *Armina-* or *Arminiya* 'Armeniens' (Sch. 137–138), but in the Aramaic translation it is written אררט <'rrṭ> *Urarṭu* (Beckwith forthcoming-b), traditionally misread "Ararat".

15. Schmitt (2012d): the full name is "written ^{m}*Bar-ta-tu-a* . . . ^{LUGAL}*šá* ^{KUR}*Iš-ku-za*)", i.e., 'Bartatua, King of Scythia'. Schmitt notes this was the time of the Assyrian king Asarhaddon (r. 680–669). Cf. Endnote 49.

16. Ivantchik (2018).

At some time shortly thereafter the Scythians assumed rule over the large territory known in Greek as *Mēdia* (dial. *Mādia), in Akkadian *Madai* (^{kur}*Ma-da-a-a*), in Imperial Aramaic *Mād̠ay,* in Old Persian *Māda,* which stretched over a wide curve of the Zagros Mountains from the area of Ecbatana (now Hamadân) and the Nisaean Plain to Ragā (Greek Ῥάγες, Latin *Rhages,* medieval and modern *Ray,* now a part of metropolitan Tehran) and beyond into Central Asia.

According to Herodotus (i 104), in or shortly after 648 BC,[17] "A great army of Scythians, led by their king Madyes,[18] son of Protothyes", came to the aid of their Assyrian allies[19] and defeated the attacking Medians/Medes,[20] killing the Median/Mede ruler Phraortes (Fravartiš) in the process, and thus subjugating Media.[21] However, most of the details of his story are ahistorical, including the failed attack on Nineveh led by the mythical Phraortes who left his son Cyaxares an orphan, in accord with the latter's lost heroic foundation myth. Cyaxares, though probably in fact a child, is supposed to have resumed the attack, but was defeated by the Scythians. The account is mythologized and again suggests two competing stories developing in the text after Herodotus had finished with it. Basically, the events involving Phraortes and Cyaxares took place later during Cyaxares' overthrow of the Scythians, followed closely by the Medes' successful campaign to overthrow Assyria.[22] Despite the confusion in Herodotus' account, a generation-long period of Scythian rule in Media must have begun in or about 650 BC

17. Diakonoff (1985: 117).

18. From *madu- 'liquor; berry wine'; see Chapter 5.

19. Cf. Endnote 50.

20. Herodotus attests the change from the pre-Scythian Media of the "Medians", with their multilingual and political disunity, to the post-Scythian Media of the "Medes" or "Scytho-Medes", with their Scythian linguistic and political unity, in his positive account of the Scythians, which notes the "Medians" learning the Scythian language and customs during the period leading up to Cyaxares' coup d'état.

21. Herodotus (i 102,2). Alekseyev (2005) dates Madyes to ca. 650–600 BC, close to the dates that may be inferred from Herodotus. See Endnote 51.

22. Herodotus (i 102; i 103). The Akkadian sources make it certain that it was Cyaxares (not the Babylonians) who led the joint attack on the Assyrians, beginning in 615, and there is no mention of Scythian involvement. The Scytho-Medes captured Arrapḫa (now Kirkuk) in 615, Aššur in 614, and Nineveh in 612. For details see Zawadzki (1988).

in order to accomplish the well-attested Scythianizing linguistic and cultural creolization that happened at that time, so his date of 648 for its beginning is quite close.

Other events related to the period of Scythian rule are spottily recorded in sources written in several different ancient languages, including Greek (mainly Herodotus), and are basically historical.[23] The most significant one relates to a great southward campaign: "In the mid-620s . . . the Scythians reached the frontiers of Egypt, plundered several cities in Palestine, and routed the Cimmerians."[24] According to Herodotus (i 105), some of them turned aside on the way back to plunder the temple of Heavenly Aphrodite (perhaps Astarte, or Ishtar) at Ascalon (now Ashkelon). These Scythians must be the same as those who ruled Media at the time, though we do not know if they were or were not still Assyrian allies. The Scythian campaign (and the similar campaign of Cyaxares shortly after in Mesopotamia northwest of Babylon, discussed below) is surely connected to the sudden shift by the polytheistic Hebrews of Palestine to Heavenly God monotheism, a movement led by their prophet Jeremiah and his contemporary King Josiah at precisely this time.[25] The campaign gave the Hebrews firsthand knowledge of the Scythians.[26]

This episode and the stated period of Scythian rule in Herodotus—28 years, one generation—thus brings us to about 620.[27] The historical (mostly non-textual) evidence outside Herodotus solidly indicates that

23. See Endnote 52.

24. Ivantchik (2018), who adds the date. Herodotus appears to give the story as if it was the direct continuation of the original Scythian invasion (thus suggesting a missing passage in the text or a conflation of two original sources), but he explicitly mentions that the Scythians attacked the Egyptians and were bought off by King Psammetichus of Egypt, a contemporary of King Josiah of Judah and King Cyaxares of Media.

25. See the Epilogue.

26. The Scythians are mentioned in the Bible under the name אשכוזי *Aškuzai (misread in later times as אשכנזי Aškenazi), from Akkadian *Aškuzai* ~ *Iškuzai*, for Old Scythian *Skuδa-; cf. Endnote 45.

27. Since Cyaxares and his Scytho-Medes were in power no later than 615, when they captured the strategic Assyrian city of Arrapḫa (now Kirkuk), a period of five years is suggested to give him enough time to consolidate his rule over the extensive region of Media he had inherited, including Urartia (Armenia) and Parthia, at least.

the Scythians dominated or ruled the originally fractious region[28] of Media for several decades, during which they intermarried with the local peoples and creolized them thoroughly, unifying the Medians and others to the west and east of Media. Media and neighboring regions were dominated by the Scythian ruling group to the extent that the native peoples adopted Scythian dress, weapons, political-military organization and methods,[29] and, most importantly of all for history, the Scythian language,[30] as also shown by ancient literary accounts, including that of Herodotus, who explicitly mentions the children of Media learning Scythian. The best known and politically most powerful of these creolized regions was Scythianized Media, but the other local cultures, including Urartia, Parthia, Bactria, and other major regions of Central Asia, were also creolized by the Scythians in much the same way. As ancient writers note, most of these peoples spoke dialects of the same language, identified in Chapter 5 as Imperial Scythian.[31]

Accordingly, the Scytho-Mede prince Cyaxares ~ *Huvaχštra[32] (r. ca. 620–585/584 BC) carried out a successful coup d'état, overthrowing the Scythian rulers,[33] in about 620.[34] He became king of a new, united Scytho-Mede realm and overlord of many Scythianized vassal states in the region, including Urartia (Armenia), Parthia, Bactria, Anshan (Elam), Pārsa, and probably Areia and Arachosia. That did not mean

28. Though earlier the peoples of the region are called "the mighty Medians" in Assyrian texts (and also "the distant Medians"), they are specified as being dozens of small, independent city-states.

29. See the Prologue; cf. Vogelsang (1992).

30. See Chapter 6.

31. See Endnote 53.

32. The Old Persian transcription 𐎢𐎺𐎧𐏁𐎫𐎼 <u-v-x-š-t-r-> is usually reconstructed as Median *Huvaχštra (Schmitt 2009: 52; 2014: 70, 271), though the Akkadian transcription *Umakištar* reflects *Huvaχštar, and the Old Persian actually suggests the same thing. Cf. Skjærvø (1983: 248), who suggests an Old Persian reading Uvaχšt(a)ra from *Hvaχšt(a)ra < *hu̯a. The name is surely composed of *huva* 'good' + *χšaθra* 'realm, empire'; not with Sch. 271.

33. The repugnant cannibal feast story in Herodotus (i 106,2) is a topos; variants of it occur several times in the received text. It here tells how someone takes revenge by killing and cooking a child of an enemy, and serving it to him for dinner. It is ahistorical and non–Central Eurasian, but of uncertain origin.

34. See Endnote 54 on the date.

installation of an Assyrian-style system of rule enforced by terror—the system the Scytho-Medes had just overthrown. As heirs of the Scythian conquerors, the new rulers continued their inherited Scythian system of light feudal-hierarchical rule, which Herodotus actually describes quite accurately, and Strabo confirms.[35]

The future King Cyaxares was probably a small child or not yet born when the Scythians established their rule in Media. Although Herodotus does not give us a coherent story for him, as he does for Cyrus the Great, there are clear elements of a Cyaxares legend in his text.

The National Foundation Myth of Cyaxares

> When Phraortes (*Fravarti* 'the Fravaši', a semidivine being), the father of Cyaxares (*Huvaχštra*), is killed by invading Scythians, the young prince is orphaned. He is taken to court to be raised together with the princes of the invading people's royal family, and learns the Royal Scythian language, as well as how to hunt and shoot with the bow on horseback. He serves the Scythian king loyally and becomes a great warrior, but he is treated unjustly. He acquires a following of other young Scytho-Mede lords, and when the time is ripe they use their knowledge of the old Scythian ruling group to overthrow them.[36] Prince Cyaxares then ascends the throne as King of a righteous kingdom.[37]

As in more complete examples of the Central Eurasian National Foundation Myth, there is no clear line between myth or legend and actual history. In some stories the founding hero[38] was fully historical and met

35. Strabo (vii 4,6). See the Prologue for analysis of Herodotus' description.

36. See Endnote 55 on contradictions in the text of Herodotus (i 73,5–6).

37. This story is based on the account in Herodotus and the elements in it that accord with the typical Central Eurasian National Foundation Myth, q.v. Beckwith (2009: 1–12); see also Chapter 3 on the Cyrus story.

38. The legendary story of Deioces in Herodotus (i 96–101) is ahistorical if taken at face value. The Scytho-Mede Empire was simply the continuation of the Scythian Empire in Media and Central Asia, the former southern realm of the full Scythian Empire as a whole. The succession thus begins with Cyaxares. However, Herodotus' story of Phraortes (*Fravarti*) as a tragic Mede king, and the Mede rebels' reference to him as a former Mede king, suggests that the Scytho-Mede bards sang the epic tale of Cyaxares and could not omit his father, whom they

visitors from neighboring kingdoms who recorded their meetings with him and made alliances with him or fought against him, sometimes for decades. Although they are historical, they come out of the mythical, legendary mists of the age of epic heroes told by bards. The elements of Cyaxares' national foundation myth suggest that some of it is historical fact rather than myth, while some of it is probably myth rather than historical fact. Two key missing mythical elements are the abandonment of the orphan in the wilderness, where the animals save him (as in Justin's version of the Cyrus story), and his crossing of a body of water to reach safety (as in the Romulus story). These elements are absent in the minimal stories of some other famous nation-founders too, for example, the account of King *Bagatvana (Mo-tun) of the Hsiung-nu (East Scythians). That king was a near-contemporary of the king of the Wu-sun—who by contrast does have a complete version of the Central Eurasian National Foundation Myth (sans water crossing). Both men are quite historical, with the exception of the magical early parts of the Wu-sun king's story. However, what the defective story of Cyaxares has in common with the similarly defective story of *Bagatvana and that of several other famous Central Eurasian nation founders, including Temüjin, the founder of the Mongol Empire, is the secure historicity of the founding character and his main achievements. In short, the fact that these mythical or symbolic elements of the classic story are *missing* from Herodotus' account of Cyaxares, who is well attested in the sober Akkadian historical accounts of his conquest of Assyria, tells us that Cyaxares actually did most of what is historically credited to him.

According to the Central Eurasian National Foundation Myth,[39] the heaven-descended hero overthrows his father or another evil ruler in order to save his mother, or with the result that the mother (with her lineage) is saved. Since Cyaxares needed to have the heavenly Aria lineage in order to be a royal pretender, if his father was actually the Median Phraortes (*Fravarti*, a Persian word), his mother should have

called Phraortes (though that would be linguistically difficult), and possibly his grandfather too, Deioces. Cf. Chapter 8.

39. The most complete and detailed version of the myth in Herodotus is the long Cyrus foundation myth, the core part of which is given and discussed in Chapter 3.

been a Scythian woman. Although actual history did not by any means need to correspond exactly to the National Foundation Myth template, it is more difficult to imagine Cyaxares succeeding unless it were the other way around, i.e., it would be better if his father was a Scythian, such as Protothyes' son Madyes, and his mother was a Median, perhaps the sister or daughter of a historical Phraortes.[40] One way or another, Cyaxares must have had the indispensable *Aria* lineage of the Royal Scythians in order for him to grow up at court as a prince under their generation-long rule when, as Herodotus says, the people called themselves *Arias* 'Royals (Scythians)'.[41] It must also have been under Scythian rule that the citadel of *Agamatāna* (modern Amadân, Amadâne, now Hamadân), Greek *Ecbatana,* was built, or renamed in Scythian, as the capital.[42]

Herodotus on Scythian Rule in Media

Thus did Cyaxares grow up as a loyal, oathsworn Scythian subject like all the other subjects of the new realm the Scythians built on Median territory. That means, whatever his ancestry, he was raised *as a Scythian.* The text of Herodotus tells us about it directly and also indirectly in an imagined story that has Cyaxares, the son of earlier Median or Mede kings, ruling *at the same time* as the Scythians ruled. Although the account reveals two or more opposed ancient scribes at work on Herodotus' *Histories,* the cultural details agree exactly with what is known from the non-textual hard data.

> Cyaxares at first treated the Scythians kindly, as suppliants for his mercy; and, as he had a high regard for them, he entrusted boys to their tutelage to thoroughly learn their language and the skill of archery. As time went on, it happened that the Scythians, who were

40. The name Madyes suggests the folk-etymological story Herodotus tells about the Colchian Medea (and her son Madus, whom he does not mention) as the origin of the name *Media,* q.v. Chapter 5.

41. Herodotus (vii 62): Ἄριοι '*Arias*'.

42. On the putative builder, Deioces, the citadel's name, and the other Scythian capitals with the same name, see Chapter 8.

accustomed to go hunting and always to bring something back, once had taken nothing.[43]

The Median boys did not learn to speak fluent Scythian and shoot well (on horseback) by going to school, as Herodotus implies in his story,[44] but certainly in Central Eurasian fashion. As his account shows, they participated in *grande battue* food-gathering hunts (which were also archery practice and training for war) and certainly in Scythian military campaigns, as military service was mandatory for vassals, but the Medes did not send their children to be raised as Scythians, either out of charity toward the Scythians or out of Cyaxares' supposed high regard for them, as "Herodotus" states. The children learned these things by growing up as Scythians while the Scythians ruled Media, as the text explicitly repeats several times[45] and implies many more times.

The "Medes" thus began as "Medians", the pre-Scythian inhabitants of the geographical region of Media. Under Scythian rule the Medians were all politically Scythians. They worked and served in the army along with the other political Scythians, intermarried with the Scythians, and raised their children as Scythians too. Growing up as an *Aria*, a Royal Scythian, Cyaxares learned not only to shoot and speak like a Scythian but to ride and fight and think like one. He had to do that in order to be of any use in the Scythian army, in which he must have served, like all other young men in the realm. It was by growing up and living and fighting together with the Scythians that the Medians acquired the Scythian language, customs, dress and weapons, skills,

43. ὃς τοὺς Σκύθας τούτους τὸ μὲν πρῶτον περιεῖπε εὖ ὡς ἐόντας ἱκέτας: ὥστε δὲ περὶ πολλοῦ ποιεόμενος αὐτούς, παῖδάς σφι παρέδωκε τὴν γλῶσσάν τε ἐκμαθεῖν καὶ τὴν τέχνην τῶν τόξων. χρόνου δὲ γενομένου, καὶ αἰεὶ φοιτεόντων τῶν Σκυθέων ἐπ' ἄγρην καὶ αἰεί τι φερόντων, καὶ κοτε συνήνεικε ἑλεῖν σφεας μηδέν: Herodotus (i 73,3–4), from Perseus, tr. Godley, with minor emendations.

44. The story shortly becomes a topos-filled fantasy, but the text shows that Herodotus knew the Medes were expert archers who shot Scythian-style with Scythian bows and arrows, all on horseback, no doubt riding the Nisaean horses of Media, the most famous in the Ancient Near East. He also knew the Medes spoke Scythian, and they had learned all these things when the Scythians ruled Media.

45. Including Herodotus i 106,1; i 130,1; iv 1,1–3 (twice).

national foundation myth, belief in the God of Heaven, and feudal political structure.[46]

One of the outcomes of the acculturation and creolization process is that a new unified nation of "Medes" or "Scytho-Medes", which had not existed before, was created out of the heterogeneous "Medians" of the geographic region of Media. They spoke a new Scythian dialect, Imperial Scythian, the creole language spoken from Media to Arachosia, as Strabo tells us a little later, calling it "*Ariana*".[47] The inscriptional and textual evidence shows that it is the same language as Young Avestan, which is close to the archaic dialect of Zoroaster's *Gāthās*, Old Avestan.[48] Significantly, one of the two identifiable clans of the Medes (besides the Magi), and the only one that has a clearly Iranic name,[49] is the Ἀριζαντοί <*Arizantoi*> *Arya-zantu, which means 'the Aria Clan', i.e., the royal clan of the Scythians and their offspring.

According to Herodotus, when the Scythians allied by marriage to the Assyrians, Media came under the rule of their loyal vassals the Scythians in 648.[50] Here one Herodotus voice says that Cyaxares ruled, but tolerated the Scythians as "guests" for 28 years, whereas the other Herodotus voice says that the Scythians ruled Media at that time. The stories show that Cyaxares grew up at court as a young prince, but was subordinate to the Scythians when they ruled, meaning that the Scythians were the rulers. That would exactly follow the Central Eurasian National Foundation Myth and explain why Cyaxares had to carry out a coup d'état in order to take power. In Herodotus' story, the prince invites the Scythian leaders to a banquet and kills them.

46. See the Prologue. They also adopted Scythian clothing along with Scythian weapons. Cf. Endnote 56.

47. I.e., 'the language of the Royal ones'. See Chapter 5.

48. The Magi clan of Medes, who served the Persians as priests, no doubt mostly spoke Imperial Scythian, but many differed from the Persians religiously. In the Babylonian version of the Behistun Inscription (519 BC), the successor of Cambyses, Gaumāta, who is accused by Darius of being a polytheistic pretender and usurper, is called *ma-da-a-a . . . ma-gu-šu* 'a Mede . . . a Maguš' (Dandamayev 2012). See Endnote 57.

49. Dandamayev and Medvedskaya (2006); cf. Benveniste (1966: 83 [cited in Tav. 112]). It is Scythian by form. The other clan names appear not to be Iranic, or even Indo-European.

50. Herodotus (i 102–104); Diakonoff (1985: 117–118).

As ruler of the unified Scytho-Mede Empire,[51] King Cyaxares took control of Media and its subordinate neighbors, eventually including satrapies and sub-satrapies in at least Urartia (Armenia), Parthia, Elam, and Persis (Pārsa), as well as Bactria, Areia (Old Persian *Haraiva*, now Herat), and Arachosia.[52] The imperial feudal structure of the steppe Scythians, the Medes, and the Persians is described by Herodotus, who shows that the Persian system was a direct continuation of the earlier Scytho-Mede system, and neither Cyrus nor Darius changed it at all.[53]

After overthrowing the Scythian rulers, no source mentions Cyaxares *destroying* anything the Scythians had built. The Scythian-named capital Agamatana (*Ecbatana*), and its fabulous, but fully historical, gold-plated citadel, became his capital.[54] There is also no evidence that the Scytho-Medes changed their inherited Scythian clothing, weapons, state structure, religious beliefs, etc. The idea of doing so surely never occurred to them because by that time—at least one full generation, in places two or three generations—the Scythians (including the Cimmerians) and the native peoples had merged. The local women had married Scythian men and learned Scythian, and their children had all grown up in the local Scythian-ruled realm (as Herodotus describes) and thus learned Scythian too, so they all spoke Imperial Scythian. Under Scythian rule they became, simply, Scythians. Under Cyaxares they were Scytho-Medes, a new unified nation that had not existed before. Since the same thing had happened throughout the Empire he took over, the new creole dialects were mutually intelligible Scythian. Together they constituted the new language of the entire region, Imperial Scythian, just as the British conquest of large parts of the world in early modern times created many creolized dialects of English, most of which were mutually intelligible and have remained so.[55]

51. After commenting here on the early extreme disunity of the Zagros region (and again later in his article), Young (1988: 6) says, "Only late in the seventh century B.C. do the Medes apparently begin to become the dominant power even in Media." Cf. Endnote 58.

52. See Endnote 59.

53. See the Prologue.

54. See Chapter 8.

55. For details see Chapter 5.

A coup d'état usually entailed killing or subjugating the ruling leadership and its closest prominent supporters. Herodotus explicitly credits Cyaxares with killing some of the Scythian rulers, but no more.[56] He also reports that the surviving Scythians fled Media over the Caucasus Mountains into the North Caucasus Steppe, from which they eventually entered the Pontic Steppe and created a new, long-lasting Scythian realm,[57] though by no means did all the Scythians leave Media.[58] In his account of their migration to the north and their acquisition of the lands of the Pontic Steppe (in his story, their re-acquisition of them), Herodotus actually describes a process like what we might expect to have happened in Media under Scythian rule. He again uses a typically non–Central Eurasian story, this time about returning lords resubjugating their "slaves",[59] who would have been their vassals if the story were historical.[60] In fact, his account of Scythian youths mating with Amazon girls, and his account of the Scythians' "slaves" mating with Royal Scythian ruling clan wives while the men were in Media,[61] both actually show the process of national creolization within one generation. So despite the faux slaves, the story relates what clearly had happened in Media under Scythian rule, whether or not it really happened in the Pontic Steppe.[62]

Nevertheless, many Scythians remained in the Near East. They were there before, during, and after the period of their rule over the Medes;

56. See Endnote 60.

57. Khazanov (2016), following Herodotus (iv 1,3). Khazanov (2014: 35) says the Scythians "had to conquer or retake the territories to the east and north of the Black Sea. First, they settled, or rather resettled, in the plains of the North Caucasus. In all likelihood, they had held on to this region even during their invasions of the Near East. Their rich burial mounds (*kurgans*)—Kostromskaia, Kelermess, Ul'skii, Krasnoe Znamia, and others—were excavated in the western (Kuban River valley) and other regions of the North Caucasus." See Endnote 61.

58. Many remained in the southern Caucasus region, forming the later statelet of Sakasene or Sakasena (Dandamayev and Grantovskiĭ 2012), about which some source material exists, but there are few good studies of it. See Endnote 62.

59. According to his doubtful story they used whips (Herodotus iv 1,3; iv 3,1–4; iv 4).

60. Herodotus (iv 72,1) explicitly says the Scythians did not practice slavery, q.v. Endnotes 39 and 101.

61. Archaeology has shown the story to be ahistorical (Khazanov 2016).

62. The Greeks did not understand Central Eurasian feudal-hierarchical sociopolitical structure (see the Prologue), nor did the Chinese. The Greeks and Chinese had slaveholding societies and wrongly thought people in the subordinate levels of the foreign feudal hierarchy system were slaves.

they were still there in the 590s,[63] doing what they had been doing before the change; and as attested by their later successor state, Sacasene, at the northern edge of Media,[64] they remained in the region for centuries. In Media, most of them undoubtedly acculturated with the new "Scytho-Mede" creole ethnos they themselves had created, just as in Babylonia they assimilated to the Babylonians, as attested in Akkadian texts. They thus became Medes, or rather, many were already "Medes" because they were, more precisely, *Scytho-Medes*, half Scythian by birth. Some, like Cyaxares, belonged to the *Aria* 'royal line' clan of Scytho-Medes.[65] According to Herodotus, they had originally called themselves "*Arias*" and only later changed their name to "Medes".[66] Although that is not actually true, it is correct that the epithet of the ruling people had previously been *Aria*, 'the Royals', because that was the Royal Scythians' self-designation.

In 615 the Medes under Cyaxares attacked and captured the Assyrian city of Arrapḫa (now Kirkuk), then in 614 Tarbiṣu (a few miles from Nineveh) and Aššur, the home city of the Assyrians.[67] He had already made a treaty with Nabopolassar, king of Babylon, for a joint assault on the great, heavily fortified Assyrian capital city, Nineveh, but as the sources indicate, Nabopolassar showed up too late for the assault in 614, so instead the Medes attacked and destroyed Aššur by themselves. The two kings then conferred and made a new peace agreement.[68]

In the following year, 613, a revolt is said to have broken out, centered in Sūḫu (Suhi), in northwestern Babylonia.[69] Cyaxares attacked the rebels and destroyed their cities, their temples, and their gods (i.e., the statues). As the Medes approached Babylon, Nabopolassar huddled on

63. Diakonoff (1985: 119).

64. See Endnote 62.

65. See Chapter 5.

66. Herodotus (vii 62).

67. Kuhrt (2007, 1: 30). See Zawadzki (1988) for a careful, detailed study of Cyaxares' campaigns in the Akkadian sources.

68. *Gadd's Chronicle* says Nabopolassar arrived too late to aid the Medes in 614, but the two kings "met one another in front of the city and concluded a mutual accord and peace." Kuhrt (2007, 1: 30).

69. On the problems in the historical account, and their apparent textual solution, see Endnote 63.

the floor,[70] but hardly out of respect for or fear of the gods. It was certainly out of fear of the Medes, who are portrayed in Babylonian sources as a terrible enemy. It is quite clear in the context that the destruction was not done as a favor to the Medes' ally Babylon but rather the opposite: it was intended to frighten Nabopolassar into carrying out his commitment to the Medes' campaign against the common enemy of practically the entire Near East: the Assyrian Empire.

In the next year, 612, Cyaxares led his army to attack Nineveh. It included Elamites—as shown by the pattern of defacement of persons portrayed on bas-reliefs in the great palace of Nineveh[71]—and thus no doubt some Persians too.[72] At the last minute Babylonian forces did show up at Nineveh for the final assault.[73] Nineveh was captured and destroyed. In 610–609 the last Assyrian bastion, Ḫarrān, was taken by the Medes and Babylonians, and the Medes similarly destroyed the great temple of Ehulhul there.[74]

Cyaxares was succeeded by King Astyages[75] (r. 585–550/549), who was probably his son, as Herodotus says.[76] Astyages was campaigning in Babylonia—we do not know the reason, whether aiming to enlarge

70. The *Babil Stele* of Nabonidus (Kuhrt 2007, 1: 33). In his *Cyrus Cylinder* Cyrus the Great states that among other regions, he restored the gods and their sanctuaries from the upper Tigris to Media ("Gutium") (Briant 2002: 43), the very region where Cyaxares had destroyed them.

71. Henkelman (2003) gives details and cites the literature, concluding "at least some Elamites had joined the Median invaders".

72. See Endnote 64.

73. See Endnote 65.

74. This is established by the later account of Nabonidus, who set out to restore Ḥarrān, especially its temple of Ehulhul. He states that it was the Medes who had captured the city from the Assyrians, destroyed the temple, and retained control of the region around it for decades, preventing Nabonidus from restoring the temple. Zawadzki's (1988: 124–125 and notes) detailed analysis concludes that the Medes and Babylonians were both involved in the capture of Ḥarrān in 610–609, but that the great temple of Ehulhul was destroyed by the Medes.

75. Akkadian *Ištumegu*, perhaps representing Old Iranic *Stāvaiga or the like. See Endnote 66.

76. Herodotus (i 107,1). The typically wild account of Ctesias denies this and also claims Cyrus was a commoner son of a robber and a goatherd. He goes on to say that because Cyrus married Cyaxares' daughter Amytis, the Bactrians, who had been in rebellion against him, accepted him as the legitimate heir of Astyages (Kuhrt 2007, 1:97–98). However, that is virtually impossible as stated. Without the royal Aria lineage Cyrus could not have been a legitimate king in the Bactrians' eyes, and marrying the daughter of one could not legitimize him. Yet Cyrus really was a legitimate heir (see Chapter 4), and according to the account of Herodotus he was also the son of the Mede princess Mandane. The one useful comment in Ctesias' account is that

the realm or following in Cyaxares' iconoclastic footsteps—where he came to blows with Cyrus II, King of Anshan, a polytheist.[77] When Astyages' army mutinied, Cyrus captured him (in 550–549).[78] Cyrus was from Anshan in Elam and had an Elamite name, so he was evidently part Elamite, and the same is true of his eldest son and successor Cambyses II (r. 530–522 BC),[79] but all Greek sources agree that Cyrus was somehow related to Astyages. According to Herodotus, he was Astyages' grandson. Study of his and Darius' lineages shows that he must already have been part Scythian or Scytho-Mede from an earlier ancestor.[80] Thus Cyrus actually continued the Scytho-Mede royal line of Cyaxares and Astyages, as well as another earlier branch.

As shown in Chapter 3, Cyrus as Great King (r. 550/549–530) vastly enlarged the Scytho-Mede Empire, conquering most of Anatolia as well as Babylonia and Syria, but died after his defeat in battle in Central Asia by the Massagetae, a Scytho-Sarmatian people ruled by Queen Tomyris.[81] Cyrus' son Cambyses (r. 530–522) continued the military exploits of his father by conquering Egypt and Libya. He campaigned in Egypt from 525 to 522, when a civil war broke out in several constituent lands of the Empire, centering on religious policy.[82] He left Egypt in spring of 522 to deal with it, but died on the way in Syria that summer. He was childless, so there was no direct successor, because his also childless brother Bardiya (Greek Smerdis) had already died (evidently murdered), after which, according to all sources, a pretender or usurper known as Gaumāta had taken the throne. The modern view that Bardiya was actually still alive, reigning peacefully as king, ignores the fact that

---

according to him the Bactrians were vassals of the Medes. This is supported by studies on the organization of the imperial satrapies (see the Prologue) as well as by linguistic and sartorial evidence.

77. See Endnote 67.

78. Briant (2002: 31–33). The Akkadian sources do not clearly say how long they fought, but only that Cyrus captured Astyages in 550/549. The Classical sources agree that Cyrus spared Astyages and treated him well. That would have been almost unthinkable unless he really was a close relative.

79. Potts (2005).

80. See Chapter 4; cf. Herodotus (i 108).

81. Herodotus (i 214,3).

82. The civil war is usually referred to as a series of "rebellions". See also Chapter 3. Shahbazi (2012) discusses the pretender Gaumāta and the other "rebels" in detail.

several rebellions had already broken out well before Cambyses' return and death.[83]

Darius I "the Great" (r. 522–486 BC)[84] was the second cousin (once removed) of Cyrus, and Spearbearer—a high-ranking officer—of Cambyses in Egypt.[85] Shortly after returning from Egypt, Darius was briefed on the situation and organized or joined a group of conspirators. They went to Gaumāta's hill fortress in Media and killed him. Over the following year Darius put down a number of "rebels" who, he says, had failed to support monotheism—specifically the worship of Ahura Mazdā, the official religious policy of the Empire under his rule.[86] Darius declares himself to be a "Persian" but traces his lineage back to Achaemenes, making his Empire "Achaemenid", though it remained the same Empire that he had taken over. Nothing had changed except Darius' restoration of the pre-Cyrus religious policy. Moreover, Darius succeeded only because he was—and successfully claimed to be—a member of the same "dynasty" as Cyrus, which belonged to the *Aria* 'royal' ruling lineage. Darius was *Ariya Ariyačiça* 'an *Aria* and seed of an *Aria*', as he explicitly says in his tomb inscription[87] and as is confirmed by comparison of the family lineage he gives in his inscriptions with the lineage given by Cyrus the Great in the latter's *Cyrus Cylinder*.[88]

Herodotus says that the radical, unprecedented characteristics of the Mede Empire were due to Cyaxares himself, who thus innovated on his own an entire new civilization. If Cyaxares had carried out an "un-Scythian" reorganization of Media, or if he had "de-Scythianized" Media, we would have to agree that he must be responsible for the innovations, thus explaining the Persian Empire as a Median innovation. In that case there would be no need for Scythians or other outsiders.

83. Shahbazi (2012).

84. Schmitt (2011d); Briant (2002) does not include the period of civil war. He discusses some of the problems presented by the Behistun Inscription's account (Briant 2002: 117–121), but as none of the other contenders can be said to have ruled most of the Empire, Darius' reign should begin with his accession in 522.

85. Shahbazi (2012).

86. See Endnotes 68 and 69.

87. Naqš-i Rustam DNa.

88. See the detailed treatment in Chapter 4; cf. Shahbazi (2012).

But the putative Median innovations correspond *exactly* to the attested equivalent elements in traditional Central Eurasian culture, specifically the beliefs, practices, and physical culture of the Scythians, the very people whose extensive empire in Central and Southwestern Asia Cyaxares had just taken over by coup d'état, as Herodotus tells us. Moreover, the Scythian Empire and the Scythians' many innovations remained in place for centuries, and their one legitimate *Aria* ~ *Ariya* ~ *Ḥarya* royal line continued to exist, in name, for at least a millennium and a half.[89]

The Scythians, as Central Eurasians, fought differently, organized differently, and thought differently about their realm and how it figured in the eternal scheme of things. Although Cyaxares and his allies overthrew the Scythian *rulers* in Media, they retained the former Scythian *realm* there, and its culture, in all other respects. The empire was an organic whole from top to bottom, and each element was key to its success, so it could not really be changed. Cyrus the Great kept the Empire and the entire imperial system intact—with the exception of the religious element—when he overthrew the Mede king, Astyages. There is no evidence that Cyrus "conquered" the Empire. He simply took it over by defeating Astyages in what seems to have been a coup d'état. At any rate, he continued the Empire and greatly expanded it. But he openly supported polytheism, or possibly pluralism. Darius actually assumed power the same way, by coup d'état, but because of Cyrus' evident opposition to strict monotheism, which opposition had eventually encouraged the independent-minded, Darius had to fight many rebels to restore the unifying, strict 'public monotheism' of the Empire.[90]

A particular Central Eurasian detail is relevant here. According to Ctesias, when Cyrus defeated Astyages in 550 BC,[91] he entered the

89. See Chapter 4.

90. Cf. Endnote 69.

91. Kuhrt (2007, 1: 56–57, note 8). The *Chronicle of Nabonidus* says, on the fall of the Mede king: "King Astyages called up his troops and marched against Cyrus, king of Anšan, in order to meet him in battle. The army of Astyages revolted against him and delivered him in fetters to Cyrus. Cyrus marched against the country of Ecbatana; the royal residence he seized; silver, gold, other valuables of the country Ecbatana he took as booty and brought to Anšan." There is no reference here, or in the *Cyrus Cylinder*, to Persis. See Endnote 70.

tent of the Mede king to accept his surrender and the symbols of his rule.[92] This was certainly no ordinary tent, but the royal ancestor of the huge, magnificent tent of Xerxes I, covered with "gold and silver embroidery",[93] which was captured by the Athenians in 479.[94] The royal golden tent was a symbol of divinely ordained rulership well attested from Antiquity through the Middle Ages[95] and used down to early modern times.[96]

However, unlike earlier Ancient Near Eastern examples, or European examples, in the ancient Scytho-Mede Empire and the Persian Empire the royal golden tent (and its image, the satrap's tent) was not pitched just anywhere. It was placed in the middle of a prepared formal grassy garden known as a *paradise*,[97] which was provided with water and good drainage. The rulers of the Empire used the royal golden tent even when staying in one of the capitals. Large parts of the Persian imperial palace cities of Pasargadae and Susa were leveled to construct paradises. That is thought to explain why the Persian imperial capitals often lack residence buildings for the imperial entourage. Today the former paradise areas, no longer filled with trees and other greenery, look empty.

> The apparent emptiness of major parts of Susa [and other Persian imperial palace cities] does not necessarily indicate a reduced population. . . . [The] Achaemenid court was itinerant. Classical sources

92. Briant (2002: 188), describing Cyrus the Great's actions upon his victory over Astyages, cites a fragment of Ctesias, *FGrH* 90 F66.45. The passage may be translated, "Cyrus having entered the tent sits on the throne of Astyages, and takes his scepter. The Persians acclaim him, then one of his men, Oibaras, puts the *kidaris* ('upright crown', symbol of royalty) on him, saying, 'You are worthier than Astyages to bear (the sceptre), since God grants (it) to you on account of your virtue, and the Persians (are worthier) to rule the Medes.'" Quintus Curtius Rufus (3.11, 23), quoted in Briant (2002: 188), says that for Persians it was "an established custom that they should receive the victor in the conquered king's *tent*".

93. Translating ποικίλοισι after *LSJ*.

94. Herodotus (9.82) describes it: "When Xerxes fled from Hellas, he left to [his general] Mardonius his own tent and furnishings." From Perseus, tr. Godley, but translating Greek παρασκευή, as in *LSJ*, s.v. κατασκευή. For discussion and references see Schmid (2013).

95. Beckwith (1993: 168, note 60).

96. Allsen (2002: 12–14, 65–66).

97. See Endnote 71.

describe the spectacular royal tent, set up amidst a vast camp wherever the court halted.[98]

The luxurious, and enormous, golden tent, a symbol of the king's divinely ordained rulership, was placed in the center of the paradise, and inside it he presided over banquets, gift-bestowal, and other events. The excavations at Tell Ecbatana in Hamadân have revealed just such a paradise within the walls,[99] perhaps the very one in which Astyages' tent was pitched.[100]

But Astyages was a Scytho-Mede king. Why would the Elamite-Persians, thoroughly sedentary people, be fixated on tents, and on regular peregrination about the Empire, and on pitching the Imperial golden tent in a flat grassy space? Surely because that is what the Scythians had done. The Scythians, as a pastoral nomadic people, were accustomed to regularly peregrinate about their grassy realm, herding their animals and checking up on their satraps in the process. They surely missed their Central Eurasian homeland. The golden tent *in a grassy paradise*, including even the term *paradise* itself, an Imperial Scythian word, was new, part of the new Central Eurasian imperial cultural package transmitted not by "borrowing" or "trade" but by Scythian rule. The Scytho-Medes did the same because that is what they were accustomed to from their Scythian upbringing, even though it was in Media.[101]

It must be emphasized that throughout world history, not just in this instance, major cultural transmission normally takes place via *direct domination* of native peoples by intruders. The process is very well

98. Henkelman (2012), who here cites inter alia Briant (2002: 186–192), Henkelman (2011), and Boucharlat (2001). Cf. Boucharlat (2013). There is a substantial archaeological literature on these and related topics.

99. I am indebted to Jamsheed Choksy for kindly sending me copies of his photos taken there on July 21, 2003. For Ecbatana see Chapter 8.

100. See Endnote 72.

101. The golden tent is well attested among Central Eurasian rulers from Antiquity through the Middle Ages. For the golden tent of the Uighurs and Tibetans see Beckwith (1993: 168 and note 160). See Allsen (1997: 13–15) on the golden tents of the later Mongol khans. As for the tent's salient golden aspect, and the central symbolic role of gold itself (Walter 2013), it is well attested among the Scythians in their national foundation myth, art, and archaeology; see Chapter 1.

attested from early modern times to the present. Structurally significant cultural transmission seems rarely, if ever, to have taken place "horizontally" via "influences", "contact", or even "trade", despite scholars' fascination with such ideas today.[102] In the Scythian case, their core beliefs, practices, and customs accompanied them and were practiced by them in their new peripheral lands. The peripheral peoples, as subjects, received key elements of the rulers' culture "vertically", in situ, directly from the new ruling people, and they adopted them, including their ruling system, language, and weapons, all the way down to their clothes. In the case at hand, the subject people *became* the ruling people.[103]

From the Scythian conquest through the long Scytho-Mede-Persian Achaemenid "Dynasty", the Empire retained all of the key innovative Scythian elements that constituted it. The Scythians, though today a much ignored, misunderstood, and despised people, thus managed to accomplish a spectacular reorganization of the Ancient Near Eastern socio-political system and culture, including provision of a unifying new Imperial spoken language and radically new, elegant, clothing fashions. And except for an occasional war of succession or expansion, the Empire as a whole existed continuously, without a structural break, from the time of its Scythian foundation to the death of Alexander the Great in 323 BC.

Thus in the west the original Scythian Empire was survived by a powerful creole realm that under Scytho-Mede rule became the "Mede Empire" and eventually the "Persian" Empire. In the east it was similarly survived by a powerful creole realm that included much of what became the state of Chao, later the birth home of the First Emperor, who led the Ch'in state to victory over the other Warring States and founded the Chinese Empire.[104]

102. See Terminology, s.v. 'Silk Road'.

103. See Endnote 186.

104. See Chapter 7. The parallel development of these two Scythianized realms needs to be constantly borne in mind, as well as the long-ignored "elephant in the room" responsible for both: the Scythian Empire.

The Scythian Military Innovations and the Scytho-Medes

What we know about the Scythians both in the steppe zone and in Media tells us that when the Scythians ruled their Empire in Media and Central Asia it was unique in the Ancient Near East. Historians have traditionally asserted that the Scythians' successor realm in that region, the Mede or Scytho-Mede Empire, was like neighboring archaic Near Eastern realms such as the Assyrian Empire, so it must have developed in accord with that model, with large stone palaces and cities, which would leave the usual Ancient Near Eastern archaeological remains. But the steppe Scythians had few cities (they did have some) and left mainly barrows, or nothing, for archaeologists. The Scytho-Medes seem to have been much the same in this respect.[105] Traditional modern scholars' expectations for the Scytho-Medes are similar to the ancient approach of Ctesias to explaining the origin of the new and distinctive style of clothing adopted by the Persians from the Medes, and by them from someone else: Ctesias attributes its invention to Mesopotamian antiquity and a young Assyrian queen, Semiramis,[106] a heroic city girl from a sedentary agricultural land.

It is thus astounding that Herodotus credits Cyaxares, the first solidly historical king of Media, with practically all of the innovations in the Mede realm, which were taken over unchanged in turn by Cyrus and Darius. Herodotus (i 96–99) also ascribes the building of the famous citadel of Ecbatana to a Median ruler, though not to Cyaxares but to a legendary founder king, Deioces, who unites the disorganized Medians into a distinct nation consisting of five clans, of which one is the *Aria clan—in origin the Royal clan of the Scythians. Because of Herodotus' inaccurate dates, scholars have argued that Deioces must be identified with a very early leader who cannot be connected to the Medes. However, Herodotus is on the right track. The *actual* Medes themselves—a new, distinct nation, the Scytho-Medes—did not yet exist until the

105. See Endnote 73.

106. See Appendix B.

*Aria 'Royal Scythians' had ruled them, shaping them into a Scythian creole nation with an *Aria clan ruler and a capital city named Agamatana (Ecbatana). The Medes themselves were thus part of the Scythian package of innovations, or a product of it. I.e., the many earlier Median (or "pre-Mede") native peoples of the geographical zone called Media were the recipients of the entire Scythian tradition via Scythian rule over them, which is symbolized by Deioces in Herodotus' story. Whereas before the Scythians Media was a region with dozens of independent "city chiefs" or kinglets, most of whom have names that are clearly non-Indo-European and are unidentifiable, by the time of Darius there is no evidence of any non-Iranic-speaking people in Media or in the other regions that had been ruled by the Scythians and the Scytho-Medes after them.[107]

Under Darius and his successors, the Scythians constituted the core of the imperial army, alongside the Persians and Medes.[108] Must we really believe this was due to their arrows alone, however excellent? The Medes are known to have used Scythian arrows, but that is because they included both the Scytho-Medes and the remaining Scythians who stayed in Media. As they had all grown up under Scythian tutelage (as Herodotus tells us), the "Medes" were Scytho-Medes and necessarily expert archers, fletchers, and smiths. Moreover, bas-reliefs portraying Medes on the walls of Persepolis show them wearing Scytho-Mede clothes, bearing both the Scythian bow and bow-case (*gorytos*) and the Scythian short sword (*akinakes*).[109] The Scytho-Medes were Scythians in practically every respect.

There is thus a very good explanation for the Scythians' military importance. The reason is that they, not Cyaxares, were responsible for both the unification of Media and for its military reorganization.

107. See the Prologue.

108. Briant (2002: 747, 765–766). The core of the Persian military was essentially tripartite: Persian, Mede, Scythian, though not in that order of actual on-the-ground military importance, which, based on Greek accounts of the Persian wars, was: Scythian, Persian, Mede. At the same time it was partly a functional division of labor, as the Scythians are explicitly said by Herodotus (see below) to have constituted the cavalry of the Persian Empire.

109. Vogelsang (1992).

Herodotus remarks in passing on the Scythians and their relatives the Massagetae distinguishing "cavalry" from "infantry", while the latter category is in turn differentiated into "spearmen and archers":

> The Massagetae are like the Scythians both in the clothing they wear and the way of life they follow. They are both cavalry and infantry (having some of each kind), both archers and spearmen; and they customarily carry the *sagaris* (Scythian battle-axe).[110]

In short, although Herodotus' description may not accord perfectly with the actual battle order among the Scythians or Massagetai, the important point was that the different kinds of warriors are clearly distinguished *functionally* by their way of fighting, and are not mixed together randomly or by nation or other non-military criteria. That is what Herodotus is talking about when he later refers to this innovation, which he ascribes to Cyaxares:

> Cyaxares was the first to organize the men of Asia in companies and posted each arm apart, the spearmen and [foot-]archers and cavalry: before this they were all mingled together in confusion.[111]

The army of Cyaxares was thus ordered along strictly functional lines, though this was not, again, an innovation of Cyaxares.[112] The key feature is separation of the cavalry from the other units. There is a particular reason for this. The power of Central Eurasian cavalry came from their close-ranked rapid attack, feint, and flanking methods, much noted by Chinese historians, and the fact that they were highly trained mounted archers. Even as late as Xerxes' campaign against the Greeks (480–481), Herodotus says, "Among the barbarians [i.e., the non-Greeks (in the Persian army)], the best fighters were the Persian infantry

110. Herodotus (i 215): Μασσαγέται δὲ ἐσθῆτά τε ὁμοίην τῇ Σκυθικῇ φορέουσι καὶ δίαιταν ἔχουσι, ἱππόται δὲ εἰσὶ καὶ ἄνιπποι (ἀμφοτέρων γὰρ μετέχουσι) καὶ τοξόται τε καὶ αἰχμοφόροι, σαγάρις νομίζοντες ἔχειν; from Perseus, tr. Godley. The *sagaris* is a distinctively Scythian weapon found in Scythian burial sites across Eurasia.

111. Herodotus (i 103,1): Κυαξάρης . . . πρῶτός τε ἐλόχισε κατὰ τέλεα τοὺς ἐν τῇ Ἀσίῃ καὶ πρῶτος διέταξε χωρὶς ἑκάστους εἶναι, τούς τε αἰχμοφόρους καὶ τοὺς τοξοφόρους καὶ τοὺς ἱππέας: πρὸ τοῦ δὲ ἀναμὶξ ἦν πάντα ὁμοίως ἀναπεφυρμένα; from Perseus, tr. Godley.

112. See Endnote 74.

and the cavalry of the Sacae [the Scythians],"[113] who were archers.[114] Ssu-ma Ch'ien reports most famously and vividly the story of how the Hsiung-nu (East Scythian) prince *Bagatvana (Mo-tun)[115] trained his armored cavalry archers to shoot simultaneously at whatever he shot, maximizing their impact.[116] They could do this only if they fought as one or more cohesive units, not mixed together with slow-moving infantry who would get in the way.[117]

The radical cultural reshaping of highly fragmented early Media into a distinctive new nation, the Scytho-Medes, with a great empire, is not the only example of successful Scythianization. At the same time, at the other end of the Scythian cultural zone in Central Eurasia, the exact same thing happened in the region that became the ancient state of Chao.[118] It included adoption of Scythian dress, weapons, style of warfare, and language.

As discussed in Chapters 4 and 7, a large part of Chao had earlier been under the rule of various Central Eurasian peoples. That included the region known as *Ta Hsia* 大夏 (*Dà Xià*) 'great *Ḥarya* (*Aria*), the *Ḥarya* (*Aria*) Empire', in which the ruling *Ḥarya* ~ *Aria* 'royal lineage' must have been bilingual in Scythian and Chinese in order to deal with the Scythian realm on one side and the Chinese Warring States on the other. By the same process of creolization described for Media, the Scytho-Chinese people of the ruling *Ḥarya* ~ *Aria* lineage, 'the royals', understood the importance of the pregnant word *Ḥarya* ~ *Aria* 'the royal ones, the rightful rulers', and spread it not only throughout Chao but

113. Herodotus (ix 71,1): ἠρίστευσε δὲ τῶν βαρβάρων πεζὸς μὲν ὁ Περσέων, ἵππος δὲ ἡ Σακέων; from Perseus, tr. Godley. For detailed study of the word *Scythian* and its variants, including *Saka*, see Chapter 6.

114. Herodotus (ix 49).

115. See Chapter 4.

116. The Alans, direct descendants of the Scythians, are historically attested as continuing to practice the same highly trained mounted archery techniques in late antique and early medieval Western Europe, to stunning effect, as did the Turkic peoples in medieval East Asia. For the Alans see Bachrach (1973).

117. The appearance of the Scythians' highly distinctive arrowheads in walls across the Middle East at this time shows that Scythians or Scytho-Medes shot them there. The arrows themselves cannot tell us whether or not the shooters are to be identified as Scythians or Scytho-Medes or both.

118. See Chapter 4.

eventually among the other states of early pre-imperial China, where it became the first ethnolinguistic term for 'the Chinese' and 'the Chinese language'. There had previously been no name in the Chinese cultural area for 'the Chinese', or 'the Chinese language'. Conceptually, at least, the foreign epithet *Hsia* 夏 (*Xià*) **Ḥarya*, also transcribed as *Hua* 華 (*Huá* from *Ḥâryá), is responsible for the Chinese acquiring the idea of themselves as one distinct people with one language.

Media and Chao were four thousand miles apart, and there is no evidence that anyone knew the same thing was going on in both places at the same time.[119] Today we can read ancient sources from both West and East which show that Scythian rule in the two regions was revolutionary in the same ways. The hard data and historical sources are unambiguous. The radical changes that occurred in both places, changing them from Archaic cultures to Classical cultures, were the result of Scythian rule over them.

119. Perhaps the Scythians themselves knew, but they left no known written historical records.

3

The Scytho-Mede Persian Empire

Vogelsang says, "The Persian Achaemenid empire was built on the foundations of the Median empire. Starting in the second half of the seventh century B.C., the Medes had carved out a large realm in lands that shortly before had been engulfed by the equally Iranian Scythians and Cimmerians from the steppes of Central Eurasia."[1]

More precisely, Cyaxares, Cyrus, and Darius in turn each *took over* the Scythians' Empire based in Media, which began as a feudal "great satrapy" of the huge original Empire that had introduced so many unprecedented innovations to the ancient Middle East (as well as East Asia). Each ruler enlarged the Empire, but otherwise retained its key features—with the exception of the disastrous policies of Cyrus and his sons regarding religion. But none founded a new "dynasty". They surely did not even think of doing so. They needed to be, and were, members of the world's one and *only* legitimate *Aria* ~ *Ariya* ~ *Ḥarya* 'royal lineage' clan:[2] *amaxam taumā* 'our seed; our family/clan', as Darius says in the Behistun Inscription,[3] in which he traces his lineage back to a Scythian prince. Each of these kings made a new beginning while preserving

1. Vogelsang (1998: 208), quoted with slight stylistic modifications and "Central Eurasia" for his "Central Asia".

2. See Chapter 4, with detailed analysis of the term and concept, as well as the rulers' lineages.

3. DB 3 (108), 12 (146), etc.: 𐎠𐎶𐎧𐎶𐏐𐎫𐎢𐎶𐎠𐏐.

and continuing the Scythian Empire. They enlarged it, but at no point did they "carve out" a realm from it. The Scythians had founded the Empire, the world's first true "empire", in what became, and still is, the usual sense, and the people over whom they first ruled *became* Scythians by creolization. Each takeover was purely a "family matter". The Empire continued.

The Legitimate Royal Lineage

Because the Scythians created the imperial tradition in their Central Eurasian homeland, and founded the heavenly *Aria* lineage of royalty, they were legitimate from the outset and had no competition when they began. The historical question has been the legitimacy of their successors.

Cyaxares, according to Herodotus (i 73,3; i 102–103), was the son of a certain Phraortes (Fravarti), said to have been king of the Medians before him, and so a Median by birth, and conceivably a legitimate ruler. Herodotus, as traditionally interpreted, says Phraortes died in 653, but according to him Cyaxares only acceded to the throne in 625, leaving a gap of 28 years, during which the *Scythians* ruled Media, but also *Cyaxares* ruled at the same time. He is approximately right chronologically about the period of *Scythian* rule, but his story about the putative Mede national founder Deioces (*Dahyu-ka), and about his putative son and successor Phraortes (Fravarti) being the father of Cyaxares, is problematic.[4] Although the received *text* (not "Herodotus", the original author) is obviously confused about whether Cyaxares was ruling or the Scythians were ruling in the second half of the 7th century,[5] the story about Cyaxares taking the Scythians in as his guests is nonsense, as noted above, and in fact the other account (mixed in with the "guests" account) says simply that the Scythians ruled. Cyaxares was no doubt a small child at best when the Scythians took over, and he grew to manhood as a Scythian or half-Scythian. Without the Royal Scythian (*Aria*)

4. See, among many other critiques, Young (1988).

5. This problem is textual in nature rather than historical, but pending a textual solution, or more sources, we are stuck with the received text.

lineage, culture, and language he could not have lived at the royal court, and could not have taken over the Scythian realm as a legitimate ruler. Thus either his father or his mother must have been Scythian royalty, whereas no doubt equally important, his other parent should have been of local Median descent, to give him support from people with both heritages. Herodotus gives several clear indications that the new ruler was in fact a member of the royal *Aria* lineage of the Scythians and (Scytho-)Medes.[6]

We must also look at what Cyaxares actually did after his successful coup and accession to the throne of the Scythian Empire in Media, now the Mede Empire. As a Scythian or half-Scythian born and raised, he inherited the Scythian Empire and its ideology, including the Scythian belief in one universal Heavenly God who had created Heaven and Earth, as well as the entire feudal-hierarchical imperial system, meaning overlordship of the satrapies (from *xšathrapa-*, a Scythian word) as far to the east and southeast as Bactria and Arachosia, as well as in Urartia (Armenia) to the west and Elam (Anshan) and Pārsa 'Persis' (now Fârs) to the south. Cyaxares maintained all of the cultural innovations introduced to Media by the Scythians, most of which are noted or suggested in Herodotus' account, as discussed in the Prologue and Chapter 2. The completeness of Cyaxares' inherited system suggests that he may actually have followed the political template of the Central Eurasian National Foundation Myth by leading a rebellion of his oppressed people (the Scytho-Medes) against the unrighteous alien conquerors—the foreign-born Scythian rulers, perhaps including his own father (a frequent element of the myth), as presented above.[7] In any event, to be a legitimate ruler in the Scythian system, Cyaxares must have been at least part *Aria* '(one of legitimate) Royal lineage'. Because he did succeed to the throne, he must have been a member of the *Arizantoi* or *Arya-zantu 'the Aria (Royal) Clan' of the Scytho-Medes mentioned by Herodotus. Accordingly, he did not have a legitimacy problem.

6. Herodotus (i 101) calls it the *Arya-zantu 'Aria clan' *of the Medes*.

7. See Chapter 2. On the Central Eurasian National Foundation Myth see Beckwith (2009: 1–12).

What about Cyrus, though? In the Cyrus myth (see below), Herodotus tells us the prince was born half Persian and half royal Mede, but was raised by a herdsman in "his homeland in the mountains between Ecbatana and the Black Sea". That is an important remark because the Scythians maintained a strong presence precisely in that region long after the Scytho-Medes and Persians took over the Empire. It at least suggests a Scythian ancestry. Ctesias says Cyrus was a beggar, his father was a robber, and his mother a goatherd, so he was not royal at all. Like Herodotus, Xenophon says Cyrus was the son of a Persian prince and a grandson of Astyages through his mother Mandane.[8] Cyrus' name and his son's name (Cambyses) are both Elamite.[9] A Babylonian text describes one or both of them wearing Elamite dress at a ceremony in Babylon in 538 BC, a year after Cyrus' conquest of Babylon,[10] and the self-declared home of Cyrus was Anshan (Anzan), Elam.[11] Based on these points it might seem unlikely that Cyrus could have been an actual member of the *Aria* lineage. Nevertheless, the events involving Darius and his accession, his comments in the Behistun Inscription, and study of the lineages of Cyrus and Darius recorded in their own words (see Chapter 4) all confirm that Cyrus was in fact a member of the Scytho-Mede royal line. Therefore he was an *Aria* and legitimate ruler of the Scytho-Mede Empire.[12] Although all genuine, local contemporaneous sources indicate he was an Elamite, and none of them even mention the name 'Persian' in any spelling, that actually strengthens the case for him being a legitimate Scytho-Mede ruler, which is what he needed to be.

8. Xenophon, *Cyropaedia* (i 2.1): μητρὸς δὲ ὁμολογεῖται Μανδάνης γενέσθαι: ἡ δὲ Μανδάνη αὕτη Ἀστυάγους ἦν θυγάτηρ τοῦ Μήδων γενομένου βασιλέως. 'His mother, it is generally agreed, was Mandane; and this Mandane was the daughter of Astyages, sometime king of the Medes'. From Perseus, tr. Miller.

9. Potts (2005). He therefore could not have been a Mardian, and as usual Ctesias cannot be trusted.

10. Álvarez-Món (2009), who says it was "Cambyses' royal investiture ceremony", which "took place in the temple of Nabû at Babylon on the fourth day of the month of Nisannu (March/April) in 538 BC, a year after the Persian conquest."

11. Repeatedly declared by him in the *Cyrus Cylinder* (Kuhrt 2007, 1: 71). According to Abdi (2001), "Anshan" in this case means Elam (the country), not the ancient Elamite capital city of Anshan.

12. Cf. Endnote 75.

We have very little information on the specific religious beliefs and practices of Cyrus and his sons,[13] but we do have some, and his short "dynasty" was bracketed before and after by religious strife. In 550,[14] the Mede king Astyages led his army into northern Mesopotamia and, says the *Nabonidus Chronicle*,[15] attacked Cyrus, though it does not say why. Herodotus relates that Cyrus had long *prepared* to rebel.[16] Both sources agree that the reason Astyages lost is that his army mutinied, and the briefness of the conflict in the Akkadian description supports Herodotus' account. In view of Cyrus' actions immediately after his conquest of Babylon, it is possible that he had attacked Astyages in order to stop the destruction of the gods and their temples, as he himself suggests in his *Cyrus Cylinder* with respect to the actions of Nabonidus. Regardless of whoever started the conflict, Cyrus and Astyages fought and in 550 Cyrus won, capturing Astyages and taking over the Empire.[17] When Cyrus died, his elder son Cambyses succeeded. In 522, while Cambyses was still in Egypt—which he had conquered and added to the Empire—rebellions broke out around the Empire and he began the journey back from Egypt, but died on the way. All sources agree that when Cambyses died in 522, his younger brother Bardiya (Greek *Smerdis*) had already died or been murdered (Darius says Cambyses had ordered him to be killed). As neither prince had children, the throne was unoccupied by a legitimate claimant.

Darius, a high-ranking lord who had been Spearbearer under Cambyses during the Egyptian campaign and whose father Vištāspa was at the time sub-satrap over Parthia and Hyrcania, returned from Egypt to find that Gaumāta, a member of the Magi clan of Medes who looked

13. See Kuhrt (2007, 1: 71–72) for the *Cyrus Cylinder* on his restoration of local gods and peoples in Babylonia (which had been ravaged by Cyaxares; see Chapter 2). See further Chapter 5 (on Avestan and Median) and the Epilogue.

14. Some insist on the year 553. What is certain is that Cyrus was victorious in 550/549, after what seems to have been a short conflict. The later Greek sources which claim the conflict took three or more years appear to have been influenced by Ctesias and subsequent traditions. See Kuhrt (2007, 1: 57, note 8).

15. *The Nabonidus Chronicle*, q.v. Kuhrt (2007, 1: 50).

16. Kuhrt (2007, 1: 57).

17. It is certain only that he was successful in adding new territory to the west of the Empire he had taken over, and died while trying unsuccessfully to expand it to the east.

enough like Bardiya to pass for him, had usurped the throne when Cambyses was still in Egypt.[18] Gaumāta set himself up not in Susa or Babylon or another great city of the Empire, but in the fortress of Sikayuvati[19] in Media. Darius and six noble comrades managed to enter the fortress, where they killed Gaumāta.

In his great Behistun Inscription, Darius accuses Gaumāta of being a usurper, and that seems to be true. But it is not the only thing, or even the major thing, that was at stake. Darius mainly accuses Gaumāta (who he says was a Magus, one of the Magi) and the "rebels" of lying, of being false, of destroying the *āyadanā* 'places of worship or offering', of not worshipping Ahura Mazdā, and as stated explicitly by Xerxes, of worshipping instead the *Daivas*, or 'false Gods'.[20]

The Empire Darius took over and ruled was the same Empire as it was under Cyrus and Cambyses,[21] before them under Cyaxares and Astyages, and before them under the Scythians. Leaving aside the serious religious change under Cyrus and Cambyses, these rulers had not changed anything other than to enlarge the realm—the most famous conquests being by Cyrus and Cambyses, all in the west, including what is now Turkey, the Levant, and Egypt. The reason Cyaxares and his successors left the Empire as it was is that it was built on closely integrated and complex Central Eurasian cultural elements alien to Ancient Near Eastern cultures. It could not be changed in any major way (other than making it bigger or smaller) without bringing the entire thing crashing down, as the succession to Cambyses showed. As long as a ruler who took over the Empire from his predecessors belonged to the legitimate *Ariya* ruling lineage and left the system alone, all would be well.

18. DB 12 (145) in Sch. 43.

19. Following Sch. 243, rather than the traditional reading *Sikayauvati*.

20. Darius' statements are fully Early Zoroastrian in content and tone. Zoroaster (Zaraθuštra) is not named in any of the Old Persian inscriptions, but he is also not named in texts in other languages used in the Empire, with two notable exceptions: ancient Greek texts, which mention Zoroaster by name, and also the undated texts known as the *Young Avesta*, which are composed in Imperial Scythian and appear to have been written under the late Empire and shortly afterward (see Chapter 5). See Endnote 76.

21. Jacobs (2011).

Each of the three imperial takeovers, by Cyaxares, Cyrus, and Darius, started with a coup d'état, in which the Empire taken over remained structurally the same as the original Empire conquered by the Scythians and still ruled by the Scytho-Medes. Any new conquests were added to the existing realm by establishing standard great satrapies, sub-satrapies, etc., over each new region conquered (as many have noted), thus maintaining the inherited Scythian feudal hierarchical structure.

Today, Cyrus the Great's takeover is often contrasted with that by Darius a mere three decades later, and the claim is repeated that the entire empire rose up against Darius as an illegitimate upstart and a liar. However, the first rebellions had broken out even before the death of Cambyses, Cyrus' son and successor,[22] so the civil war was not about Darius' legitimacy, not to speak of the legitimacy of the deceased sons of Cyrus. Nor was it even about politics per se. It is explicit and resoundingly clear that it was about *religion*. The "rebels" Darius tells us a little about were anti-monotheistic. Darius says he needed to save what he calls "our" Empire, the realm of "our family, our seed". That alone makes it clear that Cyrus and Darius were both part of the same royal line, which could only be the Scytho-Mede *Aria* lineage of Cyaxares and the Scythians, so there was no question about Darius' or Cyrus' legitimacy.[23]

The only attested exception to the Imperial "non-alteration rule" was the restoration of polytheism by Cyrus. Although tolerance of polytheism, or of all religions, is not the same as suppression of monotheism, the specific point of the monotheism in question is that no other god could be treated as "God", i.e., the *one* "God" who was the head of the cosmic and worldly order and was *defined* as being One, unique. As the Hebrew example shows, it was the principle that was at stake, not the *name* of God. The minor "gods" were not a threat because their worshippers did not attempt to have them placed beside the one God as equals. But the worshippers of the *Daivas*, the "false Gods" condemned by Zoroaster, did attempt to do that. Cyrus, by denying the uniqueness

22. Shahbazi (2012).

23. The two rulers' first-person accounts of their own lineages confirm this conclusion. See Chapter 4.

of Ahura Mazdā, attacked the core of the monotheistic belief system. Even his personal version of the national foundation myth builds on his polytheistic beliefs, clearly indicating his support for, and by, the two chief *Daivas*. The polytheistic rebels took his negation of monotheism to the logical extreme. Thus Cyrus' polytheistic policies eventually threatened the continued existence of the Empire. They brought about the civil war fought by Darius to restore monotheism, as he explicitly tells us. As the civil war was not about Darius' legitimacy or that of Cyrus and his deceased sons, their legitimacy was not in question, and it is not even mentioned.

Cyrus had faced few rebellions after his coup d'état or brief familial war with his grandfather, King Astyages, no doubt because he publicly declared his support for the local religious beliefs of the Empire, shown most famously by his freeing of the Judeans in Babylonian captivity. As a result, Cyrus had been free to pursue campaigns of conquest, and did so with great success, acquiring much valuable territory that had not been part of the Empire he inherited. No one within the Empire had a problem with its expansion—certainly not Darius.

Darius vehemently condemns Gaumāta, whom he always calls "the Magus" (no doubt meaning a *Daiva* polytheist) and *false*, a *liar*. These purely Zoroastrian accusations are alone sufficient to invalidate the arguments of some historians who contend that Darius fought because he was illegitimate and had usurped the throne.

The rebellions only took place in the former Mede parts of the empire, including Pārsa,[24] but the chronology and the fact that most of the Medes and others in the Empire actually supported Darius, not the rebels—that is why Darius won—certainly indicate there was already support for Early Zoroastrianism in those regions of the Empire. More importantly, their support confirms that Darius was a legitimate contender for the throne.

There is another factor that seems to have been little noticed. Cyrus did greatly expand the empire's territory beyond its Scytho-Mede

24. See the detailed analysis of the chronology by Shahbazi (2012), who shows that the rebellion had already begun before Darius' coup. As Darius himself tells us in the Behistun Inscription, many lands rebelled again after he subdued them, so he had to subdue them once or even twice more.

foundations, but his conquests—Babylonia, most of Anatolia, Syria, and the Levant—were all in the west. When he invaded the east, attacking the Massagetae in Central Asia, he was defeated and killed.[25] His exploits were furthered by his son Cambyses, who conquered Egypt and Libya, also in the west.[26] Yet none of these *newly conquered* peoples actually rebelled when Darius took power. All of the rebels were people of Media (including its sub-satrapy of Armenia), Pārsa, and Elam, the old core of the Empire. Moreover, the armies of Darius which fought with him to suppress the rebels were Medes and Persians from those very same realms, as he repeatedly tells us, calling the Medes "my Medes" (versus the rebels' Medes), no doubt emphasizing the "*my*". Darius' campaign to end the civil war succeeded, and he restored Early Zoroastrianism as the official imperial belief system. His success was enabled by his excellent *Aria* pedigree and by strong support from his monotheistic Scytho-Mede-Persian relatives.[27]

The Teachings of Darius the Great

Darius' campaign was explicitly aimed at changing the Empire's polytheistic religious policy, which had been followed by Cyrus and Cambyses, back to its previous official monotheism. Darius openly and repeatedly declares his monotheistic beliefs:

> The Great God is Ahuramazdā, who created this earth, who created that heaven, who created man, who created happiness for man,[28] who made Darius king, one king of many, one lord of many.[29]

Ahura Mazdā[30] was the "Capital G" creator God, a unique, universal, unprecedented *type* of god in the Ancient Near East. Darius several times calls Ahura Mazdā the "greatest of the gods" and mentions "the

25. See Endnote 77 for what Tomyris said, according to Herodotus.

26. The two most important new additions made by Darius to the Empire after he restored internal peace were northwestern India (Gandhāra and Sindh) to the east and Thrace to the north.

27. See Chapter 4.

28. On this point see Lincoln (2012).

29. DNa 1–6. For the Old Persian text, translation, glosses, and commentary see Endnote 78.

30. See Endnote 79.

other gods that there are", but these "other *gods*" (whose worship was also subsidized by the Achaemenid government) were subordinate to Ahura Mazdā, who had created them and evidently everything else. They were not *Daivas,* other rival "Gods", who were a direct threat to the *one* Great God, Ahura Mazdā, and the *one* Great Empire. This explains the repeated condemnation of the rebels in Darius' Behistun Inscription, and even more explicitly in the Daiva Inscription of Xerxes I. The feudal-hierarchical structure of the imperium under Darius and the Achaemenids, in which the "Great King" (the emperor), ruled over the other "kings" in the empire (the satraps or "dukes"), who ruled over lesser rulers, according to the pyramidal hierarchy,[31] was closely parallel to the feudal-hierarchical structure of divinity.

As the apex of the divine feudal hierarchy, Ahura Mazdā was in an entirely different category from all other gods, from the many "small g" local gods to the major non–Early Zoroastrian "Gods", Mithra and Anāhitā. Zoroaster declared the "old Gods" to be *daevā* (Old Persian *daivā*) '*false* Gods'. Cyrus and Cambyses (though probably not Bardiya) clearly supported them, as well as the "small g" gods, but *not* Ahura Mazdā. Darius explicitly comments about the rebels (and at least one Scythian people) *not worshipping* Ahura Mazdā. He says that the rebel Gaumāta, the Magus, who had impersonated Cyrus' son Bardiya, followed *drauga* 'falsehood' and destroyed the *āyadanā* 'places of worship'.[32] Darius defeated and killed Gaumāta and restored the *āyadanā* and the worship of *Ahura Mazdā,* who is the only deity mentioned by name in imperial Achaemenid inscriptions until the late imperial period. Darius' son Xerxes I says in his "Daiva Inscription" that he suppressed a breakout of the worship of *Daivas,* the chief "false Gods", commanding, "You shall *not* worship the *Daivas!*"[33] It was only under the late Achaemenid ruler Artaxerxes II (r. 405/4–359/8) that the two most important of the Medes'

31. See the Prologue.

32. DB 1.63ff.: *āyadanā tayā Gaumāta haya maguš viyaka adam niyaçārayam* 'The places of cult which Gaumāta the Magus had destroyed, I restored.' Schmitt (2009: 46). Despite some careful scholarship and some interesting theories, the exact meaning of *āyadanā* 'places of worship' (if that is what they were) remains uncertain.

33. XPh; Xerxes also mentions that he destroyed the *Daiva*-worshippers' temple with the help of Ahura Mazdā.

(specifically, the Magi's) "old believer" chief deities, Anāhitā and Mithra, were rehabilitated.[34] Temples with statues of various gods were erected around the empire, no doubt including Ecbatana's great temple of Anāhitā, which is described later as having been covered with heavy gold and silver plating.[35] Artaxerxes II thus instituted a return to Old Mazdaist[36] polytheism.

Zoroaster's "reformed" Mazdaism, Early Zoroastrianism, was monotheistic, as attested both in the Old Avestan *Gāthās* 'hymns' of Zoroaster and in the early Achaemenid inscriptions.[37] Some have argued that this is a mistake because "the Avesta" have a plurality of gods or other spirits, particularly the Aməša Spəntas. However, that is because such writers do not distinguish between the oldest texts, the *Gāthās* 'Hymns', on the one hand, and the Young Avestan texts on the other. The Aməša Spəntas do not occur at all in the actual *Gāthās* (i.e., in the strict sense), nor do the *fravašis*.[38] Scholars have long tried to make Zoroastrianism very old, but why would an archaic religion maintained by aged Magi be revolutionary? *Monotheism* is certainly old, but the special *Zoroastrian* variety could not have been old in Cyaxares' day. It must have been strikingly *new*, and when it caught on it spread like a revolutionary new religion.

It has often been claimed that the inscriptions of Darius show no evidence of his faith in "Zoroastrianism", but that is untrue from the point of view of *Early* Zoroastrianism.[39] In the Early Zoroastrianism of the *Gāthās* in Old Avestan, Zoroaster rejects all other Gods, the *Daēvas*,[40]

34. As discussed, they had been restored once before, under the rule of Cyrus and his sons and the usurper Gaumāta. Darius does not mention the word *Daiva* even once, but always calls Gaumāta and the rebels followers of 𐎭𐎼𐎢𐎥 *drauga-* 'falsehood, the lie, untruth' (Schmitt 2014: 170). This is an explicit, highly characteristic feature of Early Zoroastrianism, as in the *Gāthās*; see the Epilogue.

35. It was repeatedly plundered for its gold and silver by Alexander and the early Seleucids. See Chapter 8.

36. See Endnote 80 for one of his inscriptions.

37. Skjærvø (1999, 2005).

38. See Endnote 81.

39. Based on the earliest Greek sources on Zoroastrianism (q.v. Horky 2009; Kingsley 1990, 1995) it is clear that many Mazdaists never accepted Zoroaster's monotheistic "reform". What is important here is that some did accept it, including Darius the Great.

40. There are of course other supramundane beings in the *Gāthās*, but they are not 'gods' (and are not called 'gods'; Zoroaster speaks of 'spirits'), not to speak of 'chief gods' in the

and proclaims his faith in the One God, Ahura Mazdā 'Lord Mazdā', the Heavenly God who created the world and stands for 'truth, the true', as opposed to *drauga* 'falsehood, untruth, the lie'.[41] Although the opposite of the truth is certainly much discussed in Early Zoroastrianism, truth and falsehood are not idealized or divinized, so falsehood was not an eternal evil demon or "negative divinity" opposed to Ahura Mazdā, as developed in later times. Zoroaster tells us we have a *choice* of which path to take, and what the result of each will be when one is judged at the end of life, as shown in the Epilogue. Too many arguments about Zoroastrianism have been based on projection of Late Zoroastrianism, with its various gods, ritual practices, and dualism, back to primordial times, thus misrepresenting or even obliterating the attested Early Zoroastrianism of the *Gāthās* and the inscriptions of Darius.

Darius, like Zoroaster, is emphatic and explicit about his faith.[42] It has been noted that he also mentions in his inscriptions "the *other gods* that there are" and "*all the gods*".[43] However, these are treated very differently from Ahura Mazdā, the unique *baga văzărka* '(the One) Great God', creator of heaven and earth, who by definition can only be in a category of his own, like '(the One) Great King'.[44] The unnamed "small g" gods were thus fundamentally different. Research on scribal records from Persepolis has made it clear that besides the one Great God, Ahura Mazdā, Darius permitted the honoring of "other gods" of peoples

traditional Ancient Near Eastern sense (e.g., Babylon's chief god Marduk, Athens' chief god Athena, etc.). The other supramundane beings are also the creations of Ahura Mazdā.

41. E.g., in Yasna 37,1 and Yasna 51,7 (Humbach and Ichaporia 1994: 54–55, 96–97). Explicitly as the Creator: Yasna 44,7 "the creator of all things", Yasna 45,4 "Him, who created [this existence]", 45,7 "of these things Mazdā Ahura is the creator", 50,11 "the Giver of Existence", 51,7 "O Mazdā, who fashioned the cow, the waters, and the plants", all from Humbach and Ichaporia (1994).

42. Cf. de Jong (2010).

43. In DB 461, 462ff. (Schmitt 2014: 149) and in DPd (Schmitt 2009: 115–117), respectively; Lecoq (1997: 227–228). Some render the expression, without overt source justification, as "the gods of the royal house" (e.g., Briant 2002: 241).

44. This is stated clearly and emphatically by the monotheistic prophet Jeremiah (10:11), who says in Imperial Aramaic (see Chapter 1, Note 18), "Let the gods who did *not* make the heavens and the earth perish from the earth and from beneath these heavens!"

throughout the realm. But the *Daivas* Anāhitā and Mithra were worshipped only beginning in the reign of Artaxerxes II, who rehabilitated them.

In his Behistun Inscription, Darius says that Gaumāta was a follower of *drauga* 'falsehood, untruth'. Darius repeatedly states that he owed his rule to Ahura Mazdā, and for each rebel he defeated and killed, he repeats that the rebel 'followed falsehood' or 'he was a liar', meaning that the rebel violated the unity of the divinely created Empire, and violated the principle of the one God, the Creator. By contrast, Darius worshipped Ahura Mazdā, he followed the truth, and his statements were true. All this hardly fits any other creed but Early Zoroastrianism, which focuses on the opposition of *truth* (Avestan *aša*, Old Persian *arta*),[45] versus falsehood (*drauga*), as discussed in the Epilogue. Darius refers to the law (*dāta*) of the Great King in the same terms as "the law (*dāta*) of God (Ahura Mazdā)".[46] Darius thus openly pronounces an Early Zoroastrian declaration of faith. The one Empire, the creation of the one Great God, ruled by the one Great King, could only exist *as a unity*.

Moreover, Darius and the members of his family before and after him are *Ariyas* 'Royals, those belonging to the legitimate Royal lineage'. They are the chosen people[47] who rule the Empire, and Paradise is promised to the followers of the king's Law—the Law of God—who serve him loyally.[48] Because the Empire was a Scythian creation, and the legitimate *Ariya* ruling lineage was in origin the *Aria* ~ *Ariya* ~ *Ḥarya* lineage of Scythians, the "Royal Scythians" were Arias and legitimate, the Medes of the Scytho-Mede ruling lineage were Arias and legitimate, Cyrus and his sons (as Royal Scytho-Medes) were legitimate, and Darius was an Ariya and legitimate too, as shown in Chapter 4. What brought about the civil war was thus not legitimacy, and not simply religion in general,

45. Sch. (240, 241), which however follows the now usual reconstruction "*ṛta-". On this problematic "Indianization" of Old Persian see Endnote 117.

46. Sch. 166–167; Briant (2002: 550–551). The word *dāta* was borrowed into Hebrew and Imperial Aramaic (either from Old Persian or from Imperial Scythian) in both senses, and frequently occurs.

47. Briant (2002: 181–183); Kingsley (1995: 195); Boyce and Grenet (1991: 375).

48. Briant (2002: 128). See also Endnote 82.

it was the polytheists' rejection of Early Zoroastrianism's unique category monotheistic God, Ahura Mazdā.

Darius and his allies killed Gaumāta and reestablished the worship of their one true God, Ahura Mazdā. Darius explicitly credits his success to the help accorded him by Ahura Mazdā, whom he names over and over throughout his inscriptions. He also repeats many times that the rebels were liars and followers of falsehood, whereas he, Darius, spoke the truth and followed the truth. The overriding importance of truth and good versus falsehood and evil in the Early Zoroastrianism of the *Gāthās* is a contrast that permeates Darius' specifically Early Zoroastrian inscriptions. No other religion has this particular constellation of core features.[49]

The beliefs of Darius in his inscriptions, and of Zoroaster in his *Gāthās*, are absolutely explicit and emphatically stated. Some doubt the truth of Darius' statements about them, and almost everything else, too, because he repeats the Early Zoroastrian litany of truth and good versus falsehood and evil. He "protests too much", they say. So Darius himself is accused of being a usurper, a liar, and not a Zoroastrian. One might as well accuse Zoroaster of the same things. Such accusations do not conform to the data, and in fact, they *reject* the data. We must first understand our extant texts—the data—and then interpret the historical events they report.

A Reconstruction of the Persian Empire's Origins

With this background in mind, and based on existing data, a possible scenario may be proposed that straightens out the historical origins of the Empire and explains how it became a Persian one.

The Iranic-speaking Cimmerians and Scythians initially expanded quickly across the steppe zone of Central Eurasia in the 8th century BC, including some frontier regions with good pasturage. They followed a pattern that is historically very well attested in better known later times, with strikingly similar results.[50] Thus the little-known Cimmerian

49. Cf. the Epilogue.

50. Especially to be noted are the identical rapid conquest and spread over the same vast territory by the Huns, a Turkic-speaking people (late 4th century CE), though unfortunately

people burst suddenly into the Transcaucasus region and eastern Anatolia in the 8th century BC, followed a few decades later by the Scythians. In about 650 BC the Scythians—evidently as allies of the Assyrians—established their rule over the then highly disunited region of Media.

Their political alignment with the polytheistic Assyrians might suggest that the Scythian rulers in Media tolerated "Old Mazdaist" polytheism, but the Royal Scythians on the steppe were basically monotheistic[51] (like other Central Eurasians, including their Proto-Indo-European ancestors in early Central Eurasia) and undoubtedly maintained their beliefs while in Media. Herodotus (iv 59), in his account of the Scythian gods, says the Royal Scythians had one main god, the sky-god Zeus, called *Papaeus* (a Greek or Scytho-Greek word), but he does not give us the actual Scythian name.

His brief account of the Scythian gods is a combination of two lists. The first is a Greek list: "Hestia in particular, and secondly Zeus and Earth, whom they believe to be the wife of Zeus; after these, Apollo, and the Heavenly Aphrodite, and Heracles, and Ares." The second is a Scythian list that he matches up approximately with the first list, adding that "they make images and altars and shrines for Ares, but for no other god".[52] Yet he does not give Ares' Scythian name, nor that of Heracles, and as noted *Papaeus* is not a Scythian name either. The gods in the first list, he says, are worshipped by all Scythians, but he adds that the Royal Scythians also sacrifice to Poseidon, whom he equates in his second list with *Thagimasadas*.[53] That means *only* the Royal Scythians worshipped Thagimasadas, so he was in fact "Capital G" heavenly God.[54] *Thagimasadas* represents Scythian *Tagi Mazda, where *Tagi* is demonstrably the

poorly attested in historical sources; then, even more successfully by the Türk (mid-6th century CE), and once again by the Mongols (early 13th century CE). On the creolizing linguistic outcome of these events see Nichols (1997b), Garrett (1999), Beckwith (2009: 369–374), and Beckwith et al. (forthcoming).

51. Khazanov (2016). The "small g" gods are normal and expected too, because the Scythians had one feudal-hierarchical system in heaven-and-earth. See Endnote 83.

52. Herodotus (iv 59), from Perseus, tr. Godley.

53. See the preceding Note.

54. Cf. Khazanov (2016). Scholars have largely overlooked the multiple *textual* voices in Herodotus.

same word as *Targi* (q.v. Chapter 6). Herodotus' comment that he was exclusively a god of the Royal Scythians is crucially important, since their own "home-ruled" territory was where the sacred gold that fell down from Heaven was kept. (See the West Scythian national foundation myth, first version, in Chapter 1.) The other gods mentioned by Herodotus were categorically different, so they were lower down on the heavenly feudal hierarchy.

The uniqueness of heavenly God is attested in both main versions of the Scythian national foundation myth in Herodotus, according to which the first Scythian king (or first man), Targitaos, was the descendant of "Zeus" via his union with the daughter of the god of the Borysthenes River, so the Scythian kings belonged to the one legitimate "heavenly" *Aria* Royal line.[55] Their exclusive God could only be the One Heavenly God.

Because the Mede prince Cyaxares must have been at least part Scythian in order to be an Aria, and was thus raised at the Scythian court, he knew the rulers and others among the elite, and understood the Scythian system. As a classic example of the Central Eurasian feudal-hierarchical political structure, its unifying power depended on vassals keeping their oaths to the one Great King. That was guaranteed by their belief in the one Great God, the heavenly creator, and his promised reward of Paradise for virtuous people who followed his Law, which was also the Law of the One King.

Having grown up as a Scythian, Cyaxares himself no doubt believed in the God of Heaven, but that means he had a problem. Old Mazdaism, the native religion of most of the Magi, a clan of Medes, was polytheistic, like more or less all religious systems in the Ancient Near East, where each area had its own local "national" or "political" god (or God). Cyaxares certainly knew what the local deities meant politically: they were the guardians of the independence of the local peoples. As long as their national gods or Gods existed, those peoples were a threat to the unified Scytho-Mede Empire. By contrast, the unique, universal God of the Scythians (and all other historical Central Eurasian steppe rulers

55. See Chapter 1 for the foundation myths.

down at least to the Mongols in the Central Middle Ages) was the Heavenly creator God, who was head of the Empire: a unified thing headed on Earth by his descendant, the single 'great king'. Accordingly, Cyaxares needed a religious leader who, like him, spoke Scythian, had grown up as a Scythian, believed in the God of Heaven, and wanted to keep the Scythian imperial system intact, but opposed the old Scythian rulers. At least some of the Magi were no doubt already involved with religion on behalf of the Scythians, if only to ensure that local religious practices continued.[56] History shows that one man, a contemporary of Prince Cyaxares, felt as he did, and had monotheistic beliefs similar to those of the Prince and his companions. But the man was treated almost as an outcast by polytheists, as he tells us in his hymns, the *Gāthās*. His name was Zarathushtra, our Zoroaster.[57]

Recently many scholars have considered Zoroaster to be problematic for one reason or another, and would like to get rid of him.[58] By contrast, historians of the Achaemenids think Early Zoroastrianism formed exactly at this time.[59] At any rate Zoroaster, or an unknown man who was identical to Zoroaster and was actually *named* Zoroaster,[60] knew the Old Avestan ritual language and composed the *Gāthās* in it. Perhaps Zoroaster maintained or revived the Scythian religious belief in Heavenly God by thoroughly reshaping it. Cyaxares and his comrades, who retained the Scythian political and military system, thus followed the teachings of the inspiring Zoroaster (q.v. the Epilogue), who passed away around the time of Cyaxares' coup d'état. If this scenario is valid, Zoroaster should have lived approximately around the time of Darius' grandfather Arsames (Aršāma), the contemporary of Cyaxares. While

56. Conquerors necessarily acquire many servants among the conquered peoples. These servants attempt to mitigate the effects of the conquest on them or even to profit by it.

57. On the name *Zoroaster* ~ *Zarathushtra* see Appendix A.

58. See Endnote 84.

59. The current consensus is that the reforms attributed to the prophet Zoroaster must have occurred in or near the lifetime of Cyrus the Great, who died in 530 BC (Frye 2010; Soudavar 2010; Malandra 2009). However, Cyaxares behaved as one would expect a radical monotheist to behave, as discussed in Chapter 2. The present analysis, including the chronology, is unrelated to the traditional date of Zoroaster. For the traditional "date of Zoroaster", 558 BC (during the reign of Astyages), and its sources, see Gnoli (2003).

60. See Appendix A.

some claim there was no Zoroaster, others do not like to see him as a revolutionary (or at least a reformer) of Old Mazdaism, and believe that there are no significant differences between Old Avestan and Young Avestan. However, there are major differences not only in the languages[61] but in the different religious beliefs in the Old Avestan *Gāthās* versus the rest of the Avesta. *Early* Zoroastrianism has a categorically unique God, the *one* Great God, the heavenly creator, who must have supported Cyaxares, the one Great King of the unified Empire, as he later supported Darius. There certainly were many other gods, but as they were lower down in the feudal celestial hierarchy, they could not belong to the unique apex category of the one Great God.[62] It remains to be investigated whether Early Zoroastrianism could be specifically Scytho-Median.[63]

At any rate, the first blows on behalf of the one Heavenly God seem to have been dealt by Cyaxares, the first historical Scytho-Mede ruler. If he was the first Early Zoroastrian ruler as well, the attack of the polytheist Cyrus the Great on Cyaxares' successor Astyages makes perfect sense. A striking parallel to this first monotheistic revolution[64] is in the account of King Josiah of Judah (r. ca. 640–609 BC) and his iconoclastic campaign from ca. 622 BC on, destroying polytheistic temples and statues. That campaign is exactly parallel to the Mesopotamian campaigns of Cyaxares (r. ca. 620–585 BC).[65]

It is well known that the Magi clan, one of the five constituent clans of the Medes according to Herodotus, provided the religious specialists for the Achaemenids throughout their rule, but they were (presumably) at first restricted to the Early Zoroastrians among them.

There is actually some evidence for the above scenario. Since the time of Darius the Great and Herodotus it has been said that Gaumāta was a rebel who destroyed the *āyadanā* 'places of worship' and either reestablished polytheism or simply continued following the polytheistic

61. Hoffmann (2011) makes the linguistic differences absolutely clear.

62. About three centuries later the logical point that a *single* God-like being is a requirement for the creator of the world is argued by Aristotle, with his Prime Mover, in the *Metaphysics*; see also Epilogue, Note 101.

63. On the Median language see Endnote 85 and Chapter 5.

64. See Endnote 86 for Akhenaten.

65. See Chapter 2.

policies of Cyrus the Great. Darius and his son Xerxes in turn suppressed polytheism. That is explicitly supported by the sources.

Some historians contend that "Gaumāta" did not change anything done by Cyrus the Great or by his elder son and successor Cambyses, who had succeeded to the throne when Cyrus was killed in battle by the Massagetae (a Scytho-Sarmatian nation) in Central Asia in 530 BC. Thus Cyrus' son Bardiya (not the pretender Gaumāta) would have succeeded peacefully and ruled peacefully. The conclusion they draw is that Darius was a usurper and a liar.

However, that idea conflicts with the sources. It has been shown conclusively that rebellions had already broken out in the empire even before the death of Cambyses,[66] who died on his way back from Egypt to put down those very rebellions. In that case, at least the first rebellions had nothing to do with Darius at all. So are the statements of Darius, repeated over and over in his inscriptions, really the truth? It is certain that Darius was actually a relative of Cyrus (Darius tells us so directly and indirectly in the Behistun Inscription), so both of them were part Scytho-Mede.[67]

However, two of the most important pieces of data seem still to be undervalued. Cyrus (in the *Cyrus Cylinder*) and Darius (in his Behistun Inscription and other inscriptions) each independently record their lineage as going back to a ruler with the Elamite name *Zi-iš-pi-iš* (Old Persian *čišpiš*, Babylonian *Ši-iš-pi-iš*), best known under the Greek transcription of his name, *Teispes*.[68] All other theories and arguments must defer to that literally hard evidence. It means that Cyrus and Darius were in fact related, and it confirms that they both did have 'royal' lineage, as they claim. Their common paternal line ancestor might thus seem at first glance to be neither a Persian nor a Mede king but an Elamite, and it is known from studies of the destruction of Nineveh that there were Elamites in Cyaxares' allied army, which overthrew the Assyrians. That means the Elamites were vassals of the Medes, as all other evidence suggests, so neighboring Pārsa (part of Elam) was also a vassal, as Herodotus' story about Cyrus' father suggests. Cyrus does not

66. Shahbazi (2012).
67. Cf. Endnote 87.
68. Potts (2005).

mention his Scytho-Mede lineage (via his mother) in his *Cyrus Cylinder* genealogy. Similarly, Darius does not expressly mention his *Ariya* ~ *Aria* ~ *Ḥarya* lineage in his Behistun Inscription, but he does mention his language, which he calls *Ariya*, the classic term used by rulers throughout Central Eurasia and neighboring parts of the periphery meaning 'the Royal language' or more precisely 'the language of the Royals'. In addition to Darius' explicit connection of himself to Cyrus as members of the same "family", i.e., the same lineage, Darius' Ariya lineage is also clear from the close examination of the lineages of the related rulers of the Empire from the Scythians to Xerxes I in Chapter 4. Since everything else in Darius' account does seem to be historical and essentially correct,[69] there are no good grounds to doubt this aspect of his lineage.

The *Nabonidus Chronicle* uniquely refers to Cyrus once (the only such reference in the sources) as "King of Parsā", but the text is much later than the period it records and includes a number of other anachronisms too.[70] Cyrus acquired further legitimacy for his sons by marrying Amytis, the daughter of Astyages (the successor of Cyaxares),[71] as Ctesias and Xenophon say,[72] while according to Herodotus he married Cassandane, an "Achaemenian", daughter of Pharnaspes (whose name is Imperial Scythian) and sister of Otanes.[73] Probably he married both women, as it would have been extremely unusual, and risky, for a king to take only one wife. His sons Cambyses and Bardiya were thus born

69. Minor errors have been noted by many scholars, but more or less all of them are textual in nature.

70. Kuhrt (2007, 1: 50–51); Zawadzki (1988). The text otherwise always calls him "King of Anshan".

71. If Cyrus' mother really was Mandanes, daughter of Astyages, so that he was the latter's grandson, as Herodotus and Xenophon both claim, then Amytis was her sister and thus Cyrus' aunt. The ancient Achaemenids are famous, or infamous, for marrying their close relatives in all directions and generations.

72. Briant (2002: 33).

73. Herodotus (iii 2,2). The name Cassandane is also Median (Imperial Scythian). Her death, or that of Amytis, is recorded in the *Nabonidus Chronicle* in March, 538 (Kuhrt 2007, 1: 51). The death of Cyrus' unnamed mother (according to Herodotus, she was Mandane, daughter of King Astyages of the Medes) is recorded on April 6, 547/6 (id., 50). See Chapter 4 for details on these names.

as doubly legitimate members of the imperial royal line, though perhaps by different mothers.[74]

In short, the Empire was in origin, structure, and legitimation purely a Scythian affair formed in the north (in Media and neighboring lands, probably including Bactria and Arachosia), not in the south (in Elam ~ Pārsa). It became a Scytho-Mede empire, and then a Scytho-Mede-Persian empire. Based on the available evidence, all three post-Scythian periods were headed by a ruler—Cyaxares, Cyrus, Darius—who belonged to the Scytho-Mede royal *Aria* ~ *Ariya* "eternal royal line" both paternally and maternally. Legitimacy was not an issue for them.

Imperial proclamations by Cyrus and imperial edicts by Darius both reveal that the struggle was about religion. The inscriptions display Darius' deep monotheistic religious beliefs, which contrast very sharply with the polytheistic beliefs of Cyrus and—according to Darius and other ancient sources—those of Gaumāta. The sources unambiguously indicate that the usurper Gaumāta stood for the polytheism of the *Daivas*, with several, or even many, apex Gods, and opposed absolute monotheism based on belief in *one* apex God, Ahura Mazdā, i.e., Early Zoroastrianism. It is now known that the continuity of the Empire was already threatened by rebellions well before Darius' coup d'état, so they were not reactions to Darius, nor were the first immediately following rebellions. In each case they were the work of polytheists backed by a traditional God other than Ahura Mazdā, so they effectively stood for polytheism. It is also significant that nearly all the leaders appear to have been Medes or from "Greater Media". Since the throne was actually unoccupied by a legitimate successor, the local nationalist rebellions did threaten the Empire, which had lasted for over a century by Darius' time. Darius and his co-conspirators thus had at least two good reasons to act, but they actually had little choice. Otherwise, as Darius says, the Empire that had been ruled by his family for generations would have been lost. All of this is explicit and consistent in the contemporaneous sources.

74. Later Darius the Great married Cyrus' daughter Atossa, acquiring additional legitimacy for their eventual son Xerxes. Darius also married Bardiya's daughter. He thus reunited the two lines of the Achaemenid family.

It must be stressed that Cyrus himself actively, openly promoted polytheism. One of his best-attested acts after taking over the Empire was to capture Babylon (in 539), after which he decreed the restoration of the gods of the former Babylonian and Assyrian local realms to their home cities, and rebuilding of their temples.[75] Moreover, there is not a single mention of Ahura Mazdā or "one Great (heavenly creator) God" or the like in anything from Cyrus and Cambyses, who have Elamite names and are portrayed as Elamites (who were polytheists).[76] The two major Babylonian chronicles, one of them pro-Nabonidus, the other pro-Cyrus, agree about Cyrus' Elamite nationality and religious policy. In Herodotus' full Cyrus story the hero sacrifices huge numbers of animals in preparation for his attack on Astyages,[77] presumably because of the number of Gods involved, as each of the many constituent local polities supporting him depended on one or more local Gods.

Most famously, the Bible records that Cyrus let the Israelites return to Palestine with the command to rebuild the Temple of their tribal god:[78]

> In the Year One of King Cyrus, King Cyrus gave an order about the house of God in Jerusalem, that the house should be built.[79]

The same texts say that the building project was stopped for a long time—when, exactly, is unclear. Construction was not resumed, according to Ezra, until the reign of Artaxerxes, presumably Darius's grandson Artaxerxes I. Nevertheless it is clear that the Temple was no longer for the Hebrews' old tribal-national god, as Cyrus had presumably intended, but specifically for God, the universal creator of Heaven and Earth, called by the Persians Ahura Mazdā. The old Gods, the *Daivas*,

75. *Nabonidus Chronicle*, 21 (quoted in Kuhrt 2007, 1: 51) and the *Cyrus Cylinder* 22–26, 30–35 (quoted in Kuhrt 2007, 1: 71–72ff.).

76. Kuhrt (2007, 1: 51); Álvarez-Món (2009). The sartorial point is of course true of Darius too.

77. Herodotus 1.126, 2.

78. Cf. Endnote 88.

79. יִתְבְּאֵ בִּשְׁנַת חֲדָה לְכוֹרֶשׁ מַלְכָּא כּוֹרֶשׁ מַלְכָּא שָׂם טְעֵם בֵּית־אֱלָהָא בִירוּשְׁלֶם בַּיְתָא (Ezra 6:3, *BHS* 1420). The text does not clarify exactly which divinity is meant by 'the god' ~ 'God'. Note that the year given in the Aramaic is incorrect, as Cyrus took Babylon eleven years after his coup. Many historians have expressed doubt about the historicity of this record, but the Temple was in fact rebuilt.

were *false* gods—lies—and had to go, as Jeremiah (10:11) had proclaimed already in Cyaxares' day. Similarly in Exodus (20:2) God declares to Moses in the First Commandment that he will have "no other gods" before him, and that his people should not worship other gods. That sounds like Cyaxares and King Josiah of Judah, but *not* like Cyrus.

As it happens, we have further relevant data: the foundation myth of Cyrus the Great. Although it has been Persianized, close examination shows that it originally had little or nothing to do with Persians per se. The main version in Herodotus, supplemented by an important passage containing a key element in the Central Eurasian National Foundation Myth that is missing from the modern text of his *Histories* but is preserved in Justin, may be summarized as follows:[80]

The Foundation Myth of Cyrus the Great

The king of the Medes, Astyages, had a dream in which his daughter Mandane urinated so much she flooded his city and all of Asia. Astyages was afraid that she would give birth to a son who would overthrow him, so he married her off to a distant Persian, Cambyses. When she gave birth, Astyages ordered his minister Harpagus to take her newborn baby away and kill him. But the minister, afraid to kill a prince of the blood, ordered Mitradates, a royal herdsman, to take the child to the mountains where he lived and expose it. The herdsman brought the baby in a basket to his home in the mountains between Ecbatana and the Black Sea *and exposed the child. When he told his wife what he had done, she entreated him to bring the baby to her. Mitradates went back and found a female dog beside the infant, nursing him and protecting him from the beasts and birds of prey.* The herdsman's wife had just given birth, but their own child was stillborn, so they put their dead infant in baby Cyrus's clothes, and after exposing it in the wilderness for a few days Mitradates brought it back to Harpagus, who told Astyages the child was dead. The herdsman and his wife raised Cyrus as their own child. When the boy was ten years old the

80. See Endnote 89 for discussion of the motif in question.

secret was discovered. Astyages punished Harpagus horribly for the deception, but he sent Cyrus to his birth parents, where the boy grew up. Eventually, with the help of the wronged Harpagus, Cyrus overthrew his grandfather Astyages and established a righteous kingdom.

The story tells us that Cyrus' real mother was Mandane, a Mede princess, daughter of King Astyages of the Medes. In the story she is presented symbolically as the goddess Anāhitā, mistress of the waters, and baby Cyrus is adopted and raised by a Mede shepherd, Mitradates, whose name means 'Given by Mithra.'[81] The deities Anāhitā and Mithra (perhaps along with Mazdā) appear to have been the chief deities of the polytheistic pre-Zoroastrian Medes, since they are the ones fully rehabilitated by Artaxerxes II.[82] Herodotus' full version of the Cyrus story thus gives Cyrus an implicit divine ancestry, but it is polytheistic. In fact, it is even worse from an Early Zoroastrian point of view, as it is specifically a *Daiva* ancestry—Mithra and Anāhitā being precisely the two *Daivas* ("false Gods") so vehemently proscribed by Darius and Xerxes. The One Great God of Heaven is not mentioned at all in the Cyrus story.

Most of Herodotus' tale is of course folklore, not history. But the loremasters of Cyrus did not make it up out of whole cloth, new and unprecedented in the world. It is a traditional version of a known, crucially important story, the Central Eurasian National Foundation Myth,[83] and it has clear references in particular to the Scythian foundation myth. The protagonist in the Central Eurasian story has divine ancestry but is taken to be a real historical person, and the story always includes some actual historical data, so it is myth, legend, and history all at once, as known from other famous full examples such as the

81. Ctesias makes Cyrus a Mardian beggar, son of the highwayman Atrodates and the goatherd Argoste. His version of the Cyrus story is hardly believable, but the outlines of the "normal" version of Herodotus are perceptible in Ctesias' story, including Cyrus growing up in Media, his mother having a dream about him conquering the Near East, and so on (Stronk 2010, 1: 291–293).

82. Artaxerxes II (r. 405/4–359/8), the last major ruler of the Achaemenid Empire, rehabilitated Anāhitā and Mithra and built rich temples and statues for them, restoring polytheism, effectively demoting Ahura Mazdā, and perhaps dooming the Empire. See Endnote 80 for Berossus.

83. See Endnote 90 on the myth and early Near Eastern versions.

Koguryo, Wu-sun or *Aśvin, and Roman myths. The loremasters and propagandists of Cyrus simply modified the existing, traditional, well-known myth already associated with the Empire to make it suit the needs of Cyrus, and promulgated it. Their one major change from the original Central Eurasian myth is striking: it supports the legitimacy of Cyrus, the father of Atossa and the grandfather of Xerxes, *not* via the one Great God of Heaven but specifically via clearly identified polytheistic Gods, the chief *Daivas*.

Belief in Heavenly God is the wellspring of the Central Eurasian National Foundation Myth. In the main version of the Scythian myth recounted by Herodotus, the Scythians are the descendants of Targitaos, who is the son of the Scythians' supreme Heavenly God and the daughter of the Dnieper.[84] Targitaos had three sons. Only the youngest one, *Skulaχšaya (Greek **Scolaxaï-*)[85] 'King Skula' (i.e., "King Scytha", as Herodotus explains), was able to touch, and take home, three divine burning golden objects that fell down from Heaven, showing that he himself was a Heavenly being. He thus became the first king of the Scythians, founded the feudal Scythian Empire, and personally ruled the apex clan of the Paralata (from *Paradatā 'the ones placed ahead [of the other clans]'), the 'Royal Scythians' of Herodotus' account. From that time on, the King of the Scythians ruled as Great King, the land he personally ruled being the one where the divine gold was kept.[86]

Now consider how Cyrus' story differs from the general Central Eurasian myth, including the Scythian version. There is no explicit mention of Cyrus' Heavenly ancestry,[87] contrasting with the Scythian story and with Darius, who mentions Heavenly God (Ahura Mazdā) repeatedly throughout his many inscriptions. Yet the ruler's Heavenly God lineage, *Ariya*, is a core element of the entire Central Eurasian package. Worse,

84. Herodotus calls him Zeus; the Dnieper's Scythian name is *Borysthenes*. See Chapter 1 for the story.

85. The Greek transcription of Scythian *Skulaχšaya*. As the text of Herodotus itself makes explicit, his name must be **Scolaxaï-* in Greek, not "Colaxaï-". See Chapter 1, Note 22.

86. Herodotus (iv 5–7). Cf. Khazanov (2016: 172–176). See Endnote 91.

87. This is true even in the Moses story in Exodus (which must therefore be derived specifically from the full Cyrus story); it is otherwise full of the doings of "Capital G" God, who supports Moses.

Cyrus' *Daiva* 'false God' lineage is clear from his mother Mandane's dream that implies she was the goddess Anāhitā, mother of waters,[88] the main goddess of the pre-Zoroastrian Medes later enshrined in the Mede capital, Ecbatana,[89] while the name of Cyrus' stepfather, *Mitradates*, means 'given by Mithra', the other chief *Daiva* of the pre-Zoroastrian Medes.[90] Neither of them is the one Heavenly God of the Royal Scythians, *Targi/Tagi/Taŋri* (from *Tagri; see Chapter 6) plus *Mazda, called by Zoroaster and Darius *Ahura* ('lord') *Mazdā*. The Cyrus foundation myth thus suggests that as son of Mandane, he owed his existence to Anāhitā and Mithra, the chief gods of the non-Zoroastrian Mazdaeans. Already under the Mede kings, the *Daēvas/Daivas* 'false Gods' (undoubtedly including Anāhitā and Mithra) had been opposed by Zoroaster, assuming he is dated to that period, and they would have been suppressed by the monotheistic Cyaxares. In any case these two *Daivas* were certainly suppressed during the first century of overt Achaemenid rule (beginning with Darius I), as we know because they are never mentioned by name in the imperial inscriptions until the early 4th century, when those same two Gods, Anāhitā and Mithra, were rehabilitated by Artaxerxes II, who invokes them by name, along with Ahura Mazdā, in his inscriptions.

The association of the Empire's national foundation myth with Cyrus in particular is thus highly significant. There are also other full and partial variants of his story, while by contrast, there is no explicit Cyaxares story, though based on Herodotus there are indications that one did exist,[91] and there is no Darius story. In short, although it might seem

88. Specifically Anāhitā /Aphrodite-Ourania. See Boyce et al. (2011).

89. This "water" motif also recalls that the mother of Targitaos was the daughter of the river god. That of course relates to the Hellenized version of the Scythian foundation myth in Herodotus (4.9.1), in which Heracles (the son of Zeus) mates with a cave-dwelling "creature of double form that was half maiden and half serpent; above the buttocks she was a woman, below them a snake." This amphibious female deity is explicitly called *Echidna* in Diodorus Siculus' (ii 43,3) brief version of the Scythian foundation myth, wherein she mates with "Zeus" (the God of Heaven) to produce Scythes. Portrayals of Echidna have been found in archaeological findings from Scythia (Khazanov 2016). For the Heracles story see Chapter 1.

90. Schmidt (2006).

91. See Chapter 2 for a reconstruction.

that Cyrus needed legitimizing more than anyone,[92] legitimacy was a non-issue for him, as it was for Darius, despite their Elamite connection, because they both had solid Scytho-Mede Royal lineage. In fact, the Cyrus story actually supports the legitimacy of both kings, as it makes Cyrus half Persian too, as well as half Scytho-Mede going straight back to the Scythians, as shown in Chapter 4.

Both Cyrus and Darius explicitly say they descended from Teispes (Old Persian Čišpiš, Elamite Zi-iš-pi-iš)—Cyrus on the *Cyrus Cylinder* and Darius in his inscriptions. However, Darius traces his lineage one step further than Cyrus, to Teispes' father, Achaemenes, who thus founded the royal line of their Empire. The name Achaemenes is Imperial Scythian and means 'liegeman, vassal lord, duke'.[93] It is clearly a title or rank, "the Duke", rather than a name, so we must ask, "vassal of whom?" His date corresponds to approximately the time of Cyaxares' father or grandfather. If Teispes were purely and only Elamite, both Cyrus and Darius would be not only from the south but specifically *not* from Māda ~ Aria ~ Scythia, which is in the north; they would thus be illegitimate. Fortunately Darius does name the father of Teispes who was their shared Iranic ancestor, Achaemenes, who has a Scythian name, like most of Darius' other ancestors, including his own father Vištāspa (see Chapter 4). It is because of "the Duke" that both Cyrus and Darius were 'the seed of an eternal royal line'—the *Aria ~ Ariya ~ Ḥarya* royal lineage—and were therefore legitimate.

The hard evidence of the Akkadian sources and the Achaemenid inscriptions thus points solidly to the ultimate cause of the rebellion suppressed by Darius: Cyrus' own rebellion against Astyages. Cyrus' rebellion may have been primarily religious in nature too, aimed at restoring the *Daivas* and other gods, both Median and in general, since Cyrus did in fact restore them, as the Akkadian chronicles attest. And his story—*only* the Cyrus story—was popular with the still polytheistic Greeks,

92. Vallat (2013) argues that Cyrus was a usurper, not Darius.

93. Sch. 192 gives by far the best etymology; cf. Bar. 1744–1746 for the Avestan data. Counting by succession of rulers, Achaemenes 'the Duke' corresponds to Deioces *Dahyuka 'the Duke' (in both Old Persian and Avestan). His short-lived son in Herodotus' story, Phraortes *Fravarti, with his Persian name, was then succeeded by Cyaxares, who has a Scythian name.

Hebrews, and Iranic peoples of the empire, who copied and rewrote the story to suit their own needs. The most famous variant is the Moses story,[94] but elements of it also appear in the Greeks' Perseus story, which relates the hero to the Persians based on his name, *Perseus*, or that of his son, *Perses*, folk-etymologized to mean 'the Persian.'[95]

The monotheistic Early Zoroastrians among the Medes and Persians thus lost power under Cyrus. For them, he was a calamity. Moreover, although his immediate family could have been part Persian (as nearly all historians have tried to show), there is no hard evidence it was, while he and his son Cambyses, who have Elamite names and are described as having dressed as Elamites, seem to have been viewed, unsurprisingly, as Elamites—good polytheists.[96] By contrast, although Darius was just as much Elamite as Cyrus and Cambyses, and both rulers were part Scytho-Mede and belonged to the royal lineage, the Early Zoroastrians among the Persians saw themselves as brothers of the Early Zoroastrians among the Medes. Many of the bas-reliefs erected under Darius in Persepolis are remarkable for showing Medes and Persians—but *only* those two peoples—walking hand in hand, patting each other on the shoulder, full of affection. (See Figures 7 and 11.)

When Darius took the vacant throne, one by one he defeated, captured, and executed every "lie-following" (*Daiva*-worshipping) rebel. Significantly—leaving aside the Babylonians, who rebelled before learning of Darius' coup[97]—all of the rebels are by name or attribution natives of a realm belonging to the *pre-Cyrus* Empire—the original Empire conquered and creolized by the Scythians and Scytho-Medes.[98] Several of these realms rebelled more than once, but none of Cyrus' new additions, which were all in the polytheistic west of the Empire, actually rebelled after Darius took over.[99] In many instances a rebel leader

94. See for a recent study Zlotnick-Sivan (2004).

95. Cf. Endnote 92.

96. Kuhrt (2007, 1: 51).

97. As shown by Vogelsang (1998: 200).

98. Cf. Endnote 93.

99. Darius mentions (DB §21) that Egypt and Assyria rebelled when he was in Babylon, i.e., very early in his reign, but he evidently did not need to subdue them by force (at least at that time) and they are not mentioned again as rebelling lands.

claimed to be a direct descendant of a famous earlier ruler of the Medes or another nation. Darius finally succeeded in suppressing them, with the support of Ahura Mazdā, as he says. But Cyrus had vastly expanded the empire and reinstated polytheism—especially the *Daivas* of polytheistic Mazdaism, which still had many supporters[100]—so Darius married Cyrus' daughter Atossa, with whom he ensured that his successors also had the direct lineage of Cyrus (Darius' second cousin once removed). Their son Xerxes, the grandson of Cyrus, thus had clear double legitimacy. Just to make sure everyone got the message, Darius sent copies of his proclamations in Imperial Aramaic and other languages around the Empire, proclaiming over and over that the one Great God, Ahura Mazdā, supported him and the Empire, and was responsible for everything he did.

With God to personally authorize him, Darius needed no story, but he did need the Medes. He could not have succeeded in ruling the empire without them. They had inherited the Scythian system first, directly from its Scythian founders, they understood best how it worked, they spoke Imperial Scythian (unlike the Persians), and they especially understood the Empire's religious aspects: the Magi were Medes, and the Early Zoroastrians among them served as the official priests of the Empire. The relationship of Medes and Persians was a marriage made in Heaven. Together the two peoples spread Heavenly God monotheism around the Empire, including in Hebrew Palestine, Greek Anatolia, and northwestern India.

Thus the Scythians, not the Medes or the Persians, built the world's first superpower empires, first in the steppe, and then in amenable regions of Central Asia and the Near East, where after them their children, the ruling Scytho-Medes, referred to themselves as *Aria* ~ *Ariya* 'the Royal ones', and in northern China, where the Scytho-Chinese called

100. Besides the fact that only the original core of the Empire rebelled, the rebels represented only the polytheists among them, whom Darius refers to in pure Zoroastrian terms as "followers of the Lie" (i.e., *Daiva*-worshippers). The non-rebels who supported Darius (leaving aside those who were neutral) were monotheists who worshipped Ahura Mazdā. The polytheists outside the original core of the Empire, *as non-Mazdaists*, were simply uninvolved. In a sense, because he created the conditions that produced Darius and his Persian conspiracy, Cyrus actually did make it a "Persian" Empire.

themselves *Ḥarya* ~ *Aria* too, and where, via said Scytho-Chinese, the Chinese in general adopted *Ḥarya* as their self-appellation. Herodotus says the Scythians ruled Media for 28 years, one full generation. As the stories told by both Herodotus and Xenophon indicate, the young Cyrus was taken to Media, the land of the *Arias*, and grew up there.[101] The importance of his Median stay (whether factual or not) was perhaps to show that he was the legitimate ruler of the originally *Scythian* Empire.

After Cyrus rebelled and captured King Astyages alive, all accounts say he treated him well. The reason would seem to be that Cyrus really was related to the Mede king, as Herodotus and Xenophon claim. His defeat of the great power of the time was thus a family-internal coup d'état, not an all-out war.[102]

In 542, Nabonidus, King of Babylon (r. 556–539), finished extensive repairs and beautification of three major temples in the kingdom (not including the main temple dedicated to Marduk, in Babylon itself). To commemorate the event he buried a foundation text written in Babylonian Akkadian, the Nabonidus Cylinder, of which two copies have been found. The copy from Sippar begins:

> I, Nabonidus, the great king, the strong king, the king of the universe, the king of Babylon, the king of the four corners, the caretaker of Esagila and Ezida, for whom Sin and Ningal in his mother's womb decreed a royal fate as his destiny . . .[103]

In 539 Cyrus defeated the Babylonian forces and captured the city. He deposed Nabonidus and shortly thereafter buried a foundation document also written in Babylonian Akkadian, the now famous *Cyrus Cylinder*. The first part of the text relates how Babylon's chief god, Marduk, chose Cyrus to save his city from Nabonidus, and personally helped Cyrus

101. The stories are however quite different. The fictionalized and mostly doubtful account by Xenophon in his *Cyropaedia* has Cyrus growing up in Media, but at the luxurious royal court of Astyages in Ecbatana.

102. On the view that the coup was a three-year-long war see Kuhrt (2007, 1: 57, note 8).

103. Translation by Beaulieu (2007/2020). Esagila is the name of the great temple of the god Marduk; Ezida is the name of the great temple of the god Nabu, near Babylon.

succeed. The second part has Cyrus, "King of Anshan", state in his own words, in the first person, his titles and lineage (italicizing the key words):

> I am Cyrus, king of the world, the great king, the powerful king, king of Babylon, king of Sumer and Akkad, king of the four quarters of the world; son of Cambyses, the great king, king of the city of Anshan; grandson of Cyrus, the great king, k[ing of the ci]ty of Anshan; great-grandson of Teispes, the great king, king of the city of Anshan; *seed of an eternal royal line.*[104]

Both Nabonidus and Cyrus thus follow the long Mesopotamian tradition of such ruler's proclamations written in literary Akkadian. Cyrus does not mention his Scytho-Mede-Elamite lineage overtly, though it is the specific "eternal royal line" to which he refers.

Darius, who like Cyaxares and Cyrus before him took over the Empire by coup d'état, proclaims in the first three lines of his monumental inscription on the side of Mount Behistun (anciently *Bagastāna* 'place of god'), in Old Persian:

> I am Darius, the Great King, King of kings, king of Persia, king of the Lands, son of Hystaspes, grandson of Arsames, the Achaemenid. King Darius says: My father is Hystaspes; the father of Hystaspes was Arsames; the father of Arsames was Ariaramnes; the father of Ariaramnes was Teispes; the father of Teispes was Achaemenes. King Darius says: That is why we are called Achaemenids; *from antiquity we have been noble; from antiquity has our seed been royal.*[105]

104. The website of the British Museum (currently home of the *Cyrus Cylinder*) gives three translations of the text. The crucial last phrase (with my emphasis) represents Akkadian *zērum darium ša šarrūtim* 'the seed everlasting of kingship' (my literal translation); cf. *CAD* 21, 95b 'of lasting royal lineage', and *CAD* 3, 116b 'a descendant of an eternal royal line'. Cf. Finkel's translation (a version of the Rogers translation of 1912) "the perpetual seed of kingship". Cyrus calls himself and all his ancestors "great kings", but that term cannot have had the meaning of 'emperor', as it has in Old Persian. Cyrus' usage suggests he was not as sure of himself as modern writers assume. Otherwise, the words of Cyrus presage the later words of Darius in his tomb inscription (DNa) quoted below.

105. The text's italicized portion reads in Old Persian: 𐏃𐎨𐎠𐏐𐎱𐎽𐎢𐎻𐎡𐎹𐎫𐏐𐎠𐎶𐎠𐎫𐎠𐏐𐎠𐎶𐏃𐎹𐏐𐏃𐎨𐎠𐏐𐎱𐎽𐎢𐎻𐎡𐎹𐎫𐏐𐏃𐎹𐎠𐏐𐎠𐎶𐎠𐎧𐎶𐏐𐎫𐎢𐎶𐎠𐏐𐎧𐏁𐎠𐎹𐎰𐎡𐎹𐎠𐏐𐎠𐏃𐏐 *hacā paruviyata āmātā amahi hacâ paruviyata hayā amāxam taumā xšāyathiyā āha*. Text from Schmitt (2009: 37–38). *Hystaspes* is the Greek transcription of *Vištāspa*. Old Persian *āmātā* is

Darius thus deviates significantly from the Babylonian tradition in the *Cyrus Cylinder*, deleting several phrases, but adding "King of kings". Nevertheless he follows in the footsteps of Cyrus, spelling out the key last phrase in Old Persian, though—like the *Cyrus Cylinder*—without the word *Ariya*. Darius' Old Persian corresponds exactly to the sense of the phrase "seed of an eternal royal line" in Cyrus' Akkadian. One might suspect that either he or the scribe slipped up and omitted *Ariya* or had not yet realized the significance of that little word, but it occurs later in the same inscription and in Darius' later Tomb Inscription in Old Persian at Naqš-i Rustam:

> I am Darius, the Great King, the King of kings, the king of countries containing all kinds of people, king on this Great Earth and wide, son of Hystaspes, an Achaemenid; a Persian, son of a Persian; *an Ariya, seed of an Ariya.*[106]

The last phrase, *Ariya Ariyaciça* 'an Ariya, seed of an Ariya' in Old Persian, like the above-quoted phrase in the Behistun Inscription, 'from antiquity has our seed been royal', corresponds exactly to Cyrus' *zērum darium ša šarrūtim* 'seed of an eternal royal line' in Akkadian. The Behistun Inscription was erected so soon after Darius' victory over the rebels that it required several revisions, as is now well known, so the most probable explanation is more pedestrian: the scribes and translators understood Darius perfectly, and wrote the sense of the Behistun Inscription text out first in Elamite and Akkadian, and then—using Darius' newly created cuneiform script—in Old Persian, which language Darius explicitly calls *Ariya*. Later the scribes understood things better and included *Ariya*, the Old Persian form of the word *Aria*, in Darius' genealogy, so that the king specifically calls himself an *Ariya*. That is, for

a hapax legomenon, the etymological meaning of which is considered very uncertain (Sch. 129); my translation is based on the Akkadian version of the text (noted by Schmitt), which has *mār banî* 'nobleman' (*CAD* 10: 257).

106. DNa 13–14. The last phrase giving his lineage reads: 𐎻𐎡𐏁𐎫𐎠𐎿𐎱𐏃𐎹𐎠𐏐𐎱𐎢𐏂𐏐𐏃𐎧𐎠𐎶𐎴𐎡𐏁𐎡𐎹𐏐𐎱𐎠𐎼𐎿𐏐𐎱𐎠𐎼𐎿𐏃𐎹𐎠𐏐𐎱𐎢𐏂𐏐𐎠𐎼𐎡𐎹𐏐𐎠𐎼𐎡𐎹𐎨𐎡𐏂𐏐 *Vištāspahyā puça Haxāmanišiya Pārsa Pārsahyā puça Ariya Ariyaciça*. Text from Schmitt (2009: 101).

Cyrus' 'seed of the royal line' and Darius' own earlier equivalent of it, Darius calls himself explicitly 'seed of an *Ariya*',[107] further confirming that the word *Ariya* ~ *Aria* ~ *Ḥarya* means '(of) the (eternal) royal line'. The other texts also show that the key statement is not one in which the ruler claims he is 'noble', but the one in which he says he is 'royal'. The word *ariya* means specifically '*belonging to the legitimate (eternal) lineage of kings*', i.e., 'royal'.[108] That is why *Ariya* ~ *Aria* ~ *Ḥarya* in the Behistun Inscription refers to the *language* of the 'royal' ruling house of Darius as '*the Royal one*', a usage regularly followed by many ancient and medieval ruling peoples from Persia to Korea.

When Darius says in the Naqš-i Rustam Inscription that he is *Ariya Ariyaciça* 'an Ariya and seed of an Ariya', he means exactly that he is a legitimate ruler in the imperial lineage established by the Scythians, who referred to themselves as the 'Aria kings'. Herodotus translates it as οἱ βασιλήιοι Σκύθαι 'the Royal Scythians', but in his account of the steppe Scythians *Aria* means specifically 'the Scythians of the royal lineage'. Similarly, Ssu-ma Ch'ien, who calls the nation of Sakas (Scythians) just to the northwest of China 塞王 'the *Sakă (Scythian) *Kings*' (an odd expression in Chinese), actually means 'the *Royal* Scythians' too.[109] The ruler of each was *Ariya Ariyaciça* 'an Ariya and seed of an Ariya', as Darius says, i.e., a 'seed of the one legitimate eternal royal line (*Ariya* ~ *Aria* ~ *Ḥarya*)'. Other sources tell us that many other ancient and medieval Central Eurasian rulers did exactly the same thing.[110]

Darius repeats over and over in his Behistun Inscription that he has told the truth, he has not lied. Some have questioned the truth of some of Darius' statements, but they misunderstand what Darius is talking about. He always refers to the rebels as those who "follow falsehood", but he meant more than simply worshipping the *Daivas*. They had

107. The original says, literally, 'son of Persian', 'seed of Ariya', etc., because Old Persian does not overtly mark definiteness; the same text is also in DSe §2 (Schmitt 2009: 124).

108. My detailed article on this topic (Beckwith 2016a) thus needs to be revised accordingly.

109. On the Old Chinese reading of the name 塞 as *Sakă see Beckwith and Kiyose (2018). See also Endnote 94.

110. See Endnote 95.

brought about civil war. Darius believed that he himself stood for unity and peace. In his Susa Inscription DSe he says:

> The Lands were revolting, one killed the other; by the will of Ahuramazdā I made it so that one did not kill the other at all.[111]

The Scythians believed in their feudal-hierarchical system, the original version of the Imperial system, from absolute Heavenly creator God on down. Their system was maintained practically without change under Cyaxares, Cyrus, and Darius.[112] When Darius says he tells the Truth, and those who rebel are liars, he is talking not only about the oath of loyalty and belief in the *one great God* but also about belief in *one undivided Empire*. The "imperial system", like the ancient and modern "democratic system", is thus founded on religious-related belief in "self-evident Truths". In the Scythian imperial system continued by Darius, Truth is defined as the system of one God, one King, one Empire. Therefore, anyone who supports more than one God ~ King ~ Empire follows false gods, supports bloody civil war, and is by definition a liar. So Darius told the truth.

111. 𐎭𐏃𐎹𐎠𐎺𐏐𐎠𐎹𐎢𐎭𐏐𐎠𐎴𐎡𐎹𐏐𐎠𐎴𐎡𐎹𐎶𐏐𐎠𐎩𐏐𐎠𐎺𐏐𐎠𐎭𐎶𐏐𐎠𐎤𐎵𐎺𐎶𐏐𐎺𐏁𐎴𐎠𐏐𐎠𐎢𐎼𐎶𐏀𐎭𐎠𐏃𐎠 𐏐𐎹𐎰𐎠𐏐𐎠𐎴𐎡𐎹𐏐𐎠𐎴𐎡𐎹𐎶𐏐𐎴𐎡𐎹𐏐𐎩𐎫𐎡𐎹𐏐𐎨𐎡𐎴𐎠 Darius DSe §5, 32–36. Text from Schmitt (2009: 125–126): *dahyāva ayauda, aniya aniyam aja; ava adam akunavam vašnā Auramazdāhā yaθā aniya aniyam naiy jatiy* [Schmitt: *janti*] *cinā*.

112. See Endnotes 96 and 101.

4

One Eternal Royal Line

The Scythian royal lineage was created by the God of Heaven, *Tagri, who impregnated the daughter of Borysthenes (the Dnieper River, a god). She gave birth to *Targitaos* 'Powerful by Heaven', or in another version, *Ariapeithes* 'Father of the Arias'.[1] In all three versions of their foundation myth the semi-divine father has three sons, of whom the youngest, **Skula xšaya* 'King Scyles (Scythes)',[2] becomes the first king of the Scythians.

The legitimate royal line was transmitted across much of Eurasia by the Scythians and the peoples who were creolized by them. In some places the term *Aria* ~ *Ariya* ~ *Ḥarya* came to be used as an epithet meaning 'Royal(s)', and later became an ethnolinguistic "national" name for the adopting people, the most outstanding examples being Iran and China (see below). In the earliest period, though, when the Scythians were still ruling their vast empire and much of the periphery as well, the word continued to be used in its primary sense of '(member of, language of) the legitimate royal line', and it spread far and wide in that sense.

Now, as for the question of the Achaemenid royal line, Teispes, the common ancestor of Cyrus and Darius, obviously could not have started a lineage alone. He must have had parents of his own and he must have

1. In Greek transcription *Targitaos*, transcribing *targi* 'heaven' + *tava* 'powerful'; see Chapter 1 for the story and Chapter 6 for the reconstruction. *Ariapeithes* *Aryāpitā 'father of Arias' cannot be made into *Ariapaisa 'ornament of the Arias', as some have argued; see Endnote 138.

2. See Chapter 6 on this name and the textual problem in Herodotus.

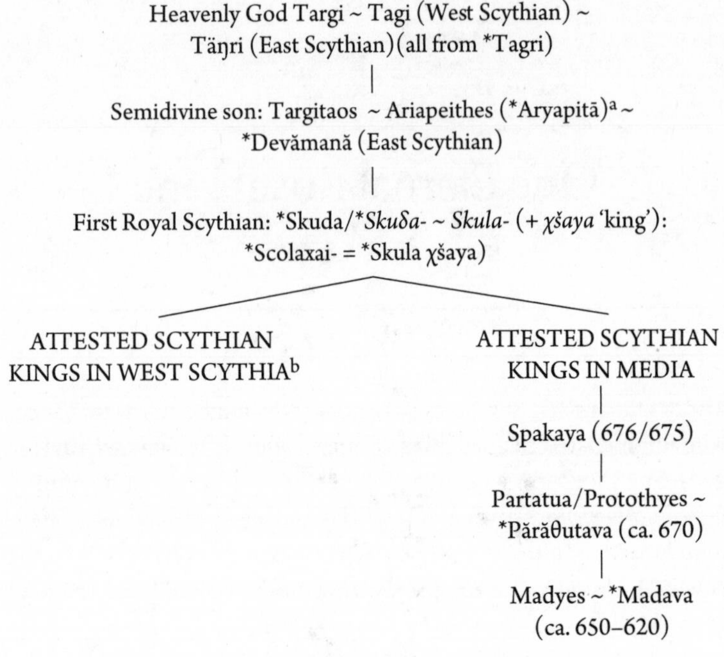

DIAGRAM 2. From Heavenly God to the Scythian Kings in Scythia.

[a] In the second, Hellenized, version, the semi-divine figure is Heracles. For the myths see Chapter 1.

[b] The history of the Scythian kings of the Pontic Steppe region is complex and most kings are poorly attested. See Alekseyev (2005).

had at least one wife. Unlike Cyrus the Great, Darius the Great traces his lineage back to the *father* of Teispes, Achaemenes ~ Haxāmaniš. The name is Scythian and means 'sworn liegeman' or the like, i.e., an Imperial feudal title, 'vassal-lord, duke'.[3] As the head of a lineage, Achaemenes could be legendary or mythological, or invented by Darius. If so, it is very odd that he has a socio-politically subordinate name. The strikingly unusual nature of his name invokes the "principle of embarrassment", which

3. Sch. 192: 'Gefolgsherr, Gefolgsmann', citing YAve *haxa-* 'Freund, Genosse usw.' and *maniš 'Denken, Sinn', therefore 'Gefolgschaftspartner (sein) Sinn'; cf. Bar. 1744: 'he who has the dedication of a friend or comrade', i.e., a 'sworn liegeman, vassal lord' or, as a title or name, 'Duke'.

supports Achaemenes' historicity. Darius would have a solidly Royal Scythian (*Aria* ~ *Ariya* ~ *Ḥarya*) lineage in the male line if it were not for Teispes. Teispes (Old Persian Čišpiš) has an Elamite name (Zišpiš) and he was King of Anshan (Elam), according to Cyrus, so he was clearly at least part Elamite.[4] Because Darius and Cyrus do not share any intervening lineage members after Teispes, there were two parallel lines, as Darius says in the Behistun Inscription,[5] each descended from Teispes and a queen, so Teispes must have had at least two queens of different regional or ethnolinguistic backgrounds. Teispes' wife who was Darius' ancestor should have been Scythian in order to account for Darius' solidly Scythian male line after Teispes, with the Scythian names Ariaramnes, Arsames, Hystaspes, and perhaps even Darius. Similarly, the queen at the head of Cyrus' lineage should have been Elamite, accounting for the solidly Elamite male line after her, with the Elamite names Cyrus (Kuraš I and II), Cambyses (Kambuzia I and II), and Smerdis (Bardiya). Darius' Scythian lineage is supported by the heavy Scythian influence on Old Persian,[6] showing additionally that the spoken language of Pārsa, formerly Elamite, was already largely Persian, as has been shown on the basis of names in the excavated documents from Persepolis.[7] For Cyrus, King of Anshan, if he really was an Elamite king in every respect, having an all-Elamite male lineage would seem ideal. By contrast, though Darius was certainly "Elamized" in some respects, he was demonstrably a Persian speaker, self-identified as a Persian, and says he was from Pārsa.[8] Nevertheless he was mostly Scythian in his male line, and he knew it—he says he was "an Ariya and seed of an

4. Potts (2005).

5. Not with Sch. 174–175. The two lineages are both attested and were in fact two parallel lines (Cyrus' lineage and Darius' lineage), as usually understood, since Darius counts the kings in *both* lineages. It is thus impossible to understand *duvitā-paranam* as meaning 'consecutively in one line', *pace* Schmitt (2009: 37–38, 91–93). It occurs twice, both times at Behistun (DB 1.9–1.11, DBa), used in exactly the same way.

6. See Chapter 5.

7. Potts (2005).

8. Unfortunately, female ancestors are not mentioned in either of the two kings' lineages. However, the female side of Darius' immediate ancestry was apparently Scythian and Persian. In the female side of Cyrus' line, which is attested in Herodotus from his mother Mandane on, all of the key women have Imperial Scythian names.

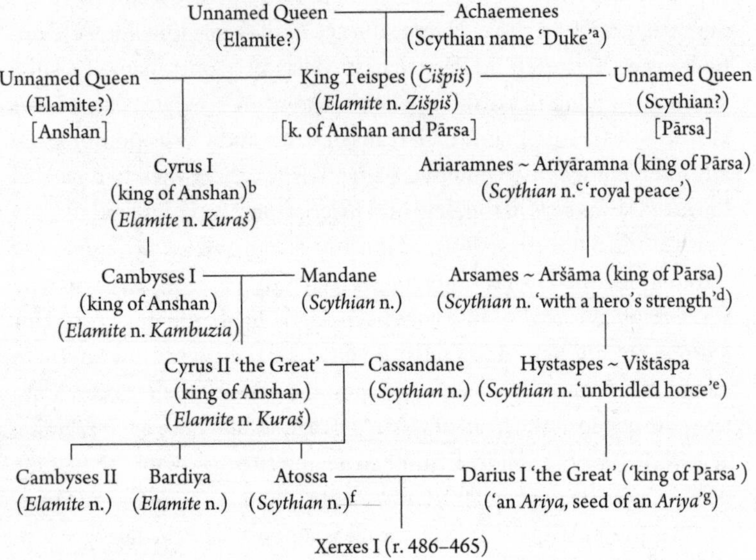

DIAGRAM 3. Lineage and Ethnolinguistic Identity from Achaemenes to Xerxes.

[a] See Chapter 4, Note 3.

[b] There is no information on his wife. Potts (2005) shows conclusively that Kuraš of Anshan ('Elam and the Elamites') was not the same king as Kuraš of Parsua ~ Parsumaš (Parsuvaš).

[c] Sch. 137 suggests 'creating peace for the Aryas'. Attested on a tombstone in Kerch, Scythia, 1st century CE (Struve 1965: 244): Ἀριαράμνης υἱὲ Ἀριαράθου χαῖρε 'Ariaramnēs son of Ariaratha. Farewell!'

[d] Sch. 238: Ave. *ărša-* 'man/hero' + *ama* 'strength'; cf. Bar. 203–204 (s.v. *aršan-*). A daughter of Darius the Great was also named *Aršāma* (Greek *Arsame*), so the name could apply to either a man or a woman.

[e] I.e., untied for a horse-race. *Vištāspa* is also the name of the lordly patron of Zoroaster in the *Gāthās*.

[f] Schmitt (2011d) identifies Greek *Atossa* as "Old Pers. *Utauθa (= Av. Hutaosā)". Old Avestan (Scythian) *Hutaosā* is the name of the sister and wife of Vištāspa in the *Gāthās*. Her name means 'with good thighs', referring to her child-bearing capacity (Bar. 1822); cf. Chapter 3, Note 75. The daughter of Cyrus, she was probably named by her mother, Cassandane, who also has an Imperial Scythian name, perhaps 'She who makes (one) become aware', from *kas-* 'become aware' + *sand-* 'cause, make' (Bar. 459–462, 1560), or 'Enlightener'. The name of Cyrus II's mother *Mandane* 'keeping in mind' is Imperial Scythian as well (Bar. 1136).

[g] Darius says the Behistun Inscription is written in *Ariya*, the 'Royal' language, which is not Scythian but Old Persian (q.v. Chapters 5 and 6). Many languages of Eurasia, most of which are not Iranic, use the term *Aria* ~ *Ariya* ~ *Ḥarya* the same way (Beckwith 2016a).

Ariya"—so a Royal Scythian (Ariya) male as lineage-head was ideal for him. Teispes was his great-great-grandfather, but Darius cites the name of Teispes' father, Achaemenes (Haxāmaniš), whose name, or rather, title, is not Persian or Elamite, but Scythian. Since Achaemenes (Haxāmaniš) and an unknown Elamite wife gave birth to Teispes, they were Darius' earliest known ancestors. Teispes in turn was the male ancestor both of Darius' branch lineage and of Cyrus' branch lineage. It would then make perfect sense that a Scythian feudal lord of the royal Aria lineage—the "Duke"—newly arrived in Elam along with a wing of the Scythian imperial army should take a local lady as his wife, as was normally, regularly done. And it would make equally good sense if the two of them agreed to have their son Teispes marry both an Elamite queen and a Scythian queen, so both queens would work to ensure the political support of their respective ethnolinguistic heritages.

Darius had to know Cyrus' own lineage in order to count the total number of kings in the Achaemenid lineage up to his own reign. Cyrus did not perhaps know Darius' lineage, but the two lineages agree. Not only do both men agree on their proximal common ancestor, Teispes (Old Persian Čišpiš, Elamite Zišpiš), the lineages make it clear that Darius was a legitimate claimant to the throne.[9] Nevertheless, the disorder and destruction of the civil war—even though strictly religious in origin—must have cast doubt on Darius' legitimacy already in Antiquity. To counter it, he married Cyrus' daughter Atossa, whose mother was Cassandane, Cyrus' favorite wife. Atossa gave birth to Xerxes I, who was thus doubly legitimate and reunited the two parallel lineages when he succeeded Darius on the throne.

Cyrus, with his male line's strong Elamite tradition and polytheistic preferences, was perhaps uninterested in the vast eastern territories of the Empire he had inherited. Those lands were solidly Scythian and Scytho-Mede ethnolinguistically and at least in part monotheistic. He no doubt wanted a polytheist at the head of the family line, so perhaps that is the reason he names only Teispes in his lineage.[10] Yet, although

9. Shahbazi (2012); cf. this chapter, Note 5, on the two lineages.

10. Of course, all we know about Teispes is his name and its occurrence in the two rulers' lineages; he might well have been a monotheist. However, Cyrus certainly would have known

Cyrus was part Elamite, King Astyages was his close relative, so Cyrus was also part royal Scytho-Mede, and thus an *Aria* and legitimate heir twice over. That is sufficient to explain how he was able to gain enough support to overthrow the king and put himself on the throne of the Mede Empire. The reason that no contemporaneous source calls Cyrus a *Persian* is that he clearly was not thought to be a Persian, and he himself does not tell us he self-identified as a Persian. So his own line too must go back one generation further to the shadowy Scythian historical figure Darius calls Achaemenes. That makes Cyrus an Achaemenid as well, and thereby an *Aria* in the male line, like Darius. Cyrus states that legitimacy (in Babylonian Akkadian) in his *Cyrus Cylinder* when he says he is 'the seed of an eternal royal line'.[11]

It is extremely unlikely that Darius simply made up the name Achaemenes ~ Haxāmaniš. As noted above, the name or title has enough "embarrassment factor" in it to indicate it is genuine. Although Achaemenes, "the Duke", must have lived long before Darius was born, the latter mentions that his grandfather Arsames was still alive when he took the throne in 522. In traditional societies, it is commonplace for aristocrats to know their ancestry much further back than that, and many know their own lineages in detail. Arsames undoubtedly knew the name of his own great-grandfather.

In order for a young woman to marry a king like Teispes, her father should have been a king himself, or a royal who had the rank of "(sub)-king" or Great Satrap in the imperial system, where the top of the hierarchy was the emperor or "Great King". The sub-kings, or subordinate-level kings—the equivalent of our "Dukes"—are thus usually referred to by scholars as "Great Satraps", and though appointed, in the Achaemenid system they were almost always members of the royal family. When Achaemenes and his Elamite wife gave birth to Teispes, they passed on the *Aria* ~ *Ariya* ~ *Ḥarya* legitimacy to him, so that eventually their heir Darius would proudly list Teispes among the names of his male lineage. Darius also counts (but does not name) the kings in the parallel lineage

that his mother was a Scytho-Mede princess with an Imperial Scythian name, and that his chief and favorite wife, Cassandane, also had an Imperial Scythian name.

11. See Chapter 3.

of Cyrus (Cyrus I, Cambyses I, Cyrus II, Cambyses II, and Bardiya) as well as those in his own line, making the total number of eight kings of his family who ruled before Darius himself. Darius is perfectly honest: his own father Vištāspa was not a king and he does not count him. We know nothing about Cyrus I of Anshan,[12] but (according to Herodotus) his son Cambyses I married Princess Mandane, the daughter of King Astyages of the Scytho-Medes,[13] who was at the time the single most powerful ruler in the entire Middle East, so Cyrus I must have been an important "king", a Great Satrap or Duke, though of course not a "Great King" (emperor), as there could only be one occupant in the top rank of the feudal hierarchy. Cambyses I and Mandane's son Cyrus II 'the Great' in turn married the noble Cassandane, whose name is also Scythian, so her children Cambyses II, Smerdis (Bardiya), and Atossa all had the Ariya lineage as well. Xerxes, son of Darius and Atossa, united both of his parents' lineages going back to their furthest known ancestor, Achaemenes, who has a Scythian name and must have been a Scythian.

As noted above, the name Achaemenes (*Haxāmaniš*), 'liegeman, duke', is literally not a name at all but a feudal title or rank. From the viewpoint of the imperial hierarchy, the rulers of Anshan (Elam) and Pārsa were "kings" (i.e., dukes, vassal kings) of the one Great King of the Scytho-Medes (and prior to that, vassal kings of the Great King of the Scythians). In English "royal" level feudal terminology, Pārsa had been a duchy, ruled by a duke. Although *duke* is a title equivalent to Great Satrap, the *rank* is explicitly that of a "sub-king" in an imperial feudal system. Perhaps, when Darius asked his grandfather about their ancestors, Arsames traced their line of kings in Pārsa back to Darius' great-great-great-grandfather and told him something like, "A powerful Ariya was he, Haxāmaniš, king under the Great King of the Ariyas (Royal Scythians)."

12. I.e., Kuraš of Anshan, who must be distinguished from Kuraš of Parsua (or Parsumaš), q.v. Endnote 64.

13. According to Herodotus (i 107ff.); comments on their relationship in Akkadian sources suggest Cyrus was indeed related to Astyages.

Darius does not actually mention that his own father Vištāspa (Hystaspes) had *not* been king; he simply omits that information. But *why* had he not become king? The members of his lineage had all been in turn king (i.e., sub-king, 'duke') of Pārsa. Cyrus and his sons had exactly the same rank: Cyrus I was king of Anshan, and Ariaramnes was king of Pārsa. So Cambyses I, and at first Cyrus II as well, were kings of Anshan, which in the feudal system meant sub-kings under their overlord the Great King of the Scytho-Mede Empire, the direct continuation of the Scythian Empire founded in Media. Even in the *Cyrus Cylinder*, after Cyrus had become Great King of the entire Empire (becoming in our tradition 'Cyrus the Great'), his primary self-identifier is "King of Anshan". He does not call himself "king of kings", and he does not mention Pārsa. But because he had rebelled against, and defeated, his maternal grandfather Astyages, the Scytho-Mede Great King, Cyrus had taken over the entire feudal-hierarchical Empire, including all the vassal kingdoms such as Pārsa, as Great King. Cyrus was about the same age as Vištāspa, his second cousin, who should have become king (i.e., sub-king or "duke") of Pārsa in his turn, but Darius' grandfather Arsames was still alive and presumably still king of Pārsa when Darius overthrew the usurper Gaumāta and became Great King. At the time, his father Vištāspa was under-satrap over Parthia and Hyrcania (i.e., sub-sub-king).[14]

When Cambyses died without male issue following his brother Bardiya's earlier death, the throne was unoccupied by a legitimate heir. But it had been usurped by a Magus, Gaumāta, even before Cambyses' death, when he was still on campaign in Egypt. Not surprisingly, rebellions had already broken out and the Empire was in danger of collapsing.[15]

14. Cf. Shahbazi (2012) and XPf 18–21. The names Pārsa and Persis 'Persia' and Parθava 'Parthia' are probably dialect forms of each other (Sch. 228), and the attested Parthian language, though much creolized, is thought to belong to the same branch of Iranic as Persian. What if Vištāspa was sent to Parthia because he knew the local language, or because he had relatives there?

15. See the interesting discussion by Vogelsang (1998). Neither now nor at the time could anyone know if the Bardiya supposedly ruling (known from reign-dates in Akkadian documents) was actually Bardiya or a usurping imposter, as he is in the story told by Darius and Herodotus.

A wise older relative, Otanes, who knew what was going on at court, briefed Darius on the situation when he got back from Egypt. At that point, as far as we know, Darius was actually *the only living legitimate pretender to the throne* in his generation.[16] He belonged to the legitimate royal line, Ariya, as far back as he could trace his lineage. He was also a high-ranking, battle-hardened veteran of Cambyses' Egyptian campaign and agreed that something needed to be done immediately to save the Empire. He believed that God, Ahura Mazdā himself, had given him and his line this one chance. Darius thanked God and seized the chance. He gathered his comrades and claimed the throne.

Darius was Cyrus' second cousin once removed, so both had the Scytho-Mede royal lineage, which Darius calls "my family". The only difficulty is caused by the other side of these rulers' familial heritage. Cyaxares was part Scythian, since he was by definition a member of the *Aria-zantu*, the 'Royal (Aria) clan' of the Scytho-Medes. Cyrus the Great was part Scytho-Mede and part unrelated Elamite, but no verifiable contemporaneous source connects him with Persis (Pārsa), then a little-known place where the people did not speak Imperial Scythian. Like Cyrus and Cambyses, Darius dressed as an Elamite, and bore Elamite weapons. His government produced mainly Elamite accounting records. But in his imperial inscriptions, which are in Old Persian, he always declares himself to be "Persian", and he refers to himself as "seed of an Ariya"—offspring of a Royal Scythian.[17]

16. This is pointed out in a careful study by Shahbazi (2012), who notes "it has been argued that Darius was not a royal prince, let alone the rightful heir. . . . As Cambyses and Bardiya had left no sons, however, the nearest to the throne would have been Aršāma [Arsames], Darius' grandfather, who was then too old to take the field. His son Vištāspa (Hystaspes) was in charge of Parthia and Hyrcania (DB 2.92–98) and could not have led an army to Media undetected." Also, though his father and grandfather were legitimate claimants to the throne, no doubt they knew that their own heir, Darius, was far more experienced in every respect and had a much greater chance of success. Moreover, Vištāspa's position as sub-satrap of Parthia and Hyrcania meant he was second or third in command of the significant forces of the Great Satrapy of Media, which included other realms as well as Parthia and Hyrcania, as Jacobs (2006) shows. And in view of Darius' dedication to Early Zoroastrianism, Vištāspa's Imperial Scythian name is surely relevant.

17. In his Tomb Inscription DNa.

One of the most interesting remarks of Herodotus (vii 62) is, "The Medes were formerly called by everyone *Arias* (Ἄριοι), but when the Colchian woman Medea came from Athens to the *Arias* they changed their name, like the Persians."[18] The last comment here must not be overlooked. Herodotus stresses elsewhere how much the Persians "borrowed" from the Medes. Did he mean to say that the Persians too originally called themselves *Arias* (Ἄριοι)? Whatever he really meant, since the Medes had earlier been Scythians *politically* (as well as culturally and linguistically), the Persians too had ultimately been Scythians *politically*.

Herodotus also lists the names of the five Median tribes,[19] of which only one is certainly Iranic linguistically, namely the Ἀριζαντοί Arizantoi, a name that is attested also in Elamite transcription; both transcribe Old Iranic *Arya-zantu- 'the Aria clan',[20] as noted above. The term *Aria ~ Ariya ~ Ḥarya* 'royal', the epithet of the ruling Royal Scythian clan, is also attested in Herodotus' minimal (third) version of the national foundation myth, which has as royal progenitor *Ariapeithes*, i.e., *Aryā-pitā- 'father of Arias'.[21] The Scythians spread the word *Ariya ~ Aria ~ Ḥarya* around Eurasia wherever they ruled or settled. It is pregnant with political significance in all regions and among all peoples where it is found, including the entire steppe zone, Southeastern Europe, Southwest Asia, and eastern Eurasia, where it is attested in many languages, including Old Chinese.[22] Thus an early group of Scythians, probably a *satrapy*

18. Herodotus (vii 62): οἱ δὲ Μῆδοι . . . πάλαι πρὸς πάντων Ἄριοι, ἀπικομένης δὲ Μηδείης τῆς Κολχίδος ἐξ Ἀθηνέων ἐς τοὺς Ἀρίους τούτους μετέβαλον καὶ οὗτοι τὸ οὔνομα. He adds, αὐτοὶ περὶ σφέων ὧδε λέγουσι Μῆδοι 'This is the Medes' own account of themselves'. From Perseus, tr. Godley. The Medea part of his story is absurd and certainly based on folk-etymology of the ethnonym, but it supports the tradition he heard that "Mede" was not the original national ethnonym. As Herodotus tells us, and the Akkadian sources confirm, before the Scythians arrived Media was strictly a geographical zone occupied by many unrelated, disunited peoples; they had no national ethnonym at all. Herodotus tells exactly the same story in his account of Deioces, his putative first Mede king. (See Chapter 8.) Their use of the word *Aria* is thus precisely parallel to its use by the early, highly disunited peoples of what became China. See Chapter 7.

19. See Endnote 97.

20. See Endnote 98.

21. Not *Aryā-paisa-, as some have proposed. See Endnote 138.

22. There are many theories about the word's ultimate origin; see Endnote 99.

(a Scythian word, from *xšaθrapā-* ~ *šaθrapā-* 'sub-king, duke') of the Scythian Empire,[23] ruled over the region of Southwestern Asia. Under Cyaxares it became the Scytho-Mede Empire.

It was not only among the Royal Scythians that a Great King (emperor) had to belong to the heavenly royal (*Aria*) line. The same lineage name marked the legitimate Great King among many other peoples after them, including West Scythians (Aria); Scytho-Medes (Aria); Persians (Ariya); East Scythians (Ḥarya) and Hsiung-nu (*Ḥără̂); Bactrians (Ḥarya) and Kushans (*Aria*); Tokharians (*Ārśi*); Türk (*Arši*); and Togon or T'u-yü-hun (*Ḥarya*).[24] There appears to be a gap between the Togon, a Serbi-Mongolic people, and the grandfather of the Mongol ruler Chinggis Khan (r. 1206–1227 CE), whose lineage was treated among steppe peoples as the only legitimate line of Great Kings down to the destruction of Central Eurasian culture in Modern times. If there was a link and it simply has not yet been recognized, a single royal line was considered to be the only legitimate one for Central Eurasian imperial rulers from the Scythians to the 19th century, about two and a half millennia. And even if there is a gap (or gaps), the idea of there being only *one* Heavenly lineage of Great Kings, legitimized by the one God of Heaven himself, permeated Central Eurasian cultures throughout historical times.

Being a member of the royal *Aria* ~ *Ariya* ~ *Ḥarya* lineage was significant in many ways, foremost of them being the requirement that to be legitimate, a ruler had to belong to that lineage by either the male or the female line, preferably both. For those who had the lineage but were unlikely ever to become kings, they could be appointed as satraps 'sub-kings, dukes', or at least could become members of the royal comitatus and live like princes at court together with the king and his sons. Having come

23. Based on later, better attested, Central Eurasian steppe empires, including those of the Türk and the Mongols. For *xšaθrapā* see Sch. 284–285.

24. In Old Tibetan ཐོ་གོན་ *Thogon* (i.e., *Togon*) in Chinese *T'u-yü-hun* 吐谷渾 (*Tǔyùhún*). The Tibetans themselves, however, nearly always call them འ་ཞ་ *Ḥaźa*, the Tibetan pronunciation of *Ḥarya*, which is also attested and precisely transcribed in Old Tibetan (Beckwith 2016a). It was the epithet of the Togon ruling clan, which the Chinese knew as the ruling clan's name, A-ch'ai 阿柴, discussed in Endnote 108.

from Heaven, they would then "go back home" to Paradise upon death[25] if they fulfilled their oaths as loyal warriors to fight to the death to defend and serve their friend, their lord.[26]

In several of his inscriptions, Darius the Great uses the adjective *Ariya*, the Old Persian form of the word,[27] in its basic meaning: 'of or relating to the one legitimate heavenly royal line'. He says of himself in the Naqš-i-Rustam Inscription that he is *Ariya Ariyaciça* 'an *Ariya* (and) seed of an *Ariya*', meaning 'an offspring of the royal line'.[28] This is confirmed by his use of this royal title formula in the same textual position as the Akkadian expression with that meaning in parallel passages by Cyrus the Great in the *Cyrus Cylinder*, and by Nabonidus in the Nabonidus Cylinder, as discussed in Chapter 3. In his great Behistun Inscription Darius also uses *Ariya* to refer to the *language* of the inscription as 'the royal one', that is, 'the language of those who belong to the legitimate royal line', the way it is used by many other peoples of Eurasia for their mostly non-Iranic and non-Indo-European languages.

Thus the word was originally innocent of any ethnolinguistic, national, or other meaning, as shown by the fact that *Aria* ~ *Ariya* ~ *Ḥarya* (and its dialect variant *Ḥărắ) was borrowed and used as an epithet by many peoples of all kinds in much of Eurasia, including the Chinese, Koreans, Türk, Togon, Tibetans, and others who were hardly "Iranian". It has long been accepted that the word did not have its modern ethnolinguistic meaning 'Iranic-speaking peoples of Iran and other Iranic-speaking countries' until Middle Persian times,[29] over half a millennium after the word's first attestation and its diffusion around much of Eurasia by the Scythians.[30]

25. Beckwith (1984a: 37).

26. Beckwith (2009: 12–23). This requirement gradually fell out of use with the spread of world religions throughout Central Eurasia in the Middle Ages.

27. The spelling "Arya" appears to be unattested in authentic texts from premodern times.

28. DNa §2; see Chapter 3, Note 107 for the Old Persian text; also in DSe §2 (Schmitt 2009: 124).

29. Not with the interpretation in Sch. 136–137.

30. See Endnote 100.

The Royal Scythian Lineage in Eastern Eurasia

The clearest key to the crucial word *Aria* ~ *Ariya* ~ *Ḥarya* '(legitimate) royal' is to be found in its little-noted history in Chinese. The first word for 'the Chinese, China', i.e., their national ethnolinguistic appellation, is earliest attested in the 4th century BC.[31] It is the adopted Scythian term *Aria* ~ *Ariya* ~ *Ḥarya*, which is transcribed phonetically in two ways, one as *Hsia* 夏 (*Xià*), in Old Chinese **Ḥaryá* *[ɣa.rya]; the other as *Hua* 華 (*Huá*), in Old Chinese **Ḥâryá* *[ɣâ.rya]. Etymologically within Chinese, these are both *ordinary everyday Chinese words*: the first, *Hsia* 夏 **Ḥaryá* [ɣa.ˈrya] means 'summer'; the second, *Hua* 華 **Ḥâryá* [ɣâ.ˈrya] means 'flower'. The two words have no etymological relationship to each other, and before the 4th century BC neither one is attested with the meaning 'Chinese, China' or anything similar. That sense appears suddenly, as if out of nowhere. They are thus manifestly two different *transcriptions* of one loanword—a foreign word.[32] However, that word obviously could not originally have been an ethnolinguistic name meaning 'Iranian' or anything of the kind. Moreover, the peoples around China who borrowed it later *from the Chinese* use it to mean 'China, Chinese', as one would expect. The Chinese thus used the term *Aria* ~ *Ariya* ~ *Ḥarya* for themselves, evidently as an epithet for their rulers, because as shown above it originally meant 'royal(s)', 'those of the legitimate ruling lineage', or the like.[33] By using the term the Chinese referred to themselves as "the rulers" in a positive way while at the same time contrasting their own "royal" lineage with their feudal subjects or with people outside their territory,[34] so they apparently saw themselves as a kind of "chosen people", as the Persians did.[35] Like other Scythianized

31. This section summarizes Beckwith (2016a), q.v. for texts and linguistic details.

32. In the earliest texts (4th century BC), *Hsia* 夏 (*Xià*) occurs much more frequently than *Hua* 華 (*Huá*), but over time the latter replaces the former as the usual form for the meanings 'China, Chinese', etc.

33. See Beckwith (2016b) and Beckwith (2018).

34. On the existence of feudalism (versus slavery) in Central Eurasia, see Endnotes 96 and 101.

35. It has been said that the ruling people of the Persian Empire considered themselves to be a kind of "chosen people" (Briant 2002: 181–183); Kingsley (1995: 195); Boyce and Grenet (1991: 375). This agrees with the way the Persian tradition appears among the early Israelites,

peoples, the Achaemenid Persians used the term *Ariya* ~ *Aria* ~ *Ḥarya* 'royal' to affirm their status as legitimate rulers, but as shown in the previous chapters they acquired their version of the term and its status by creolization and inheritance, not by simple borrowing. What about the Chinese? The key is in the expression *Ta Hsia* 大夏, in Old Chinese literally '*Great* *Ḥarya'.

The *Shih chi* reveals that the Hsiung-nu were vassals of the *Yüeh-chih* 月氏 (*Yuèzhī*) people at the time of *T'ou-man* 頭曼 (*Tóumàn*) *Dewămană, the semi-legendary founder of the Hsiung-nu realm and father of *Mo-tun* 冒頓 (*Mòdùn*) *Bagătwănă.[36] The *Yüeh-chih* 月氏 Old Chinese *Tukwar(ă)-kē/kay—transcribing *Tuχwară *kay(ă), 'the *Tuχwară kings'[37]—therefore actually ruled the Eastern Steppe at the time. Such was the political order in the region before the defeat of the Hsiung-nu in the Ordos by the armies of Ch'in shih huang ti in 215 BC and the Hsiung-nu move to the north, and it continued to be the political order until ca. 176 BC when Mo-tun *Bagătwănă (r. 209–174 BC) and his son defeated the Yüeh-chih '*Tuχwară kings',[38] who then began their famous migration. The imperial ruling clan, the Ta-Yüeh-chih 'Great' or 'Imperial' *Tuχwară kings, moved in stages far to the west, merging with *Aśvin (Wu-sun) and Saka (Scythian) peoples on the way. The resulting confederation of three nations under the leadership of the Ta-Yüeh-chih 'Great *Tukwar(ă)-*kē *Tuχwar(ă)-kings', in Greek *Tocharoi* '*Tuχ(w)ara(s)', eventually conquered Bactria and settled there.

When the Chinese envoy Chang Ch'ien reached the Yüeh-chih in Bactria in ca. 126 BC,[39] he called Bactria[40] *Ta Hsia* 大夏 (*Dàxià*), in Old Chinese literally '*Great* *Ḥarya', meaning 'the *Ḥarya* (*Aria* ~ *Ariya*) *Empire*'. This Chinese term thus refers to the (Great) Yüeh-chih or Tukwar(ă)-*kē/kay or 'Tocharoi Empire in Bactria' as *Ta-Hsia* 'the (Great) *Ḥarya Empire',

---

and perhaps with the way the Warring States period Chinese use the term *Ḥarya* for themselves in Warring States texts (Beckwith 2016b), but this particular idea requires further study.

36. For the transcriptions and Scythian etymologies of these names see Chapter 6.

37. See Endnote 102.

38. Beckwith (2009: 84–85).

39. Pulleyblank (1991b).

40. I.e., the loosely connected realm then led by the *Tuχwar(ă) (Yüeh-chih/Tocharoi) nation.

and it *also* refers to the former steppe empire of the Scythians in the east, *Ta-Hsia* 'the (Great) Ḥarya Empire'.[41] About a century later the five chiefdoms including that of the Yüeh-chih/*Tocharoi* unified as the Kushan Empire. In the Rabatak Inscription of the Kushan Empire's King Kanishka the Great (r. ca. 127–150 CE), *Aria* is the term used to refer to Bactrian, the language of the ruling lineage, in which the inscription is written.[42] Since the Kushan Empire grew out of the Yüeh-chih/*Tocharoi*-led conquest of Bactria, *Aria* effectively meant or included the ruling lineage of the Kushans.[43]

During and after the Han Dynasty period the Chinese commonly referred to the Hsiung-nu and other foreigners of the north and west as *Hu* 胡 (*Hú*). In traditional (HSR) Chinese reconstruction, it is Middle Chinese ☆ɣɔ (Pul. 126),[44] but it may be reconstructed straightforwardly as Old Chinese *ɣărấ, a regularly depalatalized Northeast Asian dialect[45] form of *ɣăryá 'royal (ones)'—the very same word that was earlier transcribed as Hsia 夏 OChi *ɣaryá ~ Hua 華 OChi *ɣâryá,[46] attested as *Ḥarya* [ɣarya] in Old Tibetan. In China by the 4th century BC the word came to be used by Chinese speakers to mean 'the Chinese, China' and was borrowed into Proto-Tibetan in that meaning, with the consonants regularly rearranged by metathesis (according to Tibetan-internal phonological rules) and the unstressed first vowel deleted, to give Old Tibetan *Rgya* 'China, Chinese'. It was also borrowed into Old Japanese and Old Koguryo, or possibly into Common Japanese-Koguryoic (both languages lack voiced onsets) as *Kara* 'China'

41. The only other option is that it refers to Bactria *as a part* of *Ta-Hsia*, the 'Great Ḥarya (Aria) Empire' ruled by someone else, but the Chinese account tells us explicitly that the Great Yüeh-chih ~ *Tukwar(ă)-kē were the ruling power in Bactria.

42. Sims-Williams (2004).

43. See further below.

44. See Chapter 6, s.v. *Ḥara, Endnotes 103 and 153; on traditional Chinese reconstruction (HSR) see Endnote 3.

45. See Endnote 103.

46. For details see Chapter 7 and Beckwith (2016a). The name *Hsiung-nu* is unrelated to the word *Hu*, it is unrelated to the name *Hun*, and the Hun language is unrelated to Hsiung-nu; see Chapter 6; cf. Shimunek et al. (2015), Beckwith (2018), and Beckwith et al. (forthcoming). By early medieval times Chinese *Hu* came to mean 'Central Eurasians, West Asians, and Indians' by birth or heritage.

from the depalatalized Hsiung-nu dialect form *Ḥărắ (transcribed in Old Chinese as *Hu* 胡).

Other names, epithets, and common nouns from the realm of the Hsiung-nu and the region of Chao are recorded in Chinese transcription. Those that have been identified so far are solidly Iranic, and the language of the Hsiung-nu itself is an eastern dialect of Scythian, as shown in Chapter 6.

When the Yüeh-chih 月氏 '*Tukwară kings' invaded Bactria (together with the Wu-sun and Saka), the Greeks called them *Tokharoi* 'Tokh(w)aras' (from *Tuχwară), confirmed by the attested Bactrian form of the name (in Greek script) from a few centuries later, <Τοχοαρα>-Toχwara- ~ Tuχwara-, corresponding very closely to the ancient Chinese transcription of their name as *Yüeh* 月 Old Chinese *Tukwar(ă)/Tokwar(ă)[47] (and also to the early medieval transcription T'u-huo-lo 吐火羅 MChi ☆Tʊχwala representing *Tʊχwara ~ *Toχwara). In short, they and the subsequent Kushan Empire became known to the Chinese as *Ta Hsia* 大夏 'Great *Ḥarya*; the *Ḥarya* Empire'. In Bactrian, the local language, the country was Τοχοαρασταν <Tokhoarastan>, i.e., *Tuχwarastan,* in Classical Arabic *Ṭukhāristān* (Ṭuχāristān), for Middle Iranic *Tuχwārastān.[48] The Rabatak Inscription of Kanishka the Great (r. ca. 127–150 CE)[49] refers to the Kushan ruler's own language, Bactrian (the Iranic language of the *Yüeh-chih* *Tukhwar(ă)-kē/-kay after their migration to Bactria),[50] as *Aria* 'the royal (one)'. Because neither Classical Greek script nor its Kushan Bactrian adaptation can indicate any "laryngeal" fricative onsets (such as the glottal fricative [h]), and the Greek vowel *α* transcribes both short and long /a/, the Greek transcription Αρια *Aria* equally represents *ariya ~ *ārya ~ *harya ~ etc.

47. See Endnote 94 on this name. Hsüan Tsang visited Balkh (ancient Bactra) in 628 or 630 CE (Beckwith 2012a: 64) and transcribes the second syllable of the word with the character *huo* 火 MSC *huŏ* < EMC *xwa$_2$ (Pul. 135), i.e., [χwa]. The many attempts to connect the name *Ta Hsia* to the name *Tukhwâră* ~ *Tocharoi* (etc.) are misguided; see Beckwith (2016a).

48. At the time of the Kushan Empire, the contemporaneous writers Bardaisan of Edessa and Clement of Alexandria refer to it as *Bactria* (Beckwith 2015: 100, note 132).

49. Bracey (2017).

50. See Endnote 104.

The Chinese evidence on the term *Ta Hsia* 大夏 'Great *Ḥarya*; the *Ḥarya* Empire' reveals that the epithet *Hsia* 夏 *Ḥarya* was also used much earlier during the Warring States period by the non-Chinese northern and western rivals of the state of Chao to the east of the great northern bend of the Yellow River as well as the non-Chinese people of Chao itself. The expression *Ta Hsia* 大夏 is used explicitly to refer to them or their homeland in a *Tso chuan* legend,[51] and again in the Lang-yeh Inscription of Ch'in shih huang ti.[52] Based on the linguistic evidence they were an early Scythian people. The highly distinctive, culturally involved meaning of *hsia* 夏 *Ḥăryá [ɣa.rya] related rulers to the hierarchical order of the Central Eurasian Culture Complex, which was characterized by an ideal imperial realm focused on a single divinely ordained ruler.[53] Confucius is quoted as saying,

> The foreigners, who have a king, are unlike the Chinese, who have none.[54]

The Warring States period *Tso chuan* states:

> I have heard that if a Son of Heaven has lost the way of good government, he should learn it among the foreigners of the four directions.[55]

One of the remaining scientific problems[56] is the Chinese form's voiced laryngeal fricative [ɣ] onset (initial consonant), written in this book as *ḥ/Ḥ except in close transcriptions [in square brackets]. The sound [ɣ]

51. The legend is about two brothers who were separated by the early culture hero Yao, one of the two brothers being sent to *Ta Hsia* 大夏 'Great *Ḥarya*'.

52. See Chapter 7.

53. Beckwith (2009, 2010).

54. 夷狄之有君，不如諸夏之亡也。*Lun-yü* 3 (from CTP), but certainly much later than Confucius. Whether it means the foreigners are better off, or the Chinese are, is much disputed; but either way it shows the Chinese were thinking about different forms of government and were looking at what the non-Chinese had.

55. 吾聞之，天子失官，學在四夷。(*Tso chuan*, Chao-kung 17, 2), from CTP. Attributed to Confucius. For the textual problem see Beckwith (2009: 74, note 64). The Scythians and others of 'royal' lineage in Central Eurasia considered their rulers to be descended from the universal creator, Heavenly God.

56. The non-apparent semantic issue is addressed below.

itself is not transcribable in ancient Greek script so it is not surprising that it is not recorded in Greek sources on the Scythians, Medes, and Persians, or in the Kushan form of the word in (Bactrian) Greek script. All write *Aria*. It is also not transcribable in Ancient Near Eastern scripts, including Old Persian, which has *Ariya*.

The usual Sanskrit form of the word, *ārya*, does not transcribe the laryngeal onset *Ḥ* either, but its former presence may be reflected in the initial long vowel,[57] since the attested onset *ḥ* agrees perfectly with the independently reconstructed onset of Old Indic *ārya*, the laryngeal *Ḥ,[58] reflecting an early Indic form *ḥarya [ɣarya] which is directly attested in the Tibetan loanword *rgyagar*[59] 'India', from an earlier *ɣăryaɣar, perhaps from an intermediary Old Chinese form *ḥăryáḥwáră [ɣăryaɣwară] corresponding to Sanskrit *āryāvarta* 'home of the Āryas, India.'[60] According to the eastern Eurasian data, that very onset, [ɣ], was fully articulated in the Eastern Steppe region dialect of Scythian at the time the word was first borrowed into Old Chinese, and was still so pronounced there in the Early Middle Ages, as directly attested by the dated Old Tibetan transcriptions of the Togon (T'u-yü-hun) forms of the word discussed below. As the absolutely earliest attested Sanskrit texts only date to the early centuries CE,[61] they do not directly transcribe the pronunciation of the word as it was half a millennium beforehand, but the initial long vowel *ā* represents a regular outcome of a lost laryngeal onset according to recent Indo-Europeanist theory.

In view of the completely consistent eastern Eurasian data from the earliest times when the Eastern Steppe was ruled by Scythians (see

57. See Endnote 105.

58. It is an 'as if' Proto-Indo-European reconstruction; see Endnotes 99 and 106. I have used *ḥ* to transcribe the onset because, as it happens, that particular transcriptional letter is one of the oldest scholarly transcriptions of the Tibetan consonant written <འ>, which is pronounced today as [ɦ] ~ [ɣ] in conservative dialects (Leongue 2018); in most prevocalic environments it has become [0] (zero, silent) in Lhasa Tibetan. By current consensus, its Old Tibetan phonetic value was [ɣ], as proposed in Beckwith (1996); cf. Hill (2009).

59. The word is earliest attested in the Khri Lde Srong Brtsan Tomb Inscription, in Phyongsrgyas, south-central Tibet, line 29 (*OTDO*), dated to the death of the honoree, 815 CE, and the Sino-Tibetan Treaty Inscription (Lhasa, dated 823), East face line 14 (*OTDO*).

60. See Endnote 107.

61. Pollock (2009: 1, 39); Beckwith (2015: 245).

Chapters 3 and 7), it is significant that the word is attested in the name of one of the western Scythian kings, Ariapeithes (r. ca. 490–460 BC) *Arya-pitā 'Aria-father',[62]—the father of King Scyles (= Skula) i.e., 'King Scytha'.[63] The Scythians are known archaeologically to have entered Western Asia and Europe from Eastern Eurasia.[64] When joined with additional evidence specifically from the Central Asian Scythians known to scholars today as "Sakas" and other Central Eurasian peoples,[65] as well as the Chinese, it is clear that the Scythians, who referred to themselves as the 'royal Scythians (Skoloti, Sakas)' and the 'Saka (Scoloti, Scythian) kings' (i.e., the 'royal Sakas'), all used the word *Ḥarya ~ Aria* in its original epithet sense, 'royal, royal one(s)', as did the Iranic and non-Iranic peoples who borrowed it from them.

Old Tibetan *Rgya* 'Chinese; China', from pre–Old Tibetan *ɣryá, from *ɣăryá by regular syncope (here, deletion of *ă) and metathesis, corresponds exactly to the Old Chinese transcription *ɣăryá now read *Hsia* 夏 'Chinese, China' as well as to *Hsia* in *Ta Hsia* 大夏 'Great *Ḥarya*' [ɣa.rya]. As noted, that name is given by the ancient Chinese to Bactria or to a larger Scythian realm including Bactria, as well as to the steppe empire of the imperial *Yüeh-chih* 月氏. *Yüeh-chih* is the modern Chinese reading of the Old Chinese transcription, 月氏 of the foreign name *Tuχwara-kay, 'the Tuχwara (or Tokhwara) kings', where 月was read *tukwár and 氏 (also written 支) was read *kē or *key/kay. According to his Lang-yeh Inscription, Ch'in shih huang ti conquered (part of) the realm of *Ta Hsia* 大夏 'Great *Ḥarya*', which must then have been under the rule of the steppe overlords of the Hsiung-nu, the Yüeh-chih 月氏 *Tuχwar-kē. Old Tibetan *rgya* 'China', from pre–Old Tibetan *ɣăryá, together with an actual transcription, *ḥarya* (see below) in an important Togon place name, attests that the *Scythian* word *Ḥarya (pronounced *ɣăryá*) was heard by the Chinese in China as *ɣăryá, written 夏 or 華, now read Hsia and Hua, respectively. Since Old Tibetan *Rgya-* in

62. This name cannot be read as *Arya-paisa 'Arya ornament'; see Endnote 138. Cf. the Scythian name of Darius' great-grandfather, *Ariyaramna* (Greek *Ariaramnes*).

63. Szemerényi (1980).

64. See Chapters 1 and 2.

65. Beckwith (2010; 2016a).

Rgyagar 'India, Indian' *also* corresponds precisely to Old Indic *Ārya-* in the early name *Āryāvarta*, as shown above, it supports Indo-Europeanists' reconstruction of Old Indic *ārya* as *Ḥarya *[ɣa.rya].[66]

This analysis confirms the identity of *Ḥarya ~ *ɣarya ~ *ārya* as the East Scythian form of the word attested in West Scythian as *aria* (and Persian *ariya*), but there is also direct *transcriptional* support for the pronunciation of the word *Ḥarya ~ *ārya* with a voiced laryngeal onset [ɣ] in the Eastern Steppe in late Antiquity and into the Early Middle Ages.

The word *ḥarya* was also borrowed into the language of the Togon (Old Tibetan *Thogon* ཐོ་གོན་, Chinese T'u-yü-hun 吐谷渾 *Tǔyùhún*), perhaps directly from the Scythians. There are two distinct Old Tibetan traditions of representing the Togon form of the word.

> The normal Old Tibetan appellation of the Togon, a Serbi-speaking[67] steppe people who migrated southwestward and settled in the Chinghai-Kansu region between 307 and 313 CE,[68] is recorded in the mid-7th century CE as *Ḥaźa* འ་ཞ་, phonetically Old Tibetan [ɣa.ʑa].[69] This word reflects a known, specifically Tibetan sound change that took place in pre–Old Tibetan and very early Old Tibetan, namely the regular change of *ryV and *lyV to Old Tibetan *ź*V (where "V" is 'any vowel'). The phonetic rules of early Tibetan did not allow the syllable onset sequences *ryV and *lyV, so Tibetan speakers regularly repaired them, making them *ź*V, as in inherited Tibeto-Burman words such as Old Tibetan *bźi* 'four' from earlier Tibeto-Burman *blyi, and also foreign words, such as the name *Źaŋźuŋ* (Zhangzhung), an Old Tibetan borrowing of a foreign name that is also recorded in the early New Persian geographical work *Ḥudūd al-'Ālam* as رانگ رنگ *r'ngrng*—read *Rângr(u)ng*, from *r^{y}aŋr^{y}uŋ ~ *räŋrüŋ.[70] In the case of

66. Mallory and Adams (1997: 213); see above. However, the word cannot be reconstructed back to PIE, so *Ḥarya is an "*as if* Proto-Indo-European" reconstruction.

67. On the Serbi-Mongolic languages, and the position of Togon among them, see Shimunek (2017a).

68. Molè (1970: xii).

69. See Endnote 108 on the Togon forms.

70. Beckwith (2012b), q.v. for the Chinese transcription of the same name.

the name *Ḥaźa* [ɣaźa], the *-źa* thus derives from earlier *-rya or *-lya. In view of the other attestations of the word for 'royal' in eastern Eurasia, it is clear that the ruling clan of the T'u-yü-hun actually called themselves *Ḥarya* 'the royals'. The Tibetans took it to be their name and pronounced it [ɣaźa]. The phone [ź] tells us that the Tibetans did not hear a foreign [ɣara], which they would have borrowed as [ɣara] and written འ་ར་ <ḥa.ra> or ག་ར་ <ga.ra>. The onset [ɣ] is also attested in Imperial Old Tibetan as the onset of the usual spelling of the genitive suffix after vowel stems, i.e., *-ḥi* འི་ [-ɣi] (now usually transcribed *-'i*), versus གྱི་ *-gyi* after consonant stems. It thus occurs with extremely high frequency throughout the language.

From the Eastern Steppe region that had formerly been called *Ta Hsia* 'Great *Ḥaryá' in Chinese, the Togon migrated southwestward in late Antiquity into what was then the region directly west of China, now the Koko Nor region of Amdo (modern northeastern Tibet; Chinese Ch'ing-hai).[71] The ruling clan, who referred to themselves as *Ḥarya [ɣa.rya], eventually came into contact with the early Tibetans, who took that to be their name, but because of Tibetan-internal phonological rules the Tibetans pronounced and wrote it *Ḥaźa* འ་ཞ་ [ɣaźa], as explained above. The ruling clan of a people from the Eastern Steppe was thus still calling itself *ɣarya ~ *Ḥarya in the Early Middle Ages, late enough that the pre–Old Tibetan speakers, when they encountered them by ca. 600 CE, learned the word, and recorded it in their earliest dated texts.[72]

The second Old Tibetan transcription set of this word deriving from the Togon dates to the end of the 7th century. The *Old Tibetan Annals I* three times records the name of an apparently important non-Tibetan place in Mdosmad (now Amdo, Chinese Ch'ing-hai), the northeastern part of the Tibetan Empire which had been part of the conquered realm of the Togon. It is transcribed under the Dragon year 692–693 as *Rgyam-śi-gar* རྒྱམ་ཤི་གར་ (line 113), an obviously Tibetanized form;

71. Molè (1970: 1–2); cf. Shimunek (2017a) on Togon and other Serbi languages.
72. See Endnote 109.

under the Snake year 717–718 as *Ryam-śï-gar* རྱམ་ཤི་གར་ (line 206); and under the Bird year 721–722 as *ḥaryam-śï-gar* འརྱམ་ཤི་གར་ (line 222).[73] These are all different attempts at transcription of the unfamiliar non-Tibetan pronunciation heard by the scribe or scribes. The third transcription begins with the exact string *ḥarya-*, which is strikingly transcribed in the "technical" way Buddhist Sanskrit came to be written in Tibetan script, i.e., as འརྱ་ *ḥarya-* [ɣa.rya], with no *tsheg* (syllable dot) after the first syllable and with vertical stacking of the letters to explicitly mark the onset of the second syllable as *ry-*. This can hardly be anything other than the native Togon pronunciation of the epithet of the Togon rulers, the very same word borrowed (as a loanword) by the pre–Old Tibetan speakers and transformed according to Old Tibetan phonology into *ḥaźa* (regularly from *Ḥarya), the usual Old Tibetan name of the Togon (T'u-yü-hun). This confirms the above analysis that the word was pronounced *Ḥarya* [ɣa.rya] by the Togon themselves.[74]

As for *Ḥarya 'Chinese; China', when the Chinese chose their first appellation for themselves in the late 5th or early 4th century BC, they chose to write it *Hsia* 夏 Old Chinese *Ḥaryá, meaning 'summer' or (less frequently) *Hua* 華 Old Chinese *Ḥâryá, meaning 'flower'. Both, as explained above, are obvious loanword transcriptions. Did the Chinese actually choose a foreign word for their own name? No, because in the beginning it could not yet have meant 'Chinese', or 'China', per se. 'China' did not yet exist, except perhaps in the imagination (there was also no name for 'the Chinese people' or 'the Chinese language' yet), and in the West (and India) the word *Aria* ~ *Ariya* has no connection to China. The popular internal etymological approach is falsified by the existence of the two distinctive Chinese character transcriptions which are etymologically unrelated to each other and have unrelated semantics,

73. All from the photographic copy of the text on the website of the International Dunhuang Project (IDP). The transliterated text is available on *OTDO*, s.v. ITJ 0750 *Old Tibetan Annals* (Version 1), but the form in line 222 is mistransliterated. Cf. Beckwith (2016a).

74. Cf. Endnote 110.

the unmistakable sign of a loanword or transcription of a foreign word. As argued in Chapter 2, the Scythian word *Ḥarya must have become known to some of the Chinese because they were bilingual in Scythian and understood what it meant.

The use of this word by many different ancient to early medieval peoples, many of whom were not speakers of Iranic languages, shows it was *not* borrowed as an ethnonym with the meaning 'Iranian' or 'early Vedic Indian immigrants from Central Asia', as often claimed. And it was also not borrowed in the meaning 'Chinese'. It must still have been an epithet meaning 'royal(s)' or the like. That explains its usage in the Old Persian, Young Avestan, Old Chinese, Old Indic, Tokharian A, Old Turkic, Togon, and other languages. Some of these languages are unattested before the Early Middle Ages, assuring us that half a millennium or more earlier, in Old Chinese times, the word *Ḥarya ~ *ārya* could only have been acquired by the Chinese *as an epithet* in its early meaning 'royal(s)', in the sense that one so characterized belonged to the legitimate 'royal' lineage, the 'chosen people' who could or should rule over everyone else.

To this long list of languages that borrowed the Scythian word, directly or indirectly, can now also be added Tibetan, which in pre–Old Tibetan times borrowed the word for 'China; Chinese', probably directly from Old Chinese *ḥarya [ɣarya].[75]

The Old Tibetan root *rgyal-* 'royal' is also clearly from *ḥarya-, with the suffixed morpheme *-l/lă (of unknown origin). From this extended root *rgyal-* 'royal' the ordinary word *rgyalpo* 'king' is derived by adding the masculine suffix *-po*.[76] Although *rgyal-* is a derived form, it preserves the original 'royal' meaning, suggesting it was borrowed in that meaning

75. As noted above, Old Tibetan *rgya-* has been canonically metathesized from earlier *grya (a disallowed onset sequence in Old Tibetan), which resulted from deletion of the unstressed first vowel *ă* in the loanform *ɣărya- during monosyllabicization in pre–Old Tibetan. See Beckwith (2016a).

76. The word *rgyalpo* 'king' is first attested in the Zhol Inscription (ca. 764 CE) as the rank of the Chinese emperor, referred to as *rgya rje* 'the Chinese feudal vassal-lord (i.e., vassal of the Tibetans)', q.v. Beckwith and Walter (2010).

earlier than the same word (in simplex form) in the later meaning (in China) of 'China, Chinese'. To summarize the above discussion:

Old Persian *Aria* = West Scythian *Aria* = Bactrian *Aria* =
Old Chinese *Ḥarya *[ɣarya] 'royal'
*Ḥarya 'royal' > *Ḥarya 'Chinese' → Old Tibetan *Rgya* 'Chinese'
*Ḥarya depalatalized > *Ḥarã́ → *Kara 'Kaya' → Old Japanese
Kara 'Chinese, Korean'
*Ḥarya → *Ḥarya* 'Togon' → pre–Old Tibetan *Ḥaźa*;
transcription in early Old Tibetan *Ḥarya*
*Ḥarya → Old Indic *Ārya* → Old Tibetan *Rgyagar* 'India'
← Old Chinese *Ḥáryaḥwárǎ ← Old Indic *Āryāwarta
(*Āryāvarta*) 'home of the Āryas, India'
*Ḥarya → pre–Old Tibetan *rgya + -l → Old Tibetan *rgya-l-*
'royal' in *rgyalpo* 'king'[77]

In view of the data and discussion above, it is concluded that the forms *Ḥarya* ~ *Aria* ~ *Ariya* ~ *Ārya* and their depalatalized forms (*Ḥarã́, etc.) represent one and the same Scythian epithet, meaning '(of or relating to) the eternal heavenly royal line'.

77. See Chapter 6, Note 65.

5

Imperial Scythian in the Persian Empire

The single most powerful and influential Scythian successor state was the Scytho-Mede-Persian Empire, which ruled a huge territory almost entirely outside the Central Eurasian steppe zone. Although Persians certainly ruled it under Darius the Great and his descendants, as shown in Chapters 2 and 3, they did not found it, nor did the Medes, whose empire had ruled much of the same territory.

The Medes, or Scytho-Medes, took over the Empire from the Scythians and continued everything built by them. In turn, Cyrus the Great, a Scytho-Mede-Elamite, took over the Empire and enlarged it considerably to the Mediterranean Sea and the Hellespont (Dardanelles) in the west, followed by his son Cambyses, who added Egypt and Libya in the southwest. Finally, a Scytho-Mede-Persian, Darius, took over the Empire and ruled it, adding a little more territory to it, especially in northwestern India and in Thrace. During good times and bad the Empire endured—on the whole, far more peacefully than the many contemporaneous Greek city-states or the many contemporaneous Chinese Warring States, which in both cases were nearly constantly at war.

But leaving aside nationalities, who, exactly, kept the Empire together in the three centuries of its existence, and how did they manage to do that? These questions are best answered by focusing on the language which was used in running it.

The Spoken Administrative Language of the Empire

At the very beginning, under the Scythians, the spoken language was of course Scythian, the language of the conquerors and their imperial administration, to the extent that their strictly feudal system had an administration. Through marrying and living together with the conquered peoples, the Scythians creolized them. The Scytho-Medes of Cyaxares, whose name is linguistically Scythian, spoke Imperial Scythian, a creole dialect of Scythian, as shown in this chapter. We have almost no significant historical information about Cyrus the Great, for whom the Greek histories are only marginally accurate, but he and his son have Elamite names, they dressed as Elamites, and they call themselves "King of Anshan (Elam)". Did they speak Elamite? What we have of their historical documents are in Akkadian, a Semitic language, not in Elamite. Finally, Darius and his son Xerxes, as Persians who also wore Elamite clothes and bore Elamite weapons, are attested to have spoken Old Persian because they dictated many imperial inscriptions, nearly all of which include copies in Old Persian (most also include versions in Akkadian and Elamite). Old Persian was so different from the Imperial Scythian language of the Medes, which was spoken outside of Pārsa (Persis, now Fârs), that the two languages were mutually unintelligible, as shown below. Excavated early administrative documents from the time of Darius are largely in Elamite, but it is known that they were mostly written by people with Old Iranic names, and it is accepted that the Medes ran most of the Imperial administration under Persian rule. That means the Medes must have known enough Persian to interact with the king and the satraps (the top level of the government), who were Persians, so the Medes also interpreted. But what language did they themselves speak, and was it the same or different from the language or languages spoken by most of the other peoples of the Empire?

Linguists early noted that a good number of Iranic but specifically *non*–Old Persian names and other words occur in the Old Persian inscriptions (from ca. 519 BC on).[1] Some have identified these words as

1. The few very short inscriptions in Old Persian putatively issued by earlier rulers are now accepted to be later compositions.

Avestan, a language traditionally defined as the Old Iranic language of the *Gāthās*, the sacred hymns of Zoroaster in Old Avestan, and also the language of a much larger body of somewhat later Zoroastrian texts in Young Avestan.[2] Unfortunately, exactly when or where the Avestan texts were composed is unknown and much disputed.

Other scholars decided long ago that the same non–Old Persian words are from a different Old Iranic language, which they called "Median".[3] They based this specifically on the *historical* importance of the Medes. Already Meillet and Benveniste note something of this:

> The religious and official vocabulary of the (Old Persian) inscriptions offers many traces of material which must be taken from a prestigious dialect and neighbor of Persian. For reasons of a historical, geographical and dialectal nature, it can only be from Median. Only the Mede Empire—which at the death of Cyaxares . . . included Persis and extended from Arachosia to Lydia—could have established in Iran the beginning of an administrative tradition and the first terms of an official vocabulary. . . . Finally, there is a striking identity between the phonetic particularities of the foreign words in Persian in the inscriptions and those of the words transmitted as Median by Greek authors.[4]

The Medes ran the imperial court, as shown long ago by Hinz, and the Persepolis bas-reliefs have many images of secular Medes, who wear a standard court version of the famous Mede outfit.[5] Media is also one of the two traditionally proposed homelands of Zoroaster (the other being Central Asia), and the father of Darius the Great has the same name as

2. They are later in part because they depend on the *Gāthās* as holy texts, which they constantly cite. See below on Skjærvø and Zoroastrianism. Briefly, the system of Darius is like the Early Zoroastrianism of the *Gāthās* in its essentials, with strict monotheism and emphasis on Truth in opposition to Falsehood. The inscriptions of Darius thus date attested Early Zoroastrianism as well as attested Avestan to no later than 519 BC. For further discussion see the Epilogue and Appendix A.

3. It must be stressed that the frequently repeated declaration to the effect that the Median language was a "north-*west* Iranian [Iranic] language" is erroneous. Media is located in northwest Iran, but the Median language belongs to the traditional "*east* Iranian [Iranic] languages". Geography, modern usages of the word *Iranian*, and widespread modern unfamiliarity with basic linguistics explain these and other errors.

4. See Endnote 111 for the French.

5. Hinz (1969: 63–114). On Mede dress see Appendix B.

Zoroaster's patron Vištāspa,[6] which is accepted to be "Avestan", not Persian. Moreover, the Magi, who produced the ancient priests of the Medes and Persians, were (or belonged to) one of the six clans or lineages of the Medes, according to Herodotus.[7] Two of the clans have recognizable names. One is clearly Scythian linguistically: the Ἀριζαντοί, or *Aria-zantu,[8] the 'Aria clan' (literally, 'the royal-lineage clan'), or the "Royal" Medes.[9] The other clan is the Μάγοι, or *Magi* clan. Greek sources say the Magi were the priests of the Great God Ahuramazdā at the Imperial court, and that Zoroaster founded the religion of Ahura Mazdā.[10] This is effectively confirmed by ancient images. A gold tablet shows a Zoroastrian Mede from the Achaemenid period carrying a stereotypical *barsom*,[11] a bundle of sticks used in Zoroastrian rituals. (See Figure 3.) A relief from the satrapal capital of Dascylium in northwestern Anatolia shows two Medes wearing the *bashlyq* and *candys*, carrying *barsoms*, beside two sacrificial animals (see Figure 12).

Both Herodotus and the inscriptions of Darius also attest to Scythians using *haoma*, a characteristic drug used by some Zoroastrians.[12] And the theonym *Mazda* is attested in Herodotus' account of the steppe Scythians in Chapter 1, as discussed in Chapter 6 as the name of Heavenly God.

It is thus clear that many of these characteristic, unique features of Zoroastrianism go back to the steppe Scythians.

6. The name means '(with) horses untied (released for the race)', Avestan *Vīštāspa-* (Schmitt 2014: 281).

7. Herodotus (i 101).

8. Cf. Benveniste (1966: 83). Greek γένος *genos* means 'clan, house, family; subdivision of an ἔθνος *ethnos*' (*LSJ*); not a 'tribe', which has very different senses in modern English.

9. See Chapter 4. In his account of the Royal Scythians Herodotus unfortunately translates the Scythian term for 'royal' without giving the word itself, but he does record it indirectly in his accounts of the Scythian national foundation myths and early Scythian history.

10. See Endnote 112.

11. Avestan *barəsman* (Kanga 1988). The ritual *barsom* is identifiable with the ritual bundle of sticks used by the Scythians' soothsayers described by Herodotus (iv 67,1).

12. The name of a Scythian people living somewhere north of the Oxus River, the *Sakā Haumavargā*, is certainly the same as the name "*Amyrgian Sakas*" in Herodotus. Everyone recognizes *hauma* in their epithet as *haoma* (Skt. *soma*), a stimulating or intoxicating drink used by Zoroastrian and Vedic priests, but the identification of the second part (*vargā* in Old Persian transcription) is disputed. See Appendix A.

FIGURE 12. Achaemenid period Magi in *candys* and *bashlyq* holding *barsoms* (Dascylium).

It has been argued convincingly that Darius's beliefs are a form of Zoroastrianism.[13] That would seemingly confirm the Avestan origin of the "Median" loanwords in Old Persian. But are Median and Avestan different languages, or the same language? If we are to seriously consider that or any language relationship proposal, we must look at the relevant data scientifically—the theory must conform to the data.[14] So, we need data. As is the case for many ancient languages, the linguistic material explicitly marked as "Scythian" in the sources is exclusively lexical, meaning "words" and a few word-like morphemes (minimal language units), such as prefixes and suffixes. We do have full texts in the same language, as will be seen, but it is not currently called "Scythian". Since much disputation concerning Old Iranic languages—and therefore their speakers and their nations—is founded on methodological or theoretical unclarity, it is necessary before proceeding to discuss the differences between the "fuzzy" categories *language* and *dialect*, and to establish the unique, crucial importance of *lexical data*, i.e., mostly "words".

Languages, Dialects, Accents[15]

Popular understanding of the differences between languages and dialects, even among scholars, varies greatly, though it is agreed that the distinctions are typically graded or fuzzy, not sharp. This chapter takes a practical approach rather than a theoretical one, and in the absence of texts for some languages it is based largely on lexical data, so it requires a little explanation.

13. Skjærvø (1999, 2005); see Endnote 113.

14. I have done my best to follow the ancient Greek thinker Myson, about whom Diogenes Laertius (i 9) says, "Εφασκε δὲ μὴ ἐκ τῶν λόγων τὰ πράγματα, ἀλλ' ἐκ τῶν πραγμάτων τοὺς λόγους ζητεῖν: οὐ γὰρ ἕνεκα τῶν λόγων τὰ πράγματα συντελεῖσθαι, ἀλλ' ἕνεκα τῶν πραγμάτων τοὺς λόγους. 'He used to say we should not investigate facts by the light of arguments, but arguments by the light of facts; for the facts were not put together to fit the arguments, but the arguments to fit the facts.' From Perseus, tr. Hicks.

15. Because the differences between languages and dialects are not absolute or precise, and the categories are truly fuzzy, they are gradable and liable to scientific analysis. Taken in isolation, a *dialect* (as a thing) is simply a *language*, but the *word* "dialect" has the explicit sense of 'a recognizable variant form of a particular language', so it is hierarchically defined. For *dialects* vs. *languages*, the salient differences are practical in nature. For more on the senses of "language" and "dialect" used in this book see Endnote 114.

TABLE 1. Dialects of Standard English, Random Lexical Sample

American	British	Australian
belief	*belief*	*belief*
beyond	*beyond*	*beyond*
cattle	*cattle*	*cattle*
dog	*dog*	*dog*
father	*father*	*father*
fortune	*fortune*	*fortune*
give	*give*	*give*
good	*good*	*good*
head	*head*	*head*
horse	*horse*	*horse*
king	*king*	*king*
man	*man*	*man*
manly	*manly*	*manly*
ornament	*ornament*	*ornament*
path	*path*	*path*
powerful	*powerful*	*powerful*
royal	*royal*	*royal*
son	*son*	*son*
spoken	*spoken*	*spoken*
sprout	*sprout*	*sprout*
strong	*strong*	*strong*
sun	*sun*	*sun*

Note: This list consists of the English glosses of my original list of Scythian words in Table 5, so they constitute a *purely random, unpredetermined* set. I have since expanded Table 5 (below in this chapter) to include words omitted by Schmitt (2003) and Mayrhofer (2006), but as I had already finished this section of the manuscript I have not incorporated the additional words into Tables 1, 2, and 3.

Within standard educated English there are closely related "dialects", for example standard American English, British English, and Australian English. We can normally communicate with people who speak another such dialect of standard educated English, despite differences in pronunciation that we call an "accent". So the words in Table 1 (all randomly selected) are the same words and sound close enough in all three dialects that we can understand them regardless of which one is our native dialect. This rule applies as well to textual examples—full sentences—as shown below for Standard English.[16]

Based on this sample, the three dialects are all the same language with minor differences—mainly "accents" or other occasional differences in pronunciation (e.g., *schedule*, in British [ʃɛdʒul], in American [skɛdʒəl] ~ [skɛdʒuʷəl)—which are not significant enough to be reflected in writing. These dialects sometimes have a different word for the same thing (e.g., British *lift*, American *elevator*), but such differences are rare enough within the context of connected speech or written text that they do not hinder general understanding. Of course, some dialects are so different that we cannot understand them at all immediately and may need ten or twenty minutes, or even days, to understand them, but they are typically not Standard English.

It is different with *different languages*, such as English, Russian, and Japanese:

English:	We're going to the library.	(*wiər goiŋ tu ðə laibrɛri*)
Russian:	Мы идём в библиотеку.	(*mɨ idjom v bibliotjeku*)
Japanese:	私たち圖書館に行きます。	(*watashitachi toshokan ni ikimasu*)

To people who know only one of these three languages, the other two sentences are completely unintelligible, though they mean exactly the same thing. And if we put our sample list of words into Russian and Japanese, as in Table 2, we will not see many lexical similarities even if the words are actually related, or loanwords.

Nevertheless, if Russians or Japanese speak fluent *Standard English* we can understand them, even if they have a foreign accent, because they speak the same *language*, Standard English.

16. Standard English (a disputed term) is the language of educated native English speakers and writers that is effectively the same in pronunciation, grammar, and lexicon, despite dialect differences, and is generally accepted and understood in native English-speaking cultures.

TABLE 2. Russian, Japanese, English Lexical Data

Russian	Japanese	English
vera	*shinnen*	*belief*
za	*mukō*	*beyond*
skot	*ushi*	*cattle*
sobaka[a]	*inu*	*dog*
otets	*otōsan*	*father*
sostojanije	*kōun*	*fortune*
datj	*ataeru*	*give*
xorošo	*yoi*	*good*
golova	*atama*	*head*
lošadj	*uma*	*horse*
korolj	*kokuō*	*king*
čelovek	*otoko*	*man*
mužestvennyj	*otokoraśī*	*manly*
ukrašenije	*hanagata*	*ornament*
putj	*michi*	*path*
mośćnyj	*chikarazuyoi*	*powerful*
tsarskij	*ōritsu*	*royal*
syn	*musuko*	*son*
govorjat	*hanaśita*	*spoken*
rostok	*me*	*sprout*
siljnyj	*tsuyoi*	*strong*
solntse	*taiyō*	*sun*

Note: To ensure impartiality, the Russian and Japanese examples have been translated by Google Translate, a free internet resource. However, in some instances I have had to pick one from among many choices.

[a] This word is generally considered to be a loan (directly or indirectly) from Scythian *spaka* 'dog'.

By contrast, English belongs to the Germanic family of languages, so its neighboring relatives, for example Icelandic and German, as in Table 3, ought to be easy for speakers of one of the other languages to understand.

However, in this case, despite some obvious similarities, even speakers of *related* languages cannot understand each other unless they study

TABLE 3. Germanic Lexical Data: German, Icelandic, English

German	Icelandic	English
Glaube	*trú*	*belief*
jenseits	*víðar*	*beyond*
Vieh	*nautgripir*	*cattle*
Hund	*hundur*	*dog*
Vater	*faðir*	*father*
Glück	*auður*	*fortune*
geben	*gefa*	*give*
gut	*góður*	*good*
Kopf	*höfuð*	*head*
Pferd	*hestur*	*horse*
König	*konungur*	*king*
Mann	*maður*	*man*
männlich	*karlmannlegur*	*manly*
Schmuck	*skraut*	*ornament*
Pfad	*leið*	*path*
mächtig	*öflugur*	*powerful*
königlich	*konunglegur*	*royal*
Sohn	*sonur*	*son*
gesprochen	*talað*	*spoken*
Spross	*spíra*	*sprout*
stark	*sterkur*	*strong*
Sonne	*sól*	*sun*

them, as in the case of Russian, Japanese, and English, which are *unrelated* languages. That is because German, Icelandic, and English do not differ at the *dialect* level but at the *language* level. The differences are mostly beyond the [ʃɛdʒul] : [skɛdʒəl] type, and belong more to the *lift*: *elevator* type. Regardless of the relationship linguists have established among them, monolingual English, Icelandic, and German speakers cannot understand each other because they speak different *languages*, not different *dialects*. Each language has a distinctive phonology ("sound system"), morphology ("grammatical form system"), syntax ("phrase and sentence grammar"), and lexicon ("words", which embody phonology, morphology, and semantics). The phonology and morphology (or morphophonology) of each language is noticeably different *at first glance* even if we have only lexical items, or *words*, because they encode most of a language's structure. And words actually provide most of the data studied by the main fields of modern theoretical linguistics.

However, if supposedly distinct languages or dialects are *formally* the same, as are the British, American, and Australian examples in Table 1, they are actually the *same language*, or the *same dialect*. That is, in practical terms, if people speaking them can understand each other despite some "accent" differences, they are actually the same language or dialect regardless of their different "language" names or political affiliations. There are many examples, such as Bosnian, Serbian, Croatian, and Montenegrin, which are all different names for the same South Slavic language formerly called Serbo-Croatian. Or Hindi and Urdu, which are the same New Indic language formerly called Hindustani. Or Farsi, Dari, and Tajiki, which are names for dialects of the same language, Persian. In Chinese, 中文 *Zhongwen*, 國語 *Guoyu*, 官話 *Guanhua*, 漢語 *Hanyu*, 普通話 *Putonghua*, and other terms, are simply synonyms for "Modern Standard Chinese (MSC)" or "Mandarin", which is based on the dialect of Nanjing.[17] Although it has numerous subdialects, many of them are mutually intelligible. However, a monolingual speaker can understand even a speaker of an aberrant dialect or subdialect, given a little time and practice, just as speakers of Modern Standard English can understand speakers of a *non-standard* English dialect, sometimes after a bit of effort and time to become accustomed to it. "Informal" types of a language are anecdotally the most difficult to understand. In Table 1 the words are identical and the dialect speakers can usually understand each other despite the "accents": they are the *same language* and essentially the *same dialect*. Yet other "dialects" can be so different, not only in phonology but also in grammar and lexicon, that the term "dialect" is a misnomer for them. This is the case for many so-called Chinese "dialects", most prominent among them Cantonese, Shanghainese, Taiwanese, and

17. Formerly spelled *Nanking*. Pekingese (the highly distinctive subdialect of Beijing and vicinity) is different enough from standard Mandarin (MSC) that it can be difficult for other Mandarin speakers to understand.

TABLE 4. Related Languages, or Dialects? Avestan, Median, and Persian Cognates

Avestan	Median	Old Persian	Gloss
aspa-	*aspa-*	*asa-*	horse
barəz-	*bărz-*	*bărd-*	to exalt; high[a]
čiθra-	*čiθra-*	*čiça-*	lineage; appearance
daēś-	*daisa-*	*daiθa-*	inform, show; showing
daēza-	*daiza-*	*daydā-*	wall
haiθiia-	*haθya-*	*hašiya-*	real, true
hazaŋra-	*hazahra-*	*hadahra-*	thousand
hu-	*hu-*	*u-*	good
kas-	*kas-*	*kaθ-*	to observe
kərəsa-	*kărs-*	*kărθ-*	skinny, meagre
mąθra-	*ma(n)θra-*	*mança-*	the word of God
maz-; mazišta-	*maz-*	*maθa-; maθišta-*	great; greatest
miθra-[b]	**miθra-*	*miça-*	treaty
paēsa-	*paisa-*	*paiθa-*	ornament
pairidaēza-[c]	*paradaisa-*[d]	*paradayda-*	enclosed garden, paradise
pasu-	*pasu-*	*paθu-*	cattle; herd animals
pərəsu-	*pǎrsu-*	*pǎrθu-*	flank, side
puθra-	*puθra-*	*puça-*	son
sāra-	*sāra-*	*θāra-*	head
sata-	*sata-*	*θata-*	hundred
saχta-	*saχta-/saχra-*	*θaχta-/θaχra-*	strong
spaka-	*spaka*[e]		dog[f]
srī-	*srī-*	*çi*	beauty
sūra-	*sūra-*	*θūra-*	strong
suχra-	*suχra-*	*Θuχra*	red
taχma-	*taχma-*	*ta(h)ma-*	brave, valiant
taoχman-	*tauχman-*	*taumā- ('family')*	seed
θrā-	*θrā-*	*çā-*	to protect
θri-/θray-	*θri-*	*çi-*	three
vaēsa-	*vaisa-*	*vaiθa-*	knight
varāza-	*varāza-*	*varāda-*	boar
vas-	*vas-*	*vaθ-*	to want, wish

Table 4. (*continued*)

Avestan	Median	Old Persian	Gloss
vīs-	*vis-*	*viθ-*	royal house; village
varəzāna-	*vărzāna-*	*vărdāna-*	city, town
vīsō.puθra	*vis(a) puθra*	*viθapuça-*	prince
vīspa-	*vispa-*	*visa-*	all, every
uruuaes-	*vrais-*	*vraiθ-*	to wander around
uruuāz-	*vrāza-*	*vrad-*	joyful
χratu-	*χratu-*	*χraθu-*	insight, wisdom
χšaθra-	*χšaθra-*	*χšaça-*	reign, kingdom
yauz-	*yaoz-*	*yaud-*	to agitate, fight
yaz-	*yaz-*	*yad-*	to worship
zana-	*zana-*	*dana-*	nation; kind, sort
zantu-	*zantu-*[g]	*dantu-*	clan, ethnos
zaotar-	*zautar*	*dautar-*	sacrificer, priest
zāta-	*zāta-*	*dāta-*	born
zaoš-[h]	*zauša-*	*dauša-*	satisfaction
zruuan-	*zărvan-, zrūn*	*dărva-*	time

[a] Most of the differences here are in modern scholars' interpretations of the ancient written forms. For example, where Tavernier has omitted an overt vowel, as in Median <*brz*>, with a supposed vocalic liquid *r̥, most scripts (including Old Persian cuneiform) always write or decree by rule at least one vowel, as in the Avestan forms. Some examples, including those in Elamite script, suggest it was an unstressed reduced vowel *ă* (schwa [ə]), so I have transcribed all such putative r̥ vowels as *ăr.* See Endnote 117.

[b] Specifically, Young Avestan. The Median word is attested in the name *Mitradates* (Tav. 249) in the Cyrus story of Herodotus, q.v. Chapter 3.

[c] Sch. 225.

[d] Sch. 225 cites the Greek form παράδεισος in Xenophon, *Anabasis* (i 2,7).

[e] The Median form is given in Herodotus (i 110) as σπάκα, thus exactly *spaka*; cf. Schmitt (2015: 253).

[f] MPer and NPer *sag* (Tav. 563), from postulated OPer *saka 'dog', is claimed by some to be the word *Saka* 'Scythian' (e.g., Tav. 604; doubted at Tav. 308). However, Scythian *spaka* 'dog' and *Saka* 'Scythian' are both very well attested (see Chapter 2), and the idea is linguistically misguided. Scythian *spaka* 'dog' is thought to be the loan source of Russian собака *sobaka* 'dog'.

[g] Tav. 552, 570, also *zana-* 'id.'

[h] Tav. 571: "derivation from Av[estan] *zaoš-* 'to care'."

Mandarin, which are in fact different languages and mutually incomprehensible. They are *related* languages but they are not mutually intelligible to monolingual speakers.[18] In other words, their relationship is like that of English, Icelandic, and German (all Germanic languages), or French, Italian, and Romanian (all Romance languages). The definition of *language* and *dialect* adopted here is thus practical in nature.[19]

Median and Avestan

The point of departure for this chapter came from using the Glossary in Tavernier's recent book[20] on Old Iranic of the Achaemenid period, in which the words he explicitly identifies here and there as "Median" in his Glossary are identical to cognate forms he cites as "Avestan".[21] Tavernier never notes any relationship among the different Old Iranic languages or dialects he cites and does not remark on anything striking about his identifications.[22] Table 4 lists only entries that Tavernier gives with equivalents explicitly said to be Median, Avestan, and Old Persian in his Glossary.[23] The list shows the identity of the Median and Avestan words vis-à-vis the cognate (but typically different) Old Persian words in his corpus. All the words in this table are genetically related—they are *cognates*—though some are Iranic-internal loans from one language to another. Their differences are strictly phonological in nature. This material thus does not compare differences such as *lift* vs. *elevator*, or *mächtig* vs. *powerful*, but only those such as [ʃɛdʒul] vs. [skɛdʒəl], both normally written *schedule*. Note that the apparent differences between some

18. See Endnote 115.

19. See also Endnote 114.

20. He does not organize his Glossary in any way other than alphabetically, so it is a random "natural" data set. His Glossary omits many forms that actually do occur in his book, so while compiling Table 4, in a few instances I have checked or supplemented his Glossary from material elsewhere in his book.

21. Tavernier (2007: 547–573). He does not distinguish Old Avestan from Young Avestan.

22. Unfortunately he ignores Scythian, the other known Old Iranic language of the period. See Endnote 116.

23. Table 4 is my work, but the raw material is from Tavernier (2007), and the identifications are his. The language of the head word in his entries is often unmentioned, perhaps because the source does not help to establish it; such examples are excluded. That has reduced the number of items in my table.

Median and Avestan cognates are mainly due to the different transcription systems and different scripts involved.

The words in the same row are all related, but not identical. Do they reflect mutually intelligible dialects, or closely related but not mutually intelligible languages? Can the lexicon alone decide?

Over 60 years ago, Benveniste[24] wrote an article on the Imperial Aramaic version of a 3rd century BC inscription of the Indian king Priyadarśi[25] in Kandahar, ancient Arachosia, in which he identifies several Old Iranic loanwords as *specifically* "Avestan". Recently a large number of Imperial Aramaic documents from late Achaemenid Bactria were discovered in which there are many "Old Iranic" loanwords.[26] Most of them belong to the same language as Avestan.[27] In an article on the name of the Scythians, Cornillot comments:

> The dialects of the Iranian speaking populations who occupied almost all of Central Asia in Antiquity were very close, to the point that they have been considered to be one and the same language, which was in turn very close to the idioms spoken in the north of Iran and in the land of the Medes, as is clear from the information given by Herodotus and Strabo. The linguistic and cultural unity of the Sakas of Central Asia and the Scythians of Europe was also as little in doubt for the Greeks as for the Persians: the former gave them all the name of Scythians (contrary to the tradition which has tended to ultimately reserve this name for the European part of the Scytho-Sakan world); the latter gave them (all) the name of Saka. From which fact one can mathematically conclude the equivalence of these two appellations.[28]

Similarly, Harmatta has compiled the Old Iranic lexical items in personal and place names from Achaemenid and post-Achaemenid Bactria that were available in 1994. He says 48 of these 56 words (i.e., 86%)

24. Benveniste (1958: 42–43).

25. The king's name is so spelled in Aramaic and similarly in his Prakrit inscriptions of the 3rd century BC. On Aśoka, a much later 'Normative Buddhist' ruler, see Beckwith (2015: 135–137, 226–250).

26. See Endnote 118.

27. See Endnote 119.

28. See Endnote 120 for the French.

"reflect another Iranian language, different from Old Persian." He concludes:

> The *overwhelming majority* of Iranian terms and names occurring in Aramaic and Greek documents of ancient Graeco-Bactria or mentioned as Bactrian in ancient Greek literature represent a language essentially identical to Avestan. *Not even a dialectal difference* can be observed between this linguistic evidence and the language of the *Avesta* . . .[29] it therefore seems very likely that Avestan was the language spoken (perhaps in several variants or dialects) and used for administration in Graeco-Bactria and other eastern Iranian countries.[30]

Benveniste and Harmatta both suggest that the people in the region were Zoroastrians, thus accounting for their "Avestan" language. The same conclusion is drawn by many specialists in Avestan and Zoroastrian studies for reasons related to the account of the civil war at the time of Darius' accession to the Imperial throne.[31] However, neither Benveniste nor Harmatta says whether he thinks the people spoke Avestan *in daily life* or only used it for religious rituals and administration. The usual view (different from Cornillot's) has it that Avestan was already a long-dead language and it had no spoken daughter languages, as the later attested Middle Iranic languages (except Middle Persian and Parthian) are considered to be "East Iranian" languages descended directly from Proto-Iranic. However, the attested lexical material in question is mostly not specifically Zoroastrian,[32] so the words were recorded when the language was still spoken in daily life—but by whom? Calling the language of the Avesta "Avestan" is like calling the language

29. My emphasis. Harmatta adds here, "the two main dialects of Avestan are both reflected by the material", possibly suggesting that some of it might be chronologically earlier than the rest of it (this should be investigated carefully by an expert in these languages), but Harmatta here probably follows many Iranists' claim that there is no significant difference between Old and Young Avestan, contra Hoffmann (2011), perhaps based on the fact that some frequent Old Iranic word *roots* are nondistinctive with respect to their affinity, and as loanwords in other languages the roots seem the same.

30. See further in Endnote 121.

31. Kellens (1998, 2012), Hoffmann (1987), Witzel (2011).

32. In addition, all indications of the influence of writing on the Avesta are many centuries later. See Endnote 122.

of this book "Bookan" instead of "English". Normally we identify languages by their speakers. What language was "Avestan"?

Because the founders of the Empire were the Scythians (not the Medians, as has been wrongly stated by historians from Antiquity on),[33] we should expect to find Scythian loanwords in Old Persian. Lubotsky notes:

> It must be borne in mind that since all three languages are closely related, it is not simple to prove borrowing. As is well known, Old Persian vocabulary contains many words which must be of Iranian but non-Persian origin. These words are usually attributed to Median, but it is in principle equally possible that they are borrowed from any other Iranian language, including Scythian.[34]

As noted earlier by Lecoq, the much-discussed Old Iranic word *farnah-* 'royal glory; personal fortune', has been equated with Avestan *χvarənah-*.[35] However, *farnah* phonetically belongs to the eastern dialect of West Scythian (Lubotsky's "Scythian-Sarmatian"), the only sub-branch of Iranic in which the regular development of word-initial *f* from earlier **p* is a characteristic feature. Avestan *χvarənah-* has long been claimed to be the same word, despite the extremely irregular phonetic correspondences. Following up on Lecoq's explanation of "the word's" origin and development, and on Skjærvø's (1983) demonstration that the Median origin theory of "the word" is impossible, Lubotsky shows that *farnah* is actually a Scythian word first attested in Assyrian sources in Median names, during and after the Cimmerian and Scythian invasions of the 8th to early 7th centuries BC.[36] Lecoq says, "As soon as we reject the Median

33. However, as shown in Chapter 2, one of the accounts in our received text of Herodotus describes the Scythians ruling Media directly for several decades before the coup of Cyaxares, and says that the Median children learned Scythian. That comment was surely added to explain why the Scytho-Medes spoke a Scythian dialect.

34. Lubotsky (2002), adding "Only when we find phonological features which are characteristic of Scythian can we be confident that we are indeed dealing with a Scythian loanword."

35. Lecoq (1987): "le *x*ᵛ*arnah* [*sic*—CIB] ne se résume pas à la seule « gloire royale », c'est aussi une fortune personnelle."

36. Already in 1922 Morgenstierne, cited in Lecoq (1987, note 14), notes, "farnah- est déjà attesté dans l'onomastique mède du VIIIᵉ siècle avant notre ère, telle qu'elle est révélée dans les documents assyriens." As remarked above, other evidence shows that the Scythian invasions began a few decades earlier and simply were not recorded until that point in time.

hypothesis, we cannot avoid that of a Scythian origin. This one admirably explains the spread of *farnah-* in western Iran, on the shores of the Black Sea, in Ossetian and even in Sogdian",[37] which later Iranic languages are direct descendants of Scythian. This conclusion is supported by the distribution and large number of early attestations of Scythian *farnah* in the Pontic Steppe, as noted by Lecoq,[38] though Lecoq's 'spread' should be emended to 'attestation' or the like, because the word was certainly transmitted internally, or historically; it was not a loanword in those languages.

However, despite the contributions of these and other scholars, the Iranic etymology of the word or words has remained disputed because of the highly irregular correspondences between Scythian *farnah-* and Avestan *χvarənah-*, which are unrelated words.[39]

Scythian, Avestan, and Median

Like ancient scholars, modern scholars rarely mention the Scythian language. The most convenient recent collection of Old Iranic etymological data, including Median and Avestan material from the Achaemenid period,[40] unfortunately ignores Scythian completely. However, even from the few Scythian examples that can be adduced from other sources, e.g., Scythian *aspa* 'horse', it is clear that Scythian patterns not with Persian (*asa* 'horse') but with Median and Old Avestan, both of which have *aspa*. Yet Median, Avestan, and Scythian are generally treated as a *language*, "Old Iranic", which includes even Old Persian and is taken to have been mutually comprehensible by its respective speakers. This is a serious problem that has long hindered the study of those peoples and their languages. In fact, the words in the small established Scythian corpus appear to be *identical* to their Median and Avestan cognates,

37. See Endnote 123.

38. Lecoq (1987), "Cette solution rendrait mieux compte du nombre relativement important de noms propres scythes en *farnah-*, attestés sur les rives de la mer Noire."

39. See Endnote 124.

40. Tavernier (2007), as noted above.

as far as they are known,[41] while Old Persian cognates are mostly different, sometimes *very* different. As shown in Chapter 6, there are also a number of words in Old Persian that do not have direct cognates at all in the other Old Iranic languages. Analysis of full texts (below in this chapter) shows the difference between the two branches of Old Iranic to be so great that the respective languages must have been mutually unintelligible.

Table 5 presents only identified Scythian lexical items that have clear cognates in Avestan,[42] based on studies by Mayrhofer[43] and Schmitt.[44] A few items they lack have been supplied, and a few problematic ones deleted, including all those marked "?" by Mayrhofer.

In addition to the items in Table 5 there are quite a few semantically identified but etymologically unidentified Scythian words, such as *akīnaka* 'short sword', attested in transcriptions across Eurasia from Greek ἀκινάκης *akinakēs* 'Scythian short sword' to Middle Iranic, especially attested Sogdian *kyn'k* kīnāk(ă) ~ kēnāk(ă) (Gharib 203, Sogdian *kyn'k* kīnāk) and closely related East Scythian (Hsiung-nu) *kēŋnâkă 'Scythian short sword', q.v. Table 7 in Chapter 6. It is significant that the physical object has a distinctive appearance (see images 3 and 7) and occurs with other characteristically Scythian objects in Scythian burials from Mongolia to Romania.

Note that some fairly early Scythian words have already undergone precocious metathesis of the Old Scythian forms. Widespread metathesis is a characteristic feature of Ossetian (Ossetian-Alanic), the lone modern descendant of Scythian in the former territory of the West Scythians.

The 31 Scythian lexical items in Table 5 share the same key diagnostic phonetic features *and* the same meanings with Avestan and Median. They are the same words. That means the crucial morphophonology of these languages—the basis for scientific historical-comparative

41. The few apparent differences are technical artifacts of the ancient transcriptions and scholars' sometimes misleading interpretations of them.

42. See Endnote 125.

43. Mayrhofer (2006). Cf. Endnote 126.

44. Schmitt (2003, 2014).

TABLE 5. Scythian and Imperial Scythian Dialects

Scythian	Avestan	Median	Gloss
a-	*a-, an-*		un-, non-
aria-/ḥarya-[a]	*airiia-*[b]	*aria-*[c]	royal, one of royal lineage
aspa	*aspa*	*aspa*	horse
dayna	*daēna-*		belief, religion; soul
dāta	*dātā*	*data*	given; placed
farnah[d]	*parənah*		fortune; abundant
gayθā	*gaēθā-*		household, herds, property
haoma-	*haoma-*	*hauma-*	soma (intoxicating liquid)
hu-	*hu-*	*hu-*	good
hvar	*huuar-*	*xvar-*	sun
mazda	*mazdā*		wisdom; God
narya	*nairiia-*	*narya*	manly
paisa	*paēsa-*	*paisa*	ornament
pant-/paθ-	*pant-/ paθ-*		path, road, way
para-	*parə-*	*para-*	across, beyond; earlier
paralata < **paradata*	*paraδāta*	*paradāta*	preceding, placed in front[e]
pita[f]	*pita(r)-*	*pita-*	father
purθa < **puθra*	*puθra-*	*puθra*	son
sarah	*sāra-*	*sāra-*	head
spaka	*spaka-*	*spaka*[g]	dog
sparga-	*sparəγa-*		a sprout, a shoot
sura	*sūra*	*sūra*	strong
syāva-	*siiāuua-*		dark-colored
tapa-	*tap-*		to burn, be warm, hot
tava-	*tauuah-*		power, powerful
uxta-	*uxta-/uxδa-*		spoken, word, proverb
vīar- < **vīra-*	*vīra-*	*vīra-*	man
xšai-	*xšaiia-*	*xšāi-*	king, prince, ruler; to rule
xšaθra-	*xšaθra-*	*xšaθra-*	kingdom, realm, rule
xšaθrapa-/šaθrapa-		*xšaθrapa*	satrap, vassal king, duke
zam[h]		*zam*	earth

TABLE 5. (*continued*)

Note: For usage of the asterisk here see Endnotes 3 and 127.

[a] As noted above, this word is not written "arya" in any ancient script.

[b] In *Airiiana, Airiianəm vaējō* < *Ārya-na (Schmitt 2012a; cf. Schmitt 2011a). See Endnote 128.

[c] In Ἀριζαντοί, or *Aria-zantu, the '*Aria* clan' of the Medes in Herodotus (i 101). See Endnote 129.

[d] This word is etymologically unrelated to Avestan *xvarənah*. See Chapter 6, s.v. Scythian dialects.

[e] The name of the royal house of the first Scythians. Benveniste (1966: 90) cited in Tavernier (2007: 263), Mayrhofer (2006: 15), q.v. for literature.

[f] See Table 7.

[g] Herodotus (i 110,1) glosses a Median woman's name (*Spakō*) as "*spaka*" which he says is the Median word for 'female dog'. His gloss is confirmed by the alternate story about her given by Herodotus himself (i 122,3), as well as by the version in Justin (q.v. Chapter 3), which refers to an actual female dog.

[h] Szemerényi (1991: 1860ff., cited in Schmitt 2014: 270), in the name *Xuāra-zam 'Khwārizm'.

linguistics—agrees, and attested Scythian, Avestan, and Median are dialects of one and the same language, like the American, British, and Australian dialects of Standard English in Table 1. Scholars have long said that Scythian, Median, Avestan, *and* Old Persian were Old Iranic "dialects" and speakers understood each other.[45] However, the Old Persian words in Table 4 are often markedly different from their Scythian, Median, and Avestan cognates, such that Persian on the one hand must be distinguished from Scythian-Median-Avestan on the other. Thus the difference is clear even in obviously related lexical data, not to speak of other *unrelated* lexical data. It is even clearer in the texts, which show that speakers of Old Persian and Imperial Scythian could not have understood each other.

The Texts and Mutual Comprehension

It has often been stated that we do not have any texts in Old Scythian and Median, which were spoken around 2,500 years ago, therefore we cannot say anything important about these languages or dialects.[46] This

45. "A la date de nos inscriptions, les dialectes étaient déjà différenciés, mais leur unité demeurait sensible et les divers Iraniens n'avaient sans doute pas besoin d'un grand effort pour se comprendre" (Meillet and Benveniste 1931: 6).

46. E.g., Meillet and Benveniste (1931: 6) "Aucune attestation directe ne nous a encore fait connaître la langue mède."

reflects the widespread assertion that we cannot do comparative-historical linguistics without texts, which means we cannot do linguistics if we only have lexical data, words. Yet the lexical material of a language encodes the morphophonology of that language. Saying we cannot study it if we only have lexical data flies in the face of scientific linguistic theory and practice.[47]

Classical comparative-historical linguistics is actually founded on careful study specifically of words and sets of words. Without at least some lexical data—*words*—it is *impossible* to say whether any two languages are related. And if the languages actually are related, we cannot say how close the relationship is if we have no words. We cannot even identify the traditionally all-important inflectional morphology (including prefixes and suffixes) of Indo-European languages, let alone determine its functions or meanings, unless it occurs along with (usually as part of) words. The *phonology* of the inflectional morphology does not differ from that of the roots with which it occurs. Accordingly, combined with their semantics, words constitute a highly distinctive and powerful linguistic dataset. It is what makes related languages easy to identify, and why it is easy to see how others are unrelated.

The question remains, however: if the lexical material shows that two or more languages are related (or unrelated), or they are the same language (or not), does that conclusion agree with the conclusion drawn from comparing full sentences, if texts are available to examine in this way?

For Old Persian and Avestan *we do in fact have texts*. What if a simple, often-repeated Old Persian sentence could not have been understood by speakers of the other so-called "Old Iranic dialects"? Consider a strictly random example, the first sentence in Darius the Great's Behistun Inscription.

47. It is like saying we cannot do neuroscience unless we have, and work with, whole bodies, or the bodies of all animals; or we cannot do physics without all the data on the whole galaxy, or the universe.

Example 1. DB 1[48]

𐎠𐎭𐎶𐏐 𐎭𐎠𐎼𐎹𐎺𐎢𐏁𐏐 𐎧𐏁𐎠𐎹𐎰𐎡𐎹𐏐 𐎺𐏀𐎼𐎣𐏐

adam *Dārayavauš* *χšāyaθiya* *văzărka*
I Darius king the Great

𐎧𐏁𐎠𐎹𐎰𐎡𐎹𐏐 𐎧𐏁𐎠𐎹𐎰𐎡𐎹𐎠𐎴𐎠𐎶𐏐

χšāyaθiya *xšāyaθiyānām*
king of kings

'I am Darius, the Great King, King of Kings'.

All the *words* in this sentence are distinctively and exclusively Old Persian. Imperial Scythian speakers could not have understood it. Only Old Persian speakers could understand it. The words and phrases in it occur very frequently in the Old Persian imperial inscriptions.

As a second example consider a sentence from an inscription of Xerxes I in Persepolis:

Example 2. XPj 2[49]

𐎰𐎠𐎫𐎡𐎹𐏐𐎧𐏁𐎹𐎠𐎼𐏁𐎠𐏐𐏈𐏐𐎡𐎶𐎶𐏐𐎫𐎨𐎼𐎶𐏐𐎠𐎭𐎶𐏐𐎠𐎤𐎢𐎴𐎺𐎶𐏐

θāti Xšayaršā χšāyaθiya: imam tacaram adam akunavam.

King Xerxes states: I built this palace.

Again, this sentence is distinctively Old Persian both by the lexicon and by its forms, such as the exclusively Old Persian stem of the verb 'to do, make'. Even with the easily recognized accusative demonstrative *imam* 'this', Imperial Scythian speakers could not have understood this sentence.

In Table 6, only *imam* 'this' is recognizable in Avestan.[50] The word *văzărka* is attested only in Old Persian[51] and has a special distribution and religious-political meaning. It meant not plain 'big, great' but 'the

48. Schmitt (2009: 36).

49. Schmitt (2009: 170); the word *xšāyaθiya* is here written with its dedicated ideographic character.

50. The pronoun *adam* 'I' is distinctively Old Persian by form, though it is clearly related to OAve *azə̄m*, YAve *azəm* 'id.'

51. It has typical Imperial Scythian morphophonology, but it is unattested in Avestan.

TABLE 6. Glossary for Old Persian Examples 1 and 2

adam	'I (pronoun, first person singular nominative)' (OAve *azə̄m*, YAve *azəm*)
Dārayavauš	proper name 'Darius (nominative singular masculine)'
xšāyaθiya	'king (nominative singular masculine)'
văzărka	'(the One) Great (adjective nominative singular masculine)'
xšāyaθiyānām	'king (genitive plural masculine)'
θāti	'says, proclaims' (third person singular present indicative active)
Xšayaršā	proper name 'Xerxes (nominative singular masculine)'
imam	'this (demonstrative pronoun accusative singular masculine)'
tacaram	'palace (accusative singular masculine)'
akunavam	'I have made (active verb first person singular imperfect)'[a]

[a] See Endnote 130.

(one, only) Great', as it is used only with the one Great King, the one Great God (Ahura Mazdā), the (one) Empire, and the (one) Earth/World.[52] Comparison of the Old Avestan sentences in the *Gāthās* with Old Persian sentences is even more striking. The great difference between Persian texts on the one hand and Avestan texts on the other confirms that Old Persian speakers and Avestan-Median-Scythian speakers could not understand each other, as suggested already by the word list in Table 4 and demonstrated by the above textual examples. This is further confirmed by the longer sentence in Endnote 78.

52. Schmitt (2014: 278). See Table 4, Old Persian *maθa-* 'great, big' (superlative *maθišta* 'greatest, biggest'), the word for generic 'great, big'. Although this Old Persian word does have cognates in Avestan, the respective forms are irregular and phonetically distinct enough that they too probably could not have been understood by non-Persian speakers.

The Empire's common *written* language was a West Semitic language, Imperial Aramaic.[53] Following that model, the name "Imperial Scythian" may be coined for the Empire's common *spoken* Old Iranic language, a Scythian dialect comprising Median and Avestan subdialects. When the Scythians and Scytho-Medes ruled the entire region in the 7th century and first half of the 6th century BC, most people (notably except for the Persians) shifted their language to Imperial Scythian, abandoning their inherited language. That is why Imperial Aramaic texts from Central Asia have many loanwords from Imperial Scythian, but few from Old Persian, as Harmatta notes. The Old Persian inscriptions too have Imperial Scythian loanwords, because Pārsa had been a vassal state of the Scythian and Scytho-Mede Empire, and even under Persian rule the Empire's administrators were Scytho-Medes who spoke Imperial Scythian. Since most of the holy texts of Zoroastrianism composed before the development of Middle Iranic literary languages are in Young Avestan, a dialect of Imperial Scythian, the latter language dominated Persian from Darius the Great to Alexander the Great, and long afterward, as shown by Benveniste and Harmatta and confirmed by the newly discovered Bactrian documents from the late Achaemenid and early Seleucid periods. It is also shown by the greatly increased number of Scythian words in Middle Persian, many of which replaced native Persian words.

The fact that linguists have not been able to find significant differences between Median and Avestan or even Scythian is paralleled by the fact that the previously heterogenous people of Media became a unified Scythian-speaking nation when the Cimmerians and Scythians ruled that former strictly geographical region and neighboring regions. As Lubotsky says, "Media was invaded by Scythian tribes and most probably many Median princes and high military officials were of Scythian descent."[54] That is because the young male Scythian warriors took wives from among the defeated, highly fragmented local

53. See Endnote 131.

54. Lubotsky (2002). See Nichols (1997a, 1997b) on the repeated conquests of Central Eurasia and immediately neighboring regions by successive Central Eurasian peoples, and the resulting creolization events.

peoples, who spoke many unrelated languages. Their wives and children learned Scythian customs and beliefs and the unifying Scythian language, as Herodotus explicitly notes.[55] Creolization or language shift takes only one generation. In about 620, the Scytho-Mede prince Cyaxares took over the Scythian realm south of the steppes and became Great King. He ruled it as the (Imperial) Scythian-speaking Mede Empire.

The Persians in Pārsa (Persis, now Fârs)[56] are not certainly mentioned in any source until the time of Darius the Great, and thus seem to have been rather isolated. Perhaps such isolation kept them, uniquely, from shifting to the Scythian language, though they did borrow many words from Imperial Scythian, showing that they were or had been under Scytho-Mede influence. Nevertheless, when Darius put up the first Old Persian inscriptions, his language was unintelligible to the Imperial Scythian-speaking peoples,[57] and vice versa, as shown. The fact that the Persians spoke a different language explains why they retained the Scythian-speaking Medes to run most of the Imperial government.[58] Lecoq (1987), following earlier scholars, stresses the indebtedness of the Persians to the Medes:

> We know that the Achaemenids, and above all Darius, placed themselves voluntarily in the tradition of a new royal absolutism, foreign to earlier Iranian thought.[59]

He adds to his "foreign to earlier Iranian thought" the comment that "the Medes themselves had borrowed from Mesopotamia". The latter point does not agree with the sources. The Medes were no doubt influenced by Mesopotamian traditions, as surely the Persians were after them, but most of the significant "borrowed" innovations were not native to Mesopotamia. Some scholars attribute them to the Urartians, or

55. Herodotus (i 73).

56. See Waters (1999) for possible earlier historical references to "Persians" further north before Darius I.

57. The Scythian influence shows up as the many Median words in the inscriptions, which are Scythian dialect words borrowed by Old Persian. Cf. Endnote 132.

58. See Endnote 133.

59. See Endnote 134 for the French.

even the Egyptians, but most of them had been acquired directly from Central Eurasian peoples during the Cimmerian and Scythian occupation of Media and Central Asia.[60] In quite the same way, as amply demonstrated by many Persepolis bas-reliefs, the Persians and Medes were inseparable from the time of Darius the Great onward—necessarily for the Persian rulers, who spoke Old Persian, the language of the ruling family. Imperial Scythian is the dialect of Scythian that developed under Scythian and Scytho-Mede rule in most of what is now Central Asia and Iran. It remained the common language of the Empire from its foundation by the Scythians in the 7th century BC down to its conquest by the Greeks in the late 4th century BC and for long afterward, as shown by Benveniste and Harmatta.[61]

The identity of Avestan, Median, and Scythian as dialects of one spoken language, Imperial Scythian, means we do after all have *texts* in Scythian and "Median": they are the Avesta. While written in two different Zoroastrian "religiolects" and thus somewhat different in lexical range from strictly secular texts, the two forms of Avestan are nevertheless simply subdialects of Imperial Scythian. That means we actually *do* know who wrote most of the Avesta,[62] and approximately when. The Scythians' Mede and Central Asian descendants who were Zoroastrians and spoke Imperial Scythian composed one of the world's great Classical literatures, the Avesta, during the Scytho-Mede-Persian Empire period and the following Hellenistic period, when documents from Central Asia attest to the continued use of Imperial Scythian.

The basic linguistic divisions within the Persian Empire are thus fairly clear: the Persian rulers and their relatives spoke Persian—at first

60. See the Prologue.

61. Avestan, the holy language of the Zoroastrian tradition, is a subdialect of Imperial Scythian preserved in two forms, Old Avestan and Young Avestan. The date and etymology of the name *Avesta* (and *Avestan*) is disputed (Kellens 2012). Without the unifying rule by speakers of a single Imperial language after the Greek conquest, each major region of the former Scytho-Mede core of the Empire developed its own daughter language. The best known of these Middle Iranic languages are Bactrian, Sogdian, Khwarizmian, and Arachosia-Sakan. Persian continued as Middle Persian, which is much more heavily Scythianized than Old Persian. The Middle Iranic languages are increasingly attested in writing from the 2nd century CE onward.

62. I.e., the Young Avestan texts. On Old Avestan see Appendix A.

Old Persian, and after the rapid changes of the Imperial period, its Middle Persian continuation. The administration was in the hands of the Medes, who spoke Imperial Scythian, which at the time of Darius and Xerxes was clearly a single language spoken throughout the Iranian and Central Asian parts of the Empire with only minor dialect differences. However, close study of the data shows that some of the most salient vocabulary items in Old Persian, the key "political" terms thought to be Median, are not attested in Avestan. They were perhaps borrowed directly from the Royal Scythians during their rule of the entire region, most of which shifted linguistically to Imperial Scythian before the time of Darius, as discussed in Chapter 6. These crucial words relating to the imperial system would thus seem likely to be specifically and directly Royal "steppe" Scythian in origin.

6

Classical Scythian in the Central Eurasian Steppes

West Scythian

The first named Scythian person mentioned in any source is King *Spakaya (Iš-pa-ka-a-a, in three Assyrian inscriptions of Esarhaddon, events of 676/675 BC). He was the leader of Scythian forces that entered the Ancient Near East at this time.[1] The root form of the name is Scythian *spaka-*, which is identical to Median *spaka* 'dog', cited by Herodotus.[2] Thus the steppe Scythian and Imperial Scythian word for 'dog' is *spaka*, as expected according to the well-established historical sound changes seen in *aspa* 'horse' and other words affected by the same rule. Since these Scythian and Median words are identical, and most of our data on early Median per se comes from study of the Old Persian inscriptions (supplemented and confirmed by Old Iranic forms transcribed in other Ancient Near Eastern scripts and Greek),[3] the language of the Classical period steppe Scythians may be called "Classical Scythian". In addition to directly attested words, some "Median" words borrowed by Old Persian, which are clearly "Old East Iranic" but are unattested in Avestan, may be Classical Scythian. They are examined later in this chapter.

1. Mayrhofer (2006: 9, "Hinweis R. Schmitt"); cf. Ivantchik (2018).
2. See Table 5 and the Cyrus story in Chapter 2.
3. This material is known as the *Nebenlieferung*, or 'secondary transmission'.

The 50 solidly attested Classical West Scythian lexical items given in Table 7 are based on recent work in Scythian etymology by Mayrhofer,[4] who provides a list of some of the best attested words with clear etymologies, given in reconstructed Old Iranic form. Most items are from Classical period Greek textual sources; a few are from inscriptions or other texts that are a little later. Editing his list to delete some speculative items and a few incorrect ones, and adding a number of items that he has overlooked, we have a small but strong list as a beginning for the study of Classical Scythian.

Classical Scythian Loanwords in Old Persian

Several key terms in the Achaemenid royal inscriptions have been classed as Median, a language attested in general mainly as loanwords into Old Persian. It is shown in Chapter 5 that this Median language is actually a dialect of Imperial Scythian (so its loanwords into Old Persian should be ordinary Imperial Scythian), and that Avestan, too (at least, Young Avestan), is a dialect of Imperial Scythian. The language thus agrees with the entire Scytho-Mede imperial assemblage of political structure, religious and mythical features, military organization and characteristic weapons, national clothing, and so on, which is actually Scythian in origin. However, some of the Median lexical items in Old Persian are unusual or problematic. A number do not occur in the Avesta in the same or similar form, if at all, but some of them are attested in steppe Scythian north of the Black Sea. It would appear, therefore, that some Scythian loans in Old Persian were borrowed directly from the Scythians before or during their rule.[5] Such terms involve the Imperial ruling elite and their political institutions. That perhaps explains why we find some of them in Imperial political documents such as the Old Persian inscriptions, where we might expect them, whereas we should not expect such terms to appear in the Zoroastrian Avesta, the almost exclusively religious texts largely written in Imperial Scythian,

4. Mayrhofer (2006).

5. See Endnote 141 for other words not discussed here.

TABLE 7. Classical West Scythian

Reconstruction	Transcription	Gloss
a-	ε-, α-	un-
(a)kīnaka[a]	(α)κινακης	Scythian short sword
anaryā	εναρεες, αναριεις[b]	unmanly ones
ariya ~ aria	αρια, αρι-[c]	one of royal lineage
aspa	ασποι[d]	a horse
dānav-[e]	Ταναις	river; the Don River
dayna	Δαινος	belief, religion
farnah[f]	Φαρνος	fortune, prosperity
gaunaka	γαυνακη, καυνακης[g]	thick jacket
gayθā̆	γοιτο-	herd; possessions
gayθā̆sūra	γοιτοσυρος	strong in herds/possessions
gav- +	γωρυτος[h]	leather quiver-bow case
haoma	*hauma-*[i]	*soma* (intoxicating liquid)
hu-	*o*	good
hva-	χο-	co-
hvadayna	χοδαινος	coreligionist
hvar/χvar	*chor-*	sun; south[j]
hvar-/χvar-sarah	*chorsari*	sunny-side (ones); southerners
**kanzuka-*[k]	κανδυς	long-sleeved coat worn on shoulders
kapa	-καπης	a fish
-lata < *data	-λαται	given, placed
maduva	Μαδυης, Μάδυς	berry wine[l]
mazda	μασαδας[m]	wisdom; God
napa-	Ναπαι	descendants, grandchildren
naryā	-ναρεες, -ναριεῖς,	manly men
pā-	-πα	to guard, protect[n]
paisa	-πισης	an ornament
pant-/paθ-	παντ-	path
pantikapa	παντικαπη	fish-path (river name)
para-	παρα-	ahead, before

Continued on next page

TABLE 7. (*continued*)

Reconstruction	Transcription	Gloss
*paralata (< *paradata)*	παραλαται	put ahead, preceding, foremost (ones)
părăθu	προτο-, *parta-/ barta-* (Akk.)	wide, far
părăθutavah	Προτοθυης, *Bartatua* (Akk.)[o]	whose power extends far
pita-	πειθης, *pitus*	father[p]
puθra	πουρθαιος/φουρτας	son[q]
sagari(s)	σαγαρις	Scythian battle-axe[r]
**sarah ~ *saraɣ(ă)*	saraɣ[s]	head; side, slope
**skuδa, skula, sugda, saka*	σκυθης, σκυλης, *sugd-*, σακα	a Scythian[t]
spaka	σπακα	a dog[u]
spakaya	*Išpakai* (Akk.)	doggie, puppy
sparga	σπαργα	a sprout, a shoot
sūra	συρο	strong
targi-, tagi- < *tagri[v]	Ταργι-, Θαγι-	Heaven (God)
tavah-	ταος	power, powerful one
uχta-	οκτα	spoken, word
vargā	*vargā*	strewers, pourers[w]
wīar ~ wīra	οιορ[x]	a man, male, human
χšaθra	χšaθra-, Akk. *kšatru*	realm, empire
**χšaθrapā- ~ šaθrapā-*	ξατραπης, σατραπης, Σατραβα-	vassal-king, duke[y]
χšaya-	ξαι-	a king, prince, ruler

Note: Hyphens are used only for morpheme divisions; *y* and *w* are used instead of their equivalents i̯ and u̯. Greek forms are given as attested in Greek, but sans diacritics. Asterisks are used only for reconstructed forms not directly based on transcriptions. Uncertain items are excluded. For non-Graeco-Latin transcriptions the source language or script is noted in parentheses.

a Schmitt (2012c): "*akīnákēs*, also *kīnákēs* 'Persian sword' (cf. Sogd. *kyn'k*)"; no etymology given. See Endnote 135.

b Herodotus (1.105.4; 4.67.2): ἐνάρεες; Pseudo-Hippocrates (Aër. 22): ἀναριεῖς (Ivantchik 2018).

c See Endnote 136.

d Mayrhofer (2006: 10). The Greek transcription is plural; *aspa* is very well attested in Imperial Scythian.

e Bar. 733–734: YAve *dānav-* 'Fluss, Strom', Ave *dānu-drājah-* 'von der Lange eines Flusses'. See below, s.v. *Dānava.

TABLE 7. (*continued*)

[f] From the eastern dialect of West Scythian, cognate to Avestan *parənah-*. See Chapter 6, s.v. Scythian dialects.

[g] *LSJ*, s.v. καυνάκης. See Appendix B.

[h] A characteristically Scythian invention, made of leather; the first part of this word is surely the well-attested common Iranic word *gav- 'cow'; the remainder is a mystery.

[i] See Appendix A.

[j] In *Chorsari* (Pliny *Nat. Hist.* vi 50), the Scythian name for 'Persians'; Mayrhofer (2006: 20–21): *hvar/n- 'sun' + *sarah- 'head'.

[k] See Endnote 137.

[l] Schmitt (2003: 12–13) suggests 'one who seeks intoxicating drink'. The Scythians liked to drink.

[m] In *Thagimasadas* 'Poseidon' and Octamasadas (see *uχta-*). Mayrhofer (2006: 14) suggests *mazatā- 'Größe' for *-masadas*, but has no suggestion for *Thagimasadas*, q.v. below. Although Mayrhofer does not suggest a connection with *mazda*, Herodotus tells us *Thagimasadas* is a god and says that only the Royal Scythians worshipped him. The sense of either 'wisdom' or 'God' works for both names. *Octamasadas*, a prince's name, is then 'word of God (Mazda)', 'spoken by God (Mazda)', or 'word of wisdom', etc.

[n] Schmitt (2003: 14); see *šaθrapā-* 'satrap' below.

[o] These are Greek and Assyrian transcriptions of a Scythian king's name; Mayrhofer (2006: 15) has "*pr̥θu-", comparing it to Ave *pərəθu-* (i.e., *părăθu-*) 'wide'; the second part, *tava-, is the Old Iranic morpheme *tav-*, *tava-*, etc. '(to be) powerful' (Mayrhofer 2006: 25, 15; Sch. 252; Bar. 638–639, 649–650; Tav. 323, 565–566, 608). It is frequently used in names.

[p] See Endnote 138.

[q] The *p-* form is attested in Herodotus and inscriptions from Olbia (western subdialect); the *f-* form is attested from Pantikapeia (eastern subdialect). The word is recorded in Scythian grave inscriptions written in Greek. Both already show the metathesis characteristic later of Ossetian.

[r] Schmitt (2012c): "*ságaris* 'Scythian battle-axe'." Herodotus (vii 64) says it is the Scythian word for 'axe'.

[s] See also Chapter 8 on East Scythian *Saraγ*, the name of Loyang (the traditional Eastern Capital of China).

[t] In Akkadian *Iškuzai* ~ *Ašguzai*, i.e., *Skuza, transcribing foreign *Skuδa, attested from 672/671 in the area of northwestern Mannea (Yusifov 1982), i.e., northwest of Media proper. The earliest Greek transcription, Σκύθης *Skythēs* in Hesiod, ca. 700 BC (Schmitt 2012b), is contemporaneous with the Akkadian transcriptions. *Pace* Schmitt, the Akkadian and Greek transcriptions represent close approximations in those languages to *Skuδa. The regional dialect alternation of *z* and *δ* (ḏ) in Imperial Aramaic is very well known, and foreign fricatives are often represented by ancient Greek aspirated stops. The word *Sug(u)da* 'Sogdian' is a form of the same name, *Skuδa (Szemerényi 1980: 6–7, 30). So too is *Sakla ~ *Saka* (Beckwith 2009: 378–380), thus not with Szemerényi's (1980: 40ff.) and others' folk etymology of *Saka*. See Endnote 139.

[u] Attested in Assyrian Akkadian as *Iš-pa-ka-a-a*, i.e., *Išpakai* *Spakaya. He was defeated by the Assyrian king Esarhaddon in 672/671. See Ivantchik (2018) and cf. the previous note.

[v] See below in this chapter s.v. *Täŋri (from *Tagri), the East Scythian form of this word.

[w] See Appendix A on *haoma* and the *Sakā Haumavargā*.

[x] See Endnote 140.

[y] Literally 'protector of the realm' (Sch. 285). The simplified onset Σ occurs in inscriptions of the Pontic Steppe region and in the best known of the Greek transcriptions (Bukharin 2013).

and such words are indeed mostly unattested in the Avestan dialects of Scythian.

SATRAP. The word *xšaθrapā* 'vassal ruler, satrap; duke', literally 'protector of the realm', has been borrowed into English as *satrap* via Greek ξατράπης *xatrapes* or σατράπης *satrapes* via the Scythian form *χšaθrapā* ~ *šaθrapā*.[6] The base of this word, *χšaθra* 'realm, empire', is very early attested in a Cimmerian ruler's name, *Sandakšatru*, reflecting Scythian *sandaχšaθra 'he who establishes the empire'.[7] The word *χšaθrapā* is the term for a "sub-king" or "duke", the vassal ruler of one of the great feudal states or 'Lands' of the Empire, the satrapies. It occurs only twice in Old Persian, in the specifically Persianized form *χšaçapāvā*. One occurrence refers to the satrap of Bactria and the other to the satrap of Arachosia,[8] places where the Imperial Scythian language is well attested.[9] Though the word is non-Persian in origin, and was long suspected to be Median or Avestan, it is unattested in Avestan, but it is attested in Greek grave inscriptions of Scythians north of the Black Sea.[10] Use of the Scythian term exclusively for these two unusually large and important Central Asian satrapies is significant because they were key contributors to Darius' successful campaign to suppress the polytheist rebels and preserve the Empire. Thus this term for one of the most crucial "feudal" features of the steppe zone Scythian imperial system, which was inherited and continued by the Mede and Persian Empire, is a solidly Scythian word.

KING. *χšāyaθiya* 'king', long considered to be highly problematic by its form, does not occur in Avestan and is attested only in Old Persian, where it occurs many times in the Achaemenid inscriptions (see

6. Bukharin (2013), who however argues against a Scythian origin.

7. The word *sanda-* 'to create, found' is well attested in Avestan (Bar. 1560–1561).

8. DB 38: 314, 45: 356 (Schmitt 2009: 65, 70), in both instances written *xšaçapāvā*. The putative Urform **xšaθrapāvāna* or **xšaθrapāna* is unattested, and Schmitt notes that the foreign transcriptions all end with *-pa*. For further discussion see Endnote 142.

9. See Chapter 5. The Persians otherwise use *dahyu-*, a word attested in both Avestan and Old Persian, with similar meaning.

10. Bukharin (2013) cites forms attesting that the word-onset cluster *xš* in *χšaθrapā* was simplified to *š* in Scythia itself, where the name *Skuδa 'Scythian' was simplified to attested *Saka* (i.e., *sk- > s). However, it did not happen that way, but via *Sakla, attested in Chinese, from *Skula, in turn from *Skuδa. However, the opposite simplification of an onset cluster occurs in East Scythian, where *χšay*(*ă*) 'king' became attested *kay*(*ă*). For details on these words see below in this chapter.

Chapter 5). Although it has mostly been treated as a loanword from Median into Old Persian,[11] it is now regularly claimed that the idea has been disproven.[12] However, the "new" proposed solution is actually an old one, as doubtful now as it was when first proposed over a century ago,[13] because it is built on a *hypothetical* word-stem for 'rule, dominate', *χšayaθa-. I.e., the form is unattested. The argument is thus ad hoc, circular, not based on hard data, and semantically unlikely: '(the) ruling one', or '(the) dominator'.[14] Moreover, if *χšāyaθiya* is not Median, it would be truly unusual for the *Mede* custodians of the Empire to have coined a *Persian* word for their ruler, the Persian king. In view of the Scythian or Scytho-Mede origin of other "Imperial" terms for rulership, it would seem more likely that this word is simply a legacy of the Royal Scythians borrowed into Persian.[15] Its root *χšā-* 'to rule' is the root of the word *χšaθra* 'realm', attested inscriptionally already in the above-noted Cimmerian-Scythian ruler's name, *Sandaχšaθra*. Moreover, there is contextual phraseological evidence for *χšāyaθiya* and several other "Imperial" words being Royal Scythian in origin, most noticeably in connection with the next word, *văzărka* 'great'.

THE ONE GREAT. The word *văzărka* 'great',[16] as Mayrhofer notes, is the "standard epithet of king, kingdom, the God Ahuramazdā, and the wide world". Scythian by form, it does not occur in Avestan. In the Old

11. E.g., Mayrhofer (1968).

12. Hoffmann (1976: 637, note 26) argues that OPer *χšāyaθiya-* is a vṛddhi-formation from **χšayaθ-* 'reign' with the suffix *-iya-* < **χšay-aθa-* 'rule, reign' (Schmitt 2014: 286–287). Cf. Lubotsky (2002: 195, note 7). It has thus been claimed to be a genuine Old Persian word.

13. See Endnote 143.

14. The actual cuneiform full-written form is 𐎧𐏁𐎠𐎹𐎰𐎡𐎹 *x-š-a-y-θ-i-y*, which can also represent *xšayθiya, among other theoretically possible readings. The word is often written with an ideograph instead.

15. Thanks to Herodotus we have a form of the Scythian word for 'king' attested within the first version of the Scythian national foundation myth (in compounds with the personal names or epithets of the three sons of the Scythian progenitor), as Scythian -ξαϊ- **χšaya-* 'king', Ave. *χšaiia-* (*χšaya-*) ~ Ved. *kṣáya-* 'ruling, ruler' (Schmitt 2003; Mayrhofer 2006), Greek transcribed Scythian -ξαϊ *xai* [ksai], a straightforward transcription of Old Iranic *χšaya*, as nearly all agree. (See also the discussion of the later East Scythian form of the word, *kay(ă), below in this chapter.) Mayrhofer notes that the proposed etymologies of the personal names of the three sons are all problematic, but that is not true of the youngest son, **Skulaχšaya*, q.v. Chapter 1, Note 22, Chapter 3, Note 85, and Endnote 91.

16. Or *vazărka*; written 𐎺𐏀𐎼𐎣, also transcribed *vazraka*, *vazṛka*, etc., by different scholars. On Indologizing transcriptions with *ṛ*, such as "*vazṛka*", see Endnote 117.

Persian inscriptions it frequently qualifies the words *χšāyaθiya* 'king'; *būmī* 'the Earth, world' (which could be a specifically Old Persian word in that sense); *baga* 'God' (in *baga văzărka* 'the one Great God', referring only to Ahuramazdā); and (twice) *χšaθra* 'the Empire'. The word *văzărka* means not simply 'great', but specifically and exclusively '*the* (one and only) *great*', and occurs *only* with these specific nouns. It is accepted to be "Median"—i.e., Imperial Scythian—by form, not Persian, yet it does not have any Avestan cognate. By contrast, the ordinary Old Persian word for 'great', OPer **maθa-* (only the superlative *maθišta* is attested)[17] does have Median and Avestan cognates.[18] The putative root of *văzărka* is often compared to YAve. *vazra-* 'mace',[19] the weapon of Mithra, and it has been related to Sanskrit *vajra-* 'weapon of Indra; strong'. However, a word meaning 'mace' or 'strong' can hardly be equated with a word meaning 'the (one and only) great', and the extension *-ka* cannot be ignored. Since the word *χšāyaθiya* 'king', a long problematic form, occurs only and with great frequency in the Old Persian inscriptions—especially in the phrase *χšāyaθiya văzărka* 'the Great King', a political title that *specifically* refers to the top of the Scythian feudal-hierarchical system—it would seem that Royal Scythian is the ultimate source not only of the regular attribute *văzărka* 'Great', but of *χšāyaθiya* 'king' as well.

GOOD FORTUNE. *farnah* '(good) fortune, prosperity'.[20] This has recently been shown to be a West Scythian word, well attested in inscriptions on the north coast of the Black Sea and in nearly all Middle Iranic and New Iranic languages, including (as a loanword) Middle Persian. Accordingly dialects of Scythian did not borrow the word, they inherited it. It is one of the earliest and best attested Scythian words, being

17. In fact, there are too many forms: Ave. *maz-* and *mas-*, and superlatives of all three: *maθišta, masišta, mazišta* 'biggest, greatest'. However, none is a superlative of *văzărka* 'the (one) great', *pace* Sch. 214.

18. Bar. 1154–1158; cf. Sch. 213–214, who however does not mention Avestan *maz-, mazišta*; see the preceding Note.

19. Sch. 278.

20. The word is well attested in Achaemenid personal names, so it was clearly borrowed into Old Persian, but in Middle Persian the word was conflated with an originally unrelated word attested in Young Avestan, *x^{v}arənah* 'glory, majesty's splendor (*Majestätsglanz*)'.

recorded in personal names of people connected with Media in the 8th century BC, at the time of the first influx of Scythian speakers into the northern Ancient Near East. However, because Akkadian has no *f*, the Akkadian transcriptions of the name actually begin with *p*, so the underlying word could be either *farnah* or **parnah*. The form *farnah* is first attested with an explicit *f* in Old Persian, but only as a compounding element in the personal name **Vindafarnah-* (Greek *Intaphernes* [*with* φ]), which occurs in the Behistun Inscription (519 BC),[21] as well as in other names in Greek and other sources. Most importantly, it is attested not long after, with *f*, in inscriptions from the *eastern* subdialect of West Scythian north of the Black Sea, while the regular *western* subdialect form with *p* (preserving the form of the etymological ancestor of both dialect forms) is attested in Avestan in *parənah-*.[22]

GOOD HORSES. **huvaspā* <*uvaspā*>, Avestan *hvaspā*[23] 'good horses'. Mayrhofer notes, "Median *aspa* mostly appears in the standard epithet used to denote the Achaemenid kingdom or Persis province *uv-aspā-u-martiyā-* having 'good horses and [good] men.'"[24] The underlying *hu(v)* element meaning 'good' in the first word is both Classical Scythian and Imperial Scythian (all three West Scythian dialects); the attested Old Persian form *u(v)* 'good' shows regular loss of *h* before *u* in that language.[25] Although *aspa* 'horse' is thus Scythian, many names of Persians include *aspa*. By contrast, the genuine Old Persian form of the word for horse, *asa-*, rarely occurs. This oddity has been passed over with little comment, but in the Persian imperial system, the cavalry was essentially the Scythian part of the army, while the Persians were spear-wielding infantry. Darius the Great characterizes the Persians' achievements as those of spear-bearers (DNa 44), and his own title under Cambyses was Spearbearer. Militarily and culturally, the horse

21. Sch. 70, 116, 175. The name is actually 𐎻𐎡𐎭𐎳𐎼𐎴𐎠 *Vidafarnā* in Old Persian because Old Persian did not allow nasals to occur in syllable-contact coda position (e.g., **vinda-*) and regularly deleted them (making *vida-*).

22. See below, s.v. Scythian Dialects.

23. Bar. 1852.

24. Sch. 264, 271.

25. Old Persian lacks *h* before the vowel *u* in inherited words. The same compound is attested with the expected *h* in Avestan *hvaspa* (Bar. 1852); see Lecoq (1987).

was still a foreign animal to most Persians, explaining why *(h)uvaspā* and many other equine words in Persian are Scythian or Scytho-Mede in origin. Very likely the epithet *originally* referred to Scythia or Media, not Persis (Persia).

ALL NATIONS. *vispazana-* (vispa-zana) '(containing) all nations', part of the royal titular formula *χšāyaθiya dahyūnām vispazanānām* 'King of the Lands of all Nations' ('König der Länder aller Stämme') in the Old Persian inscriptions. Mayrhofer notes that *-zana-*, Median by form, primarily exists in the Old Persian inscriptions in this compound with another characteristically Median form, *vispa* 'all'. The word *vispa-zana* does not occur in Avestan.[26]

MALEFACTOR. The Median word *zūra-* 'evil' in *zūrakāra-* 'malefactor, culprit' (literally 'evil-doer') in the Behistun Inscription has no known cognates,[27] but it looks Scythian by form, so *zūrakāra*, whatever its origin, is likely to be a loan from Scythian.[28]

Scythian Dialects

Previous discussion of Scythian dialects has been very limited, no doubt due to the extremely limited data on the language. More recently, scholars' observations have focused on the territory of the West Scythians living in the Pontic Steppe and North Caucasus Steppe from the 4th century BC to 3rd century CE. The inscriptions along the coast of the Black Sea distinguish between the western subdialect (centered on Olbia), which has forms with an onset transcribed in Greek as Π [p], and the eastern subdialect (centered on Tanaïs and Panticapaeum, modern Kerch), which has forms with an onset transcribed in Greek as Φ [ɸ] ~ [f], the clearest example being πουρθαιος *pourθaios* 'son' vs. φουρτας *φourtas* 'son', the ancestor of Ossetian *fyrt/furt* 'id.', from Old Scythian *puθra-, identical to Old Avestan *puθra-* 'id.', and cognate to

26. Bar. 1464. The genuine Old Persian cognate of *vispa-*, i.e., *visa-* 'all', occurs in Elamite transcriptions of Old Persian (Sch. 280, 294).

27. See Sch. 295–296.

28. See Endnote 144.

Old Indic *putra-* 'id.' as well.[29] Lubotsky, following earlier work that mostly considered the differences to be internal and chronological, notes "the sound change **p > f* was typical of eastern West Scythian dialects", or "Scytho-Sarmatian".[30] The word *farnah* is attested in the Behistun Inscription (519 BC) in the Median name *Vindafarnah* (written *Vidafarnah*). Lecoq and Lubotsky, following earlier scholars, state that the shift of onset *p to *f* in *farnah* is attested to have happened by the late 8th century BC,[31] as discussed above. That is not impossible, but the transcriptions are in Akkadian script, which has no *f*, so it can write only *p*, making the early transcriptions ambiguous. Further study shows that *farnah* is not related to the word *xᵛarənah* at all, as was previously thought, but to a word that had *p* in the earliest times and still had that phone—attested as *parənah-* in Avestan—until some unknown point (but retained in Pontic dialects down to modern times). In the Behistun Inscription (ca. 519 BC), *f* is attested in the Old Persian transcription *farnah*, and a century later in Greek transcriptions.[32] Nevertheless, the Scythians ruled Media in the mid- to late 7th century, when their language spread all over the region that is now Iran and Central Asia, where reflexes of *farnah*, with *f*, are attested in Middle Iranic languages descended from Scythian. Accordingly the Scythians who ruled Media and founded the Empire must have already spoken the *eastern* subdialect of West Scythian, and the *western* subdialect speakers must have arrived in the Pontic Steppe region earlier than the eastern subdialect speakers. Other than this internal difference within West Scythian, little has been done on Scythian dialects.[33]

Forms of the national name of the Scythians so far constitute the earliest and most precise data relevant to the topic of Scythian dialects. It is critical to note that the earliest attestations of the name in a firmly datable source are the Assyrian Akkadian transcriptions *Áš-ku-za-a-a* /

29. Bielmeier (1989: 240), Mayrhofer (2006: 26).

30. See Endnote 145.

31. Lecoq (1987); Lubotsky (2002).

32. For discussion see the section "Median and Avestan" below.

33. See Endnote 146 on earlier work.

Áš-gu-za-a-a and *Iš-ku-za(-a-a)*,[34] representing *Iškuzai* ~ *Aškuzai* (confirmed by Hebrew **Aškuza*),[35] first recorded in 676/675, contemporaneous with the occurrence of the name Σκύθας *Scythas* (Skutha-s) in Hesiod, ca. 700 BC.[36] Non-Indo-European Near Eastern languages in Antiquity, as now, mostly do not allow any onset clusters, so foreign words with such onsets have been adjusted to make them pronounceable (whereas Greek does allow onset clusters and had no problem with this name). In this case the Akkadian transcribers added an epenthetic ("helping") vowel, *a* or *i*, at the beginning of the word. Removing it and nominal suffixes leaves a name *Škuza* ~ *Skuza*, in Greek *Skutha*. In Imperial Aramaic the consonants *z* [z] and *d* [d]/[δ] distinguish two dialects, but they are sometimes interchangeable in the same dialect.[37] In view of the Near Eastern provenance also of the Scythian name transcribed in Greek it is clear that it was Scythian *Skuδa, as shown by Szemerényi.[38]

His etymology of *Skuδa from Proto-Iranic *Skuda- from Indo-European *skud-o 'shooter, archer', from Proto-Indo-European *skeud- 'to shoot'[39] is convincing for historical reasons too. Until the Central Middle Ages, when firearms were invented (in China), the normal way to 'shoot' was with a bow and arrow. Early accounts of Central Eurasian steppe peoples, whatever their identity, often refer to them as 'the archers' or 'people who draw the bow'.[40] Other etymologies that have been proposed are linguistically unacceptable.

Leaving aside the etymology, the name *Skuδa is uniquely the name of the Scythians. It has undergone regular sound changes over time and in each of its major daughter dialects.

34. Ivantchik (2018).

35. See Chapter 2, Note 6 and Endnote 45 for details. Szemerényi (1980: 7) also gives *Iškuza, Ašguzai, Askuzai.*

36. Schmitt (2012b).

37. This important feature of Ancient Near Eastern phonology, though well known to Aramaicists, has not been noted previously in connection with the name of the Scythians.

38. Szemerényi (1980: 20–21). It is no doubt cognate to English SHOOT, as he proposes. Not with Schmitt's (2003) and Mayrhofer's (2006: 16) remarks on this.

39. Watkins (2011: 81–82).

40. Cf. the similar historical remarks of Szemerényi (1980: 18–19) with regard to the Scythians specifically.

The Major Early Scythian Dialect Divisions[41]

1. Scythian *skuδa (attested in Akkadian, Greek, and Hebrew, ca. 700–600 BC) > *skula, saka*
   - lambdacization of *δ:

   > WScy subdialect *skula* 'local name of the Scythians' (Herodotus, 5th century BC)

   - epenthesis with *a* (to break up the onset cluster *sk*) + syncope (deletion of *u*):

   > *sakla- (attested in Old Chinese transcriptions)[42]

   - deletion of *l* by the Syllable Contact Law:[43]

   > *saka* 'Saka'[44]

2. Scythian *skuδa > *sugda*, *suɣla > *suŋla
   - metathesis of *u* (> *sukδa) + voicing of *k* (> *sugδa) + fortition of *δ* (> *sugda)

   > EScy dialect *sugda* 'Sogdia, Sogdian'

   - spirantization of *g*:

   > EScy dial. *suɣda* 'East Scythian; Sogdian'[45] and adjective *Suɣdīk* 'Sogdian' (~ *-ān* 'Sogdians')

   - lambdacization of *d*:

   > *Suɣlīk ~ *Suɣli ~ *Sʊgli* ~ *Suwli 'Sogdian'[46]

   > eastern EScy *suɣla 'Sogdian; early Hsiung-nu'

   - regular nasalization of velar coda before a liquid in Hsiung-nu

   > *suŋla (OChi *suŋlâ) 'eastern East Scythian; Hsiung-nu'

41. Additional abbreviations in this table: WScy 'West Scythian dialect', EScy 'East Scythian dialect'.

42. Beckwith (2009: 378–380); this material was clearly unknown to Szemerényi (1980).

43. Davis (1998); Gouskova (2004); Özçelik (forthcoming).

44. Attested from 519 BC on as [saka] in Old Persian, Akkadian, Elamite, Greek, and Old Chinese (Beckwith and Kiyose 2018), it is the most common name for the Scythians. Not with Szemerényi's (1980: 45) speculative argument that it is from an Iranic verb meaning 'to go', by extension 'roam', and means 'nomad'.

45. Kent (1950: 209) "*Sugda- Suguda- 'Sogdiana',*" citing Elamite *šu-ug-da*, Akkadian *su-ug-du*, Greek Σογδιᾱνή. Cf. Old Tibetan སོག་དག་ *Sogdag* 'Sogdian(s)' [sʊgdak] vs. Sogdian *Sugdīk* (Szemerényi 1980: 27).

46. See Endnote 147.

East Scythian

The language of the Central Eurasian people near, and in, the crucially important ancient state of Chao 趙 (*Zhào*), in the Eastern Steppe region on the northern Chinese frontier, was *Ḥarya 'Royal Scythian', as discussed above. Its Chinese-speaking population, or a significant part of it, must have been bilingual at one point, exactly parallel to the similar situation in contemporaneous Media, as described in Chapter 2. Chao was the home of Ch'in shih huang ti 秦始皇帝 (*Qín Shǐhuángdì*), the First Emperor of China. He was born and raised in the capital, *Han-tan* 邯鄲 (*Hándān*), the name of which is Scythian *Ăgámătánă, the same name as *Agamatāna* 'Ecbatana' (early modern Amadān ~ Amadāna, now Hamadân), the name of Media's capital, as discussed in Chapters 7 and 8.

The non-Chinese people of Chao and the region to the east of it, as well as the Hsiung-nu (*Suŋlâ) 匈奴 (*Xiōngnú*), whose homeland was in the Ordos steppe within the great bend of the Yellow River to the west of Chao, are all called *Hu* 胡 (*Hú*), Old Chinese *Ḥărắ [ɣə.râ] (from *Ḥarya) [ɣa.rya] 'Royal (Scythians)' in early Chinese sources, as are the *Sai* 塞 (*Sài*), Old Chinese *Sakă, i.e., Scythians, an East Scythian people living to the west of Hsiung-nu territory in what is now Kazakhstan and the Ili River region of Jungaria and southwestward into Central Asia, who spoke a dialect of Scythian usually referred to by modern scholars as *Saka*. The Sogdians also were known as Hu 胡 *Hú*, especially in the Early Middle Ages. These peoples were contiguous neighbors and archaeology has shown Hsiung-nu culture to be practically identical to western Scythian culture.[47] It is shown below that they also spoke dialects of Scythian, as has already been proposed.[48]

47. Di Cosmo (1999); Taylor et al. (2020).

48. Harmatta (1994b: 488) states, "Their royal tribes and kings (*shan-yü*) bore Iranian names and all the Hsiung-nu words noted by the Chinese can be explained from an Iranian language of Saka type. It is therefore clear that the majority of Hsiung-nu tribes spoke an Eastern Iranian language." Bailey (1985: 21–45) also proposes an Iranic origin. However, neither gives any data to support their claims. See Beckwith (2018), which the present book partly updates.

TABLE 8. Classical East Scythian

Reconstruction[a]	Transcription	Gloss
*ăɣámă (< *āgam-)	邯	come near, come alongside[b]
*ăɣámătánă	邯鄲	arrival place (capital)[c]
*bágă	冒[d]	god
*bágătvắnă[e]	冒頓	whose power is from god
*dánăva	單于	(heavenly) ocean-river; emperor
*devă	頭	god
*devămánă	頭曼	god-minded
*ḥăryá ~ *ḥâryá	夏*ḥăryá ~ 華*ḥâryá	royal, royals (*aria*)
*ḥărắ[f] < *ḥâryá	胡	royal, royals (*aria*)
*kayă/*key ~ *kē/ kē <*χšayă	皆 ~ 氏/支	king
*kēŋrâkă (< *kēŋnâkă)	徑路	Scythian short sword[g]
*sarah- ~ saráɣ(ă)	洛**săráɣ*	head; capital city[h]
*suŋlâ < *suglâ	匈奴	Scythian (Hsiung-nu)
*täŋri < *tagri	撐犁	Heaven, Heavenly God (天)
*tvắna- (< tava-)	頓	powerful, capable
*χvadâ (*χwadâ)	孤塗	lord

Note: Asterisks are used sparingly to save space. Most *Suŋlâ (Hsiung-nu) language material in Old Chinese transcription remains unidentified.

[a] These reconstructions are based both on the reconstruction of the Old Chinese transcriptions and on known Old Iranic forms (often also reconstructed). However, I have been as conservative as possible.

[b] Sch. (179): OAve, YAve *ā-gam-* (also OPer *ā-gam-*) '(heran)kommen [come nigh]', etc. Cf. Endnote 168.

[c] See Endnote 149 and especially Chapter 8.

[d] Undoubtedly also *mo* 莫 (*mò*) *bágă in the title of the Wu-sun king, K'un-mo 昆莫, perhaps 'glowing/blazing (sun-)god', from *x^{v}aēna- (Bar. 1861) + baɣa (Bar. 921) 'god'.

[e] An attested Old Iranic name, reconstructed as *Bagātvana (Tav. 140).

[f] The word *hu* 胡 *hú*, OChi *ḥará* is the depalatalized form of the preceding form, *ḥaryá*, in the depalatalizing Northeast Asian subdialect of East Scythian.

[g] See Endnote 150.

[h] Mayrhofer (2006: 21, 24); see Chapter 8, Notes 30–33.

This section focuses on the question of the language and ethnolinguistic identity of these ancient peoples of Mongolia, the Ordos and Inner Mongolia, northern Manchuria, and the north Chinese frontier, and in particular on the long-vexed issue of the language of the Hsiung-nu (*Suŋlâ),[49] whose name is first noted in Chinese sources regarding events of the year 318 BC.[50]

There is actually a considerable amount of ethnolinguistically relevant data on the *Suŋlâ (Hsiung-nu) and eastern *Sakă (塞) languages or dialects, but almost none of it has received serious attention. As with West Scythian in the steppe zone, we have almost exclusively lexical data on these languages. However, it is clear that *Suŋlâ at least is very closely related to Sogdian, which is textually attested from late Antiquity on and has been well studied by specialists in the language.[51]

Although the list of East Scythian lexical items in Table 8 is short, all of it corresponds to West Scythian lexical data. Discussion of selected examples follows the table.

The most salient and firmly established among the above lexical items are discussed below, giving only the minimum necessary linguistic information. Each is introduced first in summary form, paying special attention to historical implications, then it is discussed, focusing on philological and linguistic details. All need further study. Because most linguistic material on Hsiung-nu and other nearby languages is recorded in Chinese, which is written in holistic (partly or wholly ideographic) characters, rather than in segmental (alphabetic or syllabic) letters, the pronunciation of each transcriptional character must be reconstructed, and that is not an easy task. The analyses given here are based on a strictly scientific approach based on hard data. However, traditional reconstructions[52] of Middle Chinese and Old Chinese based on medieval

49. The Old Chinese transcription represents *Suŋlâ, reflecting the native form of the name, *Suŋla. See Endnote 148 on earlier speculations about the Hsiung-nu language.

50. Di Cosmo (1999: 960).

51. Reconstruction of Old Chinese itself needs major technical improvements in order to accord with scientific linguistics and with comparative data, including loanwords and transcriptions in both directions. For recent work toward that goal see Shimunek (2017a) and Beckwith and Kiyose (2018).

52. See Endnote 151 on HSR.

rhyme tables and "spellers" are often cited, despite their intrinsic problems, because of the paucity of attested segmental script transcriptions of Middle Chinese[53] and (even rarer) of Old Chinese forms.

ROYAL (1). *Ḥarya 'royal, of the one legitimate royal line, royals, the royal language'; in Chinese written *hsia* 夏 (*xià*), recording Old Chinese **ḥarya* [ɣăryá].[54] This is the epithet of the Scythian royal lineage, in West Scythian (transcribed in Greek script by Herodotus) as *Aria* and in Old Persian as *Ariya*.[55] Prefixed with the (Chinese) word *ta* 大 (*dà*) 'great; imperial', the Chinese term *Ta Hsia* 大夏 (*Dàxià*) 'Great *Ḥarya*' refers to the imperial realm and its people, region, and language in the northern Ordos, the lands across the Yellow River from it, and in Mongolia (4th century to late 3rd century BC). In the early 2nd century CE it refers to Bactria under *Tuχwară (*Yüeh-chih* 月氏) rule, and the Bactrian language there is later explicitly called <Aria> by Kanishka the Great (r. ca. 127–150 CE).[56] Because *both* regions are called in Chinese *Ta Hsia* 大夏 (*Dàxià*) 'Great *Ḥarya*', meaning 'the *Ḥarya* Empire', and the founders of the Kushan Empire are clearly and unambiguously identified by the Chinese with the Yüeh-chih, who were natives of eastern Central Eurasia, both regions must once have been parts of the Scythian Empire, the Imperial realm ruled by the *Ḥarya* 'Royal' clan of the Scythians. East Scythian *Ḥarya* [ɣa.rya] 'royal', equivalent to West Scythian *Aria* [a.rya] 'royal', is widely attested in eastern Eurasian languages. To summarize the key points, the 4th century BC Old Chinese 大夏 'Great *Ḥarya, *Ḥarya Empire' refers to western Chao and an undefined region north and west of the great northern bend of the Yellow River. Second century BC Old Chinese Ta-hsia 大夏 'Great *Ḥarya' meaning 'Bactria'[57] is directly confirmed by the Bactrian (Kushan Empire)

53. Many such transcriptions exist and should form the basis for Middle Chinese reconstruction. See Beckwith (2007a, 2014, 2016a, 2016b, 2017, 2018), Shimunek (2017a), and for Late Old Chinese, Beckwith and Kiyose (2018).

54. Sta. 562 has 夏 OChi *ghrāʔh, i.e., monosyllabic *ɣra-, since Starostin's long vowels should mostly be short, and vice versa, and his proposed coda is speculation; see Endnote 152.

55. See Chapter 4. In modern works the word is commonly written "arya", an ahistorical spelling.

56. Bracey (2017).

57. Beckwith (2016a); cf. Chapter 4.

inscriptional form *Aria* referring to the Bactrian language, a usage exactly equivalent to West Scythian <Aria> 'royal', an epithet for those belonging to the royal lineage and for the royal language, as discussed in Chapter 4. Thus:

> Old Persian *Aria* <Ariya> ← West Scythian *Aria* <Aria> = Bactrian Αρια *Aria* in Greek script (Bactrian and Classical Scythian) = *Ḥarya in Old Chinese (大)夏 '(Great) *Ḥarya, the Scythian Empire; northwestern Chao; the Bactrian-Kushan Empire'.

ROYAL (2). *Ḥarắ 'royal, royals'. In Imperial Antiquity the Chinese call their northern neighbors and chief rivals by their name, *Hsiung-nu* (*Suŋlâ), but often call them instead *Hu* 胡 *hú*, in Old Chinese *Ḥarắ,[58] a word that has not received much attention by linguists. Its default reference in the Han Dynasty period is actually 'Hsiung-nu'. It did *not* mean 'barbarian' and had no intrinsic pejorative sense at all.[59] It is a typically depalatalized[60] northeast Eurasian form of 夏 OChi *Ḥăryá 'royal; royal one(s)'. The linguistic area in which the depalatalization (or non-palatalization) is attested includes the land of the Tung Hu 東胡 (*Dōnghú*) 'Eastern Hu' (Eastern *Ḥărắ, i.e., 'Eastern Arias'). The Chinese qualifier *Tung* 東 'East(ern)' is clearly intended to distinguish them from the referents of the unqualified word *Hu* 胡 to their west, the Hsiung-nu. This depalatalized form *Hu* 胡 *hú*, OChi *Ḥărắ, appeared one or two centuries after the word *Ḥarya* was borrowed and transcribed into Chinese in the early 4th century BC. The word *Hu* 胡 (*hú*), Old Chinese *Ḥărắ, when it appears in Chinese sources, thus refers not only to the Hsiung-nu or East Scythians (without qualification), but

58. This word belongs to the Old Chinese 魚 'fish' rhyme. On members of that rhyme in Starostin (1989), and some recent discoveries relevant to disyllabic morphemes in Late Old Chinese, see Endnote 153.

59. The Chinese and Hsiung-nu of the time did not perhaps like each other very much, but many modern Sinologists are attached to the modern pejorative senses of the European word *barbarian*, which has no equivalent in Chinese, and have projected it onto Chinese history. See the essay on this topic in Beckwith (2009: 320–362).

60. I.e., it has lost the "palatal" feature or phone *y of *Ḥaryá/Aria 'royal(s)' and has thus become *Ḥará. This change is probably responsible for the final vowel becoming pronounced further back, producing *â. N.B.: The acute diacritic in my reconstructions marks the location of the stress accent.

also to other Scythian speakers, including the Tung Hu 'Eastern' *Ḥărấ to the east of the Hsiung-nu and also the non-Chinese peoples in the territory of Chao and vicinity, which is mentioned in Chinese in the 4th century BC *Tso chuan* as *Ta Hsia* 大夏 'Great *Ḥăryá'. Depalatalized *Ḥărấ, rather than the earlier form *Ḥăryá, thus marks the language of the slightly later Hsiung-nu and other Scythian speakers around the great northern bend of the Yellow River and immediately to the east of them.

The Scythian peoples further to the west continued to be called the *Hsia* 夏 *Ḥaryá* (i.e., the palatalized form), as attested by use of the same transcription in *Ta Hsia* 大夏 'Great *Ḥăryá' to refer to the Yüeh-chih and to Bactria. The Chinese continued to refer to the Scythian region included in the state of Chao as *Ta Hsia* 大夏 'Great *Ḥăryá' in historical contexts,[61] but to its non-Chinese population as *Hu* 胡 *Ḥărấ, suggesting that the speech of the non-Chinese people in the region of Chao had also undergone depalatalization. Thus by that time they probably spoke essentially the same East Scythian dialect spoken by the Hsiung-nu, as did the other peoples bordering on them to the east and southeast. By the Han Dynasty period all, including the Hsiung-nu, were called *Hu* 胡 *Ḥarấ.[62]

The depalatalization spread widely, affecting the Koguryo language (a close relative of Japanese) and also the Han 韓 OChi *Ḥáră[63] languages (the ancient languages of the Korean Peninsula related to the modern Korean language), as well as Chinese dialects in that region. The Chinese eventually extended usage of their transcription *Hu* 胡 *Ḥărấ as a label for many other related peoples in Central Eurasia, but particularly for the Sogdians, who were close cousins of the *Suŋla (Hsiung-nu) and other East Scythians. In other words, the Chinese actually did call the Hsiung-nu *Ḥăryá too, but they had already modified their transcription of that word to *Ḥarấ (*Hu* 胡 *Hu*) to reflect the

61. There are several historical contexts, all needing more study. See further below.

62. See Chapter 4. See Endnote 154.

63. Beckwith (2007a: 94–95, 104–105); note the accent on the first syllable. Old Chinese demonstrably had a moveable stress accent. Cf. Endnote 155.

*Suŋla's own pronunciation in their eastern subdialect of East Scythian. Thus, *Hu* 胡 *Ḥărắ 'royal; belonging to the legitimate royal line', a depalatalized form of *Ḥaryá*, was used at first for the *Suŋlâ (Hsiung-nu, eastern East Scythians) and other peoples of Northeast Asia, and was later extended to Central Asians to the west and southwest of them who were their vassals or under their influence. The Chinese phonetic transcription now read *Hu* 胡 *Hú* was in Old Chinese read **Ḥarắ* [ɣa.ˈrâ] and was used to transcribe the regularly depalatalized Northeast Asian form of the Scythian epithet *Ḥarya* [ɣa.ˈrya].[64] In summary:

> East Scythian *ḥarya [ɣa.rya] 'noble, royal; Scythian' → Old Chinese *ḥaryá 夏 / *ḥâryá 華 'royal; Chinese, China' → Proto-Tibetan *ḥarya [ɣa.ˈrya] > Old Tibetan *rgya* 'Chinese, China'; East Scythian *ḥarya → Togon[65] *ḥarya-* → Old Tibetan *ḥaźa* and, in a Togon place name, *ḥarya-* and (Tibetanized) *rgya-*; + *-l-*[66] > Old Tibetan *rgyal-* 'royal'. Late East Scythian *ḥarắ [ɣa.ˈra] '*Hu* 胡; royal' < East Scythian *ḥarya via the depalatalization characteristic of the Northeast Asian linguistic area.

*ĂɣáMăTáNă. 'The name of the capital city of the state of *Chao* 趙 (*Zhào*)', it is now read *Han-tan* 邯鄲 (*Hándān*) from Middle Chinese ☆ɣamtan,[67] from Old Chinese *Ăgámătánă,[68] and is essentially identical to the name of the capital of Media (modern *Hamadān* ~ *Amadāna* from attested *Agamatāna*) and to the name of the capital of Ch'in, Hsien-yang 咸陽 (*Xiányáng*), from Old Chinese *Ăgắmădánă from

64. For palatalization in Northeast Asia, including Chinese dialects in that region that did not undergo the Late Old Chinese palatalization, see Beckwith (2007a).

65. Togon (*T'u-yü-hun* 吐谷渾 *Tǔyùhún*) is a Serbi-Mongolic language (Shimunek 2017a) spoken in the Ordos region until the people migrated to the Ch'i-lien Mountains and Kokonor in Late Antiquity.

66. This suffix is mysterious. The existence of a Togon transcriptional *rgya* alternating with *ḥarya* in the same place name described in Chapter 4 suggests Togon as a source. Early Serbi-Mongolic had a collective human plural suffix *-l* (Shimunek and Beckwith forthcoming). Further study is needed.

67. Pul. 119, 70.

68. *Han-tan* 邯鄲 (*Hándān*) has been its name from its first attestation in the Warring States period down to the present. The characters are purely transcriptional; they have no actual Chinese etymologies.

*Ăgắmătánă (also recorded in Aramaeo-Sogdian).[69] Ch'in shih huang ti 秦始皇帝 (*Qín Shǐhuángdì*), born Chao Cheng, was raised as a prince of the Chao clan in the capital of Chao, *Han-tan* 邯鄲 (*Hándān*). He later moved to Hsien-yang 咸陽 (*Xiányáng*),[70] the Chao clan's capital city of Ch'in 秦 (Qín), where he became King and eventually unified China, becoming the 'First Emperor'. (See Chapter 7.) From its earliest history Han-tan 邯鄲 (*Hándān*) is associated with non-Chinese people; in view of the city's Scythian name, they were clearly Scythians.[71] As shown in Chapter 8, the two Chinese capital city names are transparently the same word as the Scytho-Mede city name *Agamatāna*, and all three cities were capitals, so *Agamatāna* was a Scythian word for '(the) (capital) city',[72] apparently derived from a participial form of Old Iranic *ā-gam- 'come near, come alongside'.[73]

DIVINELY-MINDED. *Devămană, the name or epithet of the legendary first ruler of the *Suŋla (Hsiung-nu, East Scythians) now read in Chinese *T'ou-man* 頭曼 (*Tóumàn*). The name is Old Iranic *Dewămană (*Devămană), from *Daivamana 'the divinely-minded'. The modern Chinese pronunciation of the transcriptional characters, *T'ou-man* 頭曼, as usual does not reflect well the Middle or Old Chinese pronunciation in important respects. Working back from contemporaneously transcribed Middle Chinese as well as Sogdian cognates, and paying attention to recent discoveries in Late Old Chinese reconstruction, it is clear that the first part of the Scythian word was *dewă (*deva*) 'god' and the second *mană 'mind, minded', a very frequent compounding element in many Old Iranic personal names.[74]

69. Imperial Aramaic transcribes Agamatana as *Ăɣămătā(nă), as shown by the Aramaeo-Sogdian and literary Sogdian transcriptions of *Hsien-yang* 咸陽. See the detailed discussion in Chapter 8; on the problematic Old Persianized form of the name see Endnote 168.

70. Hsien-yang 咸陽 (*Xiányáng*) from Middle Chinese ☆ɣəɨmjɨaŋ (Pul. 119, 360), but from Old Chinese *ĂgămădáɴăNă or the like, is the same name transcribed in a different Old Chinese dialect. See Chapter 8.

71. See Endnote 156.

72. See Chapter 8 for further discussion and for the word *Saraɣ*, apparently meaning 'imperial palace'.

73. See Endnote 157 on the etymology.

74. Beckwith (2018), Beckwith and Kiyose (2018); for examples of similar names see Tav. 596.

In attested Middle Chinese the first character *t'ou* 頭 (*tóu*) is read *'de'u* [^{n}deu] (Tak. 1988: 346), transcribing foreign [deu] ~ [dew]; the traditional (HSR) system has Early Middle Chinese ☆dəu$_1$ (Pulleyblank 1991: 311). This is precisely the inherited Sogdian word for 'god', Sog. <δyω> *dēw* (or *dēv*) from *daiva* (Gharib 150–151); both languages lost their final unstressed vowel *-ă in Late Antiquity before the Sogdian literary language developed.[75] Gharib defines simplex *dēw* negatively as "demon", but that reflects the later-introduced Zoroastrian sense; the words in which it appears as a compounding element show that Sogdian also uses the word in an unambiguously positive or neutral sense, well attested by, e.g., <δyω'kk> *dēwāk* 'heavenly' (Gharib 150); <δyω'štyč> *Dēwāštīč* (i.e., *Dēvāštīč*) 'P.N. of a Sogdian prince' (Gharib 150); and <δyωγωn> *dēw(a)γōn* 'heavenly' (Gharib 151). Sogdian *dēw* 'god' is identical to the Middle Chinese reading of 頭. The history of other old words for 'head' in Chinese suggests that in Old Chinese *t'ou* 頭 MChi *deu* [dew] (which replaced the other words in the spoken language) also had a short final vowel *ă,[76] making it *dewă, corresponding perfectly, both phonetically and semantically, to Old Persian *daiva*, Old Avestan *daēva* '(false) God' (as well as Sanskrit *deva* 'god'), all from PIE *deiwos 'god' (Watkins 2011: 22). The second character *man* 曼 (*màn*) is attested as MChi *man* (Tak. 362). Its word-final coda *n* in Middle Chinese and Mandarin could theoretically correspond in Old Chinese to either a non-labial nasal *N, or *r, including in transcriptions of foreign words, but the later Puyo-Koguryoic versions of the same word in monosyllabicized early Middle Chinese transcriptions have word-final coda ☆ŋ, corresponding to traditional Old Chinese coda *N, confirming that the word had a non-labial nasal *ɴ in it, or rather, a second syllable *n(ă), in Old Chinese.[77] Thus the second component *man(ă) corresponds to Old Iranic *manah* 'mind', which occurs

75. Beckwith (2007a), Beckwith and Kiyose (2018).

76. See Endnote 158.

77. Beckwith (2007a, 2018). Beckwith and Kiyose (2018) shows that many Old Chinese words had disyllabic root morphemes, and the second syllable was often unstressed *ă, phonetically [ə].

in compounds like this in very many names (Tav. 596).[78] The *Suŋlâ (Hsiung-nu) founder's name or title is therefore *dewămană or *devămană 'god-minded' or 'divinely-minded'. Like the later Koguryo and Türk, Hsiung-nu royal names and titles affirm that the dynasty had Heavenly origins.[79]

POWERFUL THROUGH GOD. *Bagătvắnă, the name of the first truly historical Hsiung-nu Great King. He is best known by his name's Mandarin pronunciation, *Mo-tun* 冒頓 (*Mòdùn*)[80] from HSR MChi ☆mək-twən₃ (Pul. 217–218, 84). The son of the semi-legendary *T'ou-man* *Dewămană, he is the actual historical founder (r. 209–174 BC) of the Hsiung-nu Empire per se. He has a very clearly Old Iranic name, *Bagătvănă, attested in the Near East as *Bagātvana*.[81]

The onset of the first element was actually read as a prenasalized stop, *^{m}b, in Western Han period Old Chinese, and in Middle Chinese as well. Words with this onset were often used by the Chinese to transcribe foreign words beginning with *b*. The character has long been accepted to transcribe Old Iranic *baga*, the most widespread Iranic word for 'god; lord' (Tav. 130).[82] In view of the divine genealogy claimed by the Hsiung-nu rulers,[83] and the fact that the Iranic word *baga* 'god, lord' is considered to be the loan-source (via Scythian) of Slavic *bogŭ* 'god',[84] the traditional etymology of the first element is secure. The second element, *-tun*, seems problematic,[85] but there is an overlooked possibility for it, *twăn [twən], as 頓 *-tun* belongs to

78. E.g., *Aryamanā* 'royal-minded' (Tav. 116: "having an Aryan mind"), *Dargamanā* 'long-minded' (Tav. 168), *Mazāmanā* 'great/noble minded' (Tav. 243), etc.

79. See below on the full title of the Hsiung-nu ruler.

80. See Endnote 159 on a widespread modern misreading.

81. Tav. 140. 'Powerful through god' or the like.

82. This is true of all branches of Iranic, unlike OPer *daiva* ~ OAve *daeva*, etymologically 'god', which acquired the negative meaning 'demon' under the influence of Zoroastrianism. It has been passed on to other Iranic languages, such as Sogdian, which did not originally have a negative sense for that word.

83. See this chapter, Note 101, for an epithet of the Hsiung-nu ruler which is explicit about his divine birth.

84. "OCS *bogŭ* 'god', Rus[sian] *bog* 'god' (perhaps Slavic < Iranian)" Mallory and Adams (1997: 161).

85. See Endnote 160 on another misreading.

the same rhyme in Middle Chinese and Old Chinese as *-sun* in Wu-sun 烏孫 from MChi ☆ɔ$_1$-☆swən$_1$ (Pul. 325, 297), which has suggested identification with Old Indic *Aśvin* 'the horse-rider twin gods, the Nasātyās'.[86] Old Iranic *tav-* 'to be strong, capable' (Tav. 566) is attested in *tuvāna-* 'strength' in the names Tuvāna "able, strong", Tuvānī, Tuvāniya (Tav. 328, 608), and *tvan-* 'capable' is attested in Avestan. Best of all, the word occurs together with *Baga* in an attested personal name, *Bagātvana-* 'capable through God' (Tavernier 140, 608), or perhaps 'Powerful by grace of God', echoing the sentiment of Darius I in his inscriptions.

SCYTHIAN SHORT SWORD. *Kēnakă ~ *Kīnakă, the *akinakes* (Greek *akinákēs*', also *kīnákēs*).[87] Sogdian, an ancient East Scythian dialect and Middle Iranic language, has <kyn'k> *kīnāk(ă) ~ kēnāk(ă)* (Gharib 203, Sogdian <kyn'k> *kīnāk*) with regular apocope, reflecting the alternate ancient form sans initial vowel. Leaving aside the usual Greek transcription of Classical Scythian ἀκινάκης *akinakēs with* the initial *a*, i.e., *akīnaka 'Scythian short sword', well attested in Greek (Herodotus iv 62,2–3), the earliest attestation of the word *in an Iranic language* is actually in a Buddhist Sogdian text, in which <kyn'k> renders a "Chinese" word for 'sword'.[88] However, the word is attested earlier in Chinese sources on the *Suŋlâ (Hsiung-nu, East Scythians), where it is said to be specifically the *Suŋlâ short sword. Since linguistically Sogdian and Hsiung-nu are East Scythian dialects in origin, and the *(a)kinakes* is a standard part of Scythian physical culture, the word is Scythian. The transcription, however, clearly reflects ongoing changes in Old Chinese phonology.

86. Beckwith (2009: 376–377). The reconstruction of the vowel *i* in *Aśvin is problematic, and the second syllable onset is Indic. The historical Wu-sun peoples' name is also attested in Greek (Strabo xi 8,2, etc.). Although the Greek transcription was unfortunately rather corrupt already before Strabo, its reference to the Wu-sun is solidly established by the virtually identical historical accounts of the conquest of Bactria in the Chinese and Greek sources. The reconstruction *Aśvən(ă) is thus better for Wu-sun, which is still evidently the name *Aśvin.

87. *LSJ*; Schmitt (2002/2012). The physical artifact is a standard part of the weaponry in the archaeological "Scythian Triad".

88. Schmitt (1967: 138, note 160), citing Émile Benveniste, *Textes Sogdiens édités, traduits et commentés* (Paris, 1940), 202. The text is not given by Schmitt.

In the *Han Shu*[89] (completed in 111 CE), the Hsiung-nu short sword is called *ching-lu tao* 徑路刀 (*jìnglù dāo*), i.e., '*ching-lu* short sword'. The characters *ching-lu* 徑路 transcribe the Hsiung-nu word; *tao* 刀 *dāo* 'short sword' is a Chinese word. The meaning is crystal clear, and the word is obviously close to the West Scythian form, but the phonology is problematic. The transcription consists of *ching* 徑 MChi ☆kɛjŋ$_3$ (Pul. 160) < OChi [homonym in first tone 經] *kēŋ (Sta. 583) ~ *keng (Baxter 1992: 768) + *lu* 路 MChi ☆lɔ$_3$ (Pul. 200) < OChi *graχ (Sta. 563: *rāh) ~ *grak (Baxter 1992: 775: *g-raks). The transcription is reconstructed by Pulleyblank (1999: 50) as OChi *kájŋ^h ráχ. There is of course no syllable contact problem in the original word, but the two long vowels [e:] and [a:] could perhaps have lengthened the *n* as well, producing three long moras, in which the intrusive *n* was reinterpreted as *ŋ*. Then, by analogy with the normal Northeast Asian sound change, the second syllable onset *n was reshaped as *r, to form *kēŋrāk(ă) ~ or as *l, to form LOC *kēŋlāk(ă). Despite the unclear origin of the intermediary form *kēŋnāk(ă), it is close to attested Sogdian <kyn'k> *kēnāk(ă) ~ kīnāk(ă)*,[90] the Sogdian dialect form of Classical Scythian (ἀ)κινάκης (*a*)*kinakēs*, i.e., *(a)kīnaka 'Scythian short sword'. However, the phonology of the transcription reflects the *Suŋlâ (Hsiung-nu) preference for disyllabic words of the shape CVŋ.rV(C)(ă) / CVŋ.lV(C(ă) (as in their name, *Suŋlâ), which is characteristic of the Northeast Asian linguistic area, so the received form is evidently the result of analogical reformation such as suggested here.

HEAVEN, HEAVENLY GOD. The Hsiung-nu word *Täŋri, 'Heaven (天), Heavenly God'. It is transcribed *ch'eng-li* 撐犁 (*chénglí*)—in Old Chinese *täŋri ~ *täg̃ri [tæŋgri]—and corresponds to the word *targi* 'Heavenly God' in the name of the West Scythian national ancestor,

89. *Han Shu* 94b: 3801.

90. Gharib (1995: 203). It is uncertain when, exactly, word-final unstressed *ă*—short *a* [ə]—was canonically deleted in Sogdian and several other early Middle Iranic languages. For Late Old Chinese, it appears to have been deleted around the late 3rd or early 4th century; see Beckwith and Kiyose (2018).

Targitaos, Scythian *targi-tavah 'the powerful one of God'. The only major difference between the two is metathesis (interchange of linear position) of the velar *g* in *targi* to resolve the violation of the Syllable Contact Law in Proto-Scythian *tagri.[91] East Scythian is faithful to the Proto-Scythian sequence of phones, and has nasalized *g into *ŋ to resolve the Syllable Contact Law violation.[92] Herodotus identifies *Thagimasadas,* a clear transcription of *Tagi Mazda,[93] as a god worshipped solely by the Royal Scythians, the apex clan. That divinity can only be the unnamed Heavenly creator God in the oldest version of the national foundation myth,[94] who is the Royal Scythians' ancestor god. He is indirectly identified in the name of his son, the first man or king, *Targitaos* *Targi-tavah 'the powerful one of Heaven', but also (in view of the other transcriptions) in the name *Thagi* (a normal alternative transcription of *Tagi) *Mazda,* 'Heavenly God'. Together these names thus represent Proto-Scythian *Tagri Mazdā,[95] 'Heaven God', the head of the entire heavenly-earthly feudal-hierarchical order. See further in the following section.

THE HEAVENLY LORD, THE UNIVERSE RIVER. *Täŋri Xvadâ Dānava, the full title of the *Suŋlâ (Hsiung-nu, East Scythian) ruler in the *Han Shu,* is transcribed in Late Old Chinese using six Chinese characters, containing three Scythian words. The first, *täŋri* 'Heaven, Heavenly God, just discussed above, was long ago recognized as the loan source

91. See above in this chapter. Note that metathesis is the most favored solution for such violations in West Scythian, to the extent that the late Classical period inscriptions near the Black Sea, and Scythian's modern descendant Ossetian-Alanic, are full of metathesized cognates.

92. Strictly phonologically, the East Scythian solution is well attested in many other examples from Northeast Asia, as discussed below.

93. The word *Mazda* also occurs in the name *Octamasades* (q.v. below), a son of Ariapeithes (Mayrhofer 2006: 14), thus establishing that the Greek form *masada transcribes the same Scythian word. Mayrhofer (id.), following Schmitt, reconstructs *masada-* as *mazatā 'Größe sein' ('to be great'). However, it is explicitly part of the name of the proprietary God of the apex clan, the Royal Scythians, namely *Thagimasadas,* so it is clearly *Mazdā,* the word for the very same One Great God of Early Zoroastrianism.

94. Herodotus gives the Scythian version of "Zeus" as *Papaeus,* but it is Greek, or at best Scytho-Greek.

95. The textual variant Θαμιμασάδας *Thamimasadas* in the manuscript tradition is generally considered to be of no value, but it could reflect a genuine graphic variant, *Θαγριμασάδας **Thagrimasadas.*

of the Turkic word *Täŋri* 'Heaven, Heavenly God, Tengri'; the second (identifiable even using the traditional Old Chinese reconstructions of Starostin) is the same as the Sogdian word *χwadâ* 'lord'. The third (also recognizable in Starostin's system) is effectively identified (from western sources) in Bartholomae as the Classical Scythian word for 'river'.

The full title of the Hsiung-nu ruler in the *Han Shu* is *Ch'eng-li ku-t'u ch'an-yü* 撐犁孤塗單于 (*Chénglí gūtú chányú*), glossed individually as 'The Ch'an-yü[96] the Son of Heaven', and also collectively as 'the Hsiung-nu expression for Emperor'. The same passage also notes, "As for *ch'an-yü*, it is the appearance of vastness, which is to say it is vast, like Heaven (單于者，廣大之貌也，言其象天單于然也。)."[97] Close examination shows that we cannot accept the gloss of the second element as 'son'. However, there are still clearly three words in the title, which are transparently Scythian and can be identified with some certainty.[98] They are discussed individually below.

HEAVEN, HEAVENLY GOD. *Täŋri. The first two characters *Ch'eng-li* 撐犁 (*Chénglí*) correspond to the *Han shu* gloss *T'ien* 天 (*Tiān*) 'Heaven'. The transcription has long ago been recognized as representing a word best known from Turkic: Old Turkic *Täŋri* 'Heaven, *Tengri*', the name of the God of Heaven. The Hsiung-nu and Old Turkic words are identical semantically, and virtually identical phonetically. They are clearly the same word, as discussed above.

It is significant that *Täŋri* is the only word in Old Turkic with the syllable contact cluster *ŋr*, and it also does not follow Turkic word-formation rules. It is thus not a native Turkic word and has long been accepted to be a loan from some other language, which is agreed to be Hsiung-nu[99] because of the Chinese transcription.

The West Scythians' national foundation myth says their ancestor, *Targitaos*, is the son of Heavenly God and the daughter of the river

96. The characters *Ch'an-yü* 單于 *chányú* were formerly read as *Shan-yü* by Sinologists.

97. *Han Shu* 94a: 3751.

98. Unfortunately, it seems there is still not a single published fully scientific critical edition of a premodern literary Chinese text, including of course the *Han shu*.

99. Clauson (1972: 523).

god.[100] As shown above, the first part of his name, *targi*, corresponds to the first word, *tagi, in *Thagimasadas*, the name of the god worshipped only by the Royal Scythians. As he is their proprietary deity, he must be the foundation myth's God of Heaven, whose Scythian name Herodotus does not directly provide. However, *Targi* and *Tagi correspond to *Täŋri, the word for 'Heaven' and the first word in the full title of the Hsiung-nu ruler.[101]

The East Scythian (Hsiung-nu) word glossed as 'Heaven (天)' is known only in Chinese transcription. In modern pronunciation the characters are read *ch'eng-li* 撐犁 (*chēnglí*) [ʈʂʰəŋli] 'Heaven'—in Pulleyblank's idiosyncratic Middle Chinese ☆tʰraɨjŋ / ☆tʰrɛːjŋ + MChi ☆lɛj. Leaving aside doubtful details in his reconstruction,[102] the Middle Chinese onset is unvoiced, and the entire string corresponds in sound and meaning to Old Turkic *täŋri*. Neither he nor anyone else has seriously doubted that the two represent the same word, 'Heaven', the name of Heavenly God.

Altogether there are thus three attested forms of the same Scythian word for 'Heaven':

West Scythian	*targi-*	'first part of the name of the son of Heavenly God'
West Scythian	*tagi*	'first part of the name of (Heavenly) God'
East Scythian	*täŋri*	'first part of the name of the son of Heavenly God; Heaven'

These forms are all derivable directly from Proto-Scythian *tagri.

100. This is confirmed by a Chinese record of another Hsiung-nu (East Scythian) royal epithet, which reads: 天地所生日月所置匈奴大單于 (*Han Shu*, 94a, from CTP). It may be translated "'the great Hsiung-nu *ch'an-yü*, born of Heaven and Earth, established by the Sun and Moon.' However, there are no non-Chinese words in it except for *Hsiung-nu* 匈奴 and *ch'an-yü* 單于.

101. In addition, the first named East Scythian is *Dew(ă)man(ă) 'the God-minded' (see above in this section), agreeing with the legends and myths in which the first Scythian was of Heavenly origin.

102. Pul. 53, 187. Pulleyblank's transcription represents ☆ʈʰ for the word onset, which is intended to explain the Chinese word's modern Pekingese Mandarin onset [ʈʂʰ]. He himself (Pulleyblank 1984) says it is not necessary to reconstruct retroflex onsets for Middle Chinese. Unfortunately the rare character *ch'eng* 撐 (*chēng*) [ʈʂʰəŋ] has so far not been found in attested segmental transcriptions of Middle Chinese.

The Mandarin and Middle Chinese forms of 撐犁 (*chēnglí*) *Täŋri have *ŋ* for the coda of the first syllable, as in the first syllable of the name *Hsiung-nu* itself, *Suŋlâ, each representing a Northeast Asian language in which a *g/ɣ coda in syllable contact with a following liquid (r/l) onset became *ŋ, following the Syllable Contact Law. Thus *Hsiung-nu* 匈奴 *Suŋlâ, from *Suglâ/*Suɣlâ corresponds to a Sogdian dialect form *Suɣla related to the attested Sogdian forms *Suɣdīk, Suwlī,* etc. 'Sogdiana, Sogdian(s)'.[103] Analyzing the word for 'Heaven', it is clearly to be reconstructed for early East Scythian (Hsiung-nu) as *tagri, in which the *g became *ŋ* when it nasalized according to the regular eastern East Scythian syllable contact rule, producing *Taŋri ~ *Täŋri, the donor form of Old Turkic *Täŋri* 'Heaven'.

Hsiung-nu *ch'eng-li* from *Täŋri, from Proto-Scythian *tagri 'Heaven', corresponds exactly to West Scythian *Targi* 'Heaven' in the name of the first National Origin myth's 'son of Heaven' Targitaos *Targi-tavah 'Powerful one of Heaven', which has metathesized the *r* of the Proto-Scythian form *tagri to repair the violation of the Syllable Contact Law (in the string *gr).

The reconstruction of the word for '(God of) Heaven' as Proto-Scythian *Tagri is further supported by **Tagi* in Θαγιμασάδας *Thagimasadas,*[104] the Scythian name of a god worshipped only by the Royal Scythians, according to Herodotus (iv 59). The second part of the name is undoubtedly *mazdā*, in Early Zoroastrianism the name of the monotheistic creator God *Ahura Mazdā* 'Lord Mazdā',[105] well attested in the Old Avestan *Gāthās* and the Old Persian inscriptions of Darius the Great.[106] The word is also attested in a West Scythian royal prince's name, Ὀκταμασάδης Octamasades (Herodotus iv 80), the first element of which has been recognized as Old Iranic *uχta- 'spoken, word', attested in Avestan *uχda-*.[107]

103. See Endnote 147.

104. Mayrhofer (2006: 12). See also this chapter, Note 96, on the manuscript variant.

105. Or '*the Ahura* (Sanskrit *Asura* 'the older gods') Mazdā'. However, much of what has been written on this and relevant topics is based on reading beliefs and assertions drawn from late Zoroastrianism or even the Vedas into the highly uncertain text of the *Gāthās*.

106. It is also attested much earlier, no doubt as a theonym, in the name of a ruler in the Amarna Letters (Witzel 2014); see Endnotes 79 and 86.

107. Mayrhofer (2006: 14).

Since it appears *mazda* (whatever its ultimate etymology) meant in practice 'the one great creator God', the two names are 'Heavenly God' and 'Word of God', or the like. The word **Tagi* (with *r deleted to repair the violation of the Syllable Contact Law in Proto-Scythian *Tagri) is thus the Royal Scythian dialect form of the same word as *Targi* and the East Scythian dialect form *Täŋri, all from *Tagri 'Heaven'.

LORD. *χvadâ. The second two characters, *ku-t'u* 孤塗 (*gūtú*), require discussion of the glosses. Giele (2010: 256, note 132) says:

> The 'So-yin,' after quoting these lines [i.e., the full six character title], adds a report from the *Hsüan-yen ch'un-ch'iu* 玄晏春秋: "Shih An read the *Han shu* and did not understand this word [i.e., *Ch'an-yü*]. There was a Hu 胡 [Hsiung-nu] slave next to him who said to him: 'This is what the Hu call Son of Heaven ["emperor"].'"

In the *Han Shu*'s character-by-character Chinese gloss of the Hsiung-nu title, *ku-t'u* 孤塗 (*gūtú*) is Chinese 子 'son', but that is clearly a misunderstanding by the ancient glossator. The comment of the Hsiung-nu informant applies only to *ch'an-yü* 單于, which has the holistic Chinese gloss 天子 'the emperor (lit., son of heaven)', so we do not know what the second two-character element *ku-t'u* 孤塗 means. Although it could of course mean 'son', and many scholars have proposed many identifications with words in many languages, without success, closer examination shows it to be a clear Old Chinese transcription of a different word entirely.

The word consists graphically of two parts, written *ku* 孤 (*gū*) from MChi ☆kɔ$_1$ plus t'u 塗 (*tú*) MChi ☆dɔ$_1$ (Pul. 110, 311), respectively from OChi *k^{w}â[108] and OChi *dâ.[109] That gives OChi *k^{w}âdâ. Old Chinese did not have the onset phone [χ], so foreign words with that sound needed to be transcribed using the unvoiced velar stop, *k. OChi *k^{w}âdâ thus reflects either foreign *k^{w}ada or, in the Iranic context, no doubt *χ^{w}adâ ("x^{v}adâ" ~ "kh^{w}adâ") 'lord'. That fits the phonology of the

108. Cf. Sta. 561 狐 [MSC *hú* 'fox'] OChi *g(h)wā [i.e., *ɣwā] for *ɣwa → (loaned to) Tibetan ཝ་ *wa* (from earlier འྭ་ *ɣ^{w}a*) 'fox', an accepted loanword from early Chinese.

109. For *t'u* 塗 MSC *tú* 'road' cf. its homonym and synonym *t'u* 途 MSC *tú*, attested MChi 途 *do* (Tak. 310), 'road'. Both should go back to LOC *dâ. Pulleyblank (1999) reconstructs the word as OChi *kwala.

transcription, it makes perfect sense, and the word is well attested in Sogdian, a Middle Iranic offshoot of western East Scythian.[110]

The first part of the Hsiung-nu title is thus *Täŋri *χ^{w}adâ 'Heaven(ly) Lord'.

RIVER, OCEAN, UNIVERSE-RIVER. *Dānăva. The third pair of characters, *ch'an-yü* 單于 *chányú* constitutes the usual, normal word for 'the emperor' or 'the great king' of the Hsiung-nu, very well attested in Chinese sources. Its literal meaning and etymology have remained unclear. The gloss by the "Hu [i.e., Hsiung-nu] slave (of the Chinese official)" quoted above says the entire six-character string is 'the Hsiung-nu "word" for "Emperor" (天子)'. However, the expression 天子, though literally 'Son of Heaven', is the ordinary Chinese honorific term for 'the Emperor (*of China*)', which as noted is a holistic term. From the standpoint of the Hsiung-nu (*Hu*) slave here, it meant 'the *Hsiung-nu* Emperor', i.e., the Ch'an-yü. Thus the individual word-by-word glosses are unreliable. They have been added later by someone who did not know the language transcribed very well, if at all.[111]

The main element in the title is *ch'an-yü* 單于 (*chányú*) written *ch'an* 單 (*chán*) from MChi ☆dʑian$_1$ (Pul. 48), with a voiced onset. It is normally read in Chinese *tan* 單 (*dān*) < MChi ☆tan$_1$ (Pul. 70) plus *yü* 于 (*yú*) from MChi ☆wuă (Pul. 381) from OChi *wa.[112] The reading *ch'an* 單 *chán* here is a "Hsiung-nu reading" used only for this one specific foreign word, so the affrication which has developed in the transcriptional character reading is no doubt from a Chinese dialect. As there are other parallel examples, e.g., *ch'eng-li* = *täŋri* (with unvoiced onset), we expect *ch'an-* to go back to theoretical Old Chinese *dan- or *dar- (with voiced onset as in the Middle Chinese 'Hsiung-nu' reading). The character *tan* 單 is one of the most frequently occurring in Mandarin, as well as in Literary Chinese, and such ordinary characters were preferentially

110. Gharib (1995: 435) Sogdian *xwd'w* 'king, lord', read by Gharib as *xuδāw*; equated with Sogdian *xwt'w* 'king, lord', read *xutāu, xutāw* (id., 440).

111. For another example of this practice see the Chinese glosses to the Chieh Prophecy, which is in Archaic Turkic (Shimunek et al., 2015).

112. Sta. 561–564, Rhyme Class XIII. This character does not occur in a *Shih ching* rhyme, but many characters in which it is a phonetic do occur.

used to transcribe foreign words. Also, it has recently been discovered that many (perhaps most) Old Chinese substantive words or morphemes were disyllabic and typically ended in a short unstressed vowel, *ă.[113] That indicates the Old Chinese voiced onset reading *dană for the transcriptional character *tan* 單.[114] As the second character reading in Old Chinese was clearly *wa, transcriptional *ch'an-yü* 單于 MSC *chányú* is *danăwa, or in Iranist spelling, *danava. It is a perfect transcription of the Avestan (Imperial Scythian dialect) word *dānav(a)- ~ dānu-* 'river, stream',[115] attested in Greek as Τάναϊς *Tanaïs*, representing *Dānav- 'the (great) River', the name of the great central river of West Scythia, the Don (from *Dān-). The Hsiung-nu ruler's title or epithet, *Ch'an-yü*, is thus Scythian *Dānava 'the (great) river'.

A word for 'river' or 'ocean' may seem odd as the title or epithet of the ruler of a great empire, but in Central Eurasia many rulers' titles or epithets are exactly the word for a 'great river' or 'sea, ocean'.

For example, the name or epithet *Attila* is transparently a form of the name *Attila ~ Atil ~ Itil ~ Etel* (and no doubt *Etzel*) 'the Volga River'—a truly vast river. The name or epithet of the youngest of his three sons and successors, Dengizikh, means '(the one of) the sea/ocean'. The same word, *deŋ(g)iz*, in the Middle Mongol *e > i* dialect is *Chinggis* [čiŋgis] 'sea, ocean',[116] the title of Chinggis Khan (popularly known in English as "Genghis Khan"), i.e., 'Ocean Khan',[117] while *dalai* in *Dalai Lama* 'Ocean Lama', is Mongolian for 'sea, ocean'.[118] In this case, if *ch'an-yü*

113. Beckwith and Kiyose (2018).

114. See Endnote 161.

115. Bar. (733–734) *dānav-* 'Fluss, Strom [river, stream]'. The Scythian word for '(great) river', *dānu* (Watkins 2011: 15) → Greek *Tanaïs* 'the Don River'; cf. Chapter 6, Note 92 and Endnote 154.

116. Underlyingly *tiğis [tiŋgis] (the string *ti is regularly attested as *či* in Mongolian). The *e*-dialect form is attested in Middle Mongolian as *teŋgis* 'sea', and is a loan from Turkic *teŋgiz / teŋiz ~ deŋgiz / deŋiz* 'sea, ocean'. The alternate Turkic forms could have developed from either *teŋiz/deŋiz* or from *teŋgiz/deŋgiz*, as both are attested. They also exhibit the well-known unsolved "t/d problem" in Turkic.

117. On this identification see Beckwith (2009: 415) and especially Baumann (2012).

118. The Classical Tibetan equivalent, རྒྱ་མཚོ་ *rgyamtsho* 'ocean', forms part of the long reign name of each Dalai Lama. The tradition of transcribing, but not actually translating, the title of the 'paramount ruler' in almost any language goes back at least to the Early Middle Ages, when it was part of diplomatic protocol. Well known examples in the Early Middle Ages include the

does evoke more or less what the Chinese gloss says, 'something vast', the likelihood historically, based on the comparative evidence of other great Central Eurasian rulers' names or epithets, is that a large body of water is meant. In the case of the Hsiung-nu, their homeland in the Ordos was centered on the great northern bend of the Yellow River, one of the world's largest rivers, and their realm at its height extended to the Pacific Ocean. The Scythians (including the Hsiung-nu), the Türks, and the Mongols had approximately this same geographical homeland. *Ch'an-yü* is the normal, ubiquitous title of the Hsiung-nu ruler in Chinese sources, so it is comparable to *chiŋgis* 'ocean' in Temüjin's title *Chiŋgis Khan*, i.e., 'Ocean Khan'. What remains is the etymology and semantics of *ch'an-yü* within Scythian.

A sentence in the Middle Turkic *Oğuz-Nameh* (13th century) reads: *Munda İtil müren*[119] *degen bir dalay bar érdi* 'Here there was a great sea (*dalay*) called "the Itil River".'[120] The word for 'river' in Scythian is attested in Avestan (an Imperial Scythian dialect) as *dānav-* 'river, in compounds *dānu-*'. It is attested in the names of the greatest rivers in western Scythian territory: the just discussed *Don* (< ancient *dān-, attested in ancient Greek as Τάναϊς *Tánaïs*,[121] reflecting Scythian *Dānava-*),[122] the Dnieper and Dniester,[123] and undoubtedly the *Danube* (Latin *Danuvius*), the greatest river of Western Europe. The Chinese transcription *ch'an-yü* 單于 can be reconstructed as 單 MChi *tan (Pul. 70, 48) < OChi *dan(ă)

---

titles of the rulers of the Chinese, Old Turkic, and Old Tibetan empires. In the case of the Hsiung-nu, we see it half a millennium earlier.

119. The word *müren* 'river' here is a loanword from Mongolian.

120. Clauson (1972: 502), from Bang and Rachmati (1932: 694 lines 157–158), my translation. *Itil* is a variant of the name *Atil* 'the Volga River'.

121. Long before Herodotus' time Classical Greek script had entirely lost the capacity of directly representing the phone [w] (formerly written with the letter <ϝ>, called the "digamma") so it often must be reconstructed. This is a clear example. Its traditional Iranistic transcription is "v", though the phone in question, [w], was certainly not articulated as [v] in Old Iranic languages.

122. Bar. 733, 734: YAve *dānav-* 'Fluss, Strom'; . . . *dānu-drājah-* 'von der Länge eines Flusses ('the length of a river'), so lang wie die Flüsse' ('as long as the rivers'); cf. Vasmer (1923: 74), who derives *Don* from Scythian *dānu* 'water, river', citing Ossetian (a direct descendant of Scythian), which has *don* 'water, river'.

123. The *Dnieper*, Late Greek Δάναπρις *Danapris*, from Scythian **dānu-apara* 'river in the rear, farther river (**apara*, farther)', in earlier Antiquity, including Herodotus, usually called the *Borysthenes* (von Bredow 2006), and the Dniester (Rus. *Dnestr*) from Scythian **dānu-nazdya* 'nearer river, river in front', from *nazdya-, 'nearer') (Watkins 2011: 15).

with voiced onset (*d-) as discussed above + 于 OChi *wa (Sta. Rhyme 13), giving *danăwa, exactly corresponding to Avestan-dialect Imperial Scythian *dānava 'great river', for the East Scythian (Hsiung-nu) ruler's chief title or epithet. This identification appears to be confirmed by Old Turkic *taluy* 'sea, ocean' and Middle Mongolian *dalai* 'sea, ocean; large body of water', which seem to be variant forms of one word. Clauson identifies Old Turkic *taluy* as an obvious loanword from some other language.[124] The long-puzzling *T* of the Greek transcription *Tanaïs* 'Don River' (instead of the expected **Danais*, with *D*) may well be connected to the unexplained interchange of *t* and *d* in word onset position in the Turkic and Mongolic languages, which later replaced the Iranic descendants of Scythian.[125]

The medieval Turkic and Mongolian words for 'sea, ocean', such as the Middle Mongolian dialect word *Chiŋgis*, via *Tingiz from Turkic *Teŋgiz/Deŋgiz ~ Teŋiz/Deŋiz* 'ocean, sea', normally do not have the literal meaning 'oceanic' or 'vast', except implicitly; rather they refer to the "ocean-river" of ancient geography-cosmology, which included our galaxy, the "River of Stars" or Milky Way. The word *taluy* formed part of the Old Turkic expression *taluy ögüz* 'ocean river' or 'ocean stream', from *taluy* 'ocean, sea' plus *ögüz* 'river', indicating the ocean continuing as a river into the heavens as the Milky Way. As it is boundless, like the ocean-river of stars stretching across the heavens, it effectively means 'the universe'.[126] In concert with the Scythians' idea of their royal line being of Heavenly descent, Scythian *dānava-* too must have the same heavenly reference. And a 'great river', especially one that includes the Milky Way, the river of Heaven, is certainly vast. So the Hsiung-nu ruler's title, today read *ch'an-yü* 單于 (*chányú*) in Chinese, is an Old Chinese transcription of East Scythian *dānava* 'the Universe-River', which is, as the gloss says, 'the image of vastness'.

124. Clauson (1972: 502). *Taluy* is strikingly un-Turkic phonologically, and is undoubtedly a loanword. However, Clauson's specific proposal, based on an early Sinologist's speculation, is quite unlikely.

125. The problem and the lexical relationships are clear. What is needed is a dedicated historical phonological and dialectological study.

126. Baumann (2012). I am indebted to Brian Baumann for kindly sending me a copy of his extremely interesting, learned article on this topic.

KING. *χšay ~ *χšayă, 'king; ruler'. West Scythian *χšayă* is attested in Greek transcription as ξαι- *ksai*- 'king; to rule'. The word is attested also in the second element *-chih* 氏/支 (*-zhī*), Old Chinese *kay(ă) ~ *kē from *χ(š)ay(ă)-, in the name of the Iranic former rulers of the Eastern Steppe and overlords of the Hsiung-nu, the *Yüeh-chih* 月氏 / 月支 'the Tuχwară kings'. The construction of the latter name is exactly parallel to that of *Sai wang* 塞王 'the Saka (Scythian) kings', Herodotus' Greek translation "the Royal Scythians", and many other parallel Central Eurasian examples.[127] The word also occurs as the second element *-chih* 氏 in the title of the Hsiung-nu queens, Yen-chih 閼氏 *Yān-zhī* '*Ar kings/rulers',[128] and is alternately written as 支 (MChi dial. *ke[129] from OChi *kē[130] or *key from earlier *kay in the name *Yüeh-chih* 月氏 / 月支. It is the same word as 'king', since the imperial queens also certainly came from a royal lineage. The East Scythian form of the word **χ(š)ay(ă) 'king' is thus attested only after it had undergone simplification of the onset cluster *χš* to *χ*, regular fortition of *χ* to *k*, with eventual umlaut of *a to *e because of the coda *y.[131] It is attested as a loanword in Archaic Koguryo *key in *makrikey [莫離支], a compound of *mak(ă)ri 'true

127. See Chapter 4, Endnote 94, Beckwith (2010), and Lincoln (1991).

128. Pul. 355, glossing it "queen of the Xiongnu". However, Karlgren (1957: 85 §270a) gives for 閼 the forms "[OChi] *ât*, [MChi] *ât*, [MSC] *o*" and glosses the Chinese word, which occurs in the *Chuangtzu*, as 'obstruct, stop'. See Endnote 162. Its form remains obscure.

129. Attested in Archaic Japanese as **key* 'queen' (*JDB* 246), in Old Japanese as *ki* (Kōno 1987). The two Middle Chinese reconstructions of Pulleyblank (Pul. 404: 氏 *tɕiă/*tɕi 支 *tɕiă/*tɕi) represent Central dialect forms and ignore the widespread use of 支 for [ke] in Chinese transcriptions of foreign words even in Early Middle Chinese times (Beckwith 2007a), and it was still pronounced [ki] in recent Mandarin dialects (Kar. 228).

130. Sta. 567: 支 *ke (i.e., *kē in my system, which agrees with Pulleyblank's for vowel length in that Starostin's system has long where we have short and vice versa). However, in view of the Old Koguryo form of the word, it is likely that the northern Old Chinese reading of 支 was *kăy or the like; see below. On the radical changes undergone by Chinese in the transition from Late Old Chinese to pre–Middle Chinese, see Beckwith (2016a, 2017), Shimunek (2017a), and Beckwith and Kiyose (2018).

131. However, this could well be a transcriptional chimera based on strictly Chinese developments. The reading *kē/*kī (or the like) is well attested in early Chinese transcriptions of foreign words and is an accepted reconstruction of a Middle Chinese dialect reading that is not attested in HSR materials (which are from the Sung Dynasty, a millennium after the Hsiung-nu Empire broke up). In Modern Standard Chinese the character 支 or 氏 *in these words* is always read *chih* [ʈʂɨ] (*zhī*). The popular reading of 氏 in 月氏 as *shih* (*shì*)—its reading for the *Chinese* word meaning 'clan; sir', etc.—is incorrect in these words.

(正)' + *key [支] 'king (王)', and well attested in Old Koguryo as ☆kăy/☆key [皆] 'king' and in Old Japanese *ke* (from *kay) 'king' (王).[132]

The proximal homeland of the Japanese-Koguryoic speakers was in the southeastern reaches of Hsiung-nu territory. They were for centuries dominated by the East Scythians, including the historical Hsiung-nu. Since Japanese-Koguryoic also disallows both fricative onsets and onset clusters, that explains the Koguryo forms attested in Chinese transcription.[133] Classical Scythian *xšay* is thus attested in late East Scythian as *kay based on attested Old Koguryo *kay/*key and Old Japanese *ke* (from *kay), both of which are from Common Japanese-Koguryoic (CJK) *kay. This establishes that CJK did not split until after the historically known Hsiung-nu influence over at least some of the people who spoke that ancestral form of the Japanese-Koguryoic languages.[134]

(EASTERN) EAST SCYTHIAN, Hsiung-nu. *Suŋlâ, the Old Chinese reading of the transcription 匈奴 now read *Hsiung-nu* (*Xiōngnú*), is the native pronunciation of the name *Scythian* in the eastern East Scythian dialect spoken by the people we know as "Hsiung-nu". The name derives straightforwardly from the dialect form **Suɣla* 'Sogdian (East Scythian)', from Old Iranic *Sugda* ~ *Suɣda* 'Sogdian (East Scythian)', from

132. The usual transcription is 皆, for which Pul. 153 has *early* "Early Middle Chinese" ☆kəɨj and *later* "Early Middle Chinese" ☆kɛːj. The first (older) of these forms is an alternate way of transcribing ☆kăɨj. Since this reconstruction of 皆 applies to the Early Middle Chinese period it represents contemporaneous Old Koguryo *kăy 'king'. As it is an alternate transcription of the word for 'king' written 支 *kē, and since the Late Old Japanese transcriptions (Kōno 1987) with Old Japanese *ke* are regularly from earlier *kay ~ *kai *within Japanese*, the Japanese-Koguryoic words for 'king' are loans from East Scythian *kay(ă), which is from Old Scythian *χšayă* 'king'. On the Japanese-Koguryoic forms see Beckwith (2007a: 122–125, 250), which now needs to be revised to incorporate the new data and findings discussed here.

133. I.e., the Japanese-Koguryoic languages, and Hsiung-nu before them, did not allow word-onset consonant clusters as in *xšay*, so they simplified the word to *kay; the vowel later umlauted to give *key ~ *kē.

134. Old Koguryo *kay ~ *key 'king' is very well attested, as is its Japanese cognate *ki* from Old Japanese *ke*, from *kay. Attested Archaic Koguryo *ka 'clan chief' and Puyo-Koguryo *ka 'king' appear to have undergone deletion of the coda *y. (For the Japanese-Koguryoic data and discussion see Beckwith 2007a.) This *ka is in turn likely to be the loan source of Serbi (Hsien-pei) *ka and thus perhaps of the Serbi title *kaɣan 'Great King, Emperor' (precise etymology still uncertain), which is first attested as 可汗 among the Serbi in *Chin shu* 晉書 125 (Shimunek 2017a: 367–368, note 443). Nevertheless, the transcriptions ending in *y* dominate, so the Scythian loanword appears to be primary in the Northeast Asian linguistic area.

Old Scythian *Skuδa 'Scythian'.[135] Transcriptions of the late adjective form *sugli- 'Sogdian' reflect the unconditioned canonical change of δ to *l* in Sogdian (and East Scythian generally). The resulting *Suɣla[136] triggered the Syllable Contact Law, which in Northeast Asia regularly changed a preceding syllable coda *g/ɣ to *ŋ* before a liquid (*r* or *l*). The result is the name *Suŋla '*Hsiung-nu*', which etymologically is the same word as *Sugda* ~ **Suɣla* 'Sogdia, Sogdian, (western) East Scythian', all late forms of *Skuδa* 'Scythian'.[137] The closeness of the two ethnonyms mirrors the closeness of their two dialects within Scythian, as shown in this section.

> The Old Chinese transcription *Hsiung-nu* 匈奴 *Suŋlâ for *Suŋla straightforwardly corresponds to the general East Scythian dialect form *Suɣla-, from *Suɣda-* ~ *Sug(u)da* 'Sogdia', ultimately from *Skuδa 'Scythian' (Szemerényi 1980). *Suŋla is specifically '*Eastern* East Scythia(n)'. The modern reading 'Hsiung-nu 匈奴 (*xiōngnú*), is from MChi ☆xuawŋ (Pul. 346)[138] ~ attested MChi *huŋ* (Tak. 416) + MChi ☆nɔ₁ (Pul. 227) ~ attested MChi *la*[139] from OChi *suŋlâ.[140]

> Sogdian *Suɣda* ~ *Suɣla* 'Sogd, Sogdian' from (Old Persian transcription) *Sug(u)da* 'Central Asian Scythian' from Old Scythian *skuδa 'archer, Scythian' (Early Greek transcription Σκύθης Scythes [*skutʰa-*]) *skuδa Classical Scythian (Greek transcriptions) Σκύλης

135. Szemerényi (1980: 21) derives it from PIE *skud-o 'shooter, archer' from PIE *skeud- 'shoot, chase, throw', cognate to English *shoot-* (Watkins 2011: 81), thus 'archer'. Szemerényi's solution is completely regular, makes perfect phonological sense, and is supported semantically by a millennium of Central Eurasian steppe peoples after the Scythians who similarly were called, or called themselves, "the Archers", most famously the Mongols. Not with Mayrhofer (2006) and Schmitt (2018).

136. In "part of the Sogdian area" (Szemerényi 1980: 27), citing Andreas (1910), which I have not seen. However, the sound change in East Scythian is apparently restricted to word-internal positions.

137. Szemerényi (1980).

138. See Endnote 163.

139. In *Lolad*, an Old Tibetan transcription of the ethnonym now read *Nu-la* 奴剌 (*Núlá*) (Beckwith 1993: 236).

140. I.e., attested in eastern dialects of Sogdian. See Endnote 147. On Old Chinese dialects see Beckwith (2008, which now needs revision) and cf. Beckwith and Kiyose (2018).

> *Scula-* [skula] ~ Σκολα- *Scula-* [skula] in (emended) Σκολάξαϊ- 'King Skula', after whom the West Scythians called themselves Σκολότοι Skolotoi [skula-ta-] 'Scythians'.[141] As Szemerényi rightly notes, the latter is a Scythian plural of the same name as Σκύλης Skula, 'Scythian'. A syncopated and epenthesized version of Skula, attested as *Sakla, became *Saka* by operation of the Syllable Contact Law.[142] The form *Saka* had already replaced most of the other forms derived from *Skuda, except *Sugda*, by the time of the Behistun Inscription (519 BC).

In sum, based on all available data, the ancient Hsiung-nu, like the ancient Sogdians, were Scythian in culture, called themselves Scythians, and spoke Scythian. They were Scythians.

Distribution of the East Scythian Dialects

The *depalatalizing/non-palatalizing* isogloss mentioned above separates the early Scythian speakers around the northeast corner of the great northern bend of the Yellow River region, which was called *Ta Hsia* 大夏 (*Daxià*) 'Great **Ḥăryá*', from early people to the south and southeast of them called *Hu* 胡 (*Hú*) *Ḥărắ.[143] The depalatalizing/non-palatalizing feature applies to many languages in that region—not only to early forms of Scythian, but also to Japanese-Koguryoic, the early northeastern dialects of Chinese, and the Koreanic (non-Puyo-Koguryoic) languages of the southern Korean Peninsula, which are known in Antiquity as the

141. For the textual error (deletion in Herodotus of the Σ onset in the third son's name at this point so that it appears in the received text as Κολάξαϊ-), see Chapter 1.

142. Beckwith (2009: 378–380). That is, speakers of some Scythian dialects could not pronounce the onset cluster *sk* in the Old Scythian form of the name, so they broke it up by inserting an epenthetic vowel, making it *Sakula; deleted the vowel *u* (perhaps to be faithful to the original disyllabic form of the name), resulting in *Sakla, which has an egregious violation of the Syllable Contact Law (though it is attested in Old Chinese transcription); and by repairing said violation produced *Saka*, the subsequently almost universal Scythian name for 'Scythian' to the end of their recorded history as a people. See above for other examples of the Syllable Contact Law, and references.

143. By contrast, the original palatalized form *Ḥarya* 'Royal' is the well attested epithet of the Togon kings, Serbi speakers who migrated from that region in late Antiquity to what is now Ch'ing-hai (Qinghai) and Kansu (Gansu), as discussed above. Cf. Beckwith (2016a).

Han languages, where *Han* 韓 (*Hán*) 'Korea, Korean', in Middle Chinese read ☆ɣan₁ (Pul. 118), is transparently from **Ḥárǎ* [ɣara] 'royal'.[144]

The name 匈奴, now read "Hsiung-nu", thus reflects the early East Scythian dialect in which the *k of the early Scythian name *skuδa is voiced and the transcriptionally attested *δ either hardens to *d* or becomes *l* (Szemerényi 1980: 27), exactly as in dialect forms of the name of the Sogdians. The Hsiung-nu are thus onomastically related to the eastern Scythian people whose land is already known as Sugda "Sogdiana" in the Behistun Inscription. In view of the completely Iranic nature of the Hsiung-nu lexicon, and its closeness to Sogdian—to the extent that the Chinese transcriptions have been deciphered so far—the Hsiung-nu language was an eastern East Scythian dialect.

144. Cf. Beckwith (2007a). Depalatalization and lambdacization also produced the name *Alan* from earlier *Aryāna- in the late West Scythian dialects.

7

The Scythian Empire in Chao and the First Chinese Empire

A century before the term *Ta Hsia* 大夏 (*Dàxià*) 'Great Ḥarya' is attested in the sense 'Bactria', it occurs in the Lang-yeh 琅琊 (*Lángyá*) Inscription of Ch'in shih huang ti 秦始黃帝 (*Qín Shǐhuángdì*) the 'First Emperor of Ch'in', erected in 219 BC, the second year of the new, unified Chinese realm, the Ch'in Empire.[1] In the text the name *Ta Hsia* unambiguously has its Classical sense, referring explicitly to the Central Eurasian steppe zone to the northwest of the state of Chao, and at least partly including Chao. The inscription gives the extent of 'the land of the emperor' (皇帝之土) as follows:[2]

西涉流沙。In the west it crosses over the flowing sands.
南盡北戶。In the south it encompasses the land of those whose doors face north.
東有東海。In the east it includes the Eastern Sea.
北過大夏。In the north it extends across Great Ḥarya.

1. It was his 28th year as ruler of Ch'in, not as ruler of all unified China (Kern 2000: 25, note 43); Kern does not discuss the inscription dates. The mountain is in the former state of Ch'i, which was located around the mouth of the Yellow River but included Shantung; it was the last of the Warring States to be conquered. See Kern (2007) on the siting and other historical features of the inscriptions.

2. Text from Kern (2000: 33), q.v. for his translation. For a similar characterization of the empire's extent see Nickel (2013).

Because of its explicit location in the north, it is known that the *Ta Hsia* 大夏 Great Ḥarya in this particular text cannot refer to Bactria, which was far to the west "over the flowing sands", in a region not to be reached by the Chinese for another century. The term also does not refer solely to "the area between the Yellow River and the Fen 汾 River in present western Shanhsi 山西", i.e., part of the former state of Chao, the First Emperor's birthplace, though it certainly included that area.[3] The text specifies that the locations mentioned are all conquests of regions lying *beyond* the home territory of the Chinese speaking peoples, and all are suitably vast geographical territories, not minor realms or provinces. *Ta Hsia* in the inscription thus refers to a generic ethno-geographical region corresponding to one of the four cardinal directions around the ideal central realm, Chung-kuo 中國 (*Zhōngguó*) the 'Middle Kingdom',[4] whose Chinese-speaking peoples had started referring to themselves as *Hsia* 夏 (*Xià*) or *Hua* 華 (*Huá*)—Old Chinese *Ḥarya—the 'royals', the 'ruling people', over a century before the Ch'in Empire, and had rapidly made it the first recorded name for 'the Chinese' as an ethnolinguistically distinct nation.[5]

The regions mentioned in the inscription are all specifically non-Chinese, and *Ta Hsia*, 'Great *Ḥarya*' or '*Ḥarya* Empire', here refers to the steppe zone[6] of Central Eurasia, which is to say Central Eurasia par excellence from the larger Eurasian continental point of view. Although in 219 BC Ch'in shih huang ti had not yet sent his general Meng T'ien

3. Kern (2000: 33, note 77) follows Chavannes (1897, 2: 148–149) for both conclusions, adding correctly that accordingly, "Ta-hsia is already mentioned in *Tso chuan*"; cf. Beckwith (2016a).

4. In Warring States texts, when the context marks number reference for the word *Chung-kuo* 中國, it is always singular (Beckwith 2016a). The long popular Sinological idea that there was no unified China yet, so the word must be a sort of plural—"the Central States" or the like—is thus falsified by the sources themselves. The *idea* of a unified China existed; Warring States philosophers have much to say about it, and 中國 appears in Chinese texts at about the same time as *Hsia* 夏 OChi *Ḥarya, the first name for 'China, Chinese'.

5. See Chapter 4. For the Warring States texts, and their interpretation on this topic, see Beckwith (2016a).

6. From the Chinese perspective, as in the inscription, it is in the north, though from a world-geography standpoint it is the "Eastern Steppe".

north to attack the Hsiung-nu in the Ordos,[7] in 222 Ch'in had already defeated and conquered Chao's northern remnant, which was in the steppe zone—that is, it was in Ta-Hsia 'Great *Ḥarya*'. Accordingly, conquest of part of Ta Hsia was evidently equated by the ruler's officials as tantamount to having conquered it all. In any case, it was clearly the most important part for the First Emperor personally, who after his victory in the war with Chao had taken revenge on the people of Chao for his family's suffering there.

Ta Hsia 大夏 'Great *Ḥarya*' is thus used in this inscription to refer to the realm of the salient ethnolinguistic region to the north and northwest of the Chinese: the steppe home of the Central Eurasian nomads, whose physical culture in Antiquity is known from archaeology to be Scythian. The people who spoke the dialect recorded in the word Hsia 夏 *Ḥarya* were in the process of being replaced *politically* in the area of the Ordos and Mongolia by the Hsiung-nu, ethnically mixed speakers of an eastern subdialect of *East* Scythian.[8] At the same time the Scythians in the Western Steppe had already been largely supplanted politically by their Scytho-Sarmatian cousins, who spoke an eastern subdialect of *West* Scythian.[9]

History of the term Ta Hsia 大夏 'Great Ḥarya'

The earliest datable reference to Ta Hsia 大夏 (Dàxià) 'Great Ḥarya (*Ariya* ~ *Aria*)' in Chinese is in the *Tso chuan*, in a legend projected into highest antiquity but actually dating to the 4th century like the rest of the text.[10] In it, the mythical Chinese culture-founder Yao is said to have separated two quarreling brothers, sending one of them to Ta Hsia 大夏,[11]

7. He did so in 215 BC; see Di Cosmo (1999: 892, 964), q.v. also for the earlier history of Central Eurasian peoples north of the Chinese.

8. For the archaeology see Di Cosmo (1999). The ethnolinguistic affinities of the Hsiung-nu ruling clan itself have recently been established (Beckwith 2018). The present book updates my previous work on this.

9. See Chapter 6.

10. On the date of the *Tso chuan* see Brooks and Brooks (2015: 36).

11. *Tso chuan*, Chao-kung 1 (Legge 1893, 2: 585): "Anciently, the emperor Kaou-sin had two sons, of whom the elder was called Oh-pih, and the younger Shih-ch'in. They dwelt in K'wang-lin, but could not agree, and daily carried their shields and spears against each other. The sovereign emperor (Yaou) did not approve of this, and removed Oh-pih to Shang-k'ëw, to preside

a place identified in the commentarial tradition with the northerly region of what is now Shanxi province,[12] which in the Warring States period was the mixed non-Chinese and Chinese region of the state of Chao. This story is one of the most important passages in the *Tso chuan*, as it legitimizes the target region as a part of the Chinese world, even though at the time it was still mostly non-Chinese in culture, and the rulers themselves were partly non-Chinese in origin.

Second, despite the *Shih chi*'s reputation for vague or misleading attributions of foreign peoples' origins, the very beginning of its famous account of the Hsiung-nu states, "As for the Hsiung-nu, their progenitor was a descendant of the lineage of the rulers of Hsia 夏."[13] Taken in the traditional Chinese understanding, i.e., Hsia 夏 as the legendary Hsia-ch'ao 夏朝 (Xiàcháo), 'Hsia Dynasty', the first "Chinese" dynasty of "China" in later Chinese historiography, as it has so far been taken, it is of course not true. But from the viewpoint of Central Eurasian history, and the early myth of the Hsia Dynasty that also appears in the Warring States period, it is correct.

In fact, the entire Eastern Steppe, including the original Hsiung-nu home territory in the Ordos, must have been *Ta Hsia* 大夏 'Great Ḥarya', meaning 'the Ḥarya (*Scythian*) Empire', the title of which *in Chinese* is identical to *Ta Hsia* 大夏 'Great Ḥarya'. That is, 'the (*Chinese*) Hsia 夏 (*Ḥarya*) Empire' (reinterpreted as a Dynasty) has exactly the same name as that given to the vast northern realm targeted by Ch'in shih huang ti. The name itself confirms the correctness of the *Shih chi* statement. Accordingly, the ancestors of the *people* of *Ta Hsia* 大夏 'Great *Ḥarya*, the *Aria* Empire' necessarily descended from rulers called Hsia (*Ḥarya* ~ *Aria* ~ *Ariya*) who had occupied the steppe zone region known to the Chinese as *Ta Hsia* 大夏 before the early 4th century BC. Those people were specifically the Scythians.

---

over the star Ta-ho. . . . The ancestors of Shang followed him [in Shang-k'ëw], and hence Ta-ho is the star of Shang. [Yaou also] removed Shih-ch'in to Ta-hëa, to preside over the star Sin (? in Orion). The descendants of T'ang (Yaou) followed him, and in Ta-hëa served the dynasties of Hëa and Shang." Legge's "Hëa" is Hsia 夏 and his "Ta-hëa" is *Ta-hsia* 大夏.

12. Wu (1994: 87, note 109).

13. *Shih chi* 110: 匈奴，其先祖夏后氏之苗裔也。Text from CTP; translation by Giele (2010: 237).

Ta Hsia and the State of Chao

Little attention has been paid to the state of Chao 趙 (*Zhào*) and its relationship to *Ta Hsia* 大夏. In fact, it seems not to be mentioned in English that Ch'in shih huang ti was not only a member of the Chao clan, he was born and raised in Han-tan 邯鄲 (*Hándān*), the capital of Chao, as the son of a Chaoish prince and princess. That is, both of his parents were members of the Chao clan.[14] The state of Chao's lone claim to fame in traditional accounts of early China is that the "Chinese" ruler of Chao, King Wu-ling (r. 325–299 BC),[15] forced the "Chinese" subjects of his state to learn and adopt several foreign customs: horse riding (foreign animal and skills), wearing trousers (foreign clothing practices), and shooting with the bow on horseback (foreign ways of warfare).[16] These helped Chao conquer deep into the steppe zone to the north and west, including other independent parts of Ta Hsia 大夏 'Great Ḥarya'. He thus enlarged his state and was able to threaten, if not defeat, his rivals to the south.[17]

The usual presentation of these changes in the sources is an obvious rewriting of history, perhaps in order to ensure Chao's continued acceptance as a legitimate Chinese state by making the heroes "Chinese".[18] Nevertheless, the ancient Chinese word for 'Chinese'—the first actual ethnonym or national name for 'the Chinese people'—is a Scythian

14. The traditional scurrilous stories about his (and his mother's) supposedly base origins cannot be accepted as historical, as noted by Bodde (1986: 42–43); cf. Loewe (1999: 969).

15. Di Cosmo (1999: 960).

16. *Shih chi* 43, s.v. Chao Wu-ling 趙武靈 (Zhào Wǔlíng), year 19.

17. Di Cosmo (1999: 951–952, 960–961). A fragment of the Warring States military treatise 孫臏兵法 'Sun Pin's Art of War' (4th century BC, later copy excavated in 1972) listing the uses of cavalry gives it only minor supporting roles and does not mention mounted archers (Lewis 1999: 624). However, the text is fragmentary and the work must be earlier than the manuscript. Traditionally the Chinese adopted Central Eurasian customs and mounted archery in the time of King Wu-ling of Chao. When Sun Pin's original work was written the Chinese themselves probably had not yet begun using mounted archery.

18. The stories giving a Hsia 夏 *Ḥarya pedigree to the earlier Spring and Autumn state of Chin 晉 (*Jìn*), which had been located in Shanxi, necessarily date to the Warring States period (when the idea of a Chinese "Hsia Dynasty" was invented), or more likely even later.

loanword, *Ḥarya ~ Aria 'royal(s)', normally transcribed in Old Chinese as 夏, which in modern Chinese is read *Hsia* (*Xià*).[19]

Any Chinese story about the events thus *could not distinguish* between "Chinese" royalty and "Scythian" royalty—they were the same. Whatever its motivation, the tale as understood from later Antiquity to the present obscures one of the most important events in the entire Warring States period and in all of Chinese history. The story would have us believe that King Wu-ling was a Chinese who had adopted foreign customs and then forced his people to adopt them. He was eventually successful, to the extent that they dressed, lived, and fought not like Chinese (*Hsia*) but like the Central Eurasians (*Hsia*) who lived both inside and outside Chao (*Hsia*). That interpretation is the exact opposite of the many attested examples of culture shift throughout the long history of Chinese contact with Central Eurasians, in which the foreign peoples ruling and living among Chinese ended up adopting Chinese culture. However, most such examples also record that internal struggles took place among the non-Chinese ruling class for and against Sinification, and the case of Chao is no exception.

Reanalyzing the Chao story in that light gives a principled explanation of the historical and linguistic data and provides a scenario to explain how the Chinese borrowed a foreign word, *Ḥarya, and made it their own ethnonym for themselves, the Chinese-speaking peoples.

The people of Chao lived on the frontier, a region including both northern steppe and southern agricultural zones. The state thus had both Scythian steppe zone people and Chinese agricultural-zone people, so the ancestors of the people of Chao necessarily included both peoples as well. They must have been bilingual, at least in part, but some of the people of Chao who dressed and lived and fought as Central Eurasians certainly did so *because they already were Central Eurasians* and wanted to keep the traditional Central Eurasian way of life. Immigration into the region by Central Eurasian pastoralists in the 7th century certainly resulted in creolization, as in other instances of such conquests

19. The same foreign word is also transcribed, less often, as *Hua* 華 (*Huá*), from OChi *Ḥâryá; see Beckwith (2016a) for details. That is the form which has survived to the present in the official name of China.

from Antiquity to the Modern period. As a result, the Chinese-speaking subjects of Chao became acculturated to their Scythian rulers, adopting their Central Eurasian customs, beliefs, and—at least in part—their language, surely via creolization, as in Media, so that many people in Chao must have been bilingual. The latter element is crucial: they knew what the Scythian word *Ḥarya* meant—'royal(s)'—and they knew that it referred to 'the legitimate rulers'. In Classical Chinese texts the word is usually marked with the optional "explicit collective plural" marker when it refers to people collectively.[20] It is also used (sans plural marker) to refer to the rulers' *language*, as Darius the Great uses it for the rulers' language in the Persian Empire, and as Kanishka the Great uses it for the rulers' language in the Kushan Empire. That is, the Chinese refer to the *Chinese* language as *Ḥarya* too, usually as Hsia yü 夏語 (*Xiàyǔ*) 'the *Ḥarya* language' (in which *yü* 語 is Chinese for 'speech, language'). Adoption of the Scythian word *Ḥarya*, with both of its widely attested, normal uses or meanings, marks the conscious self-identification of Chinese speakers as 'the Royals', a "chosen people" who spoke the "Royal" language, in contrast to the other peoples who lived in contact with them in all directions. This can only be the result of the transmission of Scythian culture to Chinese culture via direct rule or domination of the former over the latter in the region that included the eventual state of Chao, so that the partly bilingual, bicultural non-Chinese, as they shifted fully to Chinese linguistically, retained some key concepts and the terms for them that had not existed previously in Chinese. This is absolutely normal and commonplace in creolization throughout history.

The state of Chao 趙 (*Zhào*) was first created by partition of the Spring and Autumn state of Chin 晉 (*Jìn*) in 424 BC,[21] an event that traditionally marks the beginning of the Warring States period. Chao was accepted

20. I.e., as *chu-hsia* 諸夏 (*zhūxià*) or *chu-hua* 諸華 (*zhūhuá*) 'the royal ones; the Chinese', with the collective plural marker *chu* 諸 (*zhū*)'. It bears repeating that the new Warring States period word *Chung-kuo* 中國 (*Zhōngguó*), traditionally understood as 'the Middle Kingdom', has been treated by Sinologists as a plural, 'the Central States', but that is incorrect. See the detailed discussion, with texts, in Beckwith (2016a), on which article much of this chapter is based.

21. Brooks and Brooks (2015: 67).

as a Chinese state, as were the other two states formed out of Chin, but Chao was located on the northern frontier of the zone of Chinese civilization.[22] It must already have had a large Central Eurasian population, as well as a Chinese population, and some among both peoples must, necessarily, have been bilingual. This dichotomy, and bilingualism, could only have increased as Chao expanded further to the north and west.

Reinterpreting the traditional story, many of those among the Chao ruling class who were of Central Eurasian heritage wanted to shift to Chinese language and culture, but the conservatives among them—clearly including King Wu-ling himself—wanted to retain and expand their steppe warrior traditions, including their self-image as *Ḥaryas* 'royals', which word they must have used for themselves, as they must have referred to their homeland as *Ḥarya*, the land of the *Ḥaryas*. Like the Cyaxares story in Herodotus,[23] the traditional Chinese story about the revolution of King Wu-ling—the adoption of Central Eurasian mounted archery, trousers (footies for horse riding), and unmentioned in the texts but portrayed in tomb figurines, the short, warm, fitted *gaunaka* (Greek *kaynakes*) tunic-coat and the *bashlyq* headgear[24]—reverses the directionality of the impetus for the historical merger of Chinese language and values with Central Eurasian state traditions and practical customs. Because the "new" cultural artifacts used in Chao—and attested in Ch'in-Han period art (see Figure 13)—are classic features of Scythian culture, the innovations were introduced by the Scythians themselves. Thus both cases equally attest to the general directionality of the cultural transmission—from Central Eurasians (the Scythians)

22. It is notable that the other Chao-clan state, Ch'in 秦 (*Qín*), was located on the far *western* frontier of the Chinese culture zone and is known to have had a substantial non-Chinese population as well.

23. See Chapter 2.

24. See Appendix B. See also the photographs (evidently taken in a museum in China) in Reinette: Chinese Figurines and Statues from Eastern Zhou to the Tang Dynasties, http://jeannedepompadour.blogspot.com/2013/06/chinese-figurines-and-statues-from.html. Some clearly show the woolen lining of the *gaunaka*. The tunic and trousers soon became the traditional everyday dress of ordinary Chinese—emphasizing the deep impression made on them by the Scythians. King Wu-ling's changes are briefly discussed with references in Di Cosmo (1999: 960–961).

FIGURE 13. Early Han Dynasty period mounted archer in footies and *bashlyq* (tomb figurine).

to peripheral peoples (the Medians and the Chinese)—and to the historical fact that the merger did indeed happen in both places.

By contrast with the historical material, the directionality of the linguistic data can *only* be interpreted in one way: the version in which people of Central Eurasian ancestry effectively kept on claiming that they were Central Eurasian royalty even after they shifted to Chinese language and culture. That was the normal thing to do for people of aristocratic heritage, and it is attested over and over many times throughout Chinese history down to the very last dynasty, the Manchu Ch'ing 清 (*Qīng*) Dynasty, which fell in 1911, centuries after the vast majority of Manchus had shifted linguistically to Chinese and adopted Chinese culture. The aristocrats of Chao secured the place of their *Hsia* 夏 *Ḥarya* ancestry within Chinese tradition by creative reinterpretation of their ancestral (Scythian) realm, *Ta Hsia* 大夏 'Great Ḥarya, the Ḥarya

Empire', as *Hsia-ch'ao* 夏朝 'the Ḥarya Dynasty', the earliest ancestral (Chinese) dynasty. In 247, less than 50 years after the death of King Wu-ling, their own prince, Chao Cheng—who was, appropriately, half-Chaoish politically, but completely Chaoish by his family heritage—became king of Ch'in and, in 221, Ch'in shih huang ti 秦始皇帝 (Qín Shǐhuángdì) 'the First Emperor of Ch'in'. He united all of the *Hsia* 夏 *Ḥarya 'royal ones', now meaning 'the Chinese', who spoke the Hsia 夏 *Ḥarya 'royal' language, Chinese. As a merger, it was as much a victory for Scythian culture as it was for Chinese culture.

From 'Ḥarya Empire' to 'Ḥarya Dynasty' to 'China'

As shown above, during the long, fragmented Warring States period, Chinese-speaking people first began to use the Scythian word *Hsia* 夏 *Ḥarya* (in West Scythian *Aria*) to refer not only to themselves but also to their own assumed ancestors, an ethnolinguistically romanticized, imagined people who, they logically concluded, must have preceded the historical Shang Dynasty. According to later traditional Chinese conceptions, these *Hsia* ~ *Ḥarya* people must have had a monarchist system of government—as the Scythian Empire certainly did have—making the ancestral realm a Hsia Dynasty or Empire. Despite its faulty chronology the story makes perfect sense according to the Scythian and Chinese ideas, both before and during the Warring States, and later throughout Chinese history.

No evidence datable before the Warring States period has been found in which the name *Hsia* 夏appears in reference to any actual *Chinese* people or "dynasty"—no inscriptions, literary texts, or anything else.[25] Since the name is not recorded in the meaning 'the Chinese', or in the meaning 'a Chinese dynasty that preceded the Shang', or anything like that for almost the entire first millennium of written Chinese texts, *Hsia* 夏 *Ḥarya* in both "Chinese" senses can only be a creation of the

25. That is, despite many Sinologists' belief in that belief, e.g., Chang (1999: 71–73). Mair (2013: 5, 7–8) shows that the Chinese word *Hsia* 夏 is first attested in the Bronze Inscriptions and early Classical texts in the meaning "large, grand; variegated", and is later written with an additional "sun" (日) radical to express the meaning "summer". See Endnote 164.

Warring States period in which it appears *de novo*. Nevertheless, it is crucially important for understanding the development of Chinese ideas about themselves in this period. If the bilingual people of Chao were already using *Ḥarya* for themselves *in their other language*, a steppe zone language—which they called *Ḥarya* 'the royal (language)', the same way other Central Eurasian and Central Eurasianized peoples used the term—then they naturally knew that *Ḥarya* meant 'royal, belonging to the legitimate ruling lineage', and it referred to themselves and their ancestors. Since they referred to themselves as *Ḥarya*, the epithet of the "Royal" Scythians, their ancestors were of course *Ḥarya* too—Scythians. After their language and culture shift to Chinese, they kept calling themselves *Ḥarya* and naturally kept referring to their glorious ancestors as *Ḥarya*.

Chao was one of the great powers among the Warring States, so the use of this term must have spread from the elite Chao speakers of Chinese to other elite speakers of Chinese. Because Chinese speakers as a whole eventually came to call themselves Hsia 夏 (Xià) *Ḥaryá—also written *Hua* 華 (*Huá*) **Ḥâryá*—they also considered the people of the land of *Ta Hsia* 大夏 'Great *Ḥarya* ~ the *Ḥarya* Empire'[26] to be their direct ancestors. Logically that made the people of *Ta Hsia* the first *Hsia* 夏 *Ḥarya*, whose *Chinese* 'empire' or 'dynasty' *Ta Hsia* 大夏 must have preceded the Shang, the first fully historical Chinese dynasty. That was the creative innovation. Calling the imagined *Chinese* people *Hsia* 夏 (i.e., *Ḥarya* ~ *Aria* ~ *Ariya*) made the Warring States rulers of the Chinese "Ariyas and the descendants of Ariyas", as Darius I says of himself in the Naqš-i Rustam Inscription. The *Ḥarya* ~ *Aria* ~ *Ariya* lineage uniquely had imperial legitimacy. If the Chinese, like the Persians, wanted to have a real empire, they had to belong to that lineage. Fortunately, Ch'in shih huang ti, Prince Cheng of Chao, had that lineage. He thus successfully founded the first Chinese Empire.

The alternative to a late Spring and Autumn to early Warring States influence via Central Eurasia is the belief that a legendary Chinese *dynasty* known as Hsia actually existed and ruled China in the period

26. The name is mentioned for the first time in Chinese in a Warring States period text, the *Tso chuan*.

before the historical Shang dynasty. As noted by scholars, that idea is not supported by any authentic pre–Warring States evidence,[27] and it cannot explain the fact that the name is actually transcribed alternatively as either *Hsia* 夏 (*Xià*) 'summer' or *Hua* 華 (*Huá*) 'flower'. Such graphic vacillation and semantic irrelevance are telltale signs of a loanword written purely phonetically in Chinese characters. By contrast, based on both historical and linguistic data we know that there was a foreign *Ta Hsia* 大夏 'Great *Ḥarya* ~ *Aria* Empire' before and during the Warring States period, and some of its people participated prominently in the struggles among the Warring States, in the process spreading use of the epithet *Hsia* 夏 *Ḥarya* ~ *Aria* ~ *Ariya* 'the royals, the legitimate rulers'.

Not long after the appearance of the term *Ta Hsia* 大夏 in Chinese sources, the peoples of eastern East Scythia, including the Hsiung-nu, begin to be called *Hu* 胡 (*Hú*), Old Chinese *Ḥarắ (*ɣarắ), a characteristically depalatalized Northeast Asian linguistic area variant of *Ḥaryá.[28] Both words continued to be so used in the Eastern Steppe zone, and in China, from the Warring States on. In Chinese itself, they eventually changed phonetically beyond recognition when the Late Old Chinese language underwent tremendous morphophonological changes in late Antiquity, becoming 'monosyllabicized' Proto-Mandarin (the spoken language) and pre–Middle Chinese (the literary language).[29] As discussed above, the available material shows that the early Classical period non-Chinese inhabitants near Chao called in the Chinese sources *Hu* 胡 (*Hú*), Old Chinese *Ḥarắ, spoke Scythian too, as did the neighboring Hsiung-nu '(East) Scythians' who were also called *Hu* 胡 (*Hú*), Old Chinese *Ḥarắ.

Chinese speakers thus ultimately adopted the epithet 'royal (ones)'—better known to us from the West Scythians as *Aria* ~ *Ariya*—from the East Scythians, who pronounced it *Ḥarya*. The Chinese used it for themselves in the same way that the Scythians, Persians, and other peoples did

27. Mair (2013) reviews the data and the scholarly literature.

28. See Chapter 6, and for additional discussion and examples, see Beckwith (2007a).

29. Beckwith and Kiyose (2018), citing data from Chinese and from foreign transcriptions and loanwords.

at about the same time, from the mid-first millennium BC into the Middle Ages or even later. The basic idea, a fundamental element of the Central Eurasian Culture Complex, is the Scythian rulers' view of themselves as a divinely engendered 'chosen people'—the 'royal Scythians' or the 'Saka kings'—in contrast to other peoples with whom they were in conflict or over whom they ruled.[30] When this term and accompanying viewpoint had been adopted by Chinese speakers of the disunited Warring States as a way of referring to themselves as a distinctive people and culture who were ideally united in a great empire, the term developed semantically to become the first autonym for "the Chinese", and the name for their earliest ancestors. The name legitimized them as the 'royal, ruling' Chinese people,[31] and led to the conceptual unification of the Warring States inhabitants as one nation, the Chinese, and eventually one unified realm, the Chinese Empire.[32]

Ch'in shih huang ti and the Scytho-Chinese Empire

The Chinese Classical Age is usually considered to have ended in 221 BC with the victory of the king of Ch'in 秦 (*Qín*), Chao Cheng 趙政 (*Zhào Zhèng*),[33] who conquered all of the other Warring States and declared the lands he had conquered to be parts of the new unified Ch'in Empire. He proclaimed himself to be *Shih huang ti* 始皇帝 (*Shǐhuángdì*) 'First[34] Emperor', and in the Lang-yeh Inscription states that his territory included the vast regions in all four directions,

30. Beckwith (2010).

31. The word in later times, increasingly written in its early alternate form *Hua* 華 *Ḥâryá, was the default ethnonym of the Chinese nation down to modern times, though *Hsia* 夏 *Ḥaryá has remained in use too, and is the regular term for 'the Chinese language' in late Antiquity and the Early and Central Middle Ages. See Endnote 165.

32. It must be emphasized that the idea of a unified state which developed during the period was different from the old ideal of the second historical Chinese dynasty, the Western Chou (Zhou) Dynasty (ca. 1040–771) which shifted its capital to the east in 771 and is thenceforth known in later histories as the Eastern Chou Dynasty, with rapidly increasing weakness until its final disappearance in 249 BC. Cf. Endnote 166 and see further below.

33. He is actually most often referred to as Ying Cheng 嬴政 (*Yíng Zhèng*). That is a topic all its own. Cf. Note 35 below.

34. Literally, 'Beginning' or 'Starting'.

including the northern steppe region, 大夏 'the Ḥarya Empire', as quoted above.

To summarize, it is a remarkable but almost universally neglected fact that Chao Cheng 趙政 (*Zhào Zhèng*), "originally named Ying Zheng",[35] but better known as Ch'in shih huang ti, was actually born in the Scythian-named capital of Chao, *Han-tan* 邯鄲 *Hándān*, from Middle Chinese ☆ɣamtan, from Old Chinese *Ăɣámătánă, in 259 BC, as Prince of both Chao and Ch'in, and he spent his childhood there. Both sides of his family belonged to the Chao clan because both states had the same ruling family, Chao, with the same ancestral story.

It is significant that the future First Emperor was born and raised in the capital of Chao, not in Ch'in, because it was the state of Chao that had introduced the crucial new Scythian cultural elements: Scythian mounted archery, Scythian clothes, Scythian feudal state organization, and the Scythian term *Ḥarya* '(the) royal (ones)', usually written Hsia 夏 (*Xià*) in Chinese. It was the epithet of the ruling peoples of the region of Chao, which included part of the great realm known as *Ta Hsia* 大夏 'Great Ḥarya; the Ḥarya Empire', meaning 'the realm of the Royals', the Royal Scythians.

With the merger of the Scythians and Chinese in Chao—including part of the vast region referred to by the Chinese as *Ta Hsia* 'Great Ḥarya'—the Scythian epithet *Ḥarya* had become a Chinese epithet too. Similarly, far to the west, the Scythians had introduced their customs and their rulers' epithet *Aria* ~ *Ariya* to the Medes, Persians, and other peoples in the vast territory of Central Asia and the Near East which came under Scythian rule. Their Scythianized offspring, the Scytho-Medes, ruled in turn after them, and under the Persians continued to run the government. The Mede rulers, and following them the Persian rulers, also declared themselves to belong to the *Ariya* (*Aria* ~ *Ḥarya*) lineage. This is just what happened in China, specifically in Chao. Prince Cheng, who became king of the other Chao-clan state, Ch'in, was born

35. Loewe (1999: 969), like others, omits the fact of his birth in Han-tan and his childhood in Chao. One must wonder if, or why, such an important member of the Chao clan really would have been named Ying instead of Chao. It recalls the invective aimed at the ruler and his family from his lifetime to the present.

and raised not in Ch'in, but in Chao, and must have learned the entire Scythianized system of that state.

The First Emperor instituted explicitly unifying policies and practices of every kind, from *one* standardized system of weights and measures to *one* accepted philosophical school (Legalism), to *one* form of the written language. He instituted the practice of making regular imperial tours of inspection around the realm, by himself or by his representatives, to facilitate which he built imperial roads and rest stations around the empire. He also introduced a novel, genuinely feudal governing structure,[36] with appointed governors, like satraps, over the constituent provinces of the empire. And finally, unlike the Scythians in Scythia or the Scytho-Medes, but like their continuators the Achaemenid Empire and its Mauryan successor the First Emperor erected monumental inscriptions proclaiming his imperial position. The latter innovation in China sounds very much like the Achaemenids, so some scholars have noted that the First Emperor must have been influenced by the Persian Empire's main Greek successor, the Seleucid Empire.[37]

The new features of the Achaemenid, Mauryan, and Ch'in empires, including feudalism, were introduced by the Scythian Empire via Scythian rule in its period of greatness, as argued in the present book. However, the inscriptions were an innovation of Darius the Great, the first Persian ruler of the Scytho-Mede-Persian 'Achaemenid' Empire, based on Ancient Near Eastern models. They, along with the entire imperial structure, were imitated very closely by King Priyadarśi (fl. ca. 272–261) of the Mauryan Dynasty in India, who erected monumental inscriptions in Prakrit, the first known texts written in an Indic language.[38] A specifically Greek artistic influence, probably Seleucid or Graeco-Bactrian, is now considered to account for the sculptural style of both the famous army

36. I.e., a system different from what modern scholars say the Chou Dynasty had.

37. Miyazaki (1977–1978: 128–129), though his statement that the novel great inscriptions erected by Ch'in shih huang ti were not new is incorrect. There certainly were many inscriptions erected in China before the Ch'in unification, but none of them were large, grandiose public proclamations set up in prominent locations, q.v. Kern (2000). I am indebted to Yanxiao He for Miyazaki and for helpful comments on the innovations of Ch'in shih huang ti; any errors are my own.

38. Beckwith (2015: 124–137, 226–250), plus a few inscriptions in Greek and one in Aramaic.

of terra cotta warriors buried with Ch'in shih huang ti in his enormous tomb, and the gigantic bronze statues he erected at his court, also supplied with inscriptions.[39] However, it is significant that the Hsiung-nu (East Scythians) are also said to have erected bronze statues for worship of Heaven,[40] possibly with inscriptions. In addition, the ruler's innovative way of designating himself as the "First Generation" (ruler), and his son and successor as the "Second Generation" (ruler), is thought to reflect the Western practice of numbering rulers of the same name or title so as to indicate their generation, e.g., Cyrus II (Cyrus the Great), Alexander III (Alexander the Great), etc.

Looking at the data on the Central Eurasian peoples in the Warring States period from a Central Eurasian viewpoint, with attention to the parallel history of the Scythians in Media, there would seem not to be any deep mystery surrounding why Chao Cheng should have won the long struggle against all the other Warring States, so that he unified them and neighboring regions under his sole rule, forming the first actual Chinese Empire. He was born and raised in the Scythian-named capital of Chao, *Agamatana (Handan), his father was a prince of Chao, and his mother was from the Chao clan too—no doubt actually a princess—so the First Emperor had rock-solid legitimacy and knew at least the Chao version of the Scythian imperial system.

Ch'in shih huang ti 'the First Emperor of Ch'in' ended the Warring States period—the Classical Age in China—but he instituted in its place the revolutionary Scythian imperial template that had been followed by his earlier western predecessors, the Scytho-Mede-Persian successor of the Scythian Empire, and subsequently in India by another Scytho-Mede-Persian successor state, the Mauryan Empire. The First Emperor's dynasty lasted only one and a half generations and was succeeded by the Han Dynasty, which retained in its essentials the Ch'in version of the Scythian imperial system. The Han ruled China for four centuries, but Chao Cheng founded a new Imperial Age in China that lasted for two millennia.

39. Nickel (2013). I am indebted to Chen Wu for his insightful comments on the Hsiung-nu statues.

40. Shiratori (1929).

8

The Scythian Capitals of Media, Chao, and Ch'in

One among the many results of the Scythian conquest that have not previously been noticed is that in the frontier zone between Central Eurasia and the Eurasian periphery, at least three new cities appeared which have the same distinctive name, *Agamatāna.

The westernmost city was the capital of ancient Media (now western Iran). It is most familiar to us historically through an aberrant ancient Greek transcription of its name, Ἐκβάτανα *Ecbatana*,[1] but the name of the city (now *Hamadân*) is widely recorded in ancient Near Eastern sources, including the Bible, which together clearly attest the oldest form of the name: *Agamatāna*.

Herodotus (i 98–101) attributes the city's foundation to a Median culture hero, Deioces, who united the Medes, became their first king, instituted various new practices, and built Ecbatana. He concludes, "Deioces, then, united the Median nation by itself and ruled it. The Median clans are these: the Busae, the Paretaceni, the Struchates, the Arizanti, the Budii, the Magi."[2] Herodotus dates his Deioces to a period possibly

1. In Greek texts, the transcription Ἀγβάτανα *Agbatana* occurs much more frequently.

2. Δηιόκης μέν νυν τὸ Μηδικὸν ἔθνος συνέστρεψε μοῦνον καὶ τοῦτον ἦρξε: ἔστι δὲ Μήδων τοσάδε γένεα, Βοῦσαι Παρητακηνοὶ Στρούχατες Ἀριζαντοὶ Βούδιοι Μάγοι. From Perseus, tr. Godley. I have revised Godley's translation 'tribes' to 'clans'; as usual, the names are all traditionally Latinized.

corresponding to the historical time of the influx of Cimmerians (*Gimirri*, attested in Akkadian from 720–714 on) or the early Scythians a few decades later.

Many scholars now identify the name *Deioces* with *Daiukku* (in Akkadian transcription), the name of a historical city chief in Mannaea, northeast of Assyria, who was captured by Sargon II of Aššur (r. 721–705) and exiled to Syria,[3] but as the Assyrian account of the capture and exile of Daiukku is clear and decisive, the actual hero of the story in Herodotus is accepted to be legendary. However, there is no reason to think that his Deioces has anything to do with the Mannaean Daiukku. The Greek transcription Deioces has been identified by Schmitt as Old Iranic *Dahyu-ka-, which would be a title for the ruler of a *dahyu* 'Land'[4], the regular Old Persian equivalent of a *satrapy* (an English loanword from Scythian). *Dahyu-ka thus would mean 'satrap' or 'duke', like the name of the Achaemenid founder, Achaemenes. Phraortes, Deioces' successor (in one version), is identified via the Behistun Inscription as *Fravarti* 'protector of the heroic dead; angel'. But the name *Fravarti* is specifically *not* Median (Imperial Scythian). It is the Old Persian equivalent of *Fravaši*, the attested Young Avestan (Imperial Scythian) form of the word.[5] The early historical Scythians (Assyrian *Iškuzai* ~ *Aškuzai* for *Skuδā) dominated the region and assumed rule over Media and neighboring lands in Herodotus' much emphasized "twenty-eight years" of Scythian rule over Media, from ca. 648 to ca. 620.[6]

3. Schmitt (2011c).

4. Schmitt (2011c; 2014: 162–163).

5. This fact suggests that Phraortes is a later character introduced by one of Herodotus' informants. Herodotus' "Median Story", despite its Persianizing influence, confirms that the name of the city is linguistically Scythian.

6. Slightly adjusting Herodotus' dates downward. Herodotus (i 96) says his national founder Deioces was the son of Phraortes, but elsewhere gives Deioces as his father. The stories of Deioces, and partly Phraortes, essentially repeat some of the founding deeds Herodotus attributes to Cyaxares, but adds different ones of a legal nature. Only "the other Herodotus", in a few passages, contradicts his "Mede" story and gives credit to the Scythians for some of it, though they are clearly the people he should have credited for most of it. See the Prologue.

In any case, not one or two, but *three* cities named *Agamatāna appear in the respective local historical records at the same time, but very far apart. The cities were founded, or rather, refounded,[7] either by the Cimmerians, a Scythian-speaking people, or by the Scythians themselves, at some point between their historical appearance and the first actual mention of the western city by name (*Agamtana*) in Babylonian Akkadian (later usually *Agamatana*), dated 550 BC, at the time of Cyrus the Great's defeat of King Astyages and capture of the Scytho-Mede national treasury in Ecbatana. As for the eastern cities, the first mentioned in Chinese is Han-tan 邯鄲 (*Hándān*) Old Chinese *Ăɣámătánă, in 500 and 494 BC, followed by the second, Hsien-yang 咸陽 (*Xiányáng*), Old Chinese *Ăgåmădáɴă, in the middle of that century, with an Aramaeo-Sogdian transcription in an early 4th century CE letter that indicates its earlier form was Old Chinese *Aɣə́m(ə)tán(ă), as explained below. The same text records an unexpected form of the name of Loyang, *Saraɣ*.

Agamatana in the West

According to Herodotus, the city of Ecbatana (his *Agbatana*) in Media, or more precisely its citadel, had a plan[8] unparalleled before this time in the Near East:

> So he built the big and strong walls, one standing inside the next in [concentric] loops, which are now called Ecbatana [Ἀγβάτανα]. This fortress is so designed that each loop of walls is higher than the next outer loop by no more than the height of its battlements; to which plan the site itself, on a hill in the plain, contributes somewhat, but chiefly it was accomplished by skill. There are seven loops in all; within the innermost loop are the palace and the treasuries; . . . thus the battlements of five loops are painted with colors; and the

7. The site of Ecbatana was undoubtedly occupied long before this period, but archaeological work there is still stymied by the fact that the large modern city of Hamadān occupies the site.

8. Some have called early Mesopotamian constructions with highly irregular plans "circular"; cf. Chapter 8, Notes 9 and 11 and Endnote 167.

> battlements of the last two loops are coated, the one with silver and the other with gold.[9]

Polybius later says of Ecbatana:

> It was originally the royal city of the Medes, and vastly superior to the other cities in wealth and the splendour of its buildings. It is situated on the skirts of Mount Orontes, and is without walls, though containing an artificially formed citadel fortified to an astonishing strength. Beneath this stands the palace.[10]

Although Herodotus describes marvelously decorated walls around the city's citadel—of which the innermost wall, with the palace and treasury, was plated with gold—Polybius says there were no walls per se at all. The excavations show that the city's fortification walls were "concentric" in the sense of 'one within the other', but they were not circular, as they have been generally understood. The plan is irregular and angular, similar to other Median fortresses portrayed in Assyrian bas-reliefs with multiple "concentric" walls.[11] However, the gold plating is confirmed in several other ancient accounts, especially Polybius, who describes the Temple of Anāhitā there in some detail, stressing the fact that the entire building had been covered in heavy gold and silver plate, which was

9. Herodotus (i 98): πειθομένων δὲ καὶ ταῦτα τῶν Μήδων οἰκοδομέει τείχεα μεγάλα τε καὶ καρτερὰ ταῦτα τὰ νῦν Ἀγβάτανα κέκληται, ἕτερον ἑτέρῳ κύκλῳ ἐνεστεῶτα. μεμηχάνηται δὲ οὕτω τοῦτο τὸ τεῖχος ὥστε ὁ ἕτερος τοῦ ἑτέρου κύκλος τοῖσι προμαχεῶσι μούνοισι ἐστι ὑψηλότερος. τὸ μέν κού τι καὶ τὸ χωρίον συμμαχέει κολωνὸς ἐὼν ὥστε τοιοῦτο εἶναι, τὸ δὲ καὶ μᾶλλόν τι ἐπετηδεύθη. κύκλων δ' ἐόντων τῶν συναπάντων ἑπτά, ἐν δὴ τῷ τελευταίῳ τὰ βασιλήια ἔνεστι καὶ οἱ θησαυροί. . . . οὕτω τῶν πέντε κύκλων οἱ προμαχεῶνες ἠνθισμένοι εἰσὶ φαρμάκοισι: δύο δὲ οἱ τελευταῖοί εἰσὶ ὃ μὲν καταργυρωμένους ὁ δὲ κατακεχρυσωμένους ἔχων τοὺς προμαχεῶνας. Text from Perseus, tr. Godley, whose translation has misled everyone with respect to the plan-shape of the walls. The Greek word κύκλος *kyklos* 'ring, circle, surrounding, etc.' has a broader meaning than English *circle*—a precise word—so I have rendered κύκλος as "[concentric] loop' throughout. See Endnote 167.

10. Polybius (x 27), from Perseus, tr. Shuckburgh.

11. Gunter (1982). Cf. Note 9 above and Endnote 167. Truly *circular* palace-city plans are in fact stereotypically Central Eurasian, but are unknown in the Ancient Near East until the Parthians introduced the circular plan for their royal capitals some centuries later. See Beckwith (1984b) and the important updates and corrections in Beckwith (2009: 147, 147, note 23 and 394, note 28). The ruins uncovered so far at Tell Ecbatana in Hamadân have three "concentric" walls that are actually irregularly shaped and angular in plan.

plundered repeatedly by later conquerors. And the citadel is specifically noted in nearly all ancient sources that mention the city.

There is some information about the place in Aramaic, most notably Ezra (vi 2), which mentions a written record having been kept 'in Ecbatana, in the citadel of the province of Media',[12] thus explicitly mentioning 'the citadel' (*bīrəṯā*).[13] Based on these descriptions, the innovation actually was that the walls of the citadel containing the palace and treasury (and eventually the temple of Anāhitā) in the central part of the city were covered entirely with heavy gold plate. The citadel was thus characteristically Scythian in that respect. Its Scythian name is confirmed by the names of two capital cities at the Far Eastern edge of the Empire, discussed below.

The City's Name, Agamatana

The city Ecbatana is not certainly mentioned by name in any dated source until 550 BC, when Cyrus the Great overthrew the second historical Mede King Astyages (r. 585–550) and captured the Imperial treasury in Ecbatana, an event recorded in Akkadian:

> (Astyages) mustered (his army) and marched against Cyrus [Akk. *Kuraš*], king of Anshan, for conquest. . . . The army rebelled against Astyages [Akk. *Ištumegu*] and he was taken prisoner. They handed him over to Cyrus . . . Cyrus marched to Ecbatana [Akkadian *Agamtanu*, for an Iranic *Agam(a)tāna*], the royal city. The silver, gold, goods, property . . . which he carried off as booty (from) Ecbatana he took to Anshan.[14]

The Babylonian Akkadian transcriptions in this, the earliest, report represent the name as <A-gam-ta-nu>, i.e., *Agamtana*. But Akkadian also

12. בְּאַחְמְתָא בְּבִירְתָא דִּי בְּמָדַי מְדִינְתָּה (*BHS* 1420).

13. *CAL*, s.v. *byrh, byrt'* (*bīrā, bīrtā*) 'fortress; palace precinct', a loan from Akkadian *birtu*.

14. From the Nabonidus (ABC) Chronicle (Kuhrt 2007, 2: 50), with added information on original text forms in brackets from Dandamaev (1989: 17), and slight reformatting to fit the style of the present book.

transcribes the name as <A-ga-ma-ta-nu> or <A-gam-ma-ta-nu>, representing *Agamatana, Agammatana,* etc.[15] The name is attested in Imperial Aramaic as *Aḥəmət̠ā(na),*[16] as well as in Elamite as *Akmadana* (*Ak-ma-da-na*)[17] and in Greek as Ἀγβάτανα *Agbatana* ~ Ἐκβάτανα *Ekbatana,* the Elamite and Greek representing Persianized forms.

Finally, although the modern literary New Persian form of the city name, *Hamadân,* preserves the literary Old Persian onset *h,* the local pronunciation of the name in about 1730, as attested on the map by Ottens, is *Amadân,* preserving the non-Persian form of the city's ancient name. It is also recorded in recent New Persian as *Amadâna* ('old name of the city of Hamadân').[18] Since *only* Old Persian and literary New Persian transcriptions have the initial *h,* the phone is an artefact of the Old Persian folk etymologization of the original name, which did not have the *h.*

Since there is confirming evidence on the Scythian origin of the Scytho-Mede capital city's name in Chinese sources (see the next

15. Word-final *-u* is an Akkadian grammatical ending equivalent to Old Iranic *-a* in these words.

16. In the Imperial Biblical Aramaic transcription אַחְמְתָא *Aḥəmət̠ā-,* final *-na* has been dropped due to reanalysis as a native Aramaic form (here, the Aramaic first person plural pronominal suffix *-nā*). Reanalysis is a known practice affecting loanwords into Aramaic. The theoretically possible reading of *Aḥəmət̠ā-* as **Aḥmət̠ā-* is ruled out by the Chinese transcriptions of the name, as well as the early 4th century CE full Aramaeo-Sogdian form of the name, *<'ḥwmt'n>*, where the '*schwa mobile*' (the articulated schwa [ə] after the *ḥ* [χ] or [ɣ], as shown below) in the Masoretic reading is explicitly written out, but unexpectedly as <w>, i.e., a vowel that has been rounded, either due to Sogdian developments or under the influence of ancient northwestern Chinese dialects. See below for sources and discussion, and see Beckwith (forthcoming-a) for another example of the vowel shift from *<ə> to *<w>.

17. Matthew W. Stolper (p.c., March 23, 2018; any errors are mine); cf. Tavernier (2007: 69) *Ak-ma-da-na.* Elamite transcriptions nearly always (as here) follow Old Persian models very closely.

18. Ottens (ca. 1730), *Regnum Persicum Imperium Turcicum in Asia Russorum Provinciae ad Mare Caspium,* from Wikipedia Commons. The old pronunciation is confirmed by the Persian Wikipedia page امدانه *Amadāna,* which says: اَمَدانه یا آمادای یا آمادانه نام قدنم شهر همدان است '*Amadāna* or *Amādāy* or *Amādāna* is the old name of the city of Hamadān'; final *a* [æ] has become *e* in Iranian Persian. Since New Persian retains the onset <h> in the ancient name of Herat (Old Persian *Haraiva*), at least in the modern language, the <h> of *Hamadān* reflects the ancient literary folk-etymology, not the attested early modern local pronunciation of the name, sans *h.* On the Old Persian form with *h* see Endnote 168.

section), the conclusion is clear. *Agamatāna*, Classical "Ecbatana", is Scythian, and was used by Scythians as the name of at least two ancient capital cities: the capital of Media and the capital of Chao, and the latter clearly influenced the name of the capital of Ch'in.[19]

Agamatana in the East

Two other ancient cities named *Agamatāna are attested. The oldest has a written form which has continued in use unchanged (except for writing style) from Old Chinese down to the present.

Han-tan 邯鄲 (*Hándān*), now usually spelled *Handan*, the capital city of the ancient Scytho-Chinese state of Chao 趙 (*Zhào*), is first named in Chinese sources in 500 or 494 BC.[20] Like Hamadân in the West, it is an important city today. Its Old Chinese written name can be straightforwardly reconstructed from Middle Chinese ☆ɣamtan[21] as *Ăɣámătánă, transcribing a foreign *Agamatana or *Aɣamatana.[22]

> Unusually in Chinese, the characters 邯鄲 have no other meaning than 'transcription of the name Ăɣámătánă > ☆ɣamtan > *Han-tan* (*Hándān*)', so it is by definition a transcription of a foreign (non-Chinese) word. The straightforward reconstruction shows it is clearly the same name as the ancient name of modern *Hamadân* ~ *Amadân* ~ *Amadâna*, which was pronounced *Agamatāna in Imperial Scythian and neighboring languages. Both Media and Chao were Scythian or Scythianized in culture and language in the mid-first millennium BC, when the Scythians dominated Central Eurasia and the neighboring frontier zones. This shared name is first recorded at that time in historical sources on both regions, and it is clearly Scythian. Like *Agamatāna* in Media (Hamadân), *Ăgámătánă in Chao (*Hándān*)

19. Etymological proposals based on the Old Persianized transcriptions (Tavernier 2006: 26; Brown 2011; Schmitt 2014: 57, 179, 186) should thus be abandoned. Cf. the preceding Note.

20. In the *Ch'un-ch'iu*, 魯哀公 Lu Ai-kung 'Duke Ai of Lu' 1 (494), 3 (492), 4 (491). In the *Tso-chuan* slightly earlier, 魯定公 Lu Ting-kung 'Duke Ting of Lu' 10 (500) and 13 (497). The name is thus attested contemporaneously with the name of Hamadân.

21. See Endnote 169.

22. See Endnote 170 for the relevant phonological rules.

is associated with Scythians from its earliest history.[23] As noted in Chapter 7, Chao Cheng, better known as Ch'in shih huang ti 秦始皇帝 (*Qín Shǐhuángdì*) 'First Emperor of Ch'in', was born and raised in the Chao clan's capital city of Chao, Han-tan (*Hándān*)—Old Chinese *Ăgámătánă[24]—as a prince of the Chao clan.

When Chao Cheng's father became king of Ch'in, his family moved to Hsien-yang 咸陽(Xiányáng), now written *Xianyang*, Old Chinese *ĂgămădáɴĂ—transcribed in Aramaeo-Sogdian as <'ḥwmt'n> *Aḥwm*(*a*)*tān*(*a*), in Literary Sogdian with <γ>, *Aγum*(*a*)*tān*(*a*). The latter forms represent a dialect pronunciation *Aɣúm(a)tān(a) or the like for an expected *Aɣə́m(a)tān(a), the name of the Chao clan's capital city of Ch'in, which was built in the 4th century BC.[25] The early Aramaeo-Sogdian text from China uses the Imperial Aramaic transcription of the name of Ecbatana, *Aḥəməṯā*[*na*] (representing a foreign *Aɣəmatāna*) to write the name of the Ch'in capital city, Hsien-yang, with one important difference. Analysis of the difference confirms that it transcribes exactly the same Scythian name as *Amadân* ~ *Hamadân*[26] and *Handan*.

Hsien-yang 咸陽 (*Xiányáng*) from Middle *Chinese ☆ɣəɨmjɨaŋ (Pul. 119, 360); attested MChi *ham* from *ɣam (Tak. 353) + attested MChi *yaŋ* (Tak. 390) from OChi *daɴ; thus Old Chinese *Ăɣə́mădáɴă. The name is transcribed in Aramaeo-Sogdian as < 'ḥwmt'n> *Aḥum(a)-tān(a) in Sogdian Ancient Letter No. 2 (Sims-Williams 2001; cf. Takata 2010), dated ca. 311 CE, using the traditional Imperial Aramaic transcription < 'ḥmt'n> *Aḥəməṯā*[*na*] of the name *Agamatāna* "Ecbatana" (see above in this chapter), but explicitly transcribing its clearly stressed *ə* vowel as <w> [u]. This follows the vowel's pronunciation in Early Middle Chinese, ☆ə, which is transcribed <u> in at

23. See Endnote 171.

24. As the characters of *Han-tan* 邯鄲 *Hándān* are purely transcriptional and are themselves meaningless, the name has been very little folk-etymologized.

25. Hung (1999: 675). It is probably significant that both cities were the capitals of Chao clan states, so the same family ruled the two most powerful of the Warring States, both of which straddled the frontier with non-Chinese Central Eurasian people.

26. That is, *ĂgămădáɴĂ via internal reconstruction and *Aɣə́m(a)tān(a) according to the Aramaeo-Sogdian and Literary Sogdian transcriptions; see below on the vowel written <w>.

least one Old Tibetan loan or transcription from the same northwestern Chinese dialect region (Beckwith forthcoming-a). In addition, Imperial Aramaic <ḥ> is usually interpreted as [χ] in this name, but the name Hsien-yang is also frequently written in Sogdian < ‘γwmt’n>, with <γ> [g/ɣ] instead of <ḥ> [χ] (Gharib 30), and of course all Akkadian transcriptions of the name, unlike Aramaic, write a voiced <g>. Thus the Imperial Aramaic transcription actually represents *Aɣəmatā(na), and the Aramaeo-Sogdian form represents an underlying *Aɣə́matāna. The transcription in Ancient Letter No. 2 is now regularly read "*Khumdān*", but that is actually the medieval pronunciation of the name from several centuries later, after regular Sogdian aphaeresis and apocope deleted the first and last vowels, based on transcriptions in several foreign segmental scripts.[27] This *Khumdān* is usually said to be the name of the more famous capital city Ch’ang-an (now Hsi-an), but that is not correct. The Aramaeo-Sogdian name *Aɣə́m(a)tān(a) is a transcription of the name now read *Hsien-yang*, Old Chinese *Ăɣắmădáɴă, formerly the capital of Ch’in, which is to the north across the Wei River, several kilometers from Ch’ang-an. Although Han-tan 邯鄲 *Ăɣámătánă—and Hsien-yang 咸陽 OChi *Ăɣắmădáɴă, in Aramaeo-Sogdian transcription *Aɣə́m(a)tān(a)—thus have the same name as *Agamatana* "Ecbatana", each has been recorded in a different Old Chinese dialect, and in the case of *Hsien-yang*, also in one ancient foreign transcription and many medieval ones.

Saraɣ ~ Saray in the East

Another ancient city name recorded in Sogdian Ancient Letter No. 2 (line 11) is *<srγ>*, read *Saraγ*,[28] identified with *Loyang* 洛陽 (*Luòyáng*), here written traditionally as Loyang. This corresponds to the Scythian word **sarah-* ‘head’ (see Tables 7 and 8). If the two are in fact related,

27. The earliest is in Theophylactus Simocatta (early 7th century), as Χουβδάν or Χουμαδάν, followed several centuries later by Arabic *Khumdān* in many works (Takata 2010).

28. Sims-Williams (2001); Gharib 361. I am indebted to Nicholas Sims-Williams for very kindly discussing the letter with me by correspondence some years ago. Any errors here are mine alone.

as seems very likely, it is the earliest attestation of the word as a city name. Since Sogdian is a Scythian dialect, the word itself is then Scythian.[29]

Saraγ is well attested later in medieval New Persian (سرای *Sarây*) and in Turkic and Mongolic (*Saray*, also transcribed *Sarai*), most famously in the name of the Golden Horde capital on the lower Volga.[30] The meaning often given to this later word is 'palace', and of course ancient and medieval capital cities did contain at least one grand palace of the monarch.

Since *Loyang* 洛陽 is generally thought to be several centuries older than the period under consideration, and to be based on a local river name, it is quite possible that its ancient name is purely Chinese, *Lo* 洛 (*Luò*) from traditional Middle Chinese ☆lak (Pul. 203) from traditional Old Chinese *rāk (Sta. 564), for Old Chinese *rag(ă), which is identical to the name of the other great city of Media, *Ragā* in Old Persian and (*pace* Sch. 236) *Raγa* in Avestan (Imperial Scythian), now *Ray* (*Rayy*), the ancestor of the nearby modern capital Tehrān, of which it is now a part.

The Aramaeo-Sogdian transcription supports the traditional reconstruction, as well as the Scythian etymology. It has been known since Karlgren (1957) that the phonetic 各 once had onset clusters (then, and mostly still, thought to be "prefixes"), selected parts of which were lost before Middle Chinese times. Updating things a little, *Lo* 洛 in Old Chinese should be *(Că)rág(ă) or the like.[31] Thus either the

29. It could be a Sogdian folk-etymologization using the native Scythian word for 'head' (see the next footnote) in the sense 'the capital', but that requires the native name to be similar, and *rak/rag(ă) would hardly serve for that.

30. Cf. Sogdian *sr*, read *sar* 'head' (Gharib 360), *s 'r* read *sār* 'head' (Gharib 351, only one occurrence), and *s r 'y* 'head' (Gharib 360), read by Gharib *sarē*, but explicitly written *sarāy*, a reading supported by later occurrences of the name in formerly Scythian-speaking Central Eurasia. Of course the word *capital* is ultimately a derivation from the Latin word for 'head'.

31. Sta. 564: 落 *rāk, correcting the vowel length to *a, and revising the coda to *-g following Zhengzhang (1991), taking cognizance of forms in the same phonetic series with a different *Middle* Chinese onset. "C" is *any* Consonant. Kar. (202–203) has traditional OChi *glâk, but it should rather be *grâk, as it is now believed that most examples of *l* in Middle Chinese are from Old Chinese *r. Moreover, we must add back the unstressed first vowel that was later deleted, as well as the unstressed final vowel. The result is *(kă)rág(ă), perhaps representing *χărág(ă), which should be from an earlier *Saráɣ(ă)—the change in Chinese of earlier *s to

Aramaeo-Sogdian form *Saraɣ* is also a conservative earlier Old Chinese reading (like that of Xianyang) of a Chinese word *Lo* 洛 (*Luò*), OChi *sărágă (which would have regularly become *χărágă and eventually just *Lo*), or else the transcription records yet another Scythian city name of North China.[32] In any case, the highly conservative form of the name of *Lo-yang* in Sogdian Ancient Letter II, with its Old Chinese *r* (rather than Middle Chinese *l*) and its Old Chinese form of the name Hsien-yang, shows that the letter is an important source for Old Chinese reconstruction.

The city naming events in ancient West and East are very closely connected. The Scythians conquered all of Central Eurasia and most of Central Asia, conducting commerce internally and externally on a continental scale for the first time, and the Sogdians or 'people of Sugda (Scythia)', who were famous merchants, are their direct descendants. It should not therefore be surprising to hear that the Scythians founded or refounded several major cities.

The outcome of their empire-building in Media was the short-lived Scytho-Mede Empire, with its capital *Agamatāna* (now Hamadān), and the realm's continuation, the long-lived *Scytho-Mede-Persian Empire*. It was a thoroughly Scythian realm in origin and remained one, despite internal power shifts, as shown in Chapters 2 and 3. Although "the Achaemenid Persian Empire" is its usual designation today, it was simply *χšaθra* "the Empire". It spread the new Scythian institutions, practices, beliefs, and language[33] around Southwestern Eurasia.

Similarly, the outcome of the Scythians' shaping or reshaping of Chao, with its own capital *Agamatána (now *Handan*), was the eventual unifying Ch'in Dynasty, founded by Chao Cheng (*Zhào Zhèng*), prince

Middle Chinese χ is well known (see the next footnote)—in which case it is an old Scythian name for the city, the Chou (Zhou) period Chinese name of which was *Ch'eng-chou* 成周 (*Chéngzhōu*).

32. Either way it is an example of an unstressed first *syllable* *să in Old Chinese becoming *χă, undergoing a known sound change (*s > *χ), depending on environment, as attested in many examples. Thus this Aramaeo-Sogdian transcription is worth further attention on several counts.

33. See Chapter 5.

of Chao and Ch'in, better known as Ch'in shih huang ti (*Qín Shǐhuángdì*). His parents were both Chaoish royalty, and he was born and raised not in Ch'in but in the capital of Chao, *Agamatána. His Ch'in Dynasty empire, with its capital *Aɣămatāna (now Hsien-yang), was succeeded by the very long-lived Han Dynasty with a new nearby capital, Ch'ang-an 長安 (*Cháng'ān*) 'Eternal Peace', modern Hsi-an 西安 (*Xī'ān*).

The Scythians were a great people who founded the world's first empire and built the first imperial capital city in the Classical period Scytho-Mede-Persian Empire, and two of the great capital cities in Classical East Asia. The continuations of the Scythian Empire in the two regions became long-lasting, prosperous regimes: the Persian Empire and the Chinese Empire.

EPILOGUE

Scythian Philosophy and the Classical Age

The single most famous shared feature of Classical culture in all of the nations that experienced a "Classical Age" is the appearance of philosophy in the strict sense, with a capital "P": *Philosophy*. It was a new and unprecedented thing, and that particular period in the mid-first millennium BC is the only time in history that Philosophy flourished so spectacularly in those cultures. To put it another way, no other "Age of Philosophy" ever happened there before or since, and each culture's Classical Age happened at about the same time as its Age of Philosophy.[1]

Could philosophy be a Scythian invention too? The first part of this chapter shows that the Greeks, Persians, Indians, and Chinese were each taught by an early Scythian philosopher and thus experienced Scythian philosophy first-hand at about the same time, *before* there is any other sign of Philosophy per se in the lands where they taught. The second part of this chapter considers the concept of the Classical Age, an ancient period when philosophy uniquely flourished outside Central Eurasia, the Scythians' homeland.

1. Unlike previous attempts to explain the co-occurrence (discussed below), the analysis here is limited to—and based strictly on—actual data.

Scythian Philosophy

The first great philosophers of Greece, China, India, Iran, and Scythia, who flourished between approximately 600 and 400 BC, were revolutionaries. They did something entirely new and unprecedented: all of them criticized and rejected the traditional beliefs and practices of the countries where they taught. They were not just "philosophers". Each one was arguably his adoptive culture's *earliest* Philosopher—in the strict modern sense of that word[2]—with the addition that in Antiquity philosophers were expected to *practice* their philosophy. Chronologically, they are:

1. Anacharsis the Scythian, a half-Greek Scythian who taught in Greece.
2. Zoroaster, a Scythian speaker who taught in the Scytho-Mede Empire.
3. Gautama the Scythian Sage (*Gautama Śākyamuni*), who taught in northern India.
4. *Gautamă (Lao-tan ~ Laotzu), who bears a Scythian name and taught in early China.

Quite a lot has been written on each philosopher discussed here, but each is usually treated as if he belonged to a much later dominant local tradition, if he even existed. Thus Anacharsis is supposed to have been a Greek Cynic, Zoroaster a Late Zoroastrian Persian dualist, Buddha an Indian pupil of Brahmanists and Jains, and Laotzu a mystical and inscrutable Chinese political theorist.[3] However, the most striking thing about these thinkers is their unusually insightful, strictly Philosophical teachings on remarkably similar themes. Although we know almost nothing historical about them, the earliest accounts agree on one point: each of

2. We speak and write *modern* languages, and we use words in their *modern* meaning, even when we know they had different meanings in Antiquity or the Middle Ages. Our modern analyses are based on modern categories, modern thinking, and modern words, not on their ancient etymological ancestors.

3. See Endnote 172.

them was a foreigner in a country where his ideas differed from local ideas, but where he achieved success. And surely the most remarkable historical fact about them is that they were Scythians.

Anacharsis the Scythian and Greek philosophy

Half Scythian and half Greek by birth and education, Anacharsis was a Scythian prince who travelled to Greece in the 47th Olympiad (592–589 BC), where he met Solon, a lawgiver considered to be one of the earliest pre-Socratic thinkers. The Greeks greatly esteemed Anacharsis, who is often listed as one of the Seven Sages of Antiquity,[4] and Aristotle treats him as a major philosopher.[5]

The Scythian's most famous philosophical argument is reported in a number of slightly variant versions, mostly short and pithy. The best-attested one, which is considered to be genuine, reflects the kind of logic attested in Early Buddhism, including its Taoist relative (both discussed below). It reports in an indirect quotation what Anacharsis said:

> He wondered why among the Greeks the experts contend, but the non-experts decide.[6]

The basic point of this comment is epistemological and sceptical, calling into question the basis of our entire cognitive ability, both individually and collectively. It is also a sceptical comment about the Greeks' quasi-religious political belief in "equality". The statement is thus deeply insightful not only for such an early period but for modern cultures too.

His sceptical attitude is praised by the ancient Pyrrhonists, the Classical Sceptics par excellence, who considered him to be the earliest Sceptic. Sextus Empiricus says, "Anacharsis the Scythian, they say, does

4. There are many lists. Diogenes Laertius (i 1,40) has an extensive treatment and a number of lists with different members, sometimes many more than seven of them. He also mentions the Seven Sages at numerous other points in his work.

5. See Epilogue, Note 11.

6. Diogenes Laertius i 8,103 (Hicks 1925: 1:106–107: θαυμάζειν δὲ ἔφη πῶς παρὰ τοῖς Ἕλλησιν ἀγωνίζονται μὲν οἱ τεχνῖται, κρίνουσι δὲ οἱ μὴ τεχνῖται. See Kindstrand (1981: 119, 150–151) and the very interesting expanded version of the same argument quoted in Sextus Empiricus, *Adversus mathematicos* vii, 1, 55–59 (2005: 13–14), q.v. Beckwith (2015: 2–3).

away with the apprehension that is capable of judging every skill, and strenuously criticizes the Greeks for holding on to it."[7] In his comedy *The Frogs*, the playwright Aristophanes, who lived about two centuries after Anacharsis,[8] dwells exactly on the issue of judging, using a scale to measure the "weight" of the dramatic poems of Aeschylus and Euripides.[9] Yet the judges are not poets—the relevant experts—quite as Anacharsis notes two centuries earlier. He thus seems to be the first in Greece to suggest the philosophical question known as the Problem of the Criterion *as* a philosophical problem that entailed dealing with entities such as ethical antilogies.[10] Other statements of his, whether genuine or simply accretions to the Anacharsis tradition, also focus on striking anomalies. Some are discussed by Aristotle, who shows them to be logically structured. For example, an ethical remark attributed to Anacharsis addresses the question of happiness, in which context Aristotle quotes him as saying, "Play, in order that you may work hard."[11] Anacharsis may thus be considered the spiritual founder of Greek logical-epistemological Scepticism.[12]

Although Thales, Solon, and others are said to be the earliest Greek philosophers, they were not "Philosophers" per se, in our modern strict sense of the word, but rather in the sense of a "wise man" or "lawgiver", frequently a "natural philosopher"—which meant a natural scientist, or

7. Beckwith (2015: 3, note 6).

8. Aristophanes lived ca. 455–ca. 385.

9. See Griffith (2013) and Henderson (2002) on Aristophanes' *Frogs* and on weighing in ancient Greek culture in general; cf. Beckwith (2015: 27, note 22). Since judging is thought to be a major theme running through Classical Greek culture and its literature, the observation of Anacharsis was perhaps not uttered in a vacuum; yet that literature was all written *long after* Anacharsis and his observations. Cf. below on the mention in the *Gāthās* of Zoroaster of a scale to "weigh" a soul after death.

10. An antilogy is an opposed pair of contraries such as *true* and *false*, *just* and *unjust*, etc.

11. Aristotle, *Nicomachean Ethics* 10.6 (1176b.30): παίζειν δ' ὅπως σπουδάζῃ. Aristotle says the epigram of Anacharsis is "right" and explains, "For amusement is a form of rest; but we need rest because we are not able to go on working without a break, and therefore it is not an end [a *telos* or goal], since we take it as a means to further activity." From Perseus, tr. Rackham (1934).

12. For Pyrrho, the actual founder of Greek scepticism, see Beckwith (2015). Much later the Cynics took Anacharsis as one of their heroes, but Martin (1996) shows that he could not have been a Cynic. His analysis of the related proposal that he is a purely legendary creation of the Cynics shows that theory to be untenable as well. See Endnote 173.

often, an engineer or inventor.[13] We know very little about Anacharsis or the other earliest thinkers in the Greek world, but it is clear that in the Classical period itself Anacharsis was viewed mainly as a Philosopher in the modern sense. Accordingly, though this might not be a popular idea in some quarters,[14] Anacharsis the Scythian seems to be the earliest actual Greek philosopher.[15]

Zoroaster and Persian Philosophy

Zoroaster, or *Zaraθuštra* (Zarathushtra), presents himself as an outsider in an unidentified region which later became a part of the Scytho-Mede-Persian Empire. One of the few things that may be historical about him is that he composed the famous *Gāthās,* or 'Hymns', in a lofty archaic form of a language that is today called Old Avestan. But *Avestan* simply means 'the language of the *Avesta,* the corpus of ancient Zoroastrian texts'. Old Avestan is actually an archaic dialect of Imperial Scythian, the spoken administrative language of the Scytho-Mede Empire and later the Achaemenid Persian Empire. Imperial Scythian was the native language spoken in most of Iran, in Southern Central Asia (most of what is now Afghanistan) and in Western Central Asia (now Turkmenistan, Uzbekistan, and Tajikistan).[16] That means the composers of the Young Avestan texts spoke that language, a form of *Scythian,* which is first certainly attested in the 7th century BC,[17] as shown in Chapter 5.

Zoroaster often refers to houses, and the world of his *Gāthās* is hardly the open steppe homeland of the nomadic Scythians. Moreover, the monotheistic system in the poems is revolutionary in the region where

13. The attributions of various inventions to Anacharsis are considered to be late and ahistorical.

14. See Endnote 174.

15. This supports the alternative Greek view on the origin of philosophy cited by *Diogenes Laertius* (i 1–13), which attributes it to foreigners. The very first sentence of his book reads, Τὸ τῆς φιλοσοφίας ἔργον ἔνιοί φασιν ἀπὸ βαρβάρων ἄρξαι. 'There are some who say that the study of philosophy had its beginning among the barbarians [i.e., foreigners, non-Greeks—CIB].' From Perseus, tr. Hicks.

16. See Chapter 5.

17. The Cimmerians first appear in Assyrian records in the late 8th century, but we do not have any Cimmerian names until the early 7th century.

he lives, which is dominated by polytheists who worship the Daēvas, against whom he rails. But in the steppe zone the known cultures well into the Middle Ages were predominantly monotheistic (with God the head of the hierarchical feudal order), so there should have been no conflict with his main religious teaching.[18] Thus the region from which he fled[19] was probably not the open steppe. That allows us to reject higher dates for the *Gāthās*, though the text must be earlier than the Behistun Inscription of Darius the Great, dated to ca. 519 BC, in which monotheistic (Early) Zoroastrianism is first firmly attested. Therefore we need to date Zoroaster, the *Gāthās*, and Early Zoroastrianism to *no earlier* than 720–714 BC (when the Cimmerians, a Scythian-speaking people, are first attested in the northern Ancient Near East) or 676/675 BC (when the Scythians are first attested there), but *no later* than 519 BC (the Behistun Inscription). That date range brings to mind the remarkable fact that the father of our earliest attested overt witness to Early Zoroastrianism, Darius the Great, was Vištāspa (Hystaspes), who is mentioned in the Behistun Inscription. The lone political supporter of Zoroaster in the *Gāthās* has the same Scythian name, Vištāspa. It has often been wondered if the two Vištāspas were one and the same person. Considering the strong Early Zoroastrian views of Darius, which surely continue those of his father Vištāspa, the *name* at least of the Gathic Vištāspa is no doubt to be connected to his father's *name*.

We must however doubt the folk etymologies that have been proposed for the name *Zoroaster, Zaraθuštra*, the most favored one today claiming that it means 'Decrepit Camels'.[20] Surely, as the founder of a great world religion, his name meant something else, something less

18. Also, Central Eurasians *in Central Eurasia* in Antiquity and the Middle Ages were famously liberal and tolerant of other religions.

19. In Yasna 46.1, quoted below. Unfortunately he does not tell us anything about that place, and laments being rejected by the people where he has moved.

20. Schmitt (2002), who reconstructs Old Iranic **Zarat-uštra-*, explaining it as "with old/decrepit [better: aging] camels" (Schmitt's parenthetical addition). He concludes, "in the final analysis the problem remains far from settled." Though he does suggest the possibility of an unknown dialect to explain one of the key problems, he rightly rejects it. Nevertheless, it is striking that he does not even consider any other language as possibly being the source of the name, or some part of it. Cf. the next Note.

redolent of an attempt to find an etymology, any etymology, in a hoped-for place—in this case, in Avestan itself. Moreover, whatever the name as a whole means, its first component, *Zara-*, is surely Semitic *zar'a* 'seed (of)', i.e., 'son (of)', so it is probably Ancient Near Eastern in origin.[21]

Zoroaster in the *Gāthās* is an outsider among blood-sacrificing polytheists, who constituted the majority of Ancient Near Eastern cultures. He rejected the traditional culture of worshipping statues of the gods. As Malandra notes, "Apparently, Zaraθuštra's position within his own society became so precarious that he was forced to flee."

What land to flee to?
Where should I go to flee?
From (my) family
and from (my) clan they banish me.[22]

Nevertheless, we know his teachings were successful. The first historical blows for monotheism and against polytheism in the Ancient Near East were struck by the Scythians in the mid-620s,[23] closely followed by King Cyaxares (*Huvaχštra) of the Scytho-Mede Empire in 613, and most explicitly by their contemporary King Josiah of Judah (after ca. 622 BC). All are said to have destroyed polytheistic gods (statues) and temples.[24] These historical events indicate the dramatic effect of the new monotheistic faith on its believers. After a polytheistic revival under Cyrus the Great and his son, Early Zoroastrian monotheism was restored by Darius, as he records in his 519 Behistun Inscription.

Early Zoroastrianism is a novel metaphysical-ethical system that emphatically rejects the dominant Archaic polytheistic beliefs and practices of Zoroaster's adoptive land, calling them Lies, and their gods False

21. The Near Eastern Semitic word meaning 'seed, offspring, clan member', e.g., Aramaic *zar'a*, Arabic *zar'*, 'seed', is often used in names followed by another word, in the sense 'son of X', or 'clan of X'. In this case *-štra* or *-stra* is the X, probably the word 'star' ~ the god Ištar ('Star'), Greek *astra* 'the stars' (as in the Greek form of the name), etc. See further in Appendix A.

22. Y. 46, 1–2 (Malandra 2009); cf. Humbach and Ichaporia (1994: 76–77).

23. They plundered the temple of Heavenly Aphrodite in Ascalon. See Chapter 2.

24. Zawadzki (1988) has definitively corrected earlier accounts of Cyaxares' campaign based on the text of *Gadd's Chronicle*. See Chapter 2.

Gods. Instead, Zoroaster teaches monotheism,[25] the Truth, and personal perfection. He says that humans have a choice either to be true and good, or false and bad, but after death all will be judged at the Account Keeper's Bridge, where their deeds will be weighed on a scale.[26] Zoroaster describes in his *Gāthās* what will happen to an evil person who has lied and followed Lies and False Gods:

> His soul, facing (him) at the Account Keeper's Bridge, will make him tremble, for he has strayed from the path of truth by his own actions and those of his tongue.[27]

So evil ones will be judged and cast down into darkness, but virtuous, truthful people will fare better:

> In the house of song, Ahura Mazdā, the Primal one, comes to the faithful offerers (with) the prize that Zarathushtra promised them.[28]

Those who follow Zoroaster's teachings are thus promised an afterlife in Paradise together with God, Ahura Mazdā. His basic teachings agree closely with the traditional beliefs of steppe peoples from the Scythians (at least) onward.[29]

The *Gāthās* are undated, so the earliest direct, dated, hard evidence for Zoroaster's teachings is in the inscriptions of Darius the Great and his son Xerxes. Darius explicitly equates the law of Ahura Mazdā with truth, unity, and peace in his Behistun Inscription. He makes obvious references to Zoroaster's teachings, stressing the Truth and absolute good embodied in the One Great God, Ahuramazdā, versus the Lie of the polytheistic *Daivas* or "False Gods", and the rebels who *lied* and

25. Artaxerxes II in the early 4th century BC rehabilitated the chief two *Daivas*, Anāhitā and Mithra, who with Mazdā made a trinity.

26. Yasna 31,3. Humbach and Ichaporia (1994: 35).

27. Yasna 51,13. Humbach and Ichaporia (1994: 98–99): *cinuuatō pərətå akå* | *xvāiš śiiaoθanāiš hizuuascā aṣ̌ahiiā nąsuuå paθō.*

28. Yasna 51, 14. Humbach and Ichaporia (1994: 98–99): *hiiaṯ miždəm zaraθuštrō magauuabiiō cōišt parā* | *garō dəmānē ahurō mazdå jasaṯ pouruiiō.*

29. Zoroaster made the *Truth* and the *Lie* a specific antilogy, but in the *Gāthās* there is no actual duality, such as appears in Late Zoroastrianism. Strict duality requires two equal divinities. For historically attested Late Zoroastrianism see Horky (2009).

nearly tore the Empire apart.[30] The rebels supported the *Daivas* (the word is explicitly mentioned by Darius' son and successor Xerxes) and were not true to their oath to be loyal vassals of the One Great King (and under Darius and Xerxes, loyal vassals of the One Great God, Ahuramazdā, who had created Heaven and Earth).

In short Zoroaster, who spoke a Scythian dialect and was ethnolinguistically Scythian, developed a perfectionistic, systematized version of steppe Scythian beliefs. Philosophically it is a unified religious-political system: *virtuous monarchy* both in Heaven and on Earth, valuing Truth and peaceful monarchistic Unity, while opposing Falsehood and warring polytheistic divisiveness. It thus puts great emphasis on the antilogy of "the True versus the False (the Lie)", which is the philosophical heart of early Zoroastrianism. In the Achaemenid period Zoroaster's teachings gradually merged with pre-Zoroastrian Mazdaism to become Late Zoroastrianism, the first "world religion".

Gautama Buddha 'the Scythian Sage' and Indian Philosophy

Gautama is best known as the *Buddha*, 'the Awakened One'. His other unique epithet,[31] Śākyamuni 'the Scythian Sage', marks him as a foreigner from northwestern India or Central Asia, regions known to have been ruled by the Scythians, Scytho-Medes, and related peoples who succeeded them.[32] According to tradition, Gautama left his home as a young prince and wandered to Magadha, in eastern India, where he "awoke", or was "enlightened". He taught there for the rest of his life. His teachings are radically unlike anything else known in Greece, Scythia,

30. In fact, the ideals of unity and peace were already rejected by the men who rebelled against Great King Cambyses, the son and successor of Cyrus the Great, when Cambyses was on campaign in Egypt. When Cambyses died, his relative Darius took the throne and suppressed the rebellions. He thus restored unity and peace. However, the rebellions were mainly about religion—the rebels rejected Ahura Mazdā. See Chapter 3.

31. No other Indian philosopher has an epithet marking him as a foreigner. (The same is true in Greece for Anacharsis the Scythian.) For other proposals see Endnote 175.

32. See Chapters 5 and 6.

Persia, India, or China before him. His life is widely considered to mark the beginning of history in India.

Gautama expounds a logical-epistemological system that denies the existence of a criterion to *decide* or *judge* between opposed absolute assertions or "views"—*antilogies* such as Truth vs. Falsehood, Honesty vs. Dishonesty, etc. His teachings are exclusively on ethics, particularly the problem of happiness or equanimity. Solving it involves rigorous personal physical-mental practice. He says nothing at all about metaphysical topics such as divinity or an afterlife, nor about the natural, physical world. His core teaching is known as the *Trilakṣaṇa* 'three characteristics' of all *dharmas*—ethical "things" or *constituents* of the conceptual world of our thoughts and emotions:

> All constituents are (1) 'impermanent', all constituents are (2) 'imperfect', and all constituents are (3) 'without an inherent identity'.[33]

Our earliest dated testimony of this teaching is a quotation by the Greek philosopher Pyrrho, who was in India with Alexander the Great for two years, from 327 to 325 BC. Pyrrho's Greek version gives the three in reverse order: all ethical "things" are without an inherent identity (*anātman*), they are imperfect (*duḥkha*), and they are impermanent (*anitya*). Consequently, he adds, there can be no absolute difference between *true* and *false*.[34] The three statements of the *Trilakṣaṇa*, like all Early Buddhist teachings, are resoundingly negative. Other teachings which logically derive from the *Trilakṣaṇa* include having *no* views or beliefs (about absolutes) and *not choosing* either side of any contention (based on absolutes). The unstated, but logically expected, indirect outcome of meditating on the *Trilakṣaṇa* is *nirvāṇa*, a word that refers to the extinguishing of the burning of the passions, and as a result, being undisturbed (calm).

Over the centuries, Gautama's teachings have changed into what is now known as Buddhism, a world religion, yet down to the present the chief goal of Buddhist practice (meditation) has remained the

33. *Anguttara-nikāya* iii, 134 (discussed at length in Beckwith 2015: 29ff.).
34. Beckwith (2015: 29, 32–40), q.v. for the Greek equivalents.

achievement of a deep understanding of the interconnected insights of the *Trilakṣaṇa,* the 'three characteristics'.[35]

Gautama rejected the teachings of his Scythian relatives, including Zoroaster, who stress the traditional ethical issues represented by the antilogy of the Truth versus the Lie.[36] That antilogy is a vital issue for the solemn oath of loyalty, a core element of steppe culture. The Buddha did share the fundamentally *ethical* focus of philosophy that characterizes both Anacharsis and Zoroaster, but unlike Zoroaster he uses a logical, analytical approach similar to that of Anacharsis. In their fundamentally sceptical outlook Gautama and Anacharsis are the opposite of Zoroaster.

Laotzu and Chinese Philosophy[37]

Laotzu 老子 is the traditional name of the author of the key logical-epistemological passages of the *Tao te ching* 道德經 (*Dàodéjīng*) 'the Classic of the Way and (its) Virtue'. He is thought by some to have served as a ritual specialist for the Chou Dynasty (Western Chou 1045–771 BC, Eastern Chou 771–249 BC),[38] which was founded in the western part of ancient China.[39] According to the story in the *Shih chi* he was "a senior contemporary of Confucius"[40] (549–479 BC), but left China when the Chou declined.[41] The story is impossibly ahistorical in every respect, as the historical dates of the dynasty alone show, but in Laotzu's case, leaving China when the Chou declined meant he went to the

35. Gethin (1998: 187); cf. Beckwith (2015: 33, 41–42).

36. To non-Indians today, Buddha's teachings may seem typically "Indian", but in fact they are radically different from Indian thought before or since. Buddhism disappeared from most of India 800 years ago.

37. This section has benefited greatly from a detailed article by Chan (2018)—which has an extensive, up to date bibliography—and from Nivison (1999).

38. Chan (2018) summarizes the traditional stories and sources related to them.

39. I am indebted to Nicholas Vogt (p.c., 2020) for valuable comments on the Chou; any errors are mine.

40. Chan (2018). In the story he is named *Li Erh* 李耳 (*Lǐ Ěr*). For such names see Endnote 176.

41. *Shih chi* 史記 (*Shiji*) 63 (2139–2143): 居周久之, 見周之衰, 迺遂去。至關, 關令尹喜曰 :「子將隱矣, 彊為我著書。」於是老子迺著書上下篇, 言道德之意五千餘言而去, 莫知其所終。For a full translation of the story see Henricks (2000: 133–134). The *Shih chi* was completed in ca. 90 BC.

West. In his day that meant Scythia, thus making him a *Hu* 胡 'Royal (Scythian)', because before modern times no Chinese would leave home to die. That alone indicates he either was a foreigner or was thought to be one.[42]

Laotzu was certainly not contemporary with Confucius, who seems not to have had "a philosophy featuring new ideas of his own",[43] since the one possibly innovative idea traditionally credited to Confucius, *cheng ming* 正名 (*zhèng míng*) "rectification of names", belongs to a very "late stratum" of the *Analects*,[44] which is a highly stratified, composite text.[45] It is thus not a genuine Confucian idea. Confucius was a teacher of tradition and morality, not Philosophy per se, but the material attributed directly to him is earlier than that attributed to Laotzu, so we must separate the two.

The date and place of Laotzu's birth are not even approximately known, but while he no doubt flourished after Confucius (d. 479), it was well before the earliest so far discovered ancient manuscript copy of the *Tao te ching* (dated ca. 300 BC), which features some of Laotzu's core ideas along with a great deal of later material added by many others. That suggests placing Laotzu's own floruit sometime between the early fifth and late fourth centuries.

However, there is solid evidence for Laotzu's foreignness. His Chinese "philosopher name" is extremely unusual. Ancient philosophers' names are otherwise formed by taking the man's surname or full name (which includes the surname) and adding to it *tzu* (子) (*zǐ*), which literally means 'son; child' but is used as a sort of honorific suffix for wise men and philosophers. But because *lao* 'old' in Chinese, as in English, is an ordinary everyday adjective, the name *Lao-tzu* 老子 (*Lǎozǐ*) literally means 'old boy', 'old philosopher', or 'old one'. It is thus not only unlike the many other Chinese philosopher names known to us from Antiquity, it is not an actual proper name at all. It also does not occur in

42. The story is very late and likely not historical, but it at least tells us that Chinese scholars in the Han period considered Laotzu to be non-Chinese. Cf. Chapters 4 and 7.

43. Nivison (1999: 754). In fact, one of the most famous quotes attributed to Confucius (*Lun-yü* vii, 1) is 述而不作 "I transmit, but do not create."

44. Nivison (1999: 757). Despite the intriguing term 'rectification of names', it has nothing to do with Early Taoist antilogies.

45. For the *Analects* see Brooks and Brooks (1998).

the *Tao te ching* itself. That suggests it is a later nickname for him. His usual full name, which occurs many times in the *Chuangtzu* and the *Hanfeitzu* (slightly later Classical philosophical texts), is also unique. In modern reading pronunciation, it is *Lao-tan* 老聃 (*Lǎodān*),[46] folk-etymologized as 'Old Long-ears'. The name was later Sinicized as *Li Erh* 李耳 (*Lǐ Ěr*) 'Ears Li', where Li is the everyday Chinese surname Li and *Erh* 耳(*Ěr*) is the everyday word for 'ear' or 'ears'.[47] So the name is written in several variant ways, with variant pronunciations, and with supposed meanings given in many folk etymologies, which are all doubtful, altogether demonstrating that the name is actually meaningless. These are all *characteristic, standard features of loanwords* in Chinese. So the man has a foreign name.[48] The question is, *which* foreign name?

In Antiquity the word now written 老 and read *lao* (*lǎo*) 'old' was also written as the character now written 考 and read *k'ao* (*kǎo*) 'old'. The characters *k'ao* 考 and *lao* 老 are graphically the partial reverse of each other. Moreover, the *Shih ming* 釋名 (a later Han Dynasty work), says that *lao* 老 is pronounced like *hsiu* 朽 (*xiǔ*), the phonetic of which is *k'ao* 丂 (*kǎo*). Thus in ancient times 老 (*lao*) itself was also pronounced like 考 (*k'ao*), or rather, like the Old Chinese reading of that character. Ancient and medieval scholars have therefore corrected the pronunciation of the character *Lao* 老 in this name to read like *K'ao* 考. That means, in short, that Lao-tan 老聃 *Lǎodān* was also K'ao-tan 考聃 *Kǎodān*.[49] K'ao-tan 考聃 can be straightforwardly reconstructed for Old Chinese as *Gu- ~ *Gau[50] plus *damă ~ *tamă,[51] a perfect transcription

46. Nivison (1999). It is sometimes written alternatively *Lao-tan* 老耽 (*Lǎodān*).

47. The character erh 耳 (*ěr*) 'ear(s)' is also the "significant" (or "radical") element in the character *tan* 聃 (*dān*) 'long-ear(s)'.

48. In pre-modern times foreign names were virtually never translated, so the Chinese name goes back to a transcription of a foreign name. For studies of other ancient foreign words in transcription see Beckwith and Kiyose (2018) and references therein.

49. See Endnotes 153 and 177.

50. Starostin (1989: 553–554) gives an orthodox HSR reconstruction, simply recycling the onset of the MChi form without change, but it is most unlikely that a MChi onset ☆k^h goes back to an OChi onset *k^h.

51. See Endnote 178. The early Chinese Buddhist texts were translated from Gāndhārī, not Sanskrit.

of Gāndhārī *Gudama* or Sanskrit *Gautama*, the personal name of the Buddha.[52]

None of this of course says that the historical Gudama (Gautama Śākyamuni), the Buddha, came to China in early Antiquity[53] and wrote the *Laotzu*, or *Tao te ching* 道德經 'Classic of the Way and Virtue'.[54] Nevertheless, it definitely does confirm that some knowledge of the Buddha and his teachings made their way to China, as suggested by even a cursory reading of the book,[55] as well as by its connection to Gudama (Gautama), the personal name of the Buddha. That knowledge could only have been transmitted orally by a living person who actually travelled from the West to China and wrote the *original early core* of the first Taoist classic. From here on the unambiguous traditional name *Laotzu* is used to refer to this otherwise unknown man known as *Gudama (*Gautama). It is to him that *the whole book* known as the *Tao te ching* is popularly—but inaccurately—ascribed.[56]

It is remarkable that a text written on perishable material, before the invention of modern printing methods, could have survived in such excellent condition after two millennia. But it is simply stunning that the provenanced, excavated Guodian manuscript archaeologically dated to ca. 300 BC, though loose (unbound) and unpaginated, was immediately recognized as a manuscript of the *Tao-te ching*, regardless of the differences between it and the traditionally transmitted texts of the same work dating to the early centuries CE.[57]

That indicates something very important about the text.[58] Despite the noticeable variety within the *Tao te ching*'s contents, its *non*-political chapters are remarkable for their extremely idiosyncratic thought,

52. For detailed data and discussion of the name see Beckwith (2015: 118–121).

53. However, one cannot rule out that possibility, in view of the Buddha's Scythian ethnicity.

54. Also "Classic of the Way and (its) Virtue", among many other renderings.

55. See Endnote 179.

56. The text, of course, also calls for much serious text-critical scholarship. Cf. the following Note.

57. The Guodian manuscript is written on bamboo strips with one line of characters per strip. The strips are unnumbered and there are no chapter numbers or other guides to reconstructing the text except for context (and the traditional transmitted version). See Henricks (2000: 6ff.).

58. See Endnote 180.

approach, and general tone. There is simply no precedent for them in Chinese. By contrast, the *political* chapters, though often similar to the other chapters in their "Taoist voice" and approach, mainly focus on government, like many analogous texts from the Classical period. This indicates that the original core of the book consisted of a few short and pithy logical-epistemological ethical chapters written by one and the same author, and as the work grew by gradual accretion, political chapters influenced by his thought system were added to it as well.[59] In addition, it is noteworthy that the book is written in verse,[60] unlike any other Classical period philosophical work in Chinese.[61] In sum, the original core of the book is radically different from anything else in early Chinese thought except for later works that are connected to it or derivative from it, particularly the *Chuangtzu*. From its very first line (in the traditional text), it states the basic principle going back to the Buddha:

> The Way that can be discoursed on is an impermanent Way.
> The names that can be named are impermanent names.[62]

Accordingly, the most relevant points are: the brilliant insight or conceptual germ of the Chinese classic; its author *Gautama, who is traditionally known as Laotzu or Lao-tan; and his *foreign* inspiration. There are other reasons for considering the *Laotzu* (the *Tao te ching*) to be inspired by Early Buddhism: its strictly philosophical teachings are traceable to the Buddha himself[63] (not to the later, strictly *religious* forms of Buddhism,

59. On authorship theories see the in-depth discussion in Endnote 181.

60. Starostin (1989) provides tables of the rhymes in the *Tao te ching* according to the traditional HSR system, with his own HSR reconstructions. Zoroaster's *Gāthās* and the statements of the Buddha in early Normative Buddhist sutras are also in verse.

61. However, the *Nei-yeh* 內業 (*Nèiyè* 'inner cultivation') chapter of the *Kuantzu* 管子, a work that is much later than the core of the *Tao te ching*, also rhymes (Nivison 1999: 776). Both works contain material relevant to early breath-control yoga (similar to that in the *Jade Yoga Inscription*) belonging to the 'inner cultivation' tradition, which is considered to be "Taoist".

62. *Tao te ching* 1: 道可道 非常道。名可名 非常名。Text from CTP. Or perhaps, "The dharmas that can be discussed are impermanent dharmas, the(ir) names that can be named are impermanent names," which corresponds closely to two of the three "characteristics" in the Trilakṣana. On *tao* 道 (OChi *dawʁă, which could be a metathesized form of *daʁwă) as a transcription of foreign *dharma* see Beckwith (2015: 122–123). The word *ch'ang* 常 (*cháng*) means 'constant, unchanging' or the like. Thus *fei-ch'ang* 非常 means 'impermanent'. See Endnote 182.

63. See the in-depth treatment of the distinction in Beckwith (2015).

or "Normative Buddhism", which contain much material foreign to Early Buddhism),[64] and the rest of the book has grown by accretion of the contributions of many others after Laotzu.[65] Nivison perceptively states, "Enough of the book is not about government to allow the possibility that it is a book of counsel for any wise man who would survive by not pressing for too much, [who would] be effective by being still, quiet."[66]

Finally, the specifically Early Buddhist teachings about antilogies in the oldest layer of the *Tao-te ching* could not have been composed by anyone except a person who had knowledge of the distinctive Early Buddhism of Gautama Buddha, an unusual system that *rejects* the traditional Scythian antilogy of the Truth versus the False (which Zoroaster made central to his philosophy). It is easy to imagine that a Chinese who taught these exotic ideas would have been remembered as "Gautama" from the teacher's frequent repetition of the name of the one who originally taught them, e.g.: "Master Gau(tama) says . . ."

Laotzu's core teachings are thus on logic, epistemology, and ethics. He famously proposes to resolve conflicting antilogies by saying that they are bound to each other, that they are human creations, that there are no inherent absolutes in nature:

When the whole world knows beauty as beautiful, ugly arises.
When all know good, not-good arises.
Existence and nonexistence are born together.
Difficult and easy are achieved together.
Long and short are mutually formed.
High and low are mutually completed.
Meaning and sound agree with each other.
Before and after follow each other.[67]

64. One of the most significant pieces of hard data is the *Jade Yoga Inscription*, a short text palaeographically dated to about the 4th century BC, which teaches basic breath-control yoga (Beckwith 2015: 115–117; Harper 1999: 881). See Endnote 183 on the Indian question.

65. My interpretation thus differs from the two approaches mentioned by Nivison (1999: 802).

66. Nivison (1999: 804). That of course sounds like Early Buddhism.

67. *Laotzu* 2A, Guodian *Laotzu* Chapter A:9, 天下皆知美之為美也惡已。皆知善則不善已。有無相生也,難易相成也,長短相形也,高下相盈也,意聲相和也,先後相隨也。Text from Henricks (2006: 52).

Because there is no real boundary between the antilogies, they do not exist in the natural world; they are human creations. So humans can get rid of them:

> Eliminate knowledge, get rid of distinctions![68]

What may be called 'overcategorization' is thus problematized.[69] The great later Taoist, Chuangtzu, illustrates the same point in his famous Chapter 2, "Discourse on the Equalization of Things", which is about two women:

> Mao Ch'iang and Li Chi were considered beautiful by men, but when fish saw them, they plunged into the depths; when birds saw them, they flew high in the sky; and when deer saw them, they ran away. Did any of the four really know the true principle of beauty in the world?[70]

Laotzu thus gives a logical solution to a logical problem that is at the same time an ethical problem. He is no doubt later than Confucius, who is usually said to be the earliest philosopher, but like Solon, Thales, and other early figures in Greek history, Confucius is a "wise man" concerned with other things, especially traditional morality and politics, not Philosophy in the narrow (modern) sense. Although there are other candidates for "earliest Chinese philosopher", they too mostly teach morality and general wisdom. Since the first to teach epistemology and serious logic in Chinese is clearly Laotzu, his work is the foundational text of Philosophy per se in China. It is followed, later, by others. And, unlike any of the other Chinese candidates for First Philosopher, Laotzu's system eventually developed into a major religion, Taoism.

68. Guodian A:1: 絕知棄辨, which continues, 民利百倍。"and the people will benefit one hundredfold." Text and translation from Henricks (2000: 28, 30).

69. The corresponding traditional text (*Laotzu* 19) begins 絕聖棄智 (from CTP) 'Eliminate wisdom, get rid of knowledge!' For discussion of this (clearly later) strain of thought see Nivison (1999). On categorization as an intrinsic, indispensable feature of human language and cognition in general, see Beckwith (2007c).

70. *Chuangtzu* 2 (齊物論): 毛嬙。麗姬。人之所美也。魚見之深入。鳥見之高飛。麋鹿見之決驟。四者孰知天下之正色哉。Text from CTP. Cf. Watson (1968: 46), Beckwith (2015: 113–114).

The First Philosophy

These four philosophers, Anacharsis, Zoroaster, Gautama Buddha, and Laotzu, are not only among the earliest teachers of 'philosophy' of any sort in the cultural traditions of Greece, Persia, India, and China, they are clearly the earliest *actual philosophers* in our modern strict sense of the word. All four of them have a direct Scythian connection.[71] So the basic idea of a Classical Age of Philosophy *in Eurasia as a whole* (not just in Greek culture), though long shouted down, seems indisputable. Our philosophers' life stories, while no doubt late and creative, all say that they moved from one region or country to another and they or their ancestors were immigrants in their adoptive countries, where they criticize and reject the traditional local beliefs. In each case their foreign teachings formed the foundations of a strikingly new tradition of thought that later became a stereotypical feature of their adoptive culture: Scepticism in Greek culture, Zoroastrianism in Iranic culture, Buddhism in Indic culture, and Taoism in Chinese culture. The core philosophical teachings of the *Tao te ching* are typically "Early Buddhist",[72] and they agree with other early attestations of Scythian thought discussed here. Since they are all strikingly similar, while at the same time they are radically unlike anything in attested early thought in Greece, India (the apparent adoptive home of the Buddha), Iran, or China, they should be Scythian in origin.

That in turn raises the question of Scythian philosophy *in Scythia proper*, in Central Eurasia, before our philosophers or their ancestors left home. Certainly in the broad sense, which includes religious thought, political theory, and so on, it is clear that the early Scythians shared much with the basic religious-philosophical system of Zoroaster in his *Gāthās* and in its reflection in the inscriptions of Darius and Xerxes. Although Gautama Buddha and Laotzu reject much of that system,[73] *all four philosophers' primary focus is specifically on the logic of*

71. Unlike any other Greek philosopher, Anacharsis is specifically remarked to have spoken Greek "like a Scythian". See Endnote 173.

72. As described and defined in Beckwith (2015).

73. Cf. Beckwith (2015: 110–121).

ethical antilogies, particularly True versus False.[74] That is remarkable and unusual. They all present the problems people have in dealing with such ethical conflicts, including recognizing them, distinguishing between them or not, judging other people based on them, and so on, and they do it in the same distinctive way.

In these four great thinkers we can thus perceive the lost philosophy of the Scythians at home in the vast steppe heartland of Eurasia. The Scythian focus on logical antilogies, especially True versus False, is crucial because it is the foundation of later scientific thought in the Scythian-speaking lands of Central Asia—especially part of what is now Afghanistan—which after the original Scythianization continued under Scythian, Scytho-Mede, and Persian rule. With Alexander, the same Central Asian region came under Greek rule and the literary and intellectual language was Greek for two centuries, but the Greeks were followed by the Indo-Scythian Sakas and the Kushans, who each spoke a Scythian daughter language, so one may assume direct continuity from the earlier Scythian dialects spoken there, which are attested as loanwords in written texts from the region.[75]

The earliest Buddhist literature on *abhidharma*—the study of *dharmas* 'ethical things' or 'constituents'—was written in Central Asia, mainly in Gandhāra, under the Sakas and Kushans. The "disputed questions" (*quaestiones disputatae*) method or "recursive argument method" of early science, which enabled methodical argumentation about anything, and the "monastery-college" or *vihāra* in which the method developed, were both invented by Buddhists in Central Asia under the Kushans in the 1st century CE.[76] The *dharmas* were catalogued and

74. Explicitly in the key passages by Anacharsis, Zoroaster, Buddha, and Laotzu quoted above.

75. The Kushans wrote their imperial inscriptions in the Bactrian language but in Greek script, while the Buddhists among them wrote their texts in the Gāndhārī language (a dialect of Indian Prakrit) using Kharoṣṭhī script (which is derived from Aramaic script). For Bactrian see the outstanding works of Nicholas Sims-Williams (1988/2011; 1999–2012); for Gāndhārī see the publications of the recently discovered early manuscripts from the territory of ancient Gandhāra, cited by Baums and Glass in the bibliography of their groundbreaking *Dictionary of Gāndhārī* (2020) online. On the Saka language materials see Harmatta (1994a).

76. See Beckwith (2020). They were not, however, called *vihāras* at first; see Beckwith (2017).

debated there by great Abhidharma scholars such as Vasubandhu. And when Central Asia became Islamic, philosophy and science flourished there in *madrasas*—Islamicized *vihāras*—where one of the greatest thinkers of all time, Avicenna, learned the same Central Asian scientific method of disputation, the *quaestiones disputatae* or recursive argument method, as he tells us explicitly in his (auto)biography. It consists of lists of arguments for or against each argument for or against the head argument. When Avicenna's major works began to be translated into Latin in 12th-century Spain, this "scientific method" was transmitted to medieval Europe.[77] The method was the foundation stone of the great creative age of medieval and Renaissance science,[78] and despite popular beliefs about its demise, it is still de rigueur for scientific reports in the natural sciences.[79]

The Classical Age

Since the appearance of a Classical Age of Philosophy is accounted for by the fact that the earliest actual philosophers were Scythians, those very people are indeed the answer to how it happened, as Turchin[80] and others have wondered. However, the Scythian contribution was not what most scholars have expected of a people widely stereotyped as "nomadic warriors" at best. It was not a mere "influence", or the "trading" of random ideas and things stolen from "innocent" peripheral agricultural realms,[81] and it had nothing to do with Scythian modes of warfare. Philosophy was only one part of a coherent package, the entire culture of the Scythians, which spread, via Scythian rule, to the peripheral civilizations around Eurasia. The history of the Classical Age is thus a world-level question, not a bureaucratic-level question.[82]

77. Beckwith (2012a).
78. Grant (1996, 2007).
79. Beckwith (2012a: 159–164).
80. Turchin (2012).
81. Cf. Endnote 184.
82. See further in Endnote 185.

Recently a few insightful scholars have suggested that the vast territory of the Central Eurasian steppe zone, which separated the peripheral cultures from each other, might be connected somehow to the Classical Age phenomena. Turchin asks, if Achaemenid Persia was one of the most important Classical Age civilizations, "Who influenced Persia?"[83] The archaeologist Vogelsang has argued that the Scythians played a key part in the rise and organization of the Achaemenid Empire,[84] whose Persian rulers—like its original Scythian rulers—considered themselves to be the chosen people of God.[85]

It has long been acknowledged that the Archaic period culture of native Greek speakers was "influenced" by the Archaic civilizations of Egypt and Mesopotamia, but at the same time most believe that the Greek Classical Age was something new, unique, and essentially autochthonous. Similarly, most Sinologists today still consider the same to be just as true of the Chinese Classical Age. In other words, in both cases the respective Classical Ages happened *in spite of* any foreign "influence".

Certainly the ancient civilization of the native speakers of Chinese had some acknowledged and very important, perhaps foundational, earlier influences from the north and west during the Bronze Age (late Shang Dynasty and early Western Chou Dynasty). Even earlier,[86] fundamental changes took place that would later develop into the Chinese Bronze Age. Then, two to three centuries after the fall of the Western Chou in 771, the Warring States period began, the Classical Age of Chinese culture. It is believed to have been unique and fundamentally "native" Chinese in character, but similar views are held about ancient Indian,

83. Turchin (2012) proposes: "The Medes and Persians themselves were Iranian groups that moved into the Middle East from the steppe." The present book agrees that the key changes came from the steppe culture, but specifically from the Scythians, who were also Iranic speakers, and the changes were effected specifically by creolization.

84. Vogelsang (1992).

85. Briant (2002: 181–183).

86. On the important Central Eurasian site at Shih-mao 石峁 (*Shímǎo*) in Inner Mongolia (modern Shaanxi) dated to ca. 2000 BC, see Li et al. (2018). As it happens, Shimao is located in the region later referred to by the Classical period Chinese as *Ta Hsia* 大夏 *Dàxià* 'Great *Ḥarya', but Shimao dates to the Indo-European migration period.

Persian, and Greek Classical cultures. That is, scholars have contended that there was, effectively, *no borrowing by or among any of them.*

As a result, they treat the strikingly similar structural features of what became the default imperial political system of post-Classical Antiquity (among the Romans, Greeks, Kushans, Indians, and Chinese) together with the strikingly similar Classical philosophical-religious ideas discussed above, as examples of very complex ignored "coincidences" (elephants in the room) or, alternatively, "universals" (unicorns are everywhere), which happen over and over again and have no explanation. Such all-purpose Modernist arguments aim to prevent logical, scientific thought.

Since, however, the simultaneous appearance of the same revolutionary ideas in far-flung regions of Eurasia in the Classical Age and its successor the Imperial Age are clearly *not* "coincidences", and *not* "universals", as shown in this book, Turchin and others are right. But *how,* exactly, did it happen? Although this is possibly the single most crucial issue in the history of the premodern world, scholars have not previously proposed a principled scientific theory—one based on the data—which explains it.

Looking at the hard data, the directionality of change (and thus development) of Eurasian civilization was radial, from Central Eurasia outward to the periphery: at the onset of the Classical Age, with the Scythians; at the onset of Late Antiquity, with mainly Huns and Goths in the West (in the Western Roman Empire) and mainly Serbi-Mongolic peoples in the East (in North China). It was the same at the onset of the revolutionary Middle Ages, with the Türks and Tibetans of Central Eurasia and the Franks from the Central Eurasianized north of Europe, plus the Arabs from the south (effectively on *the other side* of the periphery), and at the onset of the Renaissance, with the Mongols.[87] The beliefs,

87. Steppe zone Central Eurasians extremely rarely adopted anything from peripheral cultures, so the directionality was *not* from the periphery (Europe, the Near East, South Asia, East Asia) inward to Central Eurasia, but the opposite. See Beckwith (2009: 232–262). For the Türks and Tibetans see Beckwith (1993); for the Serbi-Mongolic peoples see Shimunek (2017a). It was only in modern times that the rulers of the peripheral regions successfully invaded, "colonized", and destroyed Central Eurasian cultures.

practices, customs, technology, and sometimes even the clothing fashions of the Central Eurasians accompanied them and were followed by them in the peripheral lands. Herodotus remarks,

> The Persians more than all men welcome foreign customs. They wear the Median dress, thinking it more beautiful than their own.[88]

He basically suggests that *fashion* is the reason for the Persian borrowing of foreign peoples' clothing styles, and elsewhere suggests the same for structural features of the Empire, as discussed in the Prologue. Certainly in the case of the Athenian women who wore the elegant Scytho-Mede-Persian *candys* for the sake of fashion, we must admit its influence in Antiquity, but the hardest of the hard evidence—the stone bas-reliefs from Persepolis and Naqš-i Rustam—shows that in general, fashion had nothing to do with it. Before early modern times, clothing style, and more or less all the rest of a people's traditional culture, was inherited and bound up together as their holistic identity. When major changes occurred, it is because conquered subjects were creolized by intermarriage with the new ruling people, so that their offspring essentially shifted to the culture of the dominant people—in the present case, the Central Eurasian culture of the Scythians, which involved changing clothing, language, religion, political system, nearly everything. By contrast, no structurally significant cultural transmission took place "horizontally" via "influences", "contact", or even "trade", despite current fascination with these ideas.[89]

The Existing Theory

There is an old scholarly tradition founded on observation of similarities among several simultaneous "Classical Ages" of Eurasia. Such observations were made over two centuries ago by Abraham Hyacinthe Anquetil-Duperron (1731–1805), but his and earlier approaches were

88. Herodotus (i 135): ξεινικὰ δὲ νόμαια Πέρσαι προσίενται ἀνδρῶν μάλιστα. καὶ γὰρ δὴ τὴν Μηδικὴν ἐσθῆτα νομίσαντες τῆς ἑωυτῶν εἶναι καλλίω φορέουσι; from Perseus online, tr. Godley. See the Prologue.

89. See Endnotes 186 and 149. However, not with Khazanov (2019).

replaced by the famous theory of the philosopher and psychologist Karl Jaspers (1883–1969) in his post–World War II book *On the Origin and Goal of History*.[90] He considered that the revolutionary changes of the Classical Age were so pivotal for world cultural development that the period deserved a special name of its own: the 'Axle Age' or 'Axial Age' (Achsenzeit), when the world "turned" dramatically in a new direction, such that religious ideas shifted to focus on *monotheistic beliefs* and *the individual*; he argues that this was a basic civilizational shift which set the affected areas of Eurasia apart from the rest of the world and lasted down to the radical changes of Modern times, his "*new* Axial Age". His book is divided into two parts, each of which deals with one of the two "Axial Ages".

Though now outdated, Jaspers' theory was and to some extent remains a brilliant *tour de force*. He himself believed that his account of the simultaneity of the radical changes he perceived was ultimately based on historical facts. But perhaps because of the relatively limited knowledge about Asian history and philosophy-religion during his formative years in the late 19th century, he did not know of any links connecting the different regional manifestations. He also rejected the idea of parallel "human social evolution", as well as any concrete cause, source, or historical connection for the simultaneous appearance of the Classical Age of Philosophy in all the noted cultures.

However, Jaspers was not a philologist, linguist, or historian, so he could not control and evaluate the primary sources and scholarship on them even when he was sympathetic to interpretations based on them. In particular, because he did not take the Scythians, Medes, and Persians into account (though he actually considers the possibility that they, or "Central Asia"—i.e., Central Eurasia—could be the explanation), he saw no historical basis for his observations and explicitly declares that the phenomena were unconnected in any concrete historical way. He even takes it one step further. He flatly rejects any theory based directly on historical "hard data". To account for the observed

90. *Vom Ursprung und Ziel der Geschichte* (Jaspers 1949a; English translation 1953); cf. Jaspers (1949b).

co-occurrences he proposes what he calls "common sociological preconditions favorable to spiritual creativeness" in the Classical Age cultures.[91]

Like Jaspers, his successors—the leading Axial Age theorists—have also not been trained philologists, linguists, or historians, so they too have mostly overlooked or misinterpreted the major primary sources. Worse, most of the discourse on the Axial Age has explicitly *avoided* the hard data, so it has excluded even the possibility of finding solutions to the many problems involved.

Thus, although Jaspers brought these issues to scholars' attention, for reasons largely beyond his control he did not succeed in keeping their attention focused on the issues. That means the problems are still unsolved, and specialist historians avoid them. Nevertheless, as noted above, it has been suggested recently by several scholars that Central Eurasia may be the answer, and that is directly relevant to a book on the Scythians. So let us wonder again about the great problems which Jaspers saw and, over a century before him, Anquetil-Duperron.

When the primary historical, linguistic, and archaeological source material is carefully studied using the best scientific methodology, and the topic is narrowed to the crucial problem alone—the *inception* of the *Classical Age* only, not the history of Antiquity as a whole—it is quite clear that Jaspers' traditional basic points about the simultaneity of the *Classical* philosophical-religious events are essentially sound, though he presents them largely outside their historical cultural setting, without reference to the actual accompanying political changes, and he does not understand the chronology.[92] In short, Jaspers was human and imperfect, and his work is imperfect, like everything else in our imperfect world. That means it is amenable to science and can be improved. Restricting the

91. Jaspers (1953: 18). Unfortunately, he later extended his earlier Axial Age period into the 1st century CE so as to include Jesus, no doubt in response to criticism of his proposal—which already included Homer (dated by him to the 8th century BC). The flaws in his *theory* and *interpretations* are still used by some to discredit the *data*, i.e., they confuse descriptions or analyses of things with the things themselves.

92. See the Prologue and Chapter 4.

"philosophers" in question to those who lived in the Classical Age solves many of the problems with his theory.

Jaspers' successors, though, have modified the theory far beyond his original general observations, virtually never on the basis of any detailed data from history, philology-linguistics, archaeology, and so forth, so that they have not improved our understanding of the period.

Most scholars today have given up on both the topic and Jaspers' theory, and avoid it. But ignoring the *data* is not an option for science, and it is still necessary to critique the theory.

Modifications of the Existing Theory

Led by the sociologist Eisenstadt, the followers of Jaspers have developed what may be called a scholarly sub-field of "Axial Age studies." They have attempted to improve on his proposal by continuing his highly theoretical approach, making it even more fully metatheoretical and sociological in character.[93] In Eisenstadt's introduction to the most prominent single post-Jaspers volume of papers on the theory, he reaffirms the founder's basic approach: "The revolution or series of revolutions, which are related to Karl Jaspers' 'Axial Age,' have to do with the emergence, conceptualization, and institutionalization of a basic tension between the transcendental and mundane orders".[94] Arnason, Eisenstadt, and Wittrock, the editors of the next major volume on the topic, agree.[95] For Bellah and Joas, the essence of their Axial Age is "the recognition of symbolicity as symbolicity, the understanding of symbolic signs as pointing to a meaning that can never be fully exhausted by these signs".[96] Arnason, Eisenstadt, and Wittrock refer, like Jaspers, to the Axial Age as marked by overarching change in "basic socio-cultural structures", but advise scholars to go further, "to de-concretize current models"—i.e., to eliminate any remaining hard data—and instead focus

93. The more recent revised Axial Age theories are nearly all by sociologists.
94. Eisenstadt (1986: 1).
95. Arnason et al. (2005: 16).
96. Bellah and Joas (2012: 4).

on "constellations of radicalized reflexivity".[97] Eisenstadt himself later says it is better to speak of "different, multiple axialities", like others generalizing the Axial Age theory into an all-purpose term, "axiality",[98] which signifies little more than 'any distinctive period of world history in general'. Gresham's Law has thus worked inexorably to a crushing conclusion.

Critics of the Existing Theory

The critics of the Axial Age approach mostly agree with its proponents. For example, like the proponents they do not base their arguments on hard data or on the cultural history of Eurasia as a whole in the Classical Age. The critics, too, accept with Jaspers that the "axial" changes occurred independently and purely internally in each instance. Accordingly, they conclude that observed similarities *could not* have anything to do with each other and—here is the "Modern scholarly turn"—they *could not really be similar*. In short, they *reject the data*.

However, Jaspers' fundamental scientific errors are, rather, that his theory does not conform to the major constituents of the relevant data, and—as he actually says—it does not in fact *explain* the data. The versions of the theory proposed by his followers, as well as the interpretations by the critics, have these same flaws. None of the prominent writers on the Axial Age, pro or con, have carefully examined all significant data and interpretations and then constructed a precise, scientific theory based on the data. They have not even proposed doing so.[99]

However, a few have nevertheless suggested, briefly and in passing, solutions based on hard data. For example, the critic Wittrock remarks, "the geographical and political space where all of the major traditions of Eurasia actually interacted is that of the Achaemenid Empire and its

97. Arnason et al. (2005: 16–17).

98. Arnason et al. (2005: 531).

99. Other critics, including Egyptologists, Mayanists, and others who work on "non-Axial" cultures, claim that much of what Jaspers and his successors have discussed is found earlier in Egypt, or as a "parallel" in Central America; why are these not Axial cultures? Following this logic, one may ask, why is Britain, an island nation very close to the Eurasian continent, not a Japanese culture?

Hellenistic and Iranian successors. In many ways, cultural traditions in the Iranian lands came to serve as direct or indirect sources of inspiration for several of the world's religions and imperial orders."[100] Unfortunately, Wittrock says no more about this other than a few remarks based on traditional ideas about Zoroastrianism and other faiths that he researches. He also *excludes* Central Eurasia, effectively preventing the discovery of a solution, and he *excludes* China, a crucial case for any such historical theory. Other papers in the same volume have touched lightly on the importance of the Achaemenid Empire, but they assume, like Wittrock, that "knowledge of key aspects of religious, and even political, practices . . . in the Achaemenid Empire . . . is lacking". These scholars, following Jaspers—who wrote seven decades ago, based mainly on scholarship from the 19th century—are thus evidently unaware of most of the hard data on these topics and the considerable relevant scholarship published in the past century. None have gone much beyond Wittrock's remarks.

In short, neither side addresses the major problems or the methodologies needed to solve them. Other scholars now work almost exclusively as specialists within one discipline and one region. This discourages thinking in terms of a sufficiently wide picture, an absolute necessity for study of a continent-spanning phenomenon. The revisions also show nearly complete loss of the original insight of Jaspers—the idea of an Axial Age—which was based on the best historical data known to him and was at first no doubt intended to conform to the data.

The Directionality of Major Structural Change

The issue of the Classical Age is inseparable from the issue of the directionality of development of civilization in Eurasia. Since it is widely thought that there was no significant influence between or among the individual major Classical cultures of the periphery of Eurasia (Greek, Persian, Indian, Chinese), either the observed similarities developed independently in each of them and spread to the Scythians' Central

100. Wittrock (2005: 76).

Eurasia homeland, where they somehow became one, or they developed in the central culture of the Scythians and spread directly or indirectly to the different peripheral regions.

Already Aristotle has pointed out the logical problem with "multiple source of unity" hypotheses.[101] In fact, the Scythians and their heirs in Central Eurasia remained essentially unchanged culturally before, during, and after the Classical Age, strongly supporting the one-source hypothesis.

Central Eurasia is not just the region from which the key *Classical Age* changes came, as some have actually wondered, it is also the source of key changes in Late Antiquity and the Middle Ages, later periods that are much better attested in the historical record.[102] These periods can be analyzed as several "re-Central Eurasianizations" of the periphery of Eurasia, with repeated introduction or restoration of Central Eurasian views and practices.[103] The restorations happened as the result of rule by Central Eurasians over peripheral regions, the same mechanism of transmission as in the Classical Revolution. The medieval period thus provides support for a general theory of how major, structural cultural transmission and change took place in the Old World from the Archaic period down to the Renaissance. The Scythians are the solution to the Axial Age problem.

In Classical studies in general, however, and in most work on the Axial Age, Classical Greece is still presented largely as an exception, a brilliant new native *European* culture in which Greeks did more or less everything by themselves without any significant outside influence on their

101. "There is either one first principle or many. If there is one, we have what we are looking for; if there are many, they are either ordered or disordered. Now if they are disordered, their products are more so, and the world is not a world but a chaos; and that which is contrary to nature exists while that which is in accordance with nature does not exist. If on the other hand they are ordered, they were ordered either by themselves or by some outside cause. But if they were ordered by themselves, they have something common that joins them, and that is the first principle." Aristotle fragment F 17 R3 *Scholia in Proverbia Salomonis* (Barnes 1984, 2: 2393).

102. For Late Antiquity and the Central Middle Ages see Beckwith (2012a); for the Early Middle Ages see Beckwith (1993). These observations no doubt apply also to the sudden spread of the Proto-Indo-Europeans across Eurasia into the periphery in the Bronze Age, q.v. Beckwith (2009).

103. Beckwith (2009: 109–111).

political structure or their philosophical-religious ideas after the Archaic period. In particular, it is believed by most Classicists that the "Axial Age shift" to a universal "political" monotheism, with a fundamentally ethical focus, did not happen among the Greeks, who kept their traditional polytheism and animal sacrifice to local deities, with the sole possible exception of Plato, until the formal establishment of Christianity centuries later. Such views are based on ignoring the data as well as much Classical scholarship.[104] For example, many Classical Age Greek *philosophers* clearly supported a monotheistic universal creator: *God* with a "capital G", who belongs to a unique category of one.[105]

Revolution in Heaven

Before the great changes of the Classical Age there were very many Greek gods or "deities", each associated typically with a particular people or place, or with one or more elements, principles, or other natural phenomena. The Greek gods and other suprahuman beings fought each other, while among peoples with a tribal or national god, their fate, and that of their god, was often decided in battle. The gods thus lived in a disordered world much like that of humans, and even though sometimes one of the gods, such as Zeus among the Greek gods, was treated as a heavenly ruler,[106] the myths show that he was not thought to have significantly more power or prestige than the other gods. His world, however lofty, was neither perfect nor universal, nor did he actually create it.[107] This was also the situation in the immediately pre-Classical period in other peripheral parts of Eurasia that we know much about.

104. See the studies on this by Kingsley (1990, 1995) and Miller 2004.

105. As noted elsewhere, Greek *philosophia* is "translated" without comment into English as *philosophy*, but the modern word is very different semantically from the ancient Greek word. Ancient philosophers were not even remotely like university teachers of "philosophy in the strict sense".

106. In the case of Greek *Zeus*, his name is from Proto-Indo-European *dyeu- 'the god of the bright sky'. The lone reconstructible Proto-Indo-European god name, it refers to Central Eurasian culture's apex creator deity, the God of Heaven. The addition of the word for 'father' gives Proto-Indo-European *dyeu-pəter (Watkins 2011: 22) 'Heaven Father'.

107. Nevertheless, Herodotus compares the Persians' monotheistic Heavenly God with Zeus specifically (see the Prologue).

Central Eurasia, especially the steppe zone, was different. Throughout history down to fairly recent times, the attested primary religious belief of well-known steppe peoples was in one powerful God who created and controls Heaven, Earth, and humankind, and determines where people go after death.[108] Other "small g" spiritual beings, "gods", existed, but they were unrelated to the apex divinity, "God", because he belonged to an entirely different, unique *kind* of category.

This structuring of the divine realm precisely mirrors the political restructuring of much of Eurasia in the Classical period to follow the political and religious beliefs of the Central Eurasian Culture Complex.[109] The Scytho-Mede-Persian emperor's title "(the One) Great King, King of Kings"[110] meant that in practice he sometimes actually left local rulers in place, though besides demoting them to be subordinate to the imperial throne, he further demoted them by appointing intermediary governors—satraps—above them, just as the Scythians did (Vogelsang 1992: 312–314) and as later Central Eurasian conquerors did.

The political revolution on Earth was thus paralleled by a revolution in Heaven. With the spread of the new feudal-hierarchical system among peripheral peoples of non-Central Eurasian background, the restructuring eventually allowed, or demanded, the conversion of the category of any other gods into members of the new hierarchical heavenly polity, as "*Aməša Spənta*", "angels", "saints", "spirits", "demons", etc., but in any case still categorically different lower-ranking beings. Any proposed alternative

108. These are characteristics of Ahura Mazdā in the *Gāthās*. The name *Ahura Mazdā* is thought by most Iranists to mean 'the Wise Lord' or 'Lord Wisdom' (Boyce 1984/2011). However the very early attestation of *Mazda* as (probably) a divine name in the Amarna Letters, and among the Scythians (transcribed in Greek as *Masada-*) in the name of the Royal Scythians' proprietary deity, altogether suggest that its primary meaning was 'God', regardless of its etymological meaning.

109. The feudal-hierarchical system was certainly a novelty in the Near East, but not in Scythia, its home, just as it was a novelty in the former Western Roman Empire when it was introduced there by the Germanic, Iranic, and Hunnic peoples of Central Eurasia after the empire had effectively become unable to govern itself. Their reintroduction of the Central Eurasian Culture Complex to Europe north of the Mediterranean resulted in spread of the well-known medieval feudal system, under which Europe developed into a major, distinctive, world cultural region (Beckwith 1993: 173–196; 2009: 12–23, 109–111).

110. See Chapter 5.

or additional "Gods" were direct challenges to the categorical uniqueness of the One Great God.

Accordingly, the change in the heavenly order was often accompanied by violence on Earth. King Josiah of Judea (traditional dates 640–609) is said to have discovered in the Temple a "book of the law", generally thought to be *Deuteronomy*, in 622 (approximately when Cyaxares overthrew the Scythian ruling group in Media). The book revealed that the Hebrews' traditional religious practices were wrong. Josiah set out to fix things, and in particular, to get rid of all the many other traditional gods except Yahweh, both within the Temple in Jerusalem and across the land, in a campaign of destruction that was "the most intense puritan reform in the history of Judah".[111] It is hardly coincidental that the prophet Jeremiah, who preached strict monotheism, was the contemporary of Josiah, and it is difficult not to associate Josiah's campaign with the similar destruction of temples and gods in upper Mesopotamia carried out by Cyaxares in 613 and again in Ḫarrān in 610.[112] The reign of Josiah ended when he was killed (traditionally in 609) by the polytheistic Egyptians. That was followed soon after by the Babylonians' destruction of Jerusalem and exile of leading Judean families to Babylon in 597. In or shortly after 539, Cyrus the Great captured Babylon and sent the Judean exiles home. The Temple was eventually rebuilt, but later, evidently under Artaxerxes I. Judea, then a province of the Persian Empire, was ruled politically by Persian governors, and religiously by priests.[113] For two centuries, Palestine remained under Persian rule and very strong Persian religious influence, resulting in the reshaping of both spheres of life there.

Megasthenes, a Seleucid envoy from Arachosia who went to the Mauryan Empire in 305–304 BC to negotiate a treaty, wrote a book, the *Indica*, in which he reports, "The Brahmanists say that the world . . . was created by God (*ho theos*), who rules it and pervades all of it . . . and they have much to say about the soul".[114] These ideas are identical to Early Zoroastrian teachings; they have no systemic antecedents in the religion of

111. Finkelstein and Silberman (2001: 277ff.), citing 2 Kings 23:2–20.

112. See Chapter 2.

113. Finkelstein and Silberman (2001: 298–310).

114. Strabo (xv 1,59).

the *Rig Veda*.[115] The other major outcome of the introduction of Early Zoroastrianism was its *rejection* by the Buddha, Gautama *Śākyamuni* 'the Scythian Sage', founder of Buddhism, particularly in his rejection of the central Zoroastrian teaching of an absolute distinction between the Truth and the Lie. His advice was, "Have *no* views!"[116] The earliest written texts in any Indic language, the Major Inscriptions of the Mauryan king Devānāṃpriya Priyadarśi, proclaim the *Dharma* 'law' of the king, and announce the ruler's adoption of an early form of popular Buddhism—the "*Dharma*". The king promises that people who are loyal and do good deeds will go to Heaven.[117]

The onset of the unprecedented Classical Age thus followed upon Scythian monotheism; monotheistic Early Zoroastrianism; Anacharsis' introduction of Scythian philosophy to the Greeks; the teachings of the Buddha, 'Sage of the Scythians' (which rejected Early Zoroastrianism); Early Brahmanism (which accepted it);[118] and Laotzu's introduction of the Buddha's Scythian philosophy to China, as discussed in the first section of this chapter.

As noted above, we still hear that the Greeks, all by themselves, changed the barely imaginable world of Archaic Antiquity into the Classical Age, evidently through sheer genius. In the usual modern view, all this happened for unknown, local, traditional, internal reasons. Certainly, we are told, no significant advances had anything to do with foreigners, not to speak of 'barbarians' (a Modern pejorative misinterpretation of the usual Greek word for 'foreigners').

Even specialists in the Ancient Near East mostly believe that the Scythians and Medes left essentially no mark, at all, on the region. Why has practically no one commented on the peculiar negative remark in

115. They are found in early Brahmanist texts, but those texts also include many elements derived from Buddhism, so they are later (Beckwith 2015: 8, 10, note 36).

116. Beckwith (2015: 16 and passim).

117. Beckwith (2015: 131–133). This belief is attested also in Megasthenes' account of the Early Buddhists, which says that "some" of the Śramaṇas (Buddhist practitioners) used belief in the afterlife as a way to encourage people to be pious (id., 73, 80, 90, 92).

118. The *contemporaneously attested* forms of several of these Indian philosophical-religious systems, though described in Antiquity (mainly in Greek), have only recently been analyzed and elucidated (Beckwith 2015), though much work remains to be done on them.

the received text of Herodotus to the effect that the Scythians in Media, and everywhere else, were worthless vandals? Because they agree with it.[119] The Medes (i.e., the Scytho-Medes) have actually fared even worse, with an entire volume of papers dedicated to the proposition that the Mede Empire did not even exist.[120] So should we forget about the Scythians and Medes, and believe that Cyrus the Great (a *good barbarian*) singlehandedly invented the gigantic, unprecedented Persian Empire? And the Greeks (a nation of geniuses) single-handedly created Classical civilization out of nothing? As did the Chinese?

Or should we *not* ignore or bury or misrepresent the data like this? Certainly the Greeks developed a very brilliant culture, but something is wrong with the current historical account, which is full of elephants and unicorns. It does not conform to the data and it makes no sense as history. Let us instead base our histories on actual data, science, and logic as well. If we do that maybe we will be able to understand not only the Scythians, Medes, and Persians, but the Greeks, and even the Chinese.

The Scythians, a nomadic herding people from the steppes, spread their complex and highly innovative culture into the peripheral Eurasian world of late Archaic Antiquity by directly ruling over parts of it. Its introduction to Southeastern Europe, the Near East, South Asia, and East Asia at the same time and in the same ways effectively produced the great shared cultural flowering known as the Classical Age.

119. E.g., Diakonoff (1985: 118).
120. Lanfranchi et al. (2003).

APPENDIX A

Zoroaster and Monotheism

Zoroaster

The founder of Zoroastrianism, the first "world religion", is a mystery in almost every respect. There is no historical, direct evidence on his dates. Of the two traditional places of origin posited for him and his teachings, Schmitt has disproved the traditional theory that says he was from Khwarizmia in Central Asia.[1] That leaves us with the other traditional theory, which says that Zoroaster was from Media, and with whatever linguistics and his *Gāthās* 'hymns' might tell us (assuming he composed them). Finally, his name, while still a mystery, is at least susceptible to examination.

Some modern scholars want to get rid of Zoroaster. They argue he did not exist. Yet such arguments largely ignore the *Gāthās*, our only authentic contemporaneous source on Zoroaster the man, who often speaks in the first person and refers to his daughter Pouručistā and to a lord, Vištāspa, who supported him. The *Gāthās* are poetry and sometimes use another voice, a poetic practice that has been used to argue against Zoroaster as the author, even though poets famously tend to address themselves in their poetry and write in other voices. Moreover, most of the Avestan texts are ritual in nature, and refer to the participants as well, making identification of a "speaker's voice" often difficult, if not impossible. [2]

1. Schmitt (1989).

2. Malandra (2009) meticulously clears up the objection. In my reading, the *Gāthās* seem to be the work of one poet, a religious man with deep convictions who calls himself *Zaraθuštra*, our Zoroaster.

It is also often asserted nowadays that there is no difference between Old Avestan (the *Gāthās'* dialect or religiolect) and Young Avestan, which is also a religiolect. Nevertheless, though they are closely related subdialects, they are not the same.[3] It is likely that Old Avestan was an archaic ritual language (or "register") used by speakers of Young Avestan, but in order to approach the question of who Zoroaster really was, we must discuss the available data on his name, his date, and the Scythian dialect of the *Gāthās,* Old Avestan.

We do not know for certain what his name, *Zaraθuštra,* means, or what language it is in. Old Persian and Avestan seem to be out of the question, despite many attempts to force his name into an Iranic mold—the current leading argument, according to which his name means 'Decrepit Camels' in "Old Iranic", is semantically peculiar and extremely unlikely for the founder of a great world religion.[4] It is also morphologically problematic. Schmitt discusses the differences between the Old Avestan (*Zaraθuštra*) and Greek (Ζωροάστρης *Zōroastrēs,* also Ζωρόαστρις *Zōroastris*) forms, but his 'decrepit camels' etymology depends after all on the name being "Old Iranic".[5] There is good reason to doubt it.

In particular, the element *zara* is surely the widespread Semitic word *zar ʿa* 'seed; progeny'[6] which is sometimes used in names in the sense 'Clan (of X)' or 'Son (of X)'. The mysterious middle element *θ* or *θu* in the Old Avestan word has remained inexplicable as an Iranic form, suggesting it is not Iranic either. Setting it aside leaves a third element, *štra* ~ *stra,* a form of the widespread Ancient Near Eastern goddess name *Ishtar* (*Ištar*), from the culture-word *star-, attested also in Avestan *star-, strə-* 'star'.[7] Ishtar was one of the chief Akkadian goddesses and the

3. For the specialist scholarship which points out the differences see Hoffmann (1987). Arguments against distinguishing the two forms of Avestan are typically based on little or no hard data.

4. See Endnote 187.

5. Schmitt (2002).

6. Common Semitic **zar ʿa* 'seed', as in Old Akkadian *zar'u,* Akkadian *zēru* 'seed (of cereals and of other plants), semen, male descendant, son' (*CAD* 21: 89, 95); Aramaic *zar ʿa* 'seed; sowing; offspring, family' (*CAL*); Arabic *zar* ʿ 'seed', etc.

7. Bar. 1598–1599. The equation of the *uštra* part of his name with the well attested word for 'camel' is clear, but that leaves *θ* stranded. However, the fact that *uštra* 'camel' is so well known suggests that the 'star' part of his name was replaced by it via folk-etymology. (Certainly the

patron of the royal family of the Mitanni kingdom, which had ruled a large territory that included western Media, until the late Bronze Age. Ishtar early came to be equated with Anāhitā (Greek Anaïtis), the chief goddess (*Daiva*) of the pre-Zoroastrian "Old Mazdaean" faith. She is also identified with Aphrodite Ourania (Heavenly Aphrodite), and with Artemis.[8] The earliest Greek forms of *Zaraθuštra*, including the one that has become the 'standard' form, *Zōroastrēs*, regularly give this part of his name as Greek *astrēs*, a form of ἀστήρ *astēr* 'star'; the Greek word is itself a form of the culture-word *star* 'star'. Assuming the first element is *zarʿa* 'seed', and the last element is 'star', it is likely that the name means 'Seed of Ishtar', 'Son of the Star', or something to that effect.[9] The dominant cultural languages of the Ancient Near East proper in the pre-Classical period were Semitic, both East Semitic (Akkadian dialects) and West Semitic (mainly Aramaic and Hebrew), though Urartian, Lydian, and other non-Semitic "national" languages of strong regional states remained in use. Semitic languages survived the Scythian conquest and continued to be spoken long after under the rule of the Scythians, Medes, Persians, Greeks, and others. The Near East (except for most of Anatolia and Iran) is still mainly Semitic speaking today. Our planets and stars were divine beings for many ancient cultures and languages, including Greek and Latin. It is thus a perfect name for a man whose teachings enlightened much of the ancient world.

We have Zoroaster's personal statements in the *Gāthās* 'Hymns' of the Avesta, in Old Avestan, so does that mean he *spoke* Old Avestan? Or did he perhaps speak Young Avestan and compose his hymns in Old Avestan, an archaic, high ritual language?[10] We do not know, but that is the most likely possibility, as it is thought to conform to the model of the Rig Veda, a corpus of oral texts which has been argued (on the basis of several loanwords) to be no older than 800 BC, meaning that either

---

Greeks identified the last syllable with the word for 'star'.) In any case, $\theta(u)$ remains a problem.

8. Boyce et al. (1989/2011).

9. Schmitt (2002) says the less frequent Greek form of Zoroaster's name, *Zōróastris*, as in Plutarch, is "secondary".

10. Suggested, in effect, by Skjærvø (2006); see the quotation below.

the texts were memorized no earlier than that point in time or that they were composed then or even later using the archaic Old Indic high ritual language. The latter alternative is far more likely than the usual, but highly unlikely, idea that the texts were composed in the second millennium BC and preserved orally, unchanged, for nearly four thousand years. The Rig Veda texts per se are not attested at all (i.e., not even in literary references or quotations) until well into the first millennium CE, and are acknowledged to have remained purely oral until the early second millennium CE. When they achieved their modern form is anyone's guess. The same analysis applies to the *Gāthās*. In any case, both "Old Avestan" and "Young Avestan", which are dialects of the same language, Scythian, should be dated approximately to the period during or after Scythian rule south of the steppe zone. The earliest firm attestation of Scythian speakers there is the appearance of the Cimmerians to the north of the Assyrian Empire in 720–714 BC in the reign of Sargon II (Sargon of Aššur), followed several decades later by the first attestation of the Scythians under the name 'Scythian' (**Skuδa*), along with several Scythian names.

The Scythian language was long considered to be attested almost exclusively as names recorded in foreign texts. However, those words are marked by specific sound changes characteristic not only of Scythian, but of Avestan and Median too, which are clearly dialects of Scythian, as shown in Chapter 5. It is theoretically possible to place Zoroaster with the earliest Scythians, in the Altai Mountains of Tuva and Western Mongolia, but he would then have been a nomad and would not refer frequently to built "houses" (OAve *dəmān-* 'house') as he does in the *Gāthās*. Also, although he praises cattle-raising, and cows themselves,[11] he does not mention horses or sheep *as domestic animals*, so it is most unlikely that he was a steppe nomad. And as noted, he is unlikely to have had problems with his teachings in a steppe zone culture.

Zoroaster's innovation in the Ancient Near East involved teaching belief in only one God of Heaven, Ahura Mazdā, the unique God who

11. He even says (Y. 31,10) that *non*-herdsmen do not "enjoy a good reputation" (Humbach and Ichaporia 1994: 35).

created the world. Zoroaster rejected the other old Gods, who are called *Daēvas* and *false* ones in the *Gāthās*. In view of the fact that Anāhitā and Mithra are the old Gods who were later rehabilitated by Artaxerxes II, the *Gāthās* evidently refer especially to Anāhitā and Mithra as Daēvas. But the people where Zoroaster lived worshipped the Daēvas. They rejected both Zoroastrianism and Zoroaster, as the prophet tells us, and they specifically did not worship Ahura Mazdā, as Darius the Great says in his Behistun Inscription. Such religious conflict places Zoroaster outside the steppe zone. The gods of the Ancient Near East were nationalistic and territorial. New gods, of whatever kind, necessarily encountered trouble.

Zoroaster tells us that he was able to achieve success only through the protection and support of one local lord, Vištāspa, who has a Scythian name. The earliest historical indication that Early Zoroastrianism was in fact a success is in 613, when Cyaxares, the first contemporaneously attested king of the Medes, devastated the temples and gods of northern Babylonia, making the Babylonian king huddle on the floor as the Medes approached Babylon. This event coincides exactly in time and outcome with the monotheistic campaign of King Josiah of Judah. Zoroaster should therefore have lived near the time of Cyaxares for his teachings to have had such a radical and dramatic effect. Since Cyaxares must have taken power in Media by around 620, a few years before his campaign that overthrew the Assyrian Empire, Zoroaster can be dated to about the same time, as proposed in Chapter 2.[12]

The Avestan language is related so closely to Vedic Sanskrit (Old Indic) that the two have been argued long ago to be almost "dialects" of each other. That is because, with the exception of some very striking (and major) specifically phonetic differences, they are nearly identical, such that sentences in one of the two "dialects" can easily be converted into the other "dialect" by following a few regular phonological rules. That should make Avestan an Indic language, not an Iranic language, and it has actually been so argued. If that were correct, perhaps one

12. Many modern historians place the floruit of Zoroaster in ca. 600 BC (close to the traditional date). Many others continue to date Zoroaster to the mid-2nd millennium BC or even earlier, but for linguistic reasons that sort of high dating is unlikely for the *Gāthās*.

could say Zoroaster spoke a phonetically Iranicized Old Indic language.[13] However, the demonstrable closeness of the two languages does not make them one language. It is unimaginable that a monolingual speaker of one of them could understand a speaker of the other, even if all the words and all the forms were identical except for said phonological differences, because those differences alone are too extreme. Moreover, it is now clear that Avestan and Median are dialects of Scythian (see Chapter 5), though a similar conclusion was suspected already in 1906 by Bartholomae, who asks incredulously, considering the extreme closeness of Avestan to Median, "Is the language of the Avesta *Median*?"[14] The probable relationship of Iranic to Indic is thus not as two chronologically early bifurcated branches of one parent language ("Proto-Indo-Iranic"), but rather as one non-bifurcated ancestral language spoken by migrating peoples who developed different creole daughter languages when they settled among people speaking other languages. That would accord with current thought among historical linguists concerning the chief way—almost the only way—languages undergo substantial changes.[15]

The "Old Avestan" language of Zoroaster's *Gāthās* remains highly problematic in general, as most would agree, but that does not tell us the hymns were composed four millennia ago out in Central Eurasia, as many still claim, rather than closer to the time when the teachings of Early Zoroastrianism first appear in historical records—in the Old Persian inscriptions[16]—at the end of the 6th century BC. That was after a century of nearly total cultural change in which the Scytho-Mede nation and the Imperial Scythian language had been formed by creolization under Scythian rule and spread with the Scythians and

13. Beckwith (2009: 365–369). The present book proposes something different; see below and Chapters 5 and 6.

14. "Ist die Sprache des Awesta m e d i s c h?" (Bartholomae 1904: 16), quoted in Rossi (2010: 300).

15. E.g., Nichols (1997a, 1997b). The proposal helps explain the problematically Indic language of the Bronze Age Mitanni rulers and their relatives in the Ancient Near East. It also helps explain the odd similarity of Old Persian to Sanskrit in some respects (p.c., Michael L. Walter, 2020).

16. Skjærvø (2005). Further support for this date is Herodotus (i 140), who mentions the Magi custom of killing as many ants, snakes, etc. "noxious" animals as possible, a well-known Zoroastrian practice.

Scytho-Medes across the Iranian Plateau and Central Asia, as shown in the Prologue and Chapters 2 and 5.

The *Gāthās* themselves ascribe the Early Zoroastrian teachings directly to a man named *Zaraθuštra*, and they represent a strong reaction against the older beliefs and practices of an earlier polytheistic faith, which has been called "Early Mazdaism". If he were dispensed with, his name would need to be replaced either with "the unknown man who wrote the works attributed to *Zaraθuštra*", or else with another random name, such as "Shakespeare". So we are stuck with Zaraθuštra (Zarathushtra) ~ Zoroaster, the apparent constituents of whose name embed him in the Ancient Near Eastern cultural world.

Ancient Greek comments on Zoroaster say he was one of the Magi, the Mede "religious specialists" of the Achaemenid Persians,[17] though he was certainly a revolutionary who opposed the views of the polytheistic mainstream Magi. But if the Greeks are right, he should have spoken the Magian language, which would thus have been a subdialect of Median. In fact, study of the available data calls for the strictly linguistic conclusion that Median and Avestan are indeed extremely similar dialects of the same language, Imperial Scythian, as shown in Chapters 5 and 6. The main distinction is that some of the lexical material traditionally identified as Median (i.e., the Scytho-Mede language) is Scythian by form, but is not attested in Avestan, so those items cannot be identified with the Avestan subdialect or subdialects, though it should be Scythian. Nevertheless, because of the relation of Imperial Scythian, Median, and Avestan as dialects of the same language, Scythian, we do have *texts* in a dialect of Scythian. The texts are known collectively as the *Avesta*, among which the *Gāthās*, in Old Avestan, are linguistically the most conservative. This is evidence for any theory about the language and homeland of Zoroaster. However, based strictly on the available data, the Median language of the Scytho-Medes, a creole dialect of Scythian, did not even exist before the Cimmerian-Scythian conquest in the late 8th to early 7th centuries. As both Avestan and Median are in fact dialects of the resulting Imperial Scythian language, they cannot

17. See Endnote 112.

be dated earlier than that event. The same goes for Zoroaster himself. He appears to have an Ancient Near Eastern name and his *Gāthās* are in an Avestan subdialect of Imperial Scythian. Thus Zoroaster was Scythian by language. In view of the revolutionary effects of the introduction of Scythian culture into Media, on the northern edge of the ancient Near East (as into Chao on the northern edge of ancient North China), Zoroaster's Scythian connections explain the revolutionary effect of his monotheistic teachings on the religious culture of Media, the home of the traditional Magi and their polytheistic beliefs.

Skjærvø, a leading scholar of the Old Iranic languages and the contents of their texts, comments on the text and transmission of the Avesta:

> The Avestan text[18] is clearly an edited and, to some degree, standardized text, as we can see, especially, from the form of the Gathic text. It must also have been changed by the oral transmitters and the manuscript scribes, who adjusted the text to the phonological systems of their own speech, which was often different from that of the original Avestan languages. . . . This makes it almost impossible to determine which of the sound changes we observe in our extant texts already belonged to the 'original' Avestan language. In particular, Old Avestan has received many Young Avestan features . . . [19]

As a speaker of the Imperial Scythian language, in particular of its Avestan subdialect, Zoroaster was probably a Scytho-Mede. The *Gāthās* explicitly reject all other gods except Ahura Mazdā, calling them *Daevā* 'false gods' (Old Persian *Daivā*).[20] We know that at least two of the

18. "The extant Avestan manuscripts go back to a prototype from ca. 1000 C.E., but the oldest preserved ones date only from the 13th and 14th centuries [CE], most of them being much later still . . ." (Skjærvø 2006).

19. Skjærvø (2006), noting, "In the extant manuscripts, the Young Avestan texts exhibit various kinds of grammatically incorrect language, which has sometimes been taken as an indication that they were composed in the post-Achaemenid period. The faulty text, however, can just as easily be ascribed to deteriorating manuscript transmission or to faulty oral transmission of the texts before they were written down, or, most likely, a combination of these two." See Endnote 188.

20. See the discussion of the Old Persian inscriptions in Chapter 2. In Old Avestan this word does not have the meaning 'demon' or the like (which it developed in dualistic-polytheistic Late Zoroastrianism), nor does Scythian attest that later sense. Sogdian, one of the best-attested

rejected gods, Anahitā and Mithra, were rehabilitated as publicly worshippable deities by the last Achaemenid king of the line of Darius the Great, Artaxerxes II (r. 404–358), who built temples and statues for them and invokes all three of them together in his inscriptions, without any explicit distinction.[21] He thus reinstituted, in principle, Old Mazdaist polytheism.[22] Pre-Zoroastrian Mazdaism was polytheistic and apparently included other "gods" inherited from the Archaic period, including the three "Gods" of Late Zoroastrianism—Anahitā, Mithra, and Mazdā. In the *Gāthās* Zoroaster vehemently rejects all other Gods except Ahura Mazdā as *Daēvas* "false Gods", and the Early Zoroastrianism of Darius the Great and his son Xerxes is equally emphatic in holding this position.

The intoxicating drink *haoma* (Young Avestan *haoma,* Sanskrit *soma*) and the ritual bundle of sticks, the *barsom* (Young Avestan *barəsman*), perhaps the two most characteristic physical features of Zoroastrianism in ancient pictorial representations, are not mentioned overtly in the *Gāthās*. Zoroaster might condemn *haoma,* using an epithet to refer to it, but the text is very short and it is likely that it simply happens not to be mentioned.[23] Both *haoma* and the *barsom* are attested among the Scythians. *Haoma* is attested in the name *Sakā Haumavargā* in the Naqš-i-Rustam Inscription of Darius the Great (ca. 490 BC), and (though less obviously) in Herodotus' Greek transcription of the same name, *Amyrgioi Sakai.* The word *haoma* is well attested in Young Avestan, and the identity of Young Avestan *haoma* and Old Indic *soma* is accepted.[24]

The meaning of the second element in *Haumavargā* is disputed. Schmitt, citing Hoffmann, concludes that it is related to Avestan *varj-* and means 'strewers', perhaps referring to the laying out of the *barsom*

---

daughter languages of Scythian, has the word in the inherited positive sense 'god' (often used in reference to rulers also). The same word does occur in the negative sense 'demon', but that sense and attendant usages entered Sogdian along with Late Zoroastrianism.

21. Brentjes (2006); for an example in one of his inscriptions see Endnote 80.

22. In so doing, he very likely doomed the Empire; see the analysis of its structure in the Prologue and Chapters 3 and 4.

23. This and the following discussion assumes that the Early Zoroastrianism of the *Gāthās* is similar to but *not identical* to the Early Zoroastrianism of Darius, unlike the assumption in Beckwith (2015).

24. Sch. 191–192.

sticks.[25] However, unqualified *haoma* (or *soma*) is a liquid. Since the Avestan (Scythian) word is also clearly equatable with Sanskrit *varja* ~ *varga* from the root *vṛj-* 'to discharge, pour or give out, emit',[26] the meaning of *vargā* here could be 'pourers' or the like. In any case, the *Sakā Haumavargā* are certainly to be equated with the *Amyrgioi Sakai* of Herodotus,[27] and they used *haoma* for something remarkable enough for it to appear in their national epithet.

The *barsom* is clearly described (but unnamed) in Herodotus' account of the Scythians on the Pontic Steppe:

> There are many diviners among the Scythians, who divine by means of many willow wands as I will show. They bring great bundles of wands, which they lay on the ground and unfasten, and utter their divinations as they lay the rods down one by one; and while still speaking, they gather up the rods once more and place them together again; this manner of divination is hereditary among them.[28]

In Achaemenid reliefs, the men holding the *barsom* are portrayed as Scytho-Medes. The implications of these connections and disconnections require careful study.

A true creole only arises from the merger of peoples speaking *two different languages* or highly distinct *dialects*. Examination of the data shows that Avestan words are present in the Old Persian inscriptions,

25. Sch. 191–192. Schmitt (2004) says "there is only one interpretation worth considering, that of Karl Hoffmann [1976], p. 612, note 6, who compared *varga-* with Av. *varj* Ved. *varj*, *vṛṇákti* 'to turn (over, away), to lay (around something),' especially with Ved. *vrnktá-barhiṣ-* 'having laid the sacrificial grass around (the fire).' He thus interpreted and translated the entire compound as 'laying *hauma*-plants (instead of the usual grass) around (the fire).' Bruno Jacobs (1982: 78, note 39a) changed this interpretation to refer to the Scythian custom of laying cannabis seeds on the blazing hot stones of their steam baths, by which they produced clouds of vapor having an intoxicating effect (see Herodotus 4.75.1)."

26. Apte (1978: 1489).

27. Problems seen by some arise from the fact that the Greek transcriptions of Old Iranic words are fundamentally *fairly* regular, just as the many English loanwords in modern Japanese mostly follow *fairly* regular rules. But Herodotus and the other Greeks were not ancient scientific linguists. Schmitt, Mayrhofer, and others have pointed out some of the many obvious mistakes in the ancient transcriptions. See Endnote 189.

28. Herodotus (iv 67), from Perseus, tr. Godley.

but they belong to the category of words identified as Median. Even in traditional Iranist publications Old Avestan is thought to be closer to Old Indic than to Old Persian, which is universally agreed to be an Iranic language. On the other side of the coin, as shown in Chapter 5, there are "Old Iranic" words in Median or Old Avestan that are not just different phonologically from genuine Old Persian words, they are *unrelated* to them, while some words which occur with great frequency in the Old Persian inscriptions are Median in form, and have been thought to be Median loanwords,[29] yet they are not attested in Avestan. They include two of the most prominent Old Persian words, *χšāyaθiya* 'King' and *văzărka* '(the one) Great' (q.v. the Prologue).

But if such problematic words are not Median loanwords, or Persianized forms of Median words, or inherited Persian forms of Proto-Iranic words, then where did they come from? It has been suggested that the clever Medes *invented* the words *χšāyaθiya* 'King' and *văzărka* '(the one) Great', to flatter Darius, or in obedience to his command. That is unlikely, so we must look beyond Media for the origin of such terms, but perhaps we do not need to look very far.

The probable source of most of these terms is indicated by Herodotus, who tells us Median children learned the Scythian language and Scythian culture directly from their Scythian rulers, as mentioned in the Prologue and Chapter 2. Mayrhofer says of his "short list" of Scythian words that the solidly established ones "display a Common Old Iranian form. This secure 'Scythian' corresponds to 'the state that we find in the ancient Iranian dialects.'"[30] Schmitt similarly says that such Scythian forms "correspond *grosso modo* to the level of development of Avestan and Old Persian."[31] Scythian is thus similar to the other "Old Iranic" languages in the traditional view—i.e., primarily Old Persian and Avestan.

29. Some are simply "Old Persianized" forms of Median loanwords, detectable because the Persian forms cannot derive directly from Proto-Iranic. The process was firmly identified by Gershevitch, whose ideas are the main topic of discussion in Mayrhofer (1968).

30. Mayrhofer (2006: 26): "zeigen gemeinaltiranische Gestalt. Dieses gesicherte 'Skythisch' entspricht somit 'dem Zustande, den wir in den altiranischen Dialekten antreffen'," quoting Vasmer (1923: 122).

31. Schmitt (2003: 6), quoted by Mayrhofer (2006: 26).

However, this should not be taken to mean that all of these speech forms were mutually intelligible dialects, as usually claimed too. Mayrhofer's constructed demonstration of the putative extreme similarity of Median and Old Persian, using Darius' Suez Inscription (DZc) in Old Persian as a basis (Mayrhofer 1968: 21), is deceptive, and unacceptable, because it takes the missing native Median *grammatical* morphology from Old Persian rather than from Young Avestan.[32] No doubt he did this because of the lack of texts conveniently pre-labelled as "Median", but as a result he has created a new hybrid faux-Median language with Median stems and Old Persian inflection.[33] Not surprisingly, then, an Old Persian speaker would have had no trouble understanding a faux-Median speaker if the faux-Median speaker was bilingual and was in on the joke, and thus used only shared cognates plus Old Persian grammar, producing something like Old Persian with an erudite Median twang. The actual contrast between the Median and Old Persian languages would have been clear if Mayrhofer had instead taken a passage in Young Avestan, a Scythian dialect (as is Median), and compared it to a text from the Achaemenid inscriptions written in Old Persian.

Because the first historically attested blows for monotheistic Zoroastrianism seem to have been struck by Cyaxares in 613, or a decade earlier by the Scythians at Ascalon, that means Zoroaster was living, or *had lived*, by that time. But his Scythian language and Ancient Near Eastern location link him to the Cimmerian and Scythian domination of Media and neighboring lands, where the Imperial Scythian language used in the Avesta must have developed. Assuming Zoroaster lived a fairly long life, as shown by the success of his teachings, his floruit was thus sometime in the 7th century BC.

32. The morphology of Avestan *roots* is practically identical to that of cognate Median forms, and often to that of Old Persian cognates, but the derivational and grammatical morphology is not identical and much else is different, as shown in Chapter 5.

33. One of the differences even between *dialects* is specifically lexical, such as British English *lift* vs. American English *elevator*. Mayrhofer (2006: 26, note 29) repeats the standard view that Median is not a "corpus language".

Monotheism versus Polytheism

The *Gāthās* of Zoroaster in Old Avestan, and the inscriptions of Darius and his son Xerxes in Old Persian—two very different, mutually unintelligible languages—present the same basic theological system. They praise and worship the One Great God, Ahura Mazdā, and do not allow any other "Gods" to be worshipped. Minor "gods" and spirits of many kinds are acknowledged, but they are categorically distinct from Ahura Mazdā, who belongs to a category of One, which in Darius' version is parallel to the unique categories of the One Great King and the One Great Empire. Study of the fragments of preserved information on the Western Steppe Scythians reveals that many things reflecting specifically Zoroastrian ideas and practices can be identified among them. One might ask, were the Scythians themselves Mazdaists or pre-Zoroastrians? We lack enough information to really know the answer, if it is really a well-formed question.

However, the problem raises an important, specifically *historical* question. *Who* followed the monotheistic system with one Heavenly God (1), and *who* followed the opposed polytheistic system with the *Daivas*, the 'other Gods' famous from the Ten Commandments (2)? By working back and forth between the various opposed groups and individuals, a clear pattern appears.

Diagram 4 is a suggestion of a theory of the historical succession of rulers in the Empire from the first historically attested Scythian people, the Cimmerians, down to the end of the Scytho-Mede-Persian empire.

Cimmerians–monotheists (1)?
enemies of the early Scythians, according to Herodotus

|

Early Scythians of Spakaya–both monotheists (1) and polytheists (2)?
eventual allies of the Assyrians (2)

|

Scythians ruling over Media: two sub-groups (1) and (2)
pro-Assyrian leading group–polytheists (2)
pro-Scytho-Mede subordinate group–monotheists (1)
sub-group (1) sacked the Daiva temple in Ascalon

|

Cyaxares–monotheist (1)
overthrew pro-Assyrian main Scythian group (2)
overthrew the Assyrians (2)
destroyed polytheistic sites in Mesopotamia, including Ḥarrān(2)

|

Astyages–monotheist (1)
attacked Cyrus–polytheist (2)

|

Cyrus–polytheist (2)

|

Bardiya–monotheist (1)?

|

Cambyses–polytheist (2)?

|

Gaumāta (usurper)–polytheist (2)

|

civil war between Mede and Persian polytheists (2) and monotheists (1)

|

Darius–monotheist (1)

|

Xerxes and other Persian kings–monotheist (1)

|

Artaxerxes II–polytheist (2)
last king in the line of Darius and last effective ruler of the Empire

Diagram 4. Monotheism versus Polytheism: People and Events.

APPENDIX B

Scythian and Scytho-Mede Dress and Weaponry

The Scytho-Medes are famous in Greek literature for their fashionable, colorful clothing. Their national dress was slim and warm, light and soft, and suitable for riding as well as for just parading about, as Aristophanes (*Wasps* 1135–1155) says when a character dresses his father in a close-fitting new garment "straight from Ecbatana". Ctesias lived in the Persian Empire for some years, so his description of Persian-adopted Mede 'riding dress' should reflect his own observations. (See Figure 8.) He imagines the ancient Assyrian queen, Semiramis (Šammu-ramāt, fl. ca. 811), designing the outfit herself—his way of emphasizing that it was a foreign, feminine outfit:[1]

> First, as she was about to go on a journey for many days, she made herself an outfit which did not allow anyone to determine whether the person wearing it was a man or a woman. This clothing was suitable for traveling in the burning heat, while it protected her complexion, and as it was fluid and youthful, it allowed her to do whatever she wanted. It was altogether so lovely that later, when the Medes

1. The adoption of the *candys* by Athenian women in the 5th century BC—part of a general "Persianizing" trend in Athens at that time (Miller 2004)—may have encouraged Ctesias' sexist view. There are many studies of Achaemenid period dress. One of the best, Walser (1966), was unfortunately unavailable to me until the present book was already in production. Its illustrations are unusually fine.

> reigned over Asia, they always wore the raiment of Semiramis, and after them the Persians did the same.[2]

Ctesias tells this as an aside within his legendary account of Semiramis. Though the story as a whole is mostly fantasy contradicted by chronology and historical evidence, his observations on the clothing itself agree with all sources and were surely based on his own eyewitness experiences in the Persian Empire in the late 5th century BC. His main point is that the Persians were effeminate because they wore women's clothing, as were the Medes, who were considered by the Greeks to be the most effeminate of all. Lenfant[3] says that the most important item of clothing in question was a cape worn by women, but also worn by men in war. However, Ctesias' full account of Semiramis' vigorous warrior-like activities, involving horse riding among other things, makes it clear that what he describes is undoubtedly the entire three-part national dress of the Medes, an outfit including trousers (which the Greeks also considered effeminate), a fitted tunic, and the *candys* (κάνδυς *kandys*), which is not a cape at all but a slender, full-length, long-sleeved coat worn on the shoulders *like* a cape. This "Mede riding costume", well attested in the sources and bas-reliefs, was adopted also by the Persians,[4] as Herodotus (i 135) and other ancient writers state. The version of this story in Justin's epitome of Pompeius Trogus (ii 1) is mostly fanciful,

2. Πρῶτον μὲν οὖν πολλῶν ἡμερῶν ὁδὸν μέλλουσα διαπορεύεσθαι στολὴν ἐπραγματεύσατο δι' ἧς οὐκ ἦν διαγνῶναι τὸν περιβεβλημένον πότερον ἀνήρ ἐστιν ἢ γυνή. Αὕτη δ' ἦν εὔχρηστος αὐτῇ πρός τε τὰς ἐν τοῖς καύμασιν ὁδοιπορίας εἰς τὸ διατηρῆσαι τὸν τοῦ σώματος χρῶτα καὶ πρὸς τὰς ἐν τῷ πράττειν ὃ βούλοιτο χρείας, εὐκίνητος οὖσα καὶ νεανική, καὶ τὸ σύνολον τοσαύτη τις ἐπῆν αὐτῇ χάρις ὥσθ' ὕστερον Μήδους ἡγησαμένους τῆς Ἀσίας φορεῖν τὴν Σεμιράμιδος στολήν, καὶ μετὰ ταῦθ' ὁμοίως Πέρσας (Ctesias, *Persica* F1b, in Diodorus Siculus ii.1,6.6, from Lenfant 2004: 30–31). Cf. Stronk (2010: 212–213). My translation largely follows Lenfant.

3. Lenfant (2004: 31, note 133), q.v. for related literature.

4. Schmitt (1990). Shahbazi (1992/2011) gives references to the scholarly literature on this topic, most of which I have not seen. Schmitt, like many others, often uses for the *candys* (or for the entire outfit) the English term "stole", borrowed from Greek στολή *stolē*, but today, at least in American English, a *stole* is typically a sort of shawl or short fur wrap covering the shoulders or torso. The graphic evidence clearly portrays a long, slender, ankle-length coat. When I was in Afghanistan in 1972 the Kazakh men there were distinguished by the elegant, saliently long *čâpân* that they wore off the shoulders—i.e., not using the sleeves. It looked almost exactly like a Scythian-Mede-Persian *candys* as shown in the Persepolis bas-reliefs.

FIGURE 14. Darius III wearing Late Achaemenid royal *bashlyq* (Alexander Mosaic).

but it includes the important addition that the outfit included the *tiara* or *kidaris* (in Greek transcription)—now referred to by scholars as a *bashlyq*—which is also implied in Ctesias' description, as it could hide a person's face almost completely, depending on what it was made from and how it was worn (see Figures 3, 5, 6, 8, and 12). In its cloth version it is a head garment more like a hijab than a "turban", but the raised golden 'royal' version of it does look vaguely like a turban, as in the Alexander Mosaic (Figure 14).

The distinctive Mede court headgear version of the stiffer Scythian and Scytho-Mede felt *bashlyq* has a spherical bowl-shape, but careful examination of the Persepolis reliefs shows that the *bashlyq*'s characteristic long side and back flaps have been pulled back and tied; the ends hanging down in back are often clearly visible (see Figures 7, 11, and 15). The *bashlyq* was made of felt, leather, or—shown most clearly in later Achaemenid period portrayals—soft cloth, which was wrapped around the head (see Figure 8).

There are two words for Median outer garments in Greek, both loanwords. The most well known is the just-discussed *candys,* a name of Iranic origin used by the Greeks for what they considered to be a Persian garment borrowed from the Medes. Schmitt explains the Greek name as from "Median **kanzu-ka-,* in Elamite *kan-su-ka,* Parthian *qnjwg,* etc., 'cloak' . . ." via "Old Persian **kantu-* . . . or 'coat thrown round the shoulders.'" More precisely, the Greek word has been borrowed from an Old Persianized form (with *d) of the Scytho-Mede word (with *z). Linguistics thus confirms the historical account.[5] In Achaemenid bas-reliefs at Persepolis it is typically shown being worn off the shoulders *as* a cloak, i.e., with the sleeves hanging free, usually by Medes or Scythians (see Figures 7 and 11).[6] It is also shown in a Persepolis relief (Figure 6) portraying Scythians bringing two of the garments to court as tribute.

The other outer garment, the καυνάκης *kaynakes,* is mentioned first (ca. 422 BC) in Aristophanes, with a great deal of implicit description.[7] The *kaynakes* was a thick, fur-lined coat (a 'Persian', as the text itself says at line 1137). It is "said to be of Persian or Babylonian make" according to *LSJ,* which gives the etymology: "Assyr[ian] *gaunakka* 'frilled and flounced mantle.'" However, it does not seem to have been anything like a mantle (large, long cloak). Aristophanes describes it as a tight-fitting garment, rather shorter than longer, like a jacket, and he explicitly says it was "straight from Ecbatana", the capital of Media, and thus a Median garment. Moreover, the word is known to be a foreign loan into Assyrian.[8] Considering Aristophanes' stress on the hairiness or wooliness of

5. The occurrence in Xenophon, *Anabasis* (1.5.8) has the earliest attestation of the word. Schmitt (1990).

6. See Figures. The relief shows two Medes wearing the *candys* and their globular "court" *bashlyq* (the court headdress being a specific national marker), each preceded by a Persian wearing typical Elamite-Persian robes and the Persian crown-like headdress.

7. Aristophanes, *Wasps* (1130–1165).

8. According to the authoritative *Chicago Assyrian Dictionary.* The lone entry reads (reformatted): *gunakku* s. 'a cloth or garment'; . . . foreign word; *šalšu ina bīti* TÚG *gu-nak-ku u* URUDU.ŠEN.TUR 'one-third share of (this) house, the g[unakku] and the small bronze pot (belong to PN)' . . . possible connection with Greek *kaunakes* [i.e., *kaynakes*] and Aram[aic] *gonakka*" (*CAD,* Vol. 5, G: 134, q.v. for source references and literature). Cf. *CAL* s.v. gwnk: *gawnaḵ* 'thick garment' in the expression "she clothed/covered him בְּגוֹנַכָּא *bəḡōnaḵā* 'with the *gōnaḵ*.'"

the garment, it is clear that Greek *kaynakes,* Assyrian *gaunakka* and Aramaic *gaunak̠* ~ *gonakka* represent the same word, Old Iranic **gaunaka-* 'hairy; the hairy one', from Avestan *gauna-* 'hair'.[9] A version of it is the garment adopted by the Chinese of Chao for horse riding and represented in many ancient Chinese tomb figurines, as in Figure 13.

The textual occurrences in Greek unfortunately do not clearly distinguish which garment is which, and usually do not use the foreign words for them at all, but—like Ctesias—they typically use generic Greek terms for 'garment' or 'cloak', etc. The unclarity is worse because both were evidently outer garments worn on top of a tunic.

Thus there appear to have been two basic variants of Median "riding dress", both including an inner tunic and trousers on the legs. Xenophon (*Cyropaedia* 8.3.10) says that "horsemen put their arms through the *candys* only when the king was inspecting them."[10] The bas-reliefs at Persepolis show the *candys* being worn off the shoulders, with empty sleeves.

The same group of Scythians bearing the *candys* as tribute are also shown holding several pairs of one-piece footed leather trousers, or "footies" (see Figure 6). Because the visible tunic openings of different peoples typically differ, the parts of the Scythian outfit that were borrowed were actually the headgear (*bashlyq* or "tiara"), the *candys,* and trousers—which for actual riding purposes were no doubt footies, but otherwise unfooted trousers—with shoes, as in portrayals of Medes and Scythians in court dress at Persepolis and as found in the early East Scythian burial at Pazyryk, or boots.[11]

Greek sources often describe a garment or outfit slightly when it is mentioned, and remark on the Persians having borrowed it from the Medes. As noted, Herodotus says "the Persians wear Median dress, considering it to be more beautiful than their own",[12] and similarly Ctesias, quoted above. The description by Aristophanes says of the tight, wooly

9. Bar. 482, Tav. 188; cf. Shahbazi (2011) for scholarly literature.

10. Shahbazi (2011), citing here Thompson (1965).

11. Cunliffe (2020: 201–207) describes the Pazyryk finds (East Scythian); see Endnote 190.

12. Herodotus (i 135): καὶ γὰρ δὴ τὴν Μηδικὴν ἐσθῆτα νομίσαντες τῆς ἑωυτῶν εἶναι καλλίω φορέουσι; from Perseus, tr. Godley.

outer garment from Ecbatana—thus a Median garment—that "some call it a *kaynakes*, but some a 'Persian.'"[13] Xenophon in the *Anabasis* "describes the candys as a purple outer garment worn by high-ranking Persians in the entourage of Cyrus the Younger; under the candys they wore costly tunics (*khitônes*), colored trousers (*anaxyrides*), and jewelry, such as necklaces and bracelets."[14] Schmitt says Xenophon in his *Cyropaedia* (1.3.2) ascribes all these items to the Medes, and says (8.3.13) that Cyrus [the Younger] wore "a solid purple (*holopórphyros*) candys over a purple tunic shot with white (the typically royal dress) and scarlet trousers . . . elsewhere these articles are combined to form the so-called 'Median stole.' . . . The currently prevailing opinion is that the candys . . . should be identified with the full-length mantle slung over the shoulders, the long empty sleeves covering the hands, that is represented often in the Persepolis reliefs".[15]

Schmitt does not mention Ctesias' creative Assyrian tale, the actual ethnic origin of which is shown, firstly, by the fact that neither the Assyrian nor the Achaemenid bas-reliefs show the Assyrians ever wearing anything remotely like the outfit he describes, and in pre-Achaemenid Assyrian reliefs the Medians wear entirely unrelated outfits, whereas Achaemenid reliefs and Greek vase paintings show the Scythians, Scytho-Medes, and related northern peoples wearing the same Scythian-derived outfit. Secondly, as noted above, a relief at Persepolis shows *Scythians* bearing tribute of the *candys* and footed trousers, showing that the key elements of "Mede" riding costume (along with the *bashlyq*) derived from the founders of the Empire, the Scythians. Thirdly, archaeological

13. Aristophanes, *Wasps* (1137), οἱ μὲν καλοῦσι Περσίδ᾽ οἱ δὲ καυνάκην; from Perseus, tr. O'Neill, Jr.

14. Schmitt (1990).

15. Schmitt (1990), who cites E. F. Schmidt, *Persepolis* I (Chicago, 1953), pls. 51, 52, 57, 58, etc., and comments, "This identification is in full agreement with the description of Pollux (*Onomasticon* 7.58), who calls the *candys* 'sleeved' (*kheiridōtós*) and 'fastened along the shoulders' (*katà toùs ṓmous enaptómenos*). Sometimes the *candys* may have been edged with fur (probably beaver). Apparently it was worn only when the climate or weather was such that the tunic (called *khitṓn* by Xenophon) and the trousers were not warm enough." Thus it seems that the fur-edged version is related to (if not the same as) the *kaynakes* (*gaunaka*). See above for corrective comments on the terms "stole" and "mantle".

excavations in Central Eurasia have found Scythians buried together with the *candys*.[16]

Ctesias' story thus transfers the creator of the garment from a Scythian or Sauromatian, perhaps a queen like Tomyris, to the early Assyrian Semiramis. He could perhaps have done this to avoid praising Tomyris, who defeated Cyrus the Great in battle, but it is more likely that he did it for the opposite reason: to *covertly* call up the story of Tomyris (whose name is vaguely reminiscent of Semiramis) among his Greek readers, who would have heard the Tomyris story via Herodotus. Ctesias thus perhaps relates the story to criticize *sotto voce* the earlier Cyrus (the Great), and thus by implication also the later Cyrus (Cyrus the Younger), with whom his royal patron Artaxerxes II was fighting a civil war. Like Schmitt in our own time, Ctesias does not mention the Scythians in this connection. Nevertheless, the Medes certainly got most of their costume from the Scythians, including its most salient elements—the *bashlyq*, *candys*, and trousers (which for actual riding were leather footies)—via the Scythians' long domination and creolization of Media, as shown sartorially by the bas-reliefs of the Assyrian and Achaemenid empires.[17]

The throne-bearer bas-reliefs at the Persian royal tombs show the stereotyped 'national' clothing of each constituent people of the Empire, as worn by a native of his satrapy, named in an inscriptional label.[18] (See Figure 15.)

The outfit worn by the Mede representative is identical to the one portrayed in the Persepolis reliefs. A deceptive difference for many figures is that in the tomb reliefs their "national" headgear is shown realistically "mashed down" by the gigantic throne, so the shapes are different from the usual ones in the Persepolis reliefs. The standard portrayal of Medes in the Persepolis reliefs shows them wearing a roughly spherical bowl-shaped "court" version of the *bashlyq* headgear, trousers with an *akinakes* (ἀκινάκης) 'Scythian short sword' pending at an angle on the right hip, and a *gōrytos* (γωρυτός) bow-and-quiver case hanging over

16. Shahbazi (2011); Cunliffe (2020).

17. And of course by the archaeology, which attests these garments among the early steppe Scythians as well as among the Ch'in-Han Chinese. Cf. Vogelsang (1992: 174–175).

18. The great work on national costumes in the Achaemenid reliefs is Walser (1966).

FIGURE 15. The Persian Empire's throne-bearers in their national costumes (Naqš-i Rustam) (after Walser 1966).

1. Persian
2. Mede
3. Elamite
4. Parthian
5. Areian
6. Bactrian
7. Sogdian
8. Choresmian (Khwarizmian)
9. Zarangian
10. Arachosian
11. Sattagydian
12. Gandharan
13. Indian
14. Saka Haumavarga (Haoma-strewing Scythian)
15. Saka Tigrakhauda (Scythian with pointed bashlyq)
16. Babylonian
17. Assyrian
18. Arab
19. Egyptian
20. Armenian (Urartian)
21. Cappadocian
22. Lydian
23. Ionian (Anatolian Greek)
24. Saka Paradraya (overseas Scythian)
25. Skudrian
26. Petasos-wearing Ionian (Greek)
27. Libyan
28. Ethiopian
29. Macan
30. Carian

9
10
11
12
13
14
23
24
25
26
27
28
30

the left hip. The Medes' standard clothing and weaponry is identical to the Scythians' from the waist down. Both are sometimes portrayed with the *sagaris* (σάγαρις) battle-axe, as in Herodotus:

> The Sacae, who are Scythians, had on their heads tall caps, erect and stiff and tapering to a point; they wore trousers, and carried their native bows, and daggers, and also axes which they call 'sagaris'. These were Amyrgian Scythians, but were called Sacae; that is the Persian name for all Scythians.[19]

Herodotus regularly calls the short sword borne by all these related peoples a 'dagger' (ἐγχειρίδιον), though the native word for the actual weapon they bore, *akīnaka*, was borrowed by the Greeks as ἀκινάκης *akinakes*, in the right meaning, 'short straight sword'.[20] It is portrayed in countless bas-reliefs and other art, and has been excavated from one end of Scythian territory to the other, always immediately recognizable by its distinctive shape.[21] All three characteristic Scythian objects—*akinakes*, *gōrytos*, and *sagaris*—are undoubtedly of Scythian origin, though the etymologies of their names remain obscure.

The man identified as a "Mede" on the tomb-bearers relief of Darius the Great at Naqš-i Rustam (Figure 15) and in the identical reliefs of Darius' successors wears this outfit, as do several others shown, including the Bactrians, Parthians, Armenians, and Cappadocians, whose Lands (satrapies) were vassal states in the Empire that the Scytho-Medes took over from the Scythians. The Scythians are attested archaeologically (across Central Eurasia as far as China) and artistically (on Persian bas-reliefs, Greek vase paintings, and Chinese tomb figurines) as having worn a version of this outfit. The Scytho-Medes ran the court

19. Σάκαι δὲ οἱ Σκύθαι περὶ μὲν τῇσι κεφαλῇσι κυρβασίας ἐς ὀξὺ ἀπηγμένας ὀρθὰς εἶχον πεπηγυίας, ἀναξυρίδας δὲ ἐνεδεδύκεσαν, τόξα δὲ ἐπιχώρια καὶ ἐγχειρίδια, πρὸς δὲ καὶ ἀξίνας σαγάρις εἶχον. τούτους δὲ ἐόντας Σκύθας Ἀμυργίους Σάκας ἐκάλεον: οἱ γὰρ Πέρσαι πάντας τοὺς Σκύθας καλέουσι Σάκας. Herodotus (vii 64), from Perseus, tr. Godley. The Amyrgian Scythians are better known as the *Sakā Haumavargā*.

20. *LSJ* from Perseus.

21. The *sagaris* too is equally distinctive.

and most of the Empire.[22] Although the Persian rulers retained their Elamite-Mesopotamian robes and headgear for formal court dress, all sources agree that they eventually adopted Mede dress, specifically the "riding outfit", for non-court use, including in battle.[23]

Clothing in the Throne-bearers Relief of Darius I's Tomb[24]

1. Scytho-Mede Court Outfit

Plain tunic (mid-calf length) with round neck; belt with *akinakes* pending at an angle from right hip and tied to the leg at the bottom edge of the tunic; trousers and shoes; court *bashlyq* flattened (by the throne) and tied back (visible tied-back line; its hanging ends can be seen on the Mede). Except for variant headgear, the outfit is worn by 2. the Mede, 4. the Parthian, 6. the Bactrian, 20. the Armenian (Urartian), and 21. the Cappadocian; and, wearing the same, but with boots up to the bottom of the tunic, 5. the Areian, 9. the Zarangian, and 10. the Arachosian.

Subgroups: A. Mede; Parthian; Bactrian; Armenian; Cappadocian.
B. Areian; Zarangian; Arachosian (difference from A: knee-high boots).

2. Scythian Outfit

Bordered mid-calf-length cutaway tunic with the sides of the opening curving down from the shoulders and inward to meet at the belted waist, then curving outward below the waist; with *akinakes* attached as in the Scytho-Mede outfit; trousers and shoes; *bashlyq*, pointed (but squashed down by the horizontal beam of the throne) or rounded. It is worn by: 7. the Sogdian, 8. the Choresmian, 14. the Saka Haumavarga, 15.

22. Hinz (1969: 63–114).
23. See Figure 8 for the Alexander Sarcophagus, and Figure 14 for the Alexander Mosaic.
24. See Figure 15, from Walser (1966), which also discusses the national dress groups.

the Saka Tigraxauda, 24. the Overseas Saka, and the same but wearing a *petasos* (a flat Greek hat like the one worn by Number 26) and barefoot: 25. the Skudrian.

Subgroups: A. Sogdian; Choresmian; Saka Haumavarga; Saka Tigraxauda; Overseas Saka.
B. Skudrian.[25]

3. *Other Nations' Outfits*

These include groups of non-Scythian peoples. A: 1. the Persian, and 3. the Elamite; B: 11. the Sattagydian, 12. the Gandharan, 13. the Indian, and 29. the Macan; C: 22 the Lydian, 23. the Ionian (Anatolian Greek), and 26. the *Petasos*-wearing Ionian (Greek).[26] D includes all those whose representative wears a unique outfit that does not belong to any other group, numbers 16, 17, 18, 19, 27, 28, 30.

Subgroups: A. 1. Persian; 3. Elamite (both with Elamite robes and Elamite sword).
B. 11. Sattagydian; 12. Gandharan; 13. Indian; 29 Macan (all wearing a short tunic, with bare legs and a sword on a scabbard hung with one or two cords across the bearer's back).

25. According to Henkelman and Stolper (2009: 291), the Skudrians appear in two different variations of the Scythian outfit. "Schmidt described the headgear of the Skudrians on tombs I, V and VI as 'a Scythian hat with the characteristic cheek flap tapering under the chin,' and a distinctive 'bluntly pointed tip.' On tomb IV, and perhaps II and III, the Skudrian wears a flat hat, a variation plausibly explained by Schmidt as an erroneous duplicate of the *petasos* of the adjacent Yauna takabara" citing Schmidt (1970: 150 and fig. 44 with table), a work inaccessible to me at the time of writing. The second variation of the Skudra outfit is in effect half Scythian and half Greek. Although the Skudrians' ethnolinguistic identity remains problematic, their basic presentation sartorially as Scythians but wearing a *petasos*, and their close textual connection with the Lycians in the Persepolis Fortification tablets, remarked by Henkelman and Stolper (2009), together strongly suggest they were a Scythian creole people of Anatolia. On their name and location see Szemerényi (1980: 24–26).

26. The outfits of Numbers 23 and 26 are identical in Walser's (1966) drawing, the only difference being that 26 has a little more hair and possibly a very slightly bigger *petasos* (hat). For a clear portrayal of a *petasos* see "Head of Hermes with petasos", a photograph of an ancient coin on Perseus.com.

C. 22. Lydian; 23. Ionian and 26. Petasos-wearing Ionian (almost identical).
D. 16. Babylonian; 17. Assyrian; 18. Arab; 19. Egyptian; 27. Libyan; 28. Ethiopian; 30. Carian.[27]

The Persepolis bas-reliefs thus show the Medes (Scytho-Medes) wearing a slightly different version of the Saka (Scythian) outfit, no doubt because a century had passed after the fall of the Scythian realm in Media, in which the ruling Scytho-Medes had modified their inherited Scythian dress. It was this modified Scytho-Median "riding costume" that was in turn adopted by the Medes' feudal vassals—copied most closely by the nations ruled directly by the Medes in the Mede Empire and later, under the Achaemenids, as sub-satrapies of Media (Parthian, Bactrian, Armenian, Cappadocian). The Mede version of the outfit was also worn by the Areians, Zarangians, and Arachosians, with the difference of their characteristic knee-high boots.

As far as we know from the archaeology, the Scythians innovated the entire original outfit and accompanying military accoutrements, from the *bashlyq* to the trousers (including the leather footie version used in riding), from the *akinakes* down to the arrowheads.[28] They define Scythian sites and do not occur in earlier cultures. The clothing is the same as the outfit famously adopted by the Chinese from the eastern Scythians in the state of Chao in the Classical period, as discussed in Chapter 7 and portrayed in tomb figurines from the Ch'in and Han dynasties (see Figure 14). The fact that the Sogdians and Khwarizmians retain the original Scythian costume in this image, and in the Persepolis bas-reliefs, indicates that those regions remained under actual or de facto steppe Scythian rule, so they were probably not integral parts of the early Scytho-Mede-Persian Empire.

27. The Carian (30) is shown at a somewhat different angle and seems different, but is perhaps arrayed the same as the Lydian.

28. See the discussion and illustrations in Cunliffe (2020: 201–207).

ENDNOTES

1. The recent popularity of the romantic term *Silk Road* has been at the expense of the geographical term *Central Asia*, which is the urbanized south-central core region of *Central Eurasia*. Much writing on the Silk Road these days omits any mention of Central Asia, not to speak of Central Eurasia, indicating that the writers know very little, if anything, about those regions and their civilizations. Some are confused by continental Europeans' use of "Central Asia" (in other languages and in English) to mean either Central Asia or Central Eurasia, or both (Central Eurasia including Central Asia). Worse, the term *Silk Road* has been pluralized by some, even from the beginning of the term's life in the mid-19th century (q.v. Mertens 2019), and taken literally to refer to actual "roads" or "highways". As if all that were not bad enough, it has been extended by others to refer also to the sea lanes which connected East Asia and the lands in between to Europe. The meaning of this term, and of a good number of other terms, has thus succumbed to the forces of Modernism (q.v. Beckwith 2009) and no longer serves its original purpose.

   Most scholarship on the commercially focused "Silk Road" starts everything with the Han Dynasty Chinese in the 2nd century BC. (We can imagine the ribbon-cutting ceremony attended by Chinese, Scythians, Persians, Greeks, and many others in their colorful best.) However, the Scythians were involved in international trade from at least the 8th–7th centuries BC, as attested by elite Scythian burial sites such as Arzhan, and later Pazyryk, that contain objects from the ancient Near East and contemporaneous early China. It cannot be stressed enough that from early Antiquity on many people actually *lived* permanently *in between* Europe, India, and East Asia—to be precise, in Central Eurasia, which includes Central Asia—and great civilizations existed there. The inhabitants mostly stayed home and did not really go anywhere. Many people still live throughout Central Eurasia as a whole, except in the fiercest deserts. And, before modern times, there were *no actual roads* at all.

   Thus the only excuse for the term *Silk Road* was and remains romance, and I have happily used it in that sense (Beckwith 2009), having in mind great books I admire with wonderful titles such as Schafer's (1963) *Golden Peaches of Samarkand*. So, romantic titles are certainly harmless enough. But for a region that remains so little known and poorly understood, including its civilization, languages, peoples, and everything else, we do need above all *scientific* archaeology, history, linguistics, and other work, and for that we need precise geographical terms like *Central Eurasia*, including its urbanized subregion, *Central Asia*.

2. The term *Historic Sinological Reconstruction* (HSR) refers specifically to the distinctive, fundamentally non-linguistic, traditional theory and method followed by most (though not all) Sinologists to reconstruct pre-modern forms of Chinese. HSR is founded on modern interpretations of descriptive material (not transcriptions) from the Sung (Song) Dynasty, half a millennium later than the target date for the HSR version of "Early Middle Chinese" (601 CE). The method then mechanically projects its results back about a millennium and a half to the early Chou (Zhou) Dynasty (ca. 1045–771 BC), the Old Chinese period in which the proponents believe their chief (if not sole) text, the *Shih ching* 詩經 (*Shijing*), was composed. Thus the method is not based on scientific linguistic theory or methodology and does not—*cannot*—produce scientifically acceptable reconstructions of early forms of Chinese. Leaving aside the problems with their dates (the *Shih ching* is much later), languages are not machines, and they can have many dialects. (Classical Chinese sources actually tell us about Chinese dialects, but dialects are discernible even in the earliest texts, the Oracle Bone Inscriptions from the Shang Dynasty.) So languages do not change in a rigid, robotic, unilinear fashion. HSR is also linked to "Sino-Tibetan", a traditional but doubtful relationship theory, the proponents of which reject almost any proposed loanwords to or from the imagined Proto-Sino-Tibetan or its supposed daughter languages. HSR similarly does not accept loanwords even from *known ancient languages* spoken near ancient China (traditional North China). Both the HSR and Sino-Tibetan traditions do, however, propose loanwords *into Chinese* from languages that are attested only in the past century or so in anthropological linguists' fieldwork. These are exclusively languages of modern southern China and Southeast Asia, very far from the ancient Chinese cultural heartland in North China. Foreign borrowings from Old Chinese are not mentioned. These and other faults mean that HSR reconstructions of Old Chinese are not, on the whole, reliable. I and a few colleagues have been working on a strictly linguistic reconstruction of Middle Chinese and Old Chinese based on transcriptions and loanwords, and we have been making progress on it, as attested by our publications, but we have other work we must do and cannot spend all our time on it. In the interim, because HSR is still the only widely used system of reconstruction for Middle Chinese and Old Chinese, I have often cited HSR forms. Cf. Endnotes 3 and 170.

3. HSR does not mark reconstructions of Middle Chinese with asterisks. In modern linguistics, no asterisk means a form is attested—known from live recordings or written records—so when HSR omits asterisks on Middle Chinese forms, they are claimed to be known. Yet the reason they must be reconstructed is obviously that they are *not* attested. That is why I innovated (Beckwith 2007a) the open star [☆] to mark reconstructions of Middle Chinese based on the HSR

method. Moreover, HSR reconstructions of *Middle* Chinese are actually based on much later medieval Chinese materials (half a millennium after the HSR date for early Middle Chinese, 601 CE). Nevertheless, I do often cite the HSR reconstructions of Pulleyblank (1991a) for ("Early") Middle Chinese, and similarly I often cite Starostin (1989) for Classical period Old Chinese (correcting both when possible based on contemporaneous foreign transcriptions in segmental scripts), simply because HSR forms are often the only ones offered as "reconstructions" by anyone so far. As for the asterisk [*], it is the standard sign used by historical linguists for forms that do not occur as such in the sources but are reconstructed on the basis of sometimes fragmentary data. Even HSR uses it, correctly, as a technical symbol to mark reconstructions of *Old* Chinese.

4. Unfortunately, the Huns are poorly known due to the unsettled conditions of that period, but recent work (Shimunek et al. 2015; Beckwith et al. forthcoming) shows they dominated the Central Eurasian steppe zone between Eastern Europe and North China long enough to be noticed by literate peoples bordering on the region.
5. Scholars have failed to distinguish the two contrasting—often directly opposed—voices in the text with regard to the Scythians (and no doubt many other topics). One striking example is "Herodotus" repeating the period of Scythian rule several times, once emphatically, "28 years, as I said!" Who was "Herodotus" arguing with? It was clearly not Herodotus arguing with himself, but rather the custodians of his text arguing with each other, i.e., one scribal tradition (neutral or pro-Scythian or pro-Scytho-Mede) arguing with another (anti-Scythian or anti-Scytho-Mede) tradition. It is no secret that the Greeks fought several serious wars with the Medes and Persians, and many Greeks developed a strongly negative view of the "Medes" (meaning both Medes and Persians). One doubts that the scribes were immune to such views.
6. The Scythians were preceded slightly by the little-known Cimmerian nation. The Cimmerians are archaeologically identical to the Scythians, and the few transcribed Cimmerian names (see Chapter 2) show that the two nations spoke the same language, Scythian. Scythian culture is attested archaeologically in Tuva over a century earlier than in Near Eastern records.
7. Many have noted the embarrassing necessity of there having been a major Mede realm for Cyrus the Great to take over, but two decades ago the very idea of there ever having been a Mede Empire at all was openly attacked by a number of scholars, culminating in a volume of papers on the issue (Lanfranchi et al. 2003). The scholars involved in this movement mainly attacked the account of Herodotus, and Herodotus in general. Their chief arguments have been carefully refuted by Tuplin (2005).
8. Diakonoff (1985: 92): "Thus, for instance, the so-called 'Scythian' arrow-heads, well studied and providing a reliable basis for a precise archaeological dating of burial mounds and strata of ruined cities, are also found as weapons of besieging armies under the walls of strongholds where the presence of Scythians is

unattested while the presence of Cimmerians (in Asia Minor during the first decades of the 7th century), of Medes (at Carchemish towards the end of the 7th century), and of Persians (in Babylon in the 6th century) has been established." This misunderstands the fact (which Diakonoff himself explicitly notes) that the artifacts of the Scytho-Medes cannot be distinguished from Scythian artifacts. And as shown in this book, the Persian Empire was largely run by Medes, who also constituted a large part of the army, as did Scythians, so where there were Persians we can expect to find Medes and Scythians too. Archaeology thus confirms that the Medes too were a Scythian people, as shown in the Prologue and Chapter 2. Moreover, Diakonoff (1985: 97, note 4) rightly adds, "It is important to note that no archaeological finds in Asia can be linked to any reliable extent with Cimmerians as *distinct* from Scythians."

9. Herodotus calls it a "dagger". All hard evidence shows it was short, but bigger and heftier than a dagger. Greek artistic portrayals often show the Scythians on foot wielding longswords. Since the Greeks (whose warriors were mainly infantry) produced much of the art, its accuracy in this regard may be doubted, but the Scythians did also have full-sized swords.
10. The Babylonian Akkadian transcription *Ištumegu* corresponds to the Greek transcription *Astyages*. In neither one is there an <r> of any kind, and the initial <i> in the Akkadian and the <a> in the Greek are (in this word and many other similar words) epenthetic "helper" vowels added to make a cluster pronounceable, as in many other examples from the Ancient and medieval to modern Near East; they are not part of the original etymological word. For example, in modern Turkish *Istanbul*, from earlier *Stamboul* (from ancient *Constantinopolis*), the onset cluster *st* in *Stamboul* was made pronounceable by adding a short unstressed vowel *i* before the cluster, making *Istanbul*. The speakers of ancient Akkadian and the language which loaned the word *Astyages* to Greek could not pronounce a word beginning with two or more consonants without adding such an epenthetic vowel, as in the Akkadian transcription of the name of the earliest known Scythian ruler, *Spakaya, and of the name *Scythian* itself (see Chapters 1 and 6). As for the <m> in the Akkadian transcription, it regularly represents foreign *w* as well as *m*, while the Greek letter (υ) (*u*, usually transcribed as <y>) very often represents a string such as *ava* or the like, as well as *u*. Thus in *Astyages* we may have a name such as the attested Old Iranic words *stavuka- 'praising (a praiser)', or *stāvaiga from *stā-* 'to stand' plus *vaiga-* 'swinger, slinger' (Tav. 315). For discussion of Old Persian transcriptions involving the doubtful putative initial vocalic liquid *ṛ see Endnote 117.
11. This theory is most clearly presented by Jacobs (2006/2011), who says it argues the genesis of the "administrative hierarchy . . . is most plausibly to be explained by the process of expansion of the Achaemenid empire. The campaigns of the two most important conquerors, Cyrus the Great and his son Cambyses, aimed at acquisition of the entire territory of the empires they were attacking. Thus, the expedition against Croesus of Lydia (r. ca. 560–546) was preceded by the

annexation of Cappadocia and followed by that of the coast of Asia Minor, and the attack on Egypt was followed by campaigns against Libya and Nubia. In other words, conquest of the ancient Oriental empires included their provinces: Lydia came with Cappadocia and the coastal provinces on the shore, Babylonia with Assyria, Media with Armenia, and so forth. As a rule, Achaemenid imperial administration involved no primary administrative (re-)organization of the conquered territories but simply adaptation of existing structures." Jacobs' model is a somewhat theorized version of the Empire's *inherited, historically attested* feudal system in Iran and Central Asia, which the rulers clearly used for the new acquisitions too, but it leaves the origin of the system itself unexplained.

12. Briant argues "vehemently" (his own word) against what he calls "feudal theories" (e.g., Briant 2002: 898, 924, 979, 1043). His discussion of "hierarchy" (Briant 2002: 307ff.) is limited to court rank, social class, etc. His vehemence is surely due to historians' inherited, dogmatic ideas about feudalism being a native, purely European institution, ruling out all other examples of the same system.
13. This loose-reined structure has characterized Central Eurasian realms down to recent times. Commenting on the recent Taliban victory in Afghanistan, Ollapally (2021) says, "the Afghan state flourished (or at least functioned reasonably) only when the country resembled a highly decentralized political entity with powerful regional powerbrokers in charge of their own affairs. This was the case much of the time prior to the 1978 communist coup against the republican Mohammed Daoud and during the earlier . . . monarchy of his cousin King Zahir Shah. The system worked because the central 'state' represented by Kabul was fragmented and non-threatening and served more as a symbol of pan-Afghan nationalism." I was there under the king, and it was a peaceful state of exactly the type Ollapally describes, so I have replaced Ollapally's "nominal" with an ellipsis.
14. Sch. 278. Although it is usually claimed that the title king of kings was borrowed from the Assyrians or Urartians, the *only* example of "king of kings" in a search of *CAD* 17 (*š* part 2) is Xerxes' title in the Akkadian version of his Van inscription: "*anāku* RN LUGAL *rabû* LUGAL *ša* LUGAL.MEŠ LUGAL *mātāte* LUGAL *napḫari lišānu gabbi* LUGAL *qaqqari rabītu rapaštu* I am Xerxes, the great king, king of kings, king over the lands, king over all nations, king over the vast wide earth VAB 3 119: 10ff." All other explicitly cited examples in Akkadian s.v. *šarru* 'king' (*CAD* 17: 76bff.) are of locutions such as 'king among kings' (*CAD* 17: 80a), which is not the same thing as 'king of kings'.
15. Others claim monotheism is an *Egyptian* idea, referring to Akhenaten's monotheistic cult, but not mentioning the famous, extensive influence of early Indo-Europeans on Egypt at precisely that time. Study of monotheism has been dominated by metatheoretical constructs representing currently fashionable ideas of what monotheism should be. It is often denied that this or that attested system could be "monotheistic" simply because it does not conform to the modern theories.

16. Despite the data and scholarship, many scholars continue to claim that *Ariya* ~ *Aria* ~ *Ḥarya* meant 'Iranian' from the very beginning, though that usually makes no sense in actual textual examples. See Chapter 4.
17. Beckwith (2010); see now Chapter 4. Words in various languages pronounced like [a.rya] ~ [ɣa.rya] that also have the precise, vital, performative meaning of the Scythian word are clearly loanwords in those languages. The *idea* was certainly present among the Imperial Mongols, but so far I am not aware of a form of the *word* in Mongolian.
18. *Hsia* 夏 (*Xià*) is the usual and most frequent writing in the early texts. In the *Tso chuan* it is interchangeable with *Hua* 華 (*Huá*) when it has the developed meaning 'Chinese'. The latter word is now pronounced *Hua* in Mandarin and is used in the sense 'China, Chinese' in the official names of both the Republic of China (now on Taiwan) and the People's Republic of China (Beckwith 2016a).
19. Diakonoff (1985: 121–122) says that Cyaxares adopted the advanced organization from his Near Eastern neighbors, the "Urartians (Sarduri II's reform of about 760–750), and the Assyrians (Tiglathpileser III's reform after 745)", who "introduced the system of a regular army fully equipped by the state and divided into strictly determined strategic and tactical units according to kinds of weapons." Unfortunately he gives no further details on the Urartian and Assyrian "reforms", and the two rulers reigned until late in that century, when the Cimmerians, a Scythian people, are recorded by name for the first time, in precisely the region of Urartu and Assyria, using their mounted archers to great effect. In view of the generally very poor coverage of foreign peoples in Akkadian sources, it is virtually certain that the Cimmerians were already there decades earlier but simply were not noted by the chroniclers. The Assyrian sources on all this—including their dating—need to be reexamined very carefully.
20. The now popular misreading "*Modu*" (which is regularly given in this Pinyin spelling) has long ago been shown to be an impossible reading for the characters which transcribe his name (Pul. 217–218). For his name and the Scythian language of the Hsiung-nu see Chapters 6 and 7; cf. Beckwith (2018). For the *Shih chi* chapter on the Hsiung-nu see Giele (2010: 237–310).
21. The other directionality is extremely unlikely. The earliest Scythian-type royal tumuli, in the Altai region, date to the 9th century BC and contain classic Scythian weapons and horse gear (Caspari et al. 2018). As remarked above, some Cimmerians or Scythians must have migrated *shortly before* the Cimmerians are attested in Assyrian records between 720 and 714, at the time of Sargon II.
22. The argument that the Urartians and Assyrians themselves made this innovation is odd. Surely the overpowering force of Cimmerian and Scythian mounted archers impelled the Urartians and Assyrians to acquire some of them by capturing them in battle, or hiring them, and incorporating them into their armies. (There are many attested examples of Central Eurasians in contact with neighboring realms joining the enemy as mercenaries.) They would then have faced the same necessity the Scythians themselves must have discovered in the steppe, namely

keeping the mounted archers together in one group (independently attested in the Chinese story of Mo-tun), and they would have had to change the usual battle order to do that. But of course the Scythians already knew about the battle order problem and its solution. The crucial contribution is the Central Eurasian innovation of the highly trained, close-ranked corps of mounted archers independently attested in the Chinese accounts. Like the people of Chao under Scythian rule, the Medians were dominated and ruled directly by the Scythians long enough to be creolized by them. The Scytho-Medes had no need to "borrow" what they had inherited and were already using. See Chapters 2 and 7.

23. Although some have claimed that the Medes, Persians, and other early Iranic speakers rode in from Central Eurasia on horseback wearing such outfits, which were supposedly a shared Iranian nomadic inheritance, such ideas are not supported by any evidence. The Assyrian bas-reliefs alone disprove it.
24. *Īrān*, from Middle Persian *Ērān* from Parthian *Aryān* from attested Imperial Scythian (Young Avestan) *Airyana-* (Bar. 198); not with Schmitt (2014: 136–137) on the word being an ethnonym from the beginning, an old argument that ignores the chronology of Kushan and the fully unknown chronology of Avestan, as well as the East Asian evidence on the word and its meanings.
25. *Chung-hua min-kuo* 中華民國 (now on Taiwan) and *Chung-hua jen-min kung-ho-kuo* 中華人民共和國 the 'Central *Hua* People's (or People's Socialist) Country', i.e., 'China', where *Hua* 華 (*Huá*) is from Old Chinese *Ḥârya (not the same as a theoretical "*Ḥārya"), an alternate Old Chinese transcription of the word usually transcribed as *Hsia* 夏 (*Xià*) *Ḥarya. See Chapter 4 and Beckwith (2016a) for details.
26. A later influx of Scythians, the *Śakas* (Sakas), conquered Southern Central Asia (now southern Afghanistan) and northwestern India (now Pakistan) at the time of the Yüeh-chih ~ Tokharoi-led conquest of Bactria, with Yüeh-chih 月氏 OChi *Tukwar(ă)-kē transcribing the foreign name *Tuχwară-kayă 'the Tokhar kings'. In Beckwith (2009: 83–84, 380–383), my identification of the Tokharoi *language* with that of the non-Iranic Indo-European *language* of ancient Eastern Central Asia (East Turkistan) today known as "Tokharian ~ Tocharian" is clearly wrong. Language names do not always belong etymologically to the language named (e.g., *French, Russian, Japanese*, and in this case *Tokharian*). The name *Tokhwar ~ *Tuχwară is no doubt Scythian, the language of the people all around the *Tuχwară in their Central Eurasian homeland, including their Hsiung-nu vassals who finally overthrew them and drove them into the West.
27. This is confirmed by the modern studies of ancient lexical data by Benveniste and Harmatta (q.v. Chapter 5). Strabo's term *Ariana* refers specifically to the original Royal language, Imperial Scythian, not Persian, so the term had not yet developed the meaning "Iranic" as a strictly ethnolinguistic term that included Persian. The history of the semantic development of this word requires further careful study.
28. Not with Briant (2002: 24), "This interpretation is based on a belief in the existence of a Median language different from Old Persian", and further, "The theory of

linguistic borrowings remains quite disputable. It proceeds from an underlying hypothesis—the assumption that the dialect words found in the vocabulary of the Old Persian inscriptions come from a Median language" (id., 25). These issues are discussed in Chapter 5.

29. It is generally accepted that the word is not reconstructible back to Proto-Indo-European. There is about a millennium between the appearance of these peoples and the earlier, attested, beginning of the migration of the Proto-Indo-European speakers in the 19th century BC (Beckwith 2009: 37). The word may or may not be an innovation of the Scythian-Cimmerian people, but it was certainly spread by them. It is not attested in Old Avestan texts, perhaps because of their brevity and highly focused religiosity, but it is attested in Old Persian, Old Chinese, and Greek sources at approximately the same time.
30. The T'u-fa 禿髮, a branch lineage of the T'o-pa 拓跋 or *Taghbach (*Tabghatch*), a Serbi-Mongolic people, are referred to as 'Saka [i.e., Scythian] miscreants', using *so* 索 (*suǒ*), Old Chinese *sakă, to transcribe the name. So too are the T'o-pa proper (Shimunek 2017a: 52, note 75). There is a whole little literature of Chinese folk-etymologies founded on the Chinese etymological meaning of the transcriptional word *so* 索 'rope'.
31. Beekes (2011: 39) adds, "The other names for gods have no cognates in other languages." In other words, the only actual divine *name* that can be reconstructed to the Proto-Indo-European language in its Central Eurasian homeland means 'Heaven (Father)'. Thus the Proto-Indo-European speakers too had only one verifiable "Capital G" God. The same is true for all well-known peoples of Central Eurasia in Antiquity and the Middle Ages before the spread there of world religions from peripheral cultures. I have spelled out Beekes' language names. Cf. Watkins (2011: 22), who also gives the traditional reconstruction *dyeu- + *pəter.
32. It is thought that Herodotus got most of his information on the Scythians from Greeks and Greek-speaking Scythians in Olbia, a port on the Black Sea, so that much of what he says must be understood through Greek or Graeco-Scythian interpreters' eyes and ears. The names are almost certainly the Olbians' answers to questions such as, "What is the Scythian name of Zeus? . . ."
33. Clauson (1972: 523) notes "*teŋrī* is a very old word, probably pre-Turkish, which can be traced back to the language of the Hsiung-nu, 3rd century BC, if not earlier. . . . It seems originally to have meant 'the physical sky' . . . and came to mean 'Heaven' as a kind of impersonal deity . . . in the earlier texts. . . . An early loan-word in Mongolian as *teŋgeri*". (I have spelled out or standardized his many abbreviations.) On the attested Archaic Turkic Hunnish language of the 4th century CE, see Shimunek et al. (2015). The word *täŋri* is by form unique in Old Turkic and is clearly non-Turkic in origin (Beckwith 2018); for details see Chapter 6.
34. Schmitt (2018): "**paisah-* 'ornament, decoration' (in *Aria-*, *Sparga-peíthēs*, slightly Grecized)." The Hellenization is modeled on native Greek names such as Διο-πείθης Diopeithes (Schmitt 2003). However, Alekseyev (2005) notes that

"Spargapeithes" lived a century or two earlier than "Ariapeithes", making Herodotus' connection of the two impossible as actual history. Schmitt (2003) and Mayrhofer (2006) argue that the second element in "*Spargapeithes*" is the same as *paisa- 'ornament', in *Spargapises* (Scythian *Spargapaisa), name of the Massagetae queen Tomyris' son killed by Cyrus the Great. In the case of this particular name they are no doubt right. It must be noted that Greek theta (θ) regularly transcribes [t] in Scythian words, not [s], so in the case of *Spargapeithes* the exception is due to Hellenization and distortion of the original second part of the man's name, as noted by Schmitt and Mayrhofer, but also to its close textual proximity to the name Ariapeithes, in which, however, the second element regularly transcribes the *t* of the genuine, well-attested Scythian word *pitā* 'father' as <θ>.

35. He is parallel to another Central Eurasian National Foundation Myth story featuring a man with a name like *Targitaos*, who is replaced by the nation-founding hero. The evil king of Alba Longa who is overthrown by Romulus and his brother (thus a two-son version of the story) in the Roman foundation myth is *Tarchetius*, whose name is phonetically not Latin. The story is in a variant of the tale recorded in Plutarch (Beckwith 2009: 4 and note 11).
36. The "Colaxais" in our Herodotus is a glaring textual error overlooked by virtually everyone. The error was pointed out already in 1888 by Abicht (Beckwith 2009: 377–378). Scholars have ignored the fact that if one reads the full text of the myth it literally does not make sense if the name is *not* Scolaxais. The many speculative etymologies of this erroneous name "Colaxais" also ignore the other variants of the Scythian national foundation myth, all of which end up with a founder named *Skula or *Skutha (both from early Scythian *Skuδa).
37. The *r* was deleted by operation of the Syllable Contact Law, which is also responsible for metathesizing the contact cluster **gr* to West Scythian *rg* and for nasalizing the *g* to *ŋ* in East Scythian. See Chapter 6. For the Syllable Contact Law see Davis (1998), Gouskova (2004), and Özçelik and Sprouse (2017).
38. Cf. Khazanov (2016: 180), who comments that the subordinate units within the *basileia* were "the same practice that existed in medieval nomadic states and is often called the *ulus* system", using the Mongol term for the feudal hierarchical structure (see the following Endnote). Khazanov suggests getting rid of the *archai*—the term is evidently not attested for Scythia outside Herodotus—but our sources on the Scythians in Scythia are extremely limited, and many essential elements of their culture are only mentioned once, or they are only attested in art or archaeology. Moreover, the historically well-attested Hsiung-nu (East Scythians) had the same feudal-hierarchical system. Eliminating the *archai* is thus not justifiable. Khazanov also does not mention the continuation of the hierarchical system under the Scytho-Medes and Persians after the period of Scythian rule.
39. Herodotus attempts several times to describe the hierarchical structure of the Scytho-Mede-Persian Empire, but clearly did not really understand it (see

Chapter 2). The mostly absurd stories he reports about supposed Scythian slaves include unlikely elements that are strikingly Greek, so he probably heard them from Greeks living in the Graeco-Scythian towns on the Black Sea coast. However, Scythians who lived among the Greeks there undoubtedly did participate in the slave trade with slaveholding Greeks and other non-Scythian neighbors. Khazanov (2016: 177–178) vacillates between saying on the one hand that the Scythians practiced slavery and it is possible that in foreign descriptions of the Scythians, the slavery "terminology was a reflection of an indigenous political lexicon", and on the other hand saying "not slavery, but various forms of tribute relations were the most important and decisive in the Scythian states."

40. The same observation is often made about the use of the term in the Normative Buddhist expression usually translated 'the Noble (*Ārya*) Eightfold Path'. It is accepted that it actually means 'the Eightfold Path of the Noble Ones (*Āryas*)', but the word "Noble" must be corrected to "Royal", as the word specifically meant they were members of the legitimate Royal clan.

41. The early Greeks, Celts, Germanic peoples, and others, as well as the Scythians, had epic poetry from their Central Eurasian ancestors, the Proto-Indo-Europeans, as is well known (Watkins 1995). Moreover, Herodotus' record of the Scythian national foundation myth and other stories is evidently based directly on oral literature reported to him by his informants (Murray 2001).

42. There is a small but growing field specializing in the epic literature and bards of the Ossetian-Alanic peoples, the principal medieval and modern descendants of the ancient Scythian-Sarmatian people in the Western Steppe (who are thought to have spoken the later Sarmatian dialect of Scythian). See Bachrach (1973) on the ancient and medieval Alans; for the traditional Ossetian sagas see May, Colarusso, and Salbiev (2016).

43. The etymology of *Dugdammē* (Akkadian) ~ *Lygdamis* (Greek), the name of *Sandaxšaθra's father, is obscure, but it is at least *Scythianized*—the Greek transcriptional form is later than the Akkadian and demonstrates the regular West Scythian–internal shift of earlier **d/δ* to later *l* in that very period (cf. Tokhtas'ev 2012; Diakonoff 1981), as attested in early Scythian *Skuda/*Skuδa 'Scythian' > later *Skula* (Szemerényi 1980), remarked already by Herodotus. The early Greek transcription <Σκυθα> *Skytha* represents foreign *skuδa, as shown by the contemporaneous Akkadian transcriptions of the same name.

44. The alternate route (via the Caucasus into northern Iran) would keep the Caucasus on their right hand. Archaeology indicates the same Scythians did traverse the Caucasus on their way north to the Pontic Steppe after the coup by Cyaxares (Khazanov 2016), and in fact the great royal burial mounds of the Pontic Steppe are among the latest Scythian monuments. As highly mobile people, it is likely that they took both routes many times. This old problem requires careful reexamination based on archaeology.

45. The Hebrew text was mistakenly copied long ago as אשכנז *'šknz*—the letters for *n* < ן/נ > and *w*/*u* < ו > being often confused in Aramaic script—and then pointed

and read as *Aškənāz*. It was reinterpreted in late Antiquity as *Scanzia* 'Scandinavia', thought to be the home of the Germanic peoples, and eventually became the name of the European Jews. See further on the name and its forms in Chapter 6.

46. It is certainly true that eventually most Near Eastern peoples adopted their advanced arrowheads. Long after Scythian power was gone, Persians and others were using them. That has recently been taken by some to "disprove" their invention by the Scythians. However, the Scythians (including the Cimmerians) were by far the earliest to use them (they are attested in their earliest known sites in the Altai), and the Scythians were probably still the only ones using them during their imperial period, because the arrowheads are part of the diagnostic "Scythian Triad" assemblage of their archaeology that clearly distinguishes Scythians from their contemporaries.
47. Cf. Justinus, *Epitome of Trogus Pompeius* 1.5.14, who says it is a "Persian" word, though that is incorrect because *sp* in Scythian, including Imperial Scythian with its Median and Avestan subdialects (q.v. Chapter 5), corresponds to *s* in Persian.
48. The account in Herodotus is problematic and the local chronicles are either fragmentary or silent in general, including about Media. In the Behistun Inscription a Mede rebel is said to have claimed he was Phraortes (Fravarti), a descendant of king Kaštariti (Xšaθrita in the inscription), whose name has been said to be based on the Scythian word *χšaθra* 'realm' (Schmitt 2014: 285). Yet Kaštariti is not a king at all in contemporaneous Akkadian sources, but only the "city lord" of Kār-kašši, one of very many little city-states in the Zagros region. His name clearly reflects his city's name, so it has nothing to do with *χšaθra* 'realm'. See Dandamayev and Medvedskaya (2006) and Diakonoff (1985), who show that the name has a non-Iranic source and has been folk-etymologized. Moreover, the Greek transcription *Phraortes* represents the same word as the name of another "rebel" king at the time of Darius the Great, namely *Fravarti*, an Old Persian word corresponding to Avestan *fravaši* 'protector spirits of the heroic dead', whose cult Boyce (2000/2012) traces back to an "Iranian Heroic Age" sometime soon after 1500 BC (cf. Schmitt 2014: 178). However, the *fravašis*, like the *Aməša Spəntas*, are not attested in the *Gāthās* (they are mentioned later, in the *Yasna Haptaŋhāiti*), and thus belong to later Zoroastrianism. Moreover, although the rebel Phraortes (*Fravarti*) claimed descent from the Mede king of that name (the putative father of Cyaxares in Herodotus' account), it is significant that his name *Fravarti*, though equivalent to the *Fravaši* in Zoroastrianism, is specifically Persian in form, not Avestan. The putative father of Cyaxares, Phraortes ~ *Fravarti*, thus seems to have been legendary even by Darius' time, and perhaps never existed outside a version of the Central Eurasian National Foundation Myth, in which Phraortes' death left Cyaxares an orphan. Also, because the *fravašis* are not attested in the *Gāthās* (the texts of strict Early Zoroastrianism), and the rebel *Fravarti* was *religiously* opposed to Darius, the rebel and his

followers should have been either "old believer" Mazdaists or the opposite, the forerunners of quasi-polytheistic Late Zoroastrianism, but in either case they no doubt worshipped the *Daivas* Anāhitā and Mithra.

49. Mayrhofer (2006: 15), following Schmitt (2003: 16ff.), reconstructs this name as "*Pṛθu-tau̯ah- 'dessen Kraft weit 'reicht',' i.e., 'whose power extends far', based on attested Avestan *pərəθu* 'breit' (wide, broad) and *tauuah-* [tavah] 'Kraft' (power). On the vowels and "ṛ" see the discussion in Endnotes 10 and 117.
50. The Assyrian annals of King Aššurbānapli record that the allies of the king in his war against Šamaššumukin, king of Babylon, in about 653 included Medians or Medes, whose homeland is referred to traditionally as "Gutium" (Diakonoff 1985: 117–118).
51. Diakonoff (1985: 119) notes that "even according to Herodotus the death of 'Phraortes' and the invasion of Media by the Scythians were close in time." However, there is no Akkadian mention of Phraortes.
52. It is not that we know so little about the Scythians and Medes in this period because there were no Scythians and Medes, as some have claimed (the fallacy of taking "absence of evidence to be evidence of absence"), but because there are almost no surviving Akkadian sources on *anything* in this period. That is, with so few contemporaneous Akkadian sources for the period, we know relatively little even about the Assyrians' and Babylonians' own history at that time, not to speak of the history of the Scythians and Medes.
53. "Old Median"—the new Scytho-Mede dialect of the Imperial Scythian language—is not a "north-west Iranian language" as often erroneously stated (evidently due to confusion of geography and linguistics). Ancient Parthia and Urartia/Armenia and their languages are problematic issues; unbiased specialist studies are needed.
54. This date is based on the unlikelihood that he would have been ready immediately to mount a successful military campaign against Assyria, then the most powerful state in the western world. The more believable of the traditional dates of Herodotus has him beginning his reign in 625 (Kuhrt 2007, 1: 38, note 10), but it is necessary to exclude the non-Medes Deioces and Phraortes (q.v. Chapter 8), as well as the idea that Cyaxares could have been "ruling" or even "reigning" during the 28 years of Scythian rule. In fact, Herodotus gives several versions of the events in this period, including two versions in which the Scythians simply ruled Media. These problems are textual, at least in part. See the following Endnote.
55. According to the story, the Scythians killed and cut up a Mede boy who was one of their "pupils", dressed the meat for dinner as they usually did with animals obtained in the hunt, and delivered it to Cyaxares' court. They then secretly fled to Alyattes, king of Lydia. The Medes unknowingly ate the hapless boy's flesh for dinner. The text of Herodotus also uses exactly the same cannibalistic motif in the main version of the Cyrus story—in that case, Harpagus the Mede's son is killed and served to his father (unknowingly) to eat, after which he was told what

he had done. The Scythians in the Cyaxares story are supposedly his *guests* in Media. The cannibalism motif is almost certainly a Greek invention.

The mostly fragmentary accounts of the Scythians in Media belong to two entirely different stories, which are largely mixed together in the received text:

The first story reports on the period of Scythian rule in Media—28 years, as explicitly noted four times in the text (once: "28 years, as I said!")—in which the young Medes are subjects of a Scythian ruler and grow up learning to speak Scythian and learning from their Scythian teachers how to shoot Scythian style—i.e., using the short composite Cimmerian bow while riding.

The second story has uninterrupted Mede rule under Cyaxares, with the Scythians as "guests" that Cyaxares invites to stay; he treats the Scythians well out of kindness. But the Scythians carry out much theft and destruction, and finally out of anger at Cyaxares for chastising them they kill one of their Mede pupils, so that he is served up to the unsuspecting king at a cannibalistic banquet.

The first story accords with the hard data, as shown in this book. The second, "guest", story is patently nonsense, as is its cannibal feast (a topos that is repeated in Herodotus). Neither the Scythians nor any other *historical* Central Eurasian steppe people are known to have practiced cannibalism. Considering the traditional Greek stress on hosting guests, and the importance of being a good guest, as well as the post–Persian War enmity against all three Iranic peoples, the second account is a later fabrication.

Significantly, the received text does not present these conflicting stories clearly *as two stories*, as the text of Herodotus often does. Instead, they are rather crudely mixed together to make *one* story.

It would be traditional, and therefore easy, to simply blame Herodotus for writing confused and contradictory historical claptrap, as some have actually claimed. However, that evaluation has turned out to be incorrect in most cases, as shown by Tuplin (2005). Like all other known ancient and medieval works that have been copied over for hundreds of years by hand (modern facsimile printing not having been invented yet), the history of Herodotus was altered by copyists' errors, interpolations, and many other changes, major and minor, over time. Although some changes no doubt crept in after the Classical period during the *millennium and a half* before the earliest surviving manuscript, others must have happened early in Antiquity, even while Herodotus was still alive or shortly afterward, since some of the changes are obvious to those who actually read the text, even if only in translation. Is that the reason scholars today neglect the "higher criticism", though they accept the "lower criticism" (critical text edition, which is important but mostly reveals minor errors)—because the higher criticism reveals *substantial* errors in the ancient texts? We need both.

56. These are shown in bas-reliefs portraying peoples from the region both before and after the event. See Appendix B.
57. It is probably significant that the word *Maguš* does not occur in Zoroaster's *Gāthās*. On this and all other issues relating to the Magi, Zoroastrianism, etc.,

there is an enormous, often polemical, literature not covered by this book. For bio-bibliographical surveys see Kellens (2012) and Malandra (2009).

58. Young also perceptively notes (id., 20), "The introduction of yet another group of Iranian people into the complex ethnic and political scene in the Zagros in the seventh century B.C. could well have had a considerable catalytic effect on events leading up to Median unity."
59. Persis (Pārsa, now Fârs) was a vassal state under the Scythians and Scytho-Medes not only because Herodotus suggests it, but because linguistics reveals that much of the official language used in the Old Persian inscriptions had already entered Old Persian via the Median (i.e., Scytho-Median) language, and apparently even earlier under the Scythians themselves (q.v. Chapters 5 and 6). Also, analysis of the royal lineages of Cyrus the Great and Darius the Great reveals they both had Scythian or Scytho-Mede ancestry, as shown in Chapter 4.
60. This is different from the Archaic Near Eastern model epitomized by the Assyrians, which did involve destruction or dispersion of defeated enemies. Another example might seem to be the Kirghiz destruction of the Uighur Empire in 840 CE (Drompp 2005), but it appears that a climatic-economic disaster was underway at the time and no one was able to build or maintain an empire; in fact, all existing empires in Eurasia either collapsed or shrank drastically at precisely the same time, between 840 and 842 CE (Beckwith 2009: 158–162); see now Di Cosmo (2018), who shows that climatic change did occur at just this time in the steppe zone, as previously postulated. Climatic studies are underway on the period of the Scythian expansion too. It is probable that climatic change was one of the factors behind the Scythian conquest, and it is equally conceivable that such change was a factor in the decline of Assyria soon after.
61. Material culture goods of Near Eastern workmanship have also been found there. Thus archaeology might support Herodotus' account with respect to a Royal Scythian migration to the north through the Caucasus. It is possible, however, that much of the Near Eastern material was acquired through trade and diplomacy.
62. Reported in Strabo (viii 8,4): "The Sacæ had made incursions similar to those of the Cimmerians and Treres, some near their own country, others at a greater distance. They occupied Bactriana, and got possession of the most fertile tract in Armenia, which was called after their own name, *Sacasene*. They advanced even as far as the Cappadocians, those particularly situated near the Euxine; who are now called Pontici." From Perseus, tr. Hamilton and Falconer, emphasis added.
63. According to *Gadd's Chronicle,* in 613 Nabopolassar led the army against Suhu and other cities in the region, which Zawadzki (1988: 110–112) shows was part of Babylonia, not part of Assyria. However, already in 616 Nabopolassar had led the army against Suhu, and *Gadd's Chronicle* says that he was victorious against them and against the Assyrians who are said to have invaded the region. In March of 615, the Assyrians and Babylonians fought at Arrapḫa (now Kirkuk), and the

Babylonians drove the Assyrians off. In May, the Babylonians attacked Aššur, but the Assyrians defeated them and drove them back to Takritain (now Tikrit), where the Babylonians took refuge in the fortress. The Assyrians returned home. Later that year (615) the Medes under Cyaxares captured Arrapḫa (Kuhrt 2007, 1: 30). The putative rebellion of Suhu in 613 was thus connected to the earlier events of 616. The 613 event would seem to show that Nabopolassar had not in fact succeeded in pacifying the Suhu region in 616. The demonstration by Zawadzki (1988) of the extensive ancient rewriting of *Gadd's Chronicle* (see the following Endnotes), and the detail concerning the Mede destruction of the gods and temples, suggests that there was no rebellion at all. The cities appear to have been attacked and partly destroyed not by the Assyrians but by the Medes, either as part of their campaign against Assyria or more likely in an attempt to force Nabopolassar to make an alliance with them to overthrow the Assyrian Empire. Further research is needed.

64. The region of Elam (Anshan) centered on Susa and the region where Persepolis was later built are accepted to have been in the process of becoming thoroughly Persian (Henkelman 2003; Potts 2005). Despite the name "Elam", then, some of the men were no doubt Persians. Potts (2005) has shown that Cyrus I of Anshan (Elam) was not the same as Cyrus of Parsumaš (i.e., Parsuvas, Parsua), a different petty kingdom, perhaps in the central Zagros region; moreover, Arukku, the eldest son of Cyrus of Parsumaš, was sent to the court of Assurbanipal, whereas the eldest son of Cyrus I of Anshan was Cambyses I, father of Cyrus the Great (Kuhrt 2007, 1: 54, note 2).
65. See the essential work of Zawadzki (1988). Among the many important emendations he makes to the historical record is his discovery that *Gadd's Chronicle* was substantially rewritten after the Babylonian break with the Medes, the revisers' aim being to diminish or eliminate any positive references to the Mede role, or sometimes any reference at all.
66. Now commonly reconstructed as *Ṛšti-vaiga- "swinging the spear, lance-hurler" (Schmitt 2011b), but the Indianizing form *ṛšti- is doubtful phonetically for Old Iranic; see Endnotes 10 and 117 on the *ṛ. Some have noted that the Babylonian chronicles never call him "King" Ištumegu, but it has been carefully and amply shown by Zawadzki (1988) that when a foreign ruler ceased to be on good terms with Babylon, the Babylonian scribes regularly deleted the title "king" when they mentioned him.
67. Babylonian inscriptions say that in Nabonidus' third year (553/552), Cyrus, king of Anzan, vassal of Astyages, king of the Umman-manda (i.e., the Medes), advanced against his lord (Schmitt 2011b). From subsequent events (and from Cyrus' religious policies) it appears that Cyrus had rebelled against Astyages, thus provoking the latter's attack. Cf. Herodotus (i 126–127), who implies the same thing, but does not actually say who attacked first. According to Diakonoff (1956: 274–275, 392–400) "the Magi supplied the Medes with court priests as early as, at least, under the last Median king Astyages, who was under some influence of the teaching of

Zoroaster" (Dandamayev 2012). However, as shown in the present book, Astyages was not in fact the last "Mede" king. (See also Endnote 70.)

68. The sequence of events suggests that Bardiya had supported monotheism. Since the murder of Bardiya and his replacement by an imposter is the overt casus belli for Darius, it makes sense for Darius to go to war on behalf of a fellow monotheist.
69. If he was a polytheist like his father, Cyrus, Cambyses' responsibility for his brother's death also makes good sense and further helps explain Darius' coup. Not with socio-political analyses (e.g., Briant 2002), which do not explain the Medes' majority support for Darius, or the latter's explicit statements throughout the Behistun Inscription that tell us it was all about religion.
70. All evidence points to Cyrus having been at least part Mede, as Herodotus and other Greek historians say. The overt statements and deeds of Darius confirm their familial connection. Potts (2005) solidly demonstrates the Elamite background of Cyrus, including his name and that of Cambyses, their Elamite customs, etc. Nevertheless, Cyrus was evidently half Elamite and half Median. His Median lineage, which is indicated by Herodotus, Xenophon, and Ctesias (though the relationship is given differently by them), explains his largely uncontested overthrow of Astyages and installation of himself on the imperial throne, as well as his unusual failure to kill Astyages, as suggested also by the *Chronicle of Nabonidus.*
71. The English word is from Greek *paradeisos,* in turn borrowed from Median (Imperial Scythian) *paridaiza* or *paridaisa* (Tavernier 2007: 560). The attested Late Old Persian form of the word, *paradayda,* derives from the expected earlier **paridaida,* an Old Persianized form of attested YAve *pairidaēza* (Sch. 225); it is thus ultimately a Scythian word.
72. Each satrapal capital was ordered to be built as a copy, somewhat smaller, of the imperial court with its accompanying paradise. The luxurious satrapal paradise in Dascylium, in northwestern Anatolia, is detailed in a first-person account by Alcibiades, who lived there for some time as a guest of the satrap Čiθrafarna (Greek *Tissaphernes*); see Stuttard (2018: 193ff.). The name *Čiθrafarna* is Imperial Scythian.
73. Urbanized people mainly left graveyards and the remains of buildings above ground, whereas Central Eurasians mainly left graveyards with huge burial mounds, which include underground buildings, and many horses and horse gear. The unspoken conclusion is that since the Central Eurasians left no aboveground stone buildings, they were not as good as the urbanites. The converse would be to claim that the urbanites were not as good as the Central Eurasians because the urbanites did not leave huge burial mounds containing large underground buildings, many horses and horse gear, etc.
74. As noted above, some historians have claimed that the Medes adopted this innovation from the Assyrians, who instituted it first, or from the Urartians. That is doubtful. Diakonoff (1985: 121) quotes the above passage of Herodotus (i 103) and explains that as usual Herodotus is wrong and that Cyaxares adopted the

advanced organization from his Near Eastern neighbors, who had adopted it earlier. Diakonoff says it appears first with the Urartians under Sarduri II (r. ca. 764–735) and the Assyrians under Tiglathpileser III (r. ca. 745–727). However, these sudden simultaneous "reforms" are hardly unconnected to the campaigns against the Cimmerians (Scythians) *by those very states* in the late 8th century, and in fact the campaigns are discussed by Diakonoff. Because the Assyrians, Urartians, and Medians had fought both against the Cimmerians and Scythians and also *alongside* them as allies or mercenaries, the contributors of the innovation to the Assyrians, Urartians, and Medians were patently the Cimmerians and Scythians, even though their presence is not explicitly recorded until shortly after the "reforms". There is an underlying assumption that *the Assyrians recorded everything that ever happened in their realm or in neighboring realms, exactly, and on time.* But they absolutely did not. One must ask, in view of the physical circumstances, how anyone could expect such a thing. Sometimes there is simply nothing for many years, or at least nothing on what we would consider to be crucial events. The old rule that "absence of evidence" is not "evidence of absence" applies. Moreover, previous interpretations of the texts can be mistaken, as shown very well by Zawadzki (1988).

75. Ctesias' scurrilous story claiming that Cyrus had worse than humble origins is intended specifically to make him sound not 'Royal', and thus illegitimate. However, in view of Ctesias' very *positive* remarks about Cyrus replacing Astyages as king (see Chapter 2, Note 93), it is likely that the text of Ctesias (now only fragments) was "modified" at least as much as the text of Herodotus.
76. As religious texts of Zoroastrianism, the *Avesta* are of course full of occurrences of the name Zoroaster, and the *Gāthās* are all about Ahura Mazdā, and only Mazdā, the Creator, whereas the Daēvas are false and evil. Significantly, Herodotus (i 131,3) says the Persians "learned later to sacrifice to the 'heavenly' Aphrodite from the Assyrians and Arabians. She is called by the Assyrians Mylitta, by the Arabians Alilat, by the Persians Mitra." From Perseus, tr. Godley. See also the Epilogue and Appendix A.
77. We have only Greek historical accounts, but one of them in Herodotus (i 214,5) is remarkable in having Queen Tomyris of the Massagetae take Cyrus' head and plunge it into a skin full of blood, declaring, "Though I am alive and have defeated you in battle, you have destroyed me, taking my son by guile; but just as I threatened, I give you your fill of blood." Herodotus adds, "Many stories are told of Cyrus' death; this, that I have told, is the most credible." Even now the anger at Cyrus for his bloody attack on the Massagetae is vivid in this ancient text.
78. The main clause of the first sentence of Darius' tomb inscription at Naqš-i Rustam (DNa 1,1–6) reads:

    𐎲𐎥𐏐𐎺𐏀𐎼𐎣𐏐𐎠𐎢𐎼𐎶𐏀𐎭𐎠𐏐𐏃𐎹𐏐𐎡𐎶𐎠𐎶𐏐𐎲𐎢𐎷𐎡𐎶𐏐
    𐎠𐎭𐎠𐏐𐏃𐎹𐏐𐎠𐎺𐎶𐏐𐎠𐎿𐎶𐎠𐎴𐎶𐏐𐎠𐎭𐎠𐏐𐏃𐎹𐏐𐎶𐎼𐎫𐎡𐎹𐎶𐏐
    𐎠𐎭𐎠𐏐𐏃𐎹𐏐𐏁𐎡𐎹𐎠𐎫𐎡𐎶𐏐𐎠𐎭𐎠𐏐𐎶𐎼𐎫𐎡𐎹𐏃𐎹𐎠𐏐𐏃𐎹𐏐
    𐎭𐎠𐎼𐎹𐎺𐎢𐎶𐏐𐎧𐏁𐎠𐎹𐎰𐎡𐎹𐎶𐏐𐎠𐎤𐎢𐎴𐎢𐏁𐏐 (Schmitt 2009: 100)

Baga văzărka Auramazdā, haya imām būmīm adā, haya avam asmānam adā, haya martiyam adā, haya šiyātim adā martiyahyā, haya Dārayavaum xšāyaθiyam akunauš.

Great God is Ahura Mazdā, who created this earth, who created that heaven, who created man, who created happiness for man, who made Darius king.

The words in this sentence marked as Avestan (i.e., Imperial Scythian) or Old Persian, are, as they occur:

Baga OPer, Ave (YAve *baγa*)
văzărka OPer
Auramazdā OPer, Ave (*Ahura Mazdā, Mazdā Ahura*)
haya OPer
imām OPer (*ima-*), Ave (OAve, YAve *ima-* Sch. 195)
būmīm OPer (*būmī-*). The word *būmī-* is Old Avestan according to Sch. (155), but it is attested only once in the *Gāthās*, in Y. 32.3, in the expression 'the seventh clime' (Bar. 969; Humbach and Ichaporia 1994: 40–41); it does not mean 'earth'. The putative other example is in Y. 37.1 (Bar. 969), which is in the Yasna Haptaŋhāiti, not in the *Gāthās*. The two occurrences in Young Avestan are based on these same two sources, OAve Y. 32.3 and Y. 37.1, respectively (Bar. 969). Otherwise, Young Avestan has *zam-* for 'earth' (Bar. 969).
adā OPer
haya OPer
avam OPer, OAve *ava-* (Sch. 191)
asmānam OPer, YAve *asman-* (Sch. 140). Old Persian *asmān-* is a "religious" loan from Avestan; the genuine Old Persian form should be *aθman-*.
adā OPer
haya OPer
martiyam OPer *martiya-* (OAve, YAve *mašiia-* Sch. 212)
adā OPer
haya OPer
šiyātim OPer *šiyāti-*, YAve *šāiti-* (Sch. 248)
adā OPer
martiyahyā OPer
haya OPer
Dārayavaum OPer *Dārayavau-*
xšāyaθiyam OPer *xšāyaθiya-*
akunauš OPer stem *-kun-*

To a monolingual Imperial Scythian speaker, this sentence would have sounded like:

'God *văzărka* Auramazdā *haya* this clime *adā haya* that heaven *adā haya martiyam adā šiyātim adā martiyahyā haya dārayavaum xšāyaθiyam akunauš.*' The parts understandable (or guessable) in Imperial Scythian would thus have been only 'God . . . Auramazdā . . . this clime . . . that heaven'; the rest would have been unintelligible. It must be added that this sentence is specifically Zoroastrian in content, and the Zoroastrian-related Avestan words in Old Persian were of course understandable to Imperial Scythian speakers who were Zoroastrians. Eliminating these words leaves only 'God . . . that heaven . . .' as what a monolingual Imperial Scythian speaker would have understood.

79. Boyce (1984) says that *Ahura Mazdā* (also *Mazdā Ahura*) is "the Avestan name with title of a great divinity of the Old Iranian religion, who was subsequently proclaimed by Zoroaster as God." The Old Persian form is *Auramazdā*. However, "Old Iranian religion" is misleading. The name *Mazda* is first attested in Indo-European language material in the Amarna Letters of the 14th century BC that is now usually taken to be "Indic" because of the problematic "Indo-Iranian" theory (Witzel 2014). Boyce's proposal (cf. Lecoq 1997: 155–156) that Zoroastrianism was a part of "the Old Iranian religion" and that veneration of Ahura Mazdā goes back to "Proto-Iranian" times is thus doubtful, based on the contemporaneous data. But if her chronology is wrong and Early Zoroastrianism was in origin a *Scythian* religious system—there may have been other Scythian religious systems with "gods" or even "Gods", as suggested by the account of Herodotus (but see Chapter 1, s.v. *Heavenly God*, and Chapter 6, s.v. *Täŋri*)—then the civil war fought among the Scytho-Medes may have continued a struggle that went back to earlier times.

80. In an inscription at Susa (A_2Sa), Artaxerxes II says: [Old Persian cuneiform]
[Old Persian cuneiform] AURAMAZDĀ *Anāhitā utā Miθra mām pa(n)tuv hacā vispā gastā* (Schmitt 2014: 192): 'May Ahura Mazdā, Anāhitā, and Mithra protect me from all evil'. Note the Imperial Scythian spelling *Miθra*. "According to Clement of Alexandria (Protrept. 5,65,3), *Berossus* . . . reported that Artaxerxes [II] had had statues of Anāhitā erected in Bactria, Ecbatana, Susa, Babylon, Damascus and Sardes" (Brentjes 2006).

81. See above. As Boyce (2012) remarks, the *fravašis* first occur in the Yasna Haptaŋhāiti, which is written in Old Avestan, but is not in verse. Its content is distinctive in many other ways by comparison with the *Gāthās*, which are all in verse. It is of course possible to write a new work even today in Classical Greek, Classical Chinese, Classical Sanskrit, and other well-known premodern languages—students of them do so on a regular basis. There is no reason that an ancient speaker of Imperial Scythian (early Young Avestan) who had memorized the *Gāthās* (which were purely oral literature until the Middle Ages) could not have composed the Yasna Haptaŋhāiti.

82. This is similar to statements in the Persian-inspired imperial inscriptions of King Priyadarśi, the great 3rd century BC Mauryan ruler who has been popularly but erroneously equated with Aśoka, a later ruler (Beckwith 2015: 124–134, 135–137, 226–250). Priyadarśi's inscriptions are modeled directly on the Achaemenid Persian inscriptions, as noted by scholars already a century ago.

83. In any case, Central Eurasian rulers such as the Scythian kings were traditionally liberal, so they would undoubtedly have tolerated or even supported Old Mazdaism. Although religious toleration by Central Eurasian governments was the norm through Antiquity and the Early Middle Ages at least (and generally down to Modern times), as widely noted, there seems to be no specialized study of it for earlier periods. There has been much discussion of Herodotus' Scythian god lists, but very little agreement on them; see Mayrhofer (2006).
84. On these issues Kellens (2015) remarks, "The time has come to imagine new ways of approach" to overcome the current "stagnation and arbitrariness". Yet the problem of Zoroaster and his dates, which continues to trouble ancient Iranian studies, is mostly the result of belief overpowering reason and the data. The *Gāthās* alone make it necessary to distinguish Zoroaster and Early Zoroastrianism from Late Zoroastrianism, while linguistics makes it clear that the *Young Avesta* are in Imperial Scythian. See Chapter 5.
85. The Scytho-Mede (or "Median") language is thought to be unknown in its own right—that is, it is believed that *no texts* survive in the language, so it is known only as a few words in Herodotus, plus some proper names. However, a good number of names and a few other words borrowed into Old Persian or recorded in Old Persian and other ancient languages have been recognized by Iranists as Median for strictly linguistic reasons (specifically, regular phonological differences from Old Persian). It has been widely believed that Median and Old Persian were mere dialects of each other, so they are often lumped together, but this is erroneous. The Median words in Old Persian are readily recognizable *because* many of them differ phonologically from equivalent inherited Iranic words in Old Persian, while some other Old Persian words which are typically Median in form (such as *văzărka*) have no cognates in Avestan. In most cases where a characteristically Median form does have attested cognates in both Old Persian and Avestan, the Median form is identical to the *Avestan* form. When a word is not found in either language, its origin could theoretically be anything, but in some cases the words are attested in Scythian. For example, Lubotsky (2002) shows that the word *farnah* is specifically Scythian. In short, the Iranic but non-Persian words in the Old Persian inscriptions belong to two or more dialects of Scythian.
86. Pharaoh Akhenaten of Egypt (r. 1353/51–1336/34 BC) also introduced monotheism, but it is exactly this particular Egyptian ruler who was powerfully influenced by historically known foreign peoples, including the ruling people of Mitanni and various subject rulers who spoke the same Indo-European language (considered to be Old Indic) attested in the Amarna Letters. Akhenaten's monotheistic revolution failed and the traditional priests restored polytheism.
87. A recent study argues that Cyrus, not Darius, was illegitimate, and essentially contends that the latter's statements about his truthfulness, his lineage, etc., really are truthful, not deceptive as many scholars now believe (Vallat 2013). Another view is that Cyrus was the legitimate local king of Anshan, but also an Achaemenid Persian (Waters 2004), as argued in the present book; see Chapter 4.

88. It has long been doubted that the document preserved in the Bible is genuine, though logic and the "principle of embarrassment" argue that it should be essentially genuine. However, much of the scholarly handling of this contentious topic is problematic; see Kuhrt (2007, 1: 73–74, note 21).
89. The story here abridges the lengthy main version in Herodotus (i 107–129), including in italics the missing passage from Justin i, 4: 7–11. Kuhrt (2007, 1: 94, note 4) says, referring to the two variants of the story (focusing on the dog or the herdsman's wife) hinted at by Herodotus, "the two stories seem to have been combined" in Justin. But the crucial point is that information found in Justin (ca. 2nd century CE) reflects a lost earlier version of the manuscript of the text of Herodotus which antedates by almost a millennium any extant manuscript (with the exception of the fragments found at Oxyrhynchus, which unfortunately do not include this passage). That version is also referred to by Herodotus himself (i 122,3). Specifically, it provides the classic Central Eurasian motif of the female canine (usually a wolf but sometimes, as here, a dog) nursing and protecting the abandoned newborn hero (see Beckwith 2009: 1–12), rather than the modified version in Herodotus in which the herdsman's wife, who nurses the baby, is *named* Spako, which we are told is Median *spaka*, meaning 'female dog'. It is thus clear that the text originally contained the dog version, perhaps as an alternate to the wife version, the connection being explained via the name. It may be that Herodotus himself related both versions and a later copyist deleted the dog version, perhaps to avoid having Cyrus the Great—who was admired by the polytheistic Greeks—being nursed by a dog.
90. Attempts to show that the story of the child abandoned in a basket or cradle was introduced by Sargon the *First*, of *Akkad*, have long ago been discredited, as the myth is dated (Wagensonner 2017) a millennium and a half after his time. It is thus about Sargon the *Second*, of *Aššur*, who ruled at the time of the Cimmerian invasion recorded for the period 720–714 BC. Several decades later the Scythians formed an alliance with the Assyrians and shortly afterward became rulers of Media. All of this interaction with Central Eurasians had profound effects on Near Eastern peoples, who acquired this striking motif and other ideas from the Cimmerians and Scythians via creolization, along with mounted archery, reorganization of the army's battle order, and much else, as summarized in the Prologue, Epilogue, and following chapters. It must also be stressed that except for the Central Eurasian motif of abandonment of the hero at birth in a basket or cradle, unknown in earlier Ancient Near Eastern myths, the rest of the *Sargon II* story has nothing at all to do with the Central Eurasian myth (q.v. Beckwith 2009: 1–12) *or with the Cyrus story's version* of that myth. The abandonment motif has often been compared to the famous one in the Moses story, which contains many other elements drawn specifically from the full Cyrus story (as told in Herodotus). In the Sargon II story the basket is waterproofed and abandoned in a river, as it is in the Moses story. Since the full Central Eurasian foundation myth includes escape of the child via a body of water (the

Roman version includes the floating basket), this particular Sargon II story motif is clearly Central Eurasian in origin.

91. The Hellenized version of the Scythian myth is interesting as well. The three objects in this case were a bow, a war-belt, and a golden bowl. The youngest son, Scythes (i.e., *Scolaxaï- 'King Skula/Skutha/Skuδa'), succeeds in stringing the bow and putting on the belt, to become the first Scythian king—appropriately, as *Skuδa* probably means 'Archer' (Szemerényi 1980). See Chapter 1 for the Scythian myths.
92. Beckwith (2009: 8). The later story of the Persian founder of the Sasanid Persian Empire goes back to the original core Central Eurasian myth, complete with dragon. For Middle Persian text and translation see Grenet (2003).
93. This includes Elam, where Āçina has an Old Persianized Mede name (Schmitt 2014: 125), and Armenia (Urartu), a sub-satrapy of Media, where Arakha (Araχa) and his father Haldita both have Urartian names (Schmitt 2014: 134).
94. The equation of these people with Herodotus' Royal Scythians is made by Bruce Lincoln (1991), whom I cite in an early article (Beckwith 2010) on the ancient and medieval "heavenly kings" of Central Eurasia. Lincoln's book also brings in the Greek transcription of the full native Saka form of the name that is partly transcribed and partly translated in Chinese as 塞王 '*Sakă Kings', namely *Sakaurakoi*, which must be the correct form of the name that appears in Strabo's account of the Tokharoi-Saka-*Aśvin confederation conquest of Bactria, where the Sakas are called *Sakaurakoi* (using the form in Lucian to correct Strabo). His account precisely parallels the Chinese accounts of the same events, with exactly the same three named participant peoples. The name "reflects an underlying Iranian **Saka-u̯ra-ka*, the **u̯ra-* element being equivalent to Khotan Saka *rre* 'King'" (Lincoln 1991: 189). These historically well-known people are precisely those called 'Saka Kings' in Chinese historical sources. Herodotus also refers to the 'Royal Scythians' as οἱ δὲ καλεόμενοι βασιλήιοι Σκύθαι 'the Scythians who are called "royal(s)" or "royal (ones)".' He explicitly describes them as the ruling Scythian clan descended from the first, semi-divine, Scythian, as he recounts in all three versions of the Scythian national foundation myth. For the significance of the royal lineage see Chapter 4.
95. E.g., Old Turkic *Aršilaš* 'the Ārya kings', a Tokharian A loan (Beckwith 2016b), was a title or epithet of the early Türk ruling lineage recorded by both the Byzantine Greeks (who correctly explain it) and the Chinese (who misunderstand it but know it is an epithet of the ruling clan). The Türk also told the Greeks and the Chinese they were descendants of the Scythians—they say explicitly *Saka*—but they clearly meant it the way Darius did: they had the *Aria lineage* and were thus the *Royal* Scythians' legitimate ruling heirs.
96. Schmitt (2011d) summarizes the Scytho-Mede-Persian imperial feudal system very well: "Society in Achaemenid Iran was feudal . . . its feudal structure, based on a personal loyalty between the king and each single subject, can no longer be doubted since Geo Widengren's *Der Feudalismus im alten Iran* (Köln and Opladen, 1969). Closely connected with the royal court was the nobility with its

large estates. The chief authorities of administration and the military, the satraps and generals, are called (in DB, passim) the king's *bandakā* 'vassals, followers' (not 'slaves,' as the OPer word has been mistranslated formerly). They bore the 'belt of vassalage' and therefore were named as 'those equipped with a binding (Oir. **banda*), a belt,' whose loyalty was generously remunerated and whose disloyalty was severely punished by the king (DB I.21ff., IV.65–67). To sum up, we may say that the people were subject to the king, as the king was subject to Ahura Mazdā. That castes or classes of society such as slaves or fully enfranchised citizens were firmly institutionalized can not be proven." (Cf. Schmitt 2014: 151.) Schmitt also notes that the system was inherited, and that is certainly correct. He also states that it was "inherited from Indo-Iranian and even Indo-European times". That point could well be correct if the steppe Scythians' feudal system was inherited from sedentary Indo-European peoples, as is certainly possible and to some extent supported by earlier research (e.g., Widengren 1969) and by the limited data we have on the comitatus among the Hittites and the Mitanni. It is possible, however, that the feudal system per se was innovated in the steppe zone by the Cimmerians and Scythians, the first known steppe nations, as their response to the problem of ruling a vast but thinly spread out nomadic realm constantly on the move. In any case, whether or not they innovated it, the system was ideal for them, and they did adopt and use it, so that it spread far and wide via the Scythian imperial conquest and creolization of peoples in other peripheral regions of Central Eurasia, the same way that it spread among the creolized Scytho-Medes of Media and their successors, as detailed in this book. Before the development of horse riding in ca. 900 BC full nomadism was not practicable on the open steppe, which is thought to have been largely unoccupied (the disputed date necessarily follows the development of full horse riding, q.v. Drews 2004). Thus as noted, feudalism per se may have developed only later, as a solution to the political problems encountered by the first steppe rulers.

97. Herodotus (i 101): "the Busae, the Paretaceni, the Struchates, the Arizanti, the Budii, the Magi," the last-named being the famous Magi, some of whom served the Persian Empire as religious specialists; their name is however of uncertain derivation. Much later, the Greeks appear to say that the Magi too are Arioi (Arias): Μάγοι καὶ πᾶν τὸ Αριον "γένος" (*LSJ*, s.v. Ἄριοι, citing "Eudem. [Eudemus Philosophus, iv B.C.] ap. [quoted in] Dam. Pr. [Damascius Philosophus] de Principiis [v/vi A.D.] 125 bis"). However, this passage just shows that the word *Aria* was already on its way to becoming an ethnonym, as it became very quickly among the Chinese.
98. Tavernier (2007: 112), citing Benveniste (1966: 83), gives the meaning erroneously as "belonging to an Aryan tribe", and cites two inscriptional forms of the word in Elamite, without any mention of the Greek form in Herodotus. But *Aria* ~ *Arya* ~ *Ḥarya* cannot have meant "Iranian" originally; it only acquired that meaning well after the Achaemenid period (Beckwith 2016a, 2016b).
99. Indo-Europeanists mostly agreed long ago that the word "Arya", i.e., attested *Ariya* ~ *Aria* ~ *Ḥarya* ~ *Ārya*, does not go back to Proto-Indo-European, and there are other problems with it. It does not occur in Old Avestan. Its

occurrences in the Rig Vedā suggest that it was introduced late into that very late-attested corpus (p.c., Michael L. Walter, 2019). For the word and its use in eastern Eurasia see Beckwith (2016a, 2016b) and Chapter 4.

100. Recently some have attempted to revive the discredited etymology of the word as having meant "Iranian" from the beginning. Some translations give, for example, 'having an Aryan mind, of Aryan reasoning' for Old Iranic *Aryamanā (Greek *Ariamenēs*) (Tav. 116), or for Old Persian *Ariyāramna-* "den Ariern bzw. Iraniern Frieden schaffend" ['creating peace for the Arians or Iranians'] (Sch. 137), but they are not supportable either linguistically or historically.

101. Foreign descriptions state incorrectly that early Central Eurasian steppe peoples, e.g., the Scythians (in Greek accounts) and the Koguryo (in Chinese accounts), viewed their subjects as "slaves". Although subordinate steppe people are sometimes referred to as "slaves" *by peripheral peoples writing in their own languages*, they are not so called by Central Eurasians themselves, when we have historical sources written by them, in the Central Eurasians' own languages, from the Early Middle Ages on.

In the Old Turkic inscriptions (mid-8th century CE) *qol* 'male servants, vassals' and *küŋ* 'female servants, vassals' (both words are often translated as 'slaves') are mentioned, but they are always Türks, and are always cited in connection with the steppe Türks' defeat and subjugation by the Chinese, after which their sons and daughters became *qol* and *küŋ* of the Chinese. As the glosses make clear, a major problem is that Old Turkic words often do not have meanings as specific as their supposed English equivalents. Nevertheless, the Türks do not speak of any other people as the Türks' servants, let alone slaves. The Kül Tigin Inscription at East 21 (Tekin 1968: 234) reads *ol ödkä qul qulliɣ bolmiš ärti*, which is translated by Tekin (1968: 267) as "At that time slaves [themselves] had slaves." (The brackets are mine—CIB.) Clauson (1972: 620) renders it "at that time (even) slaves had become slave-owners" (however, there is no word for "owners" in the text). It is generally understood as being a positive statement on "the good old days". However, the idea of "the slaves of the slaves of the slaves . . ." is *precisely* the standard *non*-steppe peoples' misunderstanding of the Central Eurasian Türks' feudal social system, in which *everyone* was "a vassal of a vassal of a vassal". All people were vassals, even the king, who was the vassal of Heavenly God. (Cf. Endnote 96 on the Scytho-Mede-Persian Empire.) The magisterial work of Doerfer (1967: 504, § 1519) argues convincingly that Old Turkic *qul* should be rendered as 'vassal' or 'dependent', not 'slave'. For texts and translations on the Central Eurasian comitatus institution (a key part of the feudal vassalage system), where the status of the individuals described is known, see Beckwith (1984a) and Beckwith (2009: 12–28).

Herodotus, who actually went to Scythia and personally met Scythians, says explicitly, "None of the Scythians have servants bought by money" (that is, chattel slaves): ἀργυρώνητοι δὲ οὐκ εἰσί σφι θεράποντες (Herodotus iv, 72,1, from Perseus, tr. Godley). The received text of Herodotus does mention Scythian "slaves" several times, and it has been argued that in fact the Scythians did have slavery after all (Taylor et al. 2020; Taylor 2021), but the two main stories in Herodotus featuring slaves are very un–Central Eurasian in character and seem to be Greek creations, while occasional references to "slaves" probably represent Greek confusion of low-ranking vassal subjects with slaves. Moreover, the highly problematic contradictions in the text have never been carefully examined by an expert in higher text criticism. Since the main stories involving slaves in Herodotus are so un–Central Eurasian in character, and Herodotus "himself" explicitly denies that the Scythians had slaves, the stories could represent alterations to Herodotus' text after "he" completed it, as in other mentioned examples where the text "argues with itself". Nevertheless, in frontier zones, such as the sedentary areas of Central Asia, slavery may have been fairly common, unlike in the steppe, and since some Central Eurasians participated in the slave trade, it could certainly suggest to an outsider that the Scythians themselves practiced slavery.

102. In Beckwith (2009: 380–383) I reconstruct this name as *Tokʷar-kē ~ *Tukʷar-kē—literally, the 'Tokʷar/Tukʷar kings'—but I have unaccountably omitted one key piece of data on the first transcriptional element, *yüeh* 月 (*yuè*) 'moon, month' (in Mandarin) from attested MChi *ŋgwar* (Tak. 372–373); cf. HSR MChi ☆ŋuat (Pul. 388). Note that the miswriting and reading of this character as *jou* 肉 (*ròu*) 'meat' is a modern popular mistake; the two words are radically different from Antiquity to the present. Some progress has been made in reconstructing Old Chinese, partly based on Old Japanese evidence (Beckwith and Kiyose 2018), so the reconstruction of this name needs to be revised in any case.

For Japanese 月 *tsuki* from OJpn *tukï ~ *tuku- 'moon, month' (*JDB* 461, 464), Martin (1987: 554) reconstructs "*tukiy from *tuku-Ci". The combining form *tuku- only occurs in compounds before *y, thus the pre–Old Japanese form was *tukuy, and with pre–Old Japanese coda *y deriving from PJpn *r(ă) following Whitman (1990), and the expected Japanese-Koguryoic final vowel, we have Proto-Japanese *tukwərə̆ or the like. The word corresponds to the Old Chinese transcription of the attested Bactrian name in the toponym Τοχοαραστaν <Tokhoarastan>, i.e., *Toχwara-* or *Tuχwara-*, as 月氏 OChi dial. *tukwar(ă) ~ tokwer(ă), in which the first element (月 'month, moon') has become Mandarin *yüeh* 月. OJpn *tukï 'month, moon' is thus ultimately a borrowing from Old Chinese 月 'month, moon'—not surprising in view of the Proto-Japanese borrowing of the Old Chinese 12-animal cycle (Kiyose and Beckwith 2008). (N.B.: *e in my Old Chinese reconstructions has different later outcomes compared to HSR *e, a doubtful vowel in that system.) For the second element, *chih* 氏 MSC *zhī* < MChi ☆tɕi (Pul. 404), also written *chih* 支 MSC *zhī*, from LOC *kē, which is attested in Archaic Koguryo and Old Koguryo as ☆key / ☆kay (usually transcribed [皆], but also [支]) in the meaning 'king', see Beckwith (2007a: 124–125). The word, with the same reading, is also attested in the title of the Hsiung-nu queens. Hsiung-nu has now been shown to be a dialect of Scythian close to Sogdian, and the Hsiung-nu were the historical intermediaries between the Chinese and the Yüeh-chih—i.e., OChi *Tukwară-kē, transcribing foreign

*Tuχwară-kay(ă)—while the Koguryo language does not allow any onset clusters. Thus the Old Koguryo word *key/*kay ~ *kē 'king' is a loan from Scythian *χšaya* 'king', which is also attested in Greek transcription, ξαι- *ksai-* <ksai>, as shown in Chapter 6.

103. On unpalatalized forms in early Northeast Asian languages, including the local dialect of Middle Chinese, see Beckwith (2007a: 93–95). To them clearly must be added depalatalized forms such as the word under consideration here. In this particular word, the backing of the second syllable vowel *a to *â in the Chinese transcriptional form *ɣărấ appears to be due to loss of the segment *y.

104. It is unknown what the *Tukhwară people spoke previously, and the point is controversial, but their early use of *Ḥarya* indicates they were Scythian speakers, and most of their name sounds strikingly Iranic (e.g., *χwar- 'sun, glory, etc.'). Thus, *not* with Beckwith (2009: 379–383), where it is argued (following many others, but that is no excuse) that their language was or had been a relative of the medieval Tokharian (or "Tocharian") languages of East Turkistan, which belong to a distinct, non-Iranic daughter language (branch) of Indo-European. That name is actually correct *historically*, but linguistically it clearly derives from later Kushan Empire (*Toχwara-*) rule over that very region.

105. Unfortunately, we do not have any datably early inscriptions or other texts in Sanskrit, and the works usually attributed to the Classical period or earlier seem in fact to be from the Gupta period or even later, while the supposedly primordial texts of the Vedas are undatable. It is quite possible that the word is a loan into Sanskrit from Saka (Kushan period) or earlier, from Classical Scythian. Vedicists do not like loanwords, but they are a fact of life; apparently all languages, no matter how remote, have loanwords in them.

106. The controversy over the Indo-European "laryngeals" is far from settled, in the opinion of unbelievers. Although an indisputably attested laryngeal is preserved in Hittite, transcribed <ḫ>, its actual *phonetic* value *is* disputable. In most laryngeal theories one laryngeal is considered to have lengthened an adjacent vowel *a* without coloring it and then disappeared itself, providing an explanation for what otherwise would seem to be inexplicable vowels (particularly long vowels) in inherited words. However, it is now widely thought that Old Indic *Ārya* and Old Iranic *Arya* are *not* Indo-European words by origin, and possibly not even "Indo-Iranian" words; thus, not with Mallory and Adams (1997: 213), among others, who reconstruct it back to a PIE *$h_4$erós ~ *$h_4$eri̯os 'member of one's own (ethnic) group, peer, freeman, (Indo-Aryan) Aryan.' However, if we take their reconstruction *$h_4$eri̯os as an "*as if* PIE" reconstruction to explain the vowel length in this word, it agrees perfectly with the data from Eastern Eurasia presented here, and thus also strengthens the case for borrowing. Possibly more important, the East Scythian form of the word, *Ḥarya*, phonetically [ɣarya], has the specific onset ɣ (or [ʁ]), not an unknowable theoretical laryngeal such as the usual Indo-Europeanist "laryngeal(s)" typically symbolized by numerals. If there is any truth to the laryngeal theory it can only be demonstrated by doing actual

linguistics—equating the postulated laryngeals with *sounds* that make sense in an early Indo-European phonological context—study of which has shown that there were no aspirate stops in PIE, among other things (Beckwith 2007b). The examples of East Scythian *Ḥarya* and Indic *Ārya* thus both firmly attest the existence of such a “laryngeal” onset phone, but the sound has been lost in West Scythian and all languages which subsequently acquired the word in the form *aria* ~ *ariya* (etc.) from West Scythian.

107. The proposed reconstruction of the second part of this word as *varta is speculative, and the name *āryāvarta* is late, but the reconstruction of the first part of the word as *Ḥarya is strongly supported by the previous Endnote and the data discussed below. Note that the Buddhist use of the term (as an epithet for the Buddha’s disciples—‘my royal ones’) is not attested until well over half a millennium after it is attested in Scythian.

108. First identified by Pelliot (1912); cf. Molè (1970: 73, note 22). The word is recorded in Chinese also. The *Sung shu* 宋書 reads: 西北諸雜種謂之為阿柴虜 ‘the mixed peoples of the northwest call them the A-ch’ai slaves’ (Shen 1974, 96: 2370, who translates the word 虜 ‘miscreants’ as ‘slaves’). The transcription A-ch’ai 阿柴 MSC *àchái* ~ *āchái* is *a-* 阿 attested MChi *ʔar* (Takata 1988: 304; Takata 2000: note 20) [MChi ☆ʔa (Pul. 23)] + *ch’ai* -柴 MChi ☆dʐaɨj/☆dʐɛːj (Pul. 47). It transcribes the pronunciation of the term by foreign intermediaries, representing a foreign *arǰay. There is another transcription of the same word, applied to an important ruler a few generations later (Shen 1974, 96: 2371), *A-ch’ai* 阿豺 (MSC *àchái* ~ *āchái*) from attested MChi *ʔar* + MChi ☆dʐəɨj/☆dʐɛːj (Pul. 47), thus *arǰăy or *arǰa. These are two Chinese transcriptions of the same Togon word, which is clearly not the actual name of the two rulers so called, but foreign versions of their shared title or epithet. Although this word is certainly related to the one underlying the Old Tibetan transcription, the differences are striking. If the early Tibetans had encountered a form *arǰa they could very easily have written it *ཨརྫ་ [ʔa.rǰa] or *ཨར་ཛ་ [ʔar.ǰa]. But they did not do so. Both Old Tibetan and Middle Chinese have a voiced fricative word-onset phoneme, so the Tibetans (unlike the Chinese) got their form, *Ḥaźa* [ɣa.ʑa], directly from the Togon (T’u-yü-hun) themselves. On the well-attested ‘entering tone’ reading (attested as final coda *-r*) of 阿 in Middle Chinese see Takata (1988: 304; Takata 2000: note 20); Beckwith (1993: 206–208); Beckwith (2016b: 42, note 16; 2017).

109. If pre–Old Tibetan speakers had encountered someone who pronounced the name *arya, as it is usually thought to have been pronounced in the West—i.e., [ʔa.rya], with a glottal stop onset as in English pronunciation and a maximized second syllable onset—they would have pronounced it *Aźa and written it as ཨ་ཞ་ *<ʔa.źa> in the *Old Tibetan Annals*. (See the preceding Endnote.) We know the Serbi did *not* pronounce it *[ɣar.ya] because the Tibetans could have pronounced it and easily written it འར་ཡ་ (ɣar.ya). In Imperial Old Tibetan, *native* Tibetan words could not begin with a vowel, or even a glottal stop (Beckwith 2006). The Tibetans could not have heard *[ʔa.źa] but mistranscribed it [ɣa.źa]

because Old Tibetan texts do not transcribe any known zero onset or glottal stop onset foreign words with the onset *ḥ* འ [ɣ] rather than with ཨ [ʔ]. Even though the glottal stop onset was foreign to the Tibetan language, the Tibetans nevertheless heard the difference, because they regularly transcribed the respective phones correctly, e.g., ʔan ཨན་ (*Old Tibetan Annals* version I, line 288) in 'the Chinese envoy (*rgya'ï pho nya*)' *ʔan da lang*', with *ʔan* probably for the well-known Chinese surname An 安 (*ān*) < MChi *ʔan (Pul. 24), and the Chinese official *ʔu ling* ཨུ་ལིང་ (Sino-Tibetan Treaty Inscription south face line 27, given also in Chinese characters as Yü Ling 於陵 (*yú líng*), with Yü 於 (*yú*) from attested MChi *ʔu* [Tak. 314–315], where the majority of transcriptions given are *ʔu*).

110. I inadvertently discovered this material in the *Old Tibetan Annals* when I had thought the manuscript of my original paper on this topic (Beckwith 2016a) was finished, and fortunately had time to add it before publication. It thus independently confirms my analysis. The variants in the *Old Tibetan Annals* suggest that the early Tibetans may have understood intuitively that their early word *rgya-* corresponded to the later, directly transcribed Togon form of the same word, *Ḥarya-*, or alternatively, the pre–Old Tibetan speakers borrowed the word from the Togon. More study is needed.

111. Meillet and Benveniste (1931: 7–8): "le vocabulaire religieux et officiel des inscriptions offre des traces nombreuses de faits qui doivent être pris à un dialecte et voisin du perse et prestigieux. Pour des raisons d'ordre historique, géographique et dialectal, il ne peut s'agir que du mède. Seul l'empire mède qui, à la mort de Cyaxare [. . .] pouvait avoir fixé dans l'Iran le début d'une tradition administrative et les premiers termes d'un vocabulaire officiel. . . . Enfin il y a une identité frappante entre les particularités phonétiques des mots étrangers au perse dans les inscriptions et celles des mots transmis comme mèdes par les auteurs grecs." Cf. also Rossi (2010: 300–301).

112. Xenophon, *Cyropaedia* (xiii 3,11). Ps. Plato, *Alcibiades* (i 122a): "the Magianism of Zoroaster, son of Ōromazes, . . . is the worship of the gods"; from Perseus, tr. Lamb. (I have revised Lamb's "magian lore" and transcribe the divine name as written in Greek, which had no "breathing" marks in the 4th century BC.) Many have remarked on the text's characterization of Zoroaster as "son of Ahuramazdā". The Scythians worshipped only one ("Capital G") God, says Herodotus, but he does not name him. Elsewhere he equates *Papaeus* (a Scytho-Greek word) with Zeus, the Greek form of *dyeu(s)-[pəter] 'heaven father, Jupiter' (Watkins 2011: 22)—the only reconstructible Proto-Indo-European god name. See Chapter 6 on Proto-Scythian *Tagri 'Heavenly God'. Cf. Horky (2009) on the related Greek material.

113. However, most arguments, whether pro or contra, do not distinguish clearly between monotheistic *Early* Zoroastrianism (with one God, Ahura Mazdā, as in the *Gāthās*) and *Late* Zoroastrianism, from Artaxerxes II (r. 404 BC–358 BC) on, which is actually polytheistic, with three Gods: Anāhitā, Mithra, and Ahura Mazdā. The system of Darius is like the *Early* Zoroastrianism of the *Gāthās* in its

essentials, with strict monotheism and emphasis on Truth in opposition to Falsehood.

114. It is often declared, without qualification, that there is no difference between a language and a dialect. That sounds exactly like a Buddhist or Pyrrhonist or Taoist statement, denying that there are any absolute (perfect) categories or that there can be any differences between categories such as True and False, Good and Bad, Beautiful and Ugly, and so on, as discussed in the Epilogue; cf. Beckwith (2015), and on categorization within language as reflecting primitive cognition, see Beckwith (2007c). However, Buddha and Pyrrho actually reject the idea of *perfection* or *absolutes*, so they argue only that there are no *absolute, perfect* categories, not that categories do not exist for humans, or that in practical daily life there are no differences between them, since if they did not exist, they would not be discussed.

Thus it is certainly true that "dialects" cannot be *absolutely* or *perfectly* distinguished from "languages", as things, but there are differences; they are simply *non-absolute, imperfect* differences. As in most things, there are gradations between them, and the categories are fuzzy. Because they are imperfect they are gradable, noticeable to the perceptive observer, and liable to scientific analysis. As Meillet (1925/1984: 82) says, "Si dégénéré que puisse être son breton, l'habitant de la région de Vannes sait s'il parle français ou breton." ('However degenerate his Breton may be, a resident of the region of Vannes knows if he is speaking French or Breton.') There is a tremendous difference between, say, Mayan and English, or Swahili and Chinese, or even neighbors such as Bulgarian and Turkish, or related neighboring languages such as French and Breton (which both descend from Proto-Indo-European). On the other hand, some "dialects" are very easy and quick to learn or adjust to (a matter of a few minutes to a few hours), while others are very difficult and take a long time to acquire (months or longer). For most adults, different "languages" cannot be picked up easily without lengthy exposure and considerable effort, though a few adults can learn even a very unusual foreign language very quickly and with relatively little effort. That indicates there are practical difference between "dialects" and "languages", and they are gradable, "grey-scale" differences.

What one needs to do is *communicate* with other people regardless of whatever tongue they speak. If people can do that despite some differences—i.e., if they *can* communicate using variant forms of one language known to both of them—these communicatively successful variant forms may be called *dialects*. If it is *not* possible for speakers to accommodate their counterparts sufficiently well, then however one *labels* any two speech forms is irrelevant, because their speakers *cannot* communicate if each speaker uses his or her own distinctive speech form. Communicatively, therefore, two mutually incomprehensible speech forms can be called *languages*, in the strict sense—i.e., ignoring labels sometimes given to them, such as the "American *language*" and the "British *language*" for *dialects* of the modern standard English language, which are in fact mutually comprehensible and often referred to instead as different *accents*. It is true that a *dialect* is a full speech form that, in isolation, is indistinguishable from a full language and it is only because there are two or more dialects that the word "dialect" is necessary. (If there is only one "dialect", it is the language, pure and simple.) That is the reason there can be no absolute distinction between the terms *dialect* and *language*. And, like languages, *dialects* (in common parlance) are usually different enough that they are often not quite understandable at first, but given a shorter or slightly longer period of contact, and perhaps a little effort, they can become understandable. The need for such effort—that is, beyond initial momentary adjustment for an unfamiliar speaker's voice or accent—and the possibility of making such adjustments without formal study, together mark the two speech forms as different *dialects*, not *languages*.

The term *languages* is used in this book to label speech forms that cannot be mutually understood without somewhat lengthy exposure and much effort, such as special study or long-term residence among native speakers. Leaving aside the many obviously cognate Old Iranic word stems, or even the lexicons in general, we do have texts in Old Persian and in Imperial Scythian (Avestan dialects), which even casual examination shows are radically different languages.

Here the term *dialects* is used to label relatively stable forms of *the same language* not distinguished purely by sociolinguistic or other features, such as religion in the case of "religiolects".

The term *accents* is used to label slight dialect differences characterized mainly by minor variations in pronunciation, such that two "subdialects" are mutually comprehensible more or less immediately, but the discrepancies mark the speakers as belonging to a different speech-group, or as non-native speakers.

As far as can be determined on the basis of the data, steppe Scythian and Imperial Scythian are two subdialects of West Scythian. Imperial Scythian consists of the Median and Avestan dialects, the latter with two "religiolect" forms, Old Avestan and Young Avestan. Other subdialects can be established as well, as shown in Chapters 5 and 6, which present data and analyses supporting this relationship theory. The theory still leaves many problems unsolved, and if viable it will no doubt need further adjustment.

115. Children under the age of about ten can effortlessly learn multiple languages as a native speaker without formally studying them, but the extent to which an individual full-grown adult can learn a foreign language without studying it differs radically from person to person, and as noted there is no sharp line distinguishing "dialects" and "languages". Most of these points have long been discussed, and are under active study. For a good introduction to general comparative-historical linguistics see Campbell (2013).

116. Tavernier's valuable book (2007) is remarkable and very useful (especially the Glossary). However, even the *word* "Scythian" (or an analogue) seems not to occur anywhere in the book, with a single partial exception, "Scyth", given as the gloss of *Saka-* (Tav. 30), which gloss is marred by acceptance of several of the

folk etymologies which pervade works on Old Iranic languages. The oddness of the "great omission" of Scythian is matched by the very same feature in the volume of papers edited by Lanfranchi et al. (2003) dedicated to the proposition that the Mede Empire did not exist. The long Table of Contents of that book does not even mention the name "Scythian". Its omission is emphasized by the fact that the title of one (very interesting) article discusses the Greek word *Sakas*, the name of a cupbearer ("*Sacas*"), but it turns out to be "Aramaic *šāqyā* 'cupbearer', a loanword from Assyrian *šāqiu* with the same meaning" (Parpola 2003: 341), so it too has nothing to do with the Scythians. Yet one must ask how an entire volume (and many other papers besides) could be published on the putative nonexistence of the Mede Empire without even mentioning the Scythians. Did they not exist either? In periods where we have no Assyrian or Babylonian sources on anything, did the Assyrians or Babylonians not exist? The limited or nonexistent *sources* on anything (at all) during this particular early ancient period have been used to establish limited or nonexistent *empires*. This commits a fundamental methodological error. Scholars have argued against the very idea of the existence of the already huge Mede Empire that Cyrus the Great took over, already fully formed, when he captured King Astyages of the Medes, successor of Cyaxares, an event solidly recorded in Akkadian sources, as well as in Greek. Although the Akkadian sources are not plentiful, they are clear and in complete agreement with Herodotus on the fact of Cyrus' defeat of Astyages and takeover of the Mede realm. But that is not all. The Akkadian sources are also very clear on the major, fully historical role earlier played by Astyages' predecessor (no doubt his father) Cyaxares in the overthrow of the Assyrian Empire in the late 7th century, an event of enormous importance in world history. Far from wondering how Cyaxares and Astyages had come by such a huge, powerful, wealthy realm, evidently without spending any time at all conquering it, the problem is ignored. So it is not surprising that the question of what the Scythians might have called their (even more overlooked) realm has been ignored too. Yet although there is sufficient evidence for every point, historians have largely ignored such questions, along with the Medes and Scythians in general. We must understand what it was that Cyrus took over, and where it came from, not create modern stories about a great founder hero creating everything *ex nihilo*.

117. The currently dominant Iranistic theory on Old Iranic argues that the letter "r(a)" 𐎼 in Old Persian often stood for an Indic-like vocalic liquid (i.e., a liquid articulated as a vowel) at the beginning of a word (or often within a word), though not always—the scholars who do this are not consistent. The now dominant Iranist transcription is "ṛ", imitating Indological practice for Sanskrit, even though in the Old Persian inscriptions the vowel in such cases is *explicitly written*, e.g., putative *ṛšti* 'spear' is actually written 𐎠𐎼𐏁𐎫𐎡 a-r-š-t-i, i.e., *aršti* or *āršti*. In any language that requires a glottal stop before a vowel in initial position, it should be written with a symbol for it, such as an aleph. So for example, the Old Persian original of the Greek transcription *Artaxerxes* (Greek <ar.ta.kser.kses>) is interpreted by

Schmitt (2014: 241) as “Ṛtaxšaçā” (representing a hypothetical Old Persian [r̥.ta.χʃa.ɕa:]), but it is actually written 𐎠𐎼𐎫𐎧𐏁𐏂𐎠 a-r$_{(a/i)}$-t$_{(a/i)}$-x-š-ç-a. Other ancient languages that transcribe the name also write the beginning *Ar-* or the equivalent, for example, Imperial Aramaic אַרְתַּחְשַׁשְׂתְּא *'artaḥšaśtə* [ʔar.taχ.ʃa.ɕtə] ‘Arataxerxes’ (with a possibly intrusive *t* and a doubly explicit final *schwa mobile*). Old Persian regularly writes out the vowel <a> before an <r> at the beginning of a word. Elamite sometimes writes <ir>, but sometimes has no <r>, while other languages do not transcribe it as *ir, and it is never transcribed as *r* alone. All this indicates that the initial vowel was *ă, i.e., schwa *[ə] in allegro speech, but short *[a] in careful speech. The better known transcriptional languages, Akkadian, Aramaic, and Greek, almost always have *a* plus a clearly written consonantal *r*. The vocalic liquid “*r̥*” has been introduced from Sanskrit into Old Persian and Median, but it is unjustified by the data. For very many attested transcriptional examples of actual *arta-* for putative *r̥ta-*, see Tav. 292–306. Cf. Endnote 10.

118. Some scholars claim that these Aramaic texts are “Iranicized” already, and were actually read in “Old Iranic” or early “Middle Iranic” (intending by this actual languages, not reconstructed proto-languages). That is incorrect for these texts, as well as for the Aramaic in the bilingual Kandahar Inscription of Priyadarśi. For the published Aramaic documents from Bactria in the Khalili Collection see Naveh and Shaked (2012), who say the same thing (2012: 52), but then immediately qualify it by saying, “This is certainly not yet the case with the documents published in this volume”. In fact, those texts are in excellent Imperial Aramaic. The Kandahar Inscription is also in Imperial Aramaic, but a late dialect of it (Beckwith forthcoming-b). The change to “Iranic” language readings did of course eventually happen in those regions.

119. Naveh and Shaked (2012: 54) state, “The Iranian loanwords in the Khalili documents may in general be characterized as deriving from Old Persian. To be precise, most words of which the Iranian etymology is clear show a phonetic form which accords with the phonology of Old Persian; *none show an unequivocal affinity with Avestan phonology*” (my emphasis). This statement explicitly contradicts Schmitt (1994: 174). Yet many of the Old Iranic words in these texts, conveniently collected by the authors in an immediately following section (Naveh and Shaked 2012: 55–60), do in fact contain diagnostic features that distinguish Old Iranic languages as either “Avestan” (i.e., Imperial Scythian), or Persian, and Naveh and Shaked do actually identify a number of forms explicitly as “Avestan”, and those explicitly marked as related to Scythian appear to outnumber those related to Persian. The prefatory statement of Naveh and Shaked is thus incomprehensible. It is necessary to reexamine the data.

120. Cornillot (1981: 30): “Les parlers des populations iranophones qui occupaient la quasi-totalité de l’Asie Centrale dans l’antiquité étaient très voisins, au point qu’on les considérait comme une seule et même langue, elle-même très proche des idiomes parlés dans le Nord de l’Iran et en pays mède, ainsi qu’il ressort des

informations données par Hérodote et Strabon. L'unité linguistique et culturelle des Saka d'Asie Centrale et des Scythes d'Europe faisait d'ailleurs aussi peu de doute pour les Grecs que pour les Perses: les premiers leur donnaient à tous le nom de Scythes (contrairement à la tradition qui a tendu à réserver ultérieurement ce nom à la partie européenne du monde scytho-sace), les seconds celui de Saka; ce qui fait que l'on peut mathématiquement conclure à l'équipollence de ces deux appellations."

121. Harmatta continues, "and the Middle Iranian development of Avestan must have been the most important language in eastern Iran on the eve of the Saka and Yüeh-chih invasion" (Harmatta 1994a). However, the names he cites are mostly from the Achaemenid period. Cf. Chapter 5, Note 29.
122. In fact, in the much later *Middle Iranic* languages of Central Asia, both the inherited words and their borrowed Zoroastrian cognates sometimes exist in the same language. For example, in Sogdian (one of the best-attested Middle Iranic languages), the inherited word *daiva* 'god'—in a positive sense—is well attested in compounds, while the exact same word in simplex form has semantically acquired the negative Late Zoroastrian sense 'demon' (Gharib 1995: 150–151).
123. My translation of Lecoq (1987): "dès l'instant où l'on rejette l'hypothèse mède, on ne peut éviter celle d'une origine scythe. Celle-ci explique admirablement la propagation de *farnah-* en Iran occidental, sur les rives de la mer Noire, en ossète et jusqu'en sogdien et en khotanais". Lecoq's (and Lubotsky's) inclusion of Khotanese in the *f*-dialect is due to the mistaken reading of the *ph* in Khotanese *phārra* as [f]. It represents [p^h] and places Khotanese in the same category with Avestan and the western subdialect of West Scythian.
124. Lecoq (1987), "Cette solution rendrait mieux compte du nombre relativement important de noms propres scythes en *farnah-*, attestés sur les rives de la mer Noire."
125. Mayrhofer (2006) and Schmitt (2003) have missed *pitā-* 'father' by ignoring other sources, choosing erroneous readings in the manuscripts of Herodotus, and uniquely interpreting Greek theta (θ) in all transcriptions of this particular word as [s], though—if correct—it would be the only example of such a transcription among Scythian words in Greek sources, as theta regularly transcribes foreign *t* or even *d*, never *s*. The textual variants are discussed by Schmitt (2003), who is quoted on this by Mayrhofer (2006: 10, note 15).
126. There are 36 items in Mayrhofer's list, which is missing about a dozen other solid Scythian words, so the total in the semantically identified Scythian lexical corpus is actually about 50. There are also many semantically unidentified words. Besides Mayrhofer and Schmitt I have used Tavernier for cognates.
127. I have omitted the omnipresent "non-linguistic" asterisk used by scholars of Old Iranic studies essentially on all forms, including those that are normal transcriptions. I have reserved the asterisk for marking reconstructions in the strict linguistic sense, as well as uncertain forms, following standard modern linguistic practice.

128. Schmitt repeats the old idea about **Arya* being an ethnonym meaning 'Iranian' or 'Indo-Iranian'. Translations and parallels in other languages (especially Akkadian) show that it meant 'royal', specifically 'heavenly (eternal) royal (line)', as shown in Chapters 2 and 4. Most scholars have long ago rejected the ethnonym idea.
129. The Greek string *ari-* is interpreted as *aria* (the Greek 'full' writing of the reconstructed word *arya) because *ari* often occurs in manuscripts instead of *aria* (Mayrhofer 2006: 10, note 15) and because the Greek vowel iota <ι> frequently transcribes Iranic *ia* and similar forms (Schmitt 2003).
130. Attested some 62 times in 33 inscriptions; from Iranic √kar 'to do, to make' (Schmitt 2014: 200–201). Among Old Iranic languages, the stem *-kunau-* occurs only in Persian; forms with the stem *kar-* are all passive verbs, or nouns, in Old Persian.
131. Also known as Official Aramaic and as Biblical Aramaic. Some scholars distinguish among the varieties or dialects these names represent, but in truth, as Rosenthal (2006: 10) says, they are all *the same language* with no major differences between them.
132. We can compare the effect to the early medieval Arabic impact on Middle Persian, which produced New Persian (Classical Persian), the language of Rudaki, Firdausi and Hafiz. It is the ancestor of modern Persian, an Arabicized Iranic language with three major modern dialects: Fârsi, Dari, and Tâjiki.
133. Herodotus' story of Cyrus' takeover of the Scytho-Mede Empire was written long after Darius had retroactively "Persianized" Cyrus. When he says that the Medes gave up their freedom to serve the Persians (Herodotus i 129), he reveals the later Achaemenid date of the story.
134. Lecoq (1987): "Nous savons que les Achéménides, et surtout Darius, se sont placés volontairement dans la tradition d'un absolutisme royal nouveau, étranger à la pensée iranienne antérieure," adding, "et que les Mèdes avaient eux-mêmes emprunté à la Mésopotamie".
135. Properly 'Scythian short sword', part of the Scythian culture complex and attested across Central Eurasia. It was not Persian but was eventually adopted by the Persians, along with the rest of Scythian costume and weaponry, as pointed out by Herodotus and other ancient writers and as is obvious from pictorial representations. See Appendix B. The East Scythian (Sogdian and Hsiung-nu) evidence (see below in this chapter) is perhaps against the initial *(a), but aphaeresis is thought to be a characteristic feature of literary Sogdian, an East Scythian dialect.
136. This word is often written αρι in Greek manuscripts instead of αρια (Mayrhofer 2006: 10, note 15; cf. Schmitt 2018, etc.); the word *ariya* ~ *aria* does not mean "Iranian" or the like until well into Middle Iranic times. See also Table 8, and Chapter 7.
137. Schmitt (1990): "Old Persian **kandu-* (beside Median **kanzu-ka-*, in Elamite *kan-su-ka*, Parthian *qnjwg*, etc., 'cloak'; cf. M. Schwartz apud I. Gershevitch, *TPS*,

1979, p. 149, note 37) or as Old Persian **kantu-* (lit. 'covering' from **kan-* 'to cover'). However, the garment is archaeologically attested among Scythians all across Central Eurasia and was a Scythian tribute item to the Persians and cannot be a Persian invention. Its name must be Scythian, transmitted by the Scytho-Medes to the Persians, who adopted the garment and Persianized the name. The Greeks then borrowed the Persianized name.

138. Mayrhofer (2006) and Schmitt (2003, 2018) discuss the forms and transcriptions, concluding that πειθης- *peithēs* is a clear Grecization of the second element in *both* names, which have influenced each other, producing "*Ariapeithēs*" and "*Spargapeithēs*". However, for the former we also have the Latin transcription *-pitus* in *Scolapitus*, not mentioned by Schmitt: "(Justin, *Epit.* 2.4.1) < **š/skula-pita(r)-* 'Scythians' father'" (Ivantchik 2018), or rather, *-pitā (*pitar is unattested in Scythian). "Ariapeithes" is explicitly said (in Herodotus' third version of the Scythian national foundation myth) to be the father of the three sons, including Scyles, the same name as *Scolaxai 'King Skula (Scyth)' in the first version, who was the first Royal Scythian and thus the first *Aria* 'royal', so his father's name *Aria-pita-* is 'father of the Arias (Royals [Scythians])', with *pita* ~ *pitā*. The much-noted name of the son of Tomyris, Σπαργαπισης Spargapisēs with regard to **-paisa* 'ornament' suggests that *Spargapeithēs* is an error for *Spargapisēs,* and indeed Mayrhofer (2006: 10) and Schmitt (2003) show that *Spargapeithēs* is a clear Grecization based on Greek names such as Διο-πείθης. "Spargapeithēs" (i.e., the early Scythian *Spargapisēs*) and *Ariapeithēs* were centuries apart, so they could not have been close relatives. Moreover, *peithēs* cannot be an actual straight *transcription* of *paisa* 'ornament', because theta (θ) never transcribes Scythian *s*—this would be the only (irregular) case (Mayrhofer 2006: 25). In addition, both Schmitt and Mayrhofer state that Scythian *ai* is regularly transcribed with simple iota (ι) alone. In short, *peithēs* is a perfectly good Greek transcription of Scythian *pita* ~ *pitā* (a word well attested in late Pontic Steppe inscriptions), which is what the text of Herodotus leads us to expect. There are thus clearly two different Scythian words here, *pita*/*pitā* 'father' and *paisa* 'ornament', and the problem is ultimately textual, not linguistic. The conflation of *pita* and *paisa* goes back to Müllenhoff, who is cited, with other scholars, by Schmitt (2003: 22); cf. Bar. 905.

139. Some of the problems seen with these forms are undoubtedly the result of their very early transcription, their rarity, and the fact that not one but several political groups are attested: Cimmerian, Scythian, and Sarmatian. There were thus at least two or three dialects even for the early language, plus East Scythian subdialects (below in this chapter).

140. Schmitt (2018) says we should not expect too much precision from ancient writers such as Herodotus, who "was neither a philologist nor a linguist", but then says this transcription is "in contrast to Herodotus' normal rendering". Certainly we cannot expect perfection, especially in view of the existence of ancient textual errors in Herodotus, but the *gloss* is unlikely to be erroneous, and it is absolutely clear.

141. The original point of departure for this section is Mayrhofer (1968: 20), revised based on Schmitt (2014), cited here as "Mayrhofer". Some items in Mayrhofer's list that are not in Schmitt (2014) are not discussed here, including *patizbay-* 'to order', *spāda* 'army (Heer)', *spāθmaida-* 'army camp (Heerlager)', *vinasta-* 'damage, harm (Schädigung)', and *ganza-* '(royal) treasury', *ganzabara* 'Schatzmeister (treasurer)'. (Tav. 422). The possibly Median term *ganzabara* is well-attested in Ancient Near Eastern transcriptions (the *Nebenlieferung* material; it is not attested in the Old Persian inscriptions), as is its Old Persian equivalent *gandabara*—attested in Elamite (Tav. 380, 422) and Aramaic (Daniel 3:2–3)—but as Mayrhofer (1968: 14) notes, "this official expression coined by the Medes was adapted to the Old Persian sound structure; it was, in the words of Gershevitch (1964: 10–11), 'Old Persianized.'" The fact of "Old Persianization" demonstrates beyond any question that the word is a loanword from another language into Old Persian (though it is unlikely that the Medes were responsible for the "Old Persianization"). Why are some words Old Persianized, while others are not, and some have both forms? This problem has been raised by others, e.g., Lecoq (1997: 49). The word's phonology is irregular, so it may belong with other Scythian "royal" loanwords that indicate the Royal Scythians spoke a different subdialect of the language.

142. Jacobs says: "Only the title *xšaça-pā-van-*, which combines *pā* (protect) and *xsaça-* (empire, sovereignty) with the suffix *-van-* and thus describes an administrator as the 'protector of empire' or 'protector of sovereignty' (Schmitt, 1976, p. 373), is found in the OP inscriptions. From the title of this official an OP **xsaça-pā-vana-* can be deduced (Hinz, 1975, p. 134). Notwithstanding this reconstructed Persian form, the Greek word *satrapeia* (*satrapēiē*) was derived from a Northwest Iranian (Median) dialect" (Jacobs 2011). Schmitt (2014) does not mention that the word is unattested in Old Avestan or Young Avestan, but says that Greek and other foreign forms reflect Old Iranic "**xšaθra-pā/ă-*, neither OPer *xšaça-pā-van-* nor **xšaθra-pā-na*." According to Dandamayev and Medvedskaya (2006), Grantovskij (1970: 154, 323–324) remarks that "the Achaemenid title for a satrap (OPer *xšaçapāvān-* 'regional administrator') existed *even prior to the emergence of the Median state* for the designation of independent chiefs [italics mine—CIB]". Cf. the review by Schmitt (2010). The word is not mentioned in the Scythian studies of Mayrhofer and Schmitt, but Σατραβάτης (*Satrabatēs*), from *χšaθrapā-*, is attested in Pontic Steppe inscriptions (Bukharin 2013). It is undoubtedly a Scythian dialect word. The simplification of the onset cluster can be compared to the simplification of the same cluster (but with a different outcome) in Scythian *χšaya* 'king' in East Scythian and the languages of the region which borrowed it from Scythian, as *kay(ă) 'king' (see Endnote 102). Note that Median is not a "Northwest Iranian" dialect linguistically.

143. The etymology is already suggested by Bartholomae (1904: 554 note), with the same explicit *vṛddhi*-formation proposal. Lubotsky (2002: note 7) summarizes the now dominant argument: "Traditionally, OP *xšāyaθiya-* 'king' has also been

seen as a non-Persian word because of its *θiya-* (allegedly from PIr. **θi̯a-* < **ti̯a-*). As Hoffmann (1976: 637, note 26) has convincingly argued, however, O[ld] P[ersian] *xšāyaθiya-* is a vṛddhi-formation derived from **xšayaθa-* 'reign' with the suffix *-iya-* < **-iHo-*." The argument is thus that *χšāyaθiya* 'king' is a purely *Persian* internal development based on the generic Old Iranic words for 'to rule', 'realm', plus normal Persian derivational morphology, but it is in fact based on a speculative unattested intermediate form.

144. OPer *dūra-* 'far, distant' is cognate to Ave. *dūra-* and OInd *dūrá-* 'id.' (Tav.), but there is no Old Persian word **dūra-* 'evil' cognate to *zūra-*, nor are there Avestan or Old Indic cognates, though Avestan has *duš-* 'bad', cognate to OPer *duš-* 'bad' and OInd *duḥ-* (as in the Buddhist Sanskrit term *duḥkha*), all from Proto-Indo-European *dus- 'bad'. In Sanskrit, final *-s regularly becomes *-r* before a voiced consonant or vowel, so it is conceivable that *zūra-* 'evil' could have been formed by analogy with *dur-* (< *dus-*) in such compounds. See Mayrhofer (1992: 736) for "Indo-Iranian" and Proto-Indo-European forms.

145. Lubotsky (2002), changing his "East Scythian" to "eastern West Scythian" because it is necessary to reserve the term "East Scythian" for the previously neglected Scythian dialects of eastern Eurasia, which are discussed in the present book.

146. Earlier work includes comments by Szemerényi (1980). Bailey (1967: viii) apparently intends to distinguish two Scythian-internal dialects, saying "certainly in the Old Persian inscriptions Suguda and Saka are clearly classed as two distinct Iranian peoples". Though he speaks of national differences, which tell us little or nothing about linguistic ones, the names *Suguda* and *Saka* do represent two different Classical period daughter dialects descended from Old Scythian, as discussed in this chapter. Mayrhofer (2006: 15) erroneously glosses Σάκαι *Saka-* as "a tribe of Scythians" rather than simply "Scythians". Herodotus explicitly says the two words refer to the same people, and that connection is solidly supported by all contemporaneous data. Cf. Endnote 120.

147. The earliest and almost the only transcription of the major eastern East Scythian ethnonym and country name is *Hsiung-nu* 匈奴 (*Xiōngnú*), representing an Old Chinese transcription *Suŋlâ, regularly from an earlier *Suɣla, in turn from *Sugda*. We do not have attestations of the expected intermediate form *Suɣla, but an adjective form, 'Sogdian', is attested as *Hsiu-li* 修利 (*Xiūlì*), MChi ☆Suw-li (Pul. 346, 188), in a translation by the famous Kuchean monk Kumārajīva shortly before 413 CE (Pelliot 1934: 36, reconstructing a MChi *Suli, which is from *Sugli, attested a little later; see below). Szemerényi (1980: 27–30) gives other related forms and analyzes the development of their ancestor, an adjective form *suγδiyaka- (from *Suɣda*) from which <swγδyk> *Suγδīk* 'Sogdian' is attested in late Antiquity in the *Sogdian Ancient Letters* (early 4th c. CE, the earliest Sogdian script attestation). The same spelling continues well into the Middle Ages (Szemerényi 1980: 28–29). Kumārajīva's transcription *Hsiu-li* 修利 (*Xiūlì*) MChi ☆Suwli dates to about the same time as the earliest Sogdian script attestation, yet already shows loss of the first syllable coda, *γ* [ɣ]. However, the earlier

form of the word is actually well recorded in a number of Chinese transcriptions by travelers, and in official histories, most notably *Su-li* 速利 (*sùlì*), attested Middle Chinese *Sogli* *[sugli] in Yi-ching (635–713 CE). Cf. *Su-yi* 粟弋 (*Sùyì*) Middle Chinese *Sʊkyik from an Old Chinese *suglik (*Chin shu* [648 CE] and *T'ung tien* [801 CE]), and as noted, Hsiu-li 修利 *Xiúlì* from ☆Suwli (Kumārajīva, 344–413 CE). I am indebted to Chen Wu for tracking down sources on this. I am responsible for any errors.

Thus the lambdacization of the *δ in Old Scythian *Skuδa 'Scythian' continued far beyond West Scythian to include the chief early East Scythian dialects, Sogdian and Hsiung-nu, as shown for Sogdian proper already by Andreas (1910), who established the unconditioned Sogdian sound change whereby *δ > l*, attested by the adjective *Suγδīk becoming *Sūlīk* 'Sogdian' (Szemerényi 1980: 27, citing Andreas). This regular sound change is what produced *Suɣla from (attested) *Suɣda*. In turn, operation of the Syllable Contact Law produced the form *Suŋla (匈奴 Old Chinese *Suŋlâ) 'Hsiung-nu' according to a well-attested rule of the Northeast Asian linguistic area: when a syllable *coda* that is a voiced velar stop or fricative (i.e., *g* or *ɣ*) precedes a liquid (*r* or *l*) syllable *onset*—as in *Suɣla—the coda changes to a velar nasal (*ŋ*), thus raising the coda's sonority and repairing the violation of the Syllable Contact Law. (For other examples see Chapter 6.) Another solution of the violation would be to simply delete the first syllable coda, which is what happened in the dialect recorded by Kumārajīva.

148. The earlier literature on possible relationships of the Hsiung-nu to other peoples is reviewed at length by Di Cosmo (2002: 163–166). The popular proposal to identify the Hsiung-nu with the Huns of Europe, first made two and a half centuries ago by Deguignes and based above all on the perceived similarity of the names *Hsiung-nu* and *Hun*, has long ago been rejected by specialists in Central Eurasian studies as implausible at best (Sinor 1990: 177–178); recent attempts do not improve on Deguignes. As for the proposal by Ligeti (1950) and others that the Hsiung-nu spoke a language related to modern Ket, a Yeniseian language, it has been conclusively falsified in Shimunek et al. (2015), Beckwith (2018), and Beckwith et al. (forthcoming), which also show that the Huns spoke an archaic Turkic language. For the archaeology, see Brosseder (2018). For Ket see the grammar by Georg (2007).
149. *Agamatana* is the name of the Chao clan capital city of *Chao*, Han-tan (*Handan*), and also the Chao clan capital city of *Ch'in*, Hsien-yang (*Xianyang*). An Old Chinese period transcription of the latter name is fortuitously preserved in an ancient Aramaeo-Sogdian transcription. See Chapter 8.
150. The identification of this word is clear, but the explanation of the Chinese transcription, representing **kēŋrâkă*, suggested to be from **kēŋnâkă*, is still uncertain; see Chapter 8. The reconstructions here are based both on the reconstruction of the Old Chinese transcription(s) and on the Old Iranic reconstruction.
151. Also known as HSR (Historic Sinological Reconstruction), it is a modern attempt to interpret late medieval quasi-linguistic data and project it back to the

Early Middle Ages and to Classical Antiquity. Founded on the work of Bernhard Karlgren (1957), it has long been followed by Sinologists attempting to reconstruct early stages of the language. As late as Starostin (1989) some practitioners would at least consider external hard data such as foreign transcriptions of Chinese and Chinese loanwords into neighboring languages, but today HSR is a closed, highly metatheoretical system.

152. The putative coda "ʔh" is Starostin's hypothetical reconstruction based on back-projection of the medieval tone categories (in which this word appears) as consonants. My reconstruction is based on attested hard data—mostly transcriptions and loanwords into neighboring languages—as well as the word's earliest occurrences in Old Chinese texts, resorting to traditional reconstructions only when we do not have such data. It has recently been shown that Old Chinese was heavily disyllabic in its root morphology (Beckwith and Kiyose 2018), thus supporting the reconstruction of *Hsia* 夏 from OChi **ḥarya* [ɣăryá], but the word is also attested in very many foreign segmental transcriptions and loanwords, which are all disyllabic. For details see Chapter 4 and Beckwith (2016a).

153. Sta. 561, 胡 (HSR) OChi *ghā, i.e., *ɣâ. The character 胡 has the phonetic *ku* 古 (*gǔ*) from (HSR) OChi *gāʔ, i.e., *gâ 'old' (based on Sta. 562–563). But 胡 belongs to the Old Chinese 魚 'fish' rhyme (as do many other words with the phonetic 古), Starostin's class XIII, in which most words are reconstructed with a liquid in them (whether *r or *l is immaterial). Old Tibetan རྒ *rga-* 'old' has been regularly metathesized from pre-OTib *gra; cf. OTib. བགྲེས་ *bgres-* 'grew old', from pre-OTib *gra-. It is uncertain whether it is a loanword or a relative of the Chinese word *ku* 古 'old', but in view of the Old Chinese forms of k'ao 考 and lao 老, discussed in the Epilogue, both of which meant 'old' in Antiquity, we can expect the Old Chinese form of 古 'old' to have a liquid in it too, as also in other words in the same rhyme which have been borrowed into neighboring languages with a liquid, such as *ma* 馬 (mǎ) from (HSR) OChi *mraɣ/*mraŋ 'horse' (properly, 'warhorse' originally), loaned to many eastern Eurasian languages) and the word *Ḥarya* itself, borrowed in two transcriptions of Scythian *Ḥarya, of which *hua* 華 OChi *ḥâryá is HSR OChi *wrā (Sta. 561)—though that reconstruction is linguistically doubtful—and *hsia* 夏 OChi *ḥaryá is HSR OChi *g(h)rāʔh, i.e., *ɣrâ- (Sta. 562), both with *r. Revising Starostin, that gives us HSR-style OChi *grâ for *ku* 古 and *ɣrâ- for *hu* 胡. However, as already shown at length (Beckwith and Kiyose 2018), even in Late Old Chinese many words are attested to be disyllabic (both in foreign loanwords from Chinese and in alternate Chinese transcriptions of foreign and Chinese words), with a movable stress accent, giving us expected OChi *ɣărắ (*Ḥarắ) for *Hu* 胡. This is solidly confirmed by its many disyllabic loanforms in Eastern Eurasian languages, as shown in Beckwith (2016a).

154. Depalatalization and lambdacization also occurred in the late Scythian dialects spoken by the Sarmatians and Alans, producing the name *Alan* from the word *Ariana* attested in Strabo (xv 2,8), q.v. the Prologue. It is unknown how far this

sound change may have spread. The word *Hu* 胡 has been widely taken to be a generic word for 'foreigner', but that only occurs later, in the Middle Ages.

155. In Modern Standard Chinese the pronunciation of *Han* 韓 (*hán*) 'Korea' is indistinguishable from the name of the Chinese Han Dynasty, *Han* 漢 (*hàn*) except for the tones in Chinese (the two are identical in standard Sino-Korean pronunciation), but the two words are written differently, and were pronounced very differently in Old Chinese.

156. Handan is earliest mentioned in the *Ch'un-ch'iu* 春秋 (*Chunqiu*) chronicle s.v. 494 BC and in the *Tso chuan* 左傳 (*Zuo zhuan*) s.v. 500 BC; see Chapter 8. As far as I know there is no specialized scholarship on the city's (and region's) early history.

157. Sch. 179: ā-gam- "(heran)kommen" in OAve, YAve, and Vedic Sanskrit. For the name Hamadān, however, Schmitt (id.) argues instead for a participle *ha(n)gmatā from *ham-gam* 'zusammenkommen'. Foremost among the major problems is the Old Persian form's onset *h*, which is unlike all the many other Near Eastern transcriptions (which have no *h*), as well as the attested early modern local form of the name, *Amadān(a)*, which if from a *ha(m)gmatāna would represent irregular loss of the *h*. See Endnote 168.

158. In particular, *t'ou* 頭 (*tóu*) 'head' is an ancient replacement for the earlier word for 'head', *shou* 首 (*shǒu*) < MChi ☆ɕuw$_2$ (Pul. 286), which merged in Antiquity with *shou* 手 (*shǒu*) 'hand/arm'. In Middle Chinese both of the latter words have rising tone, one outcome of words that had final short *ă after a fricative or approximant (here, *w) in Late Old Chinese (Beckwith and Kiyose 2018).

159. Today this name is often misread as "Mòdú" (regularly given in this Pinyin spelling), but the reading *dú* for *tun* 頓 (*dùn*) as a putative homonym of 毒 is incorrect. In Early Middle Chinese the latter is solidly ☆dəwk (Pul. 12), attested (Late) Middle Chinese *thog* [tʰʊk] (Takata 1988: 414–415), also attested in loanwords. The reading *dú* is thus impossible, and rightly rejected by Pulleyblank (1991a: 217–218).

160. The second character of *Mo-tun* 冒頓 (*Mòdùn*) was long ago suggested to be read *tur, and it was thought that the entire name corresponds to the well-known Central Eurasian culture-word *bagatur* 'hero'. The proposal has been followed by most scholars, including this writer, with the final syllable *-tun* presumably from OChi *tur or *tură, agreeing with the HSR reconstruction of *-tun*, OChi *turs, proposed to correspond to the unidentified second element in the name of the Scythian rulers Idanthyrsos *Idanturs/*Idanturš and Agathyrsos. However, the idea is now clearly incorrect on several counts. See Mayrhofer (2006: 12), citing Schmitt (2003: 8).

161. In theory it could possibly be *tară/*dară ~ *tală/dală. Starostin (579) has *tār (corresponding to the modern reading *tan* (*dān*), but something is wrong with the HSR method here, and not only here (Beckwith 2017), because there is no principled way to distinguish between his Class XXXV (元 A) rhyme and his Class XXXVIII (元 D) rhyme, as shown by the fact that the rhyme **an* of *an* 安 (*ān*) in

An-hsi 安息 *Aršakă 'Arsacids, Parthia' (元 A), should actually be the rhyme *ar (元 D), not *an, while the rhyme *an in *shan* 山 (*shān*) in *Wu-i-shan-li* 烏弋山離 'Alexandria' represents the rhyme *-an (元 A) as expected. My old proposal *darʁa (Beckwith 2009: 387, note 7) for *Ch'an-yü,* and the popular proposal *bagatur for *Mo-tun,* must both be rejected. Cf. Beckwith and Kiyose (2018).

162. It is one of the words that Karlgren has buried without explanation far from related words, in this case those with the common word and phonetic element *yü* 於 (*yú*) from MChi ☆ʔɨă (Pul. 380), which has the alternate pronunciation *wu* 於 MSC *wū* from MChi ☆ʔɔ (Pul. 324). All of these Middle Chinese and Old Chinese reconstructions are doubtful, but if there is any reality behind Karlgren's **ât* it would be ☆ɔr in Middle Chinese (not his "*·â*") and presumably **âr* in late Old Chinese, as supported by the MChi reading ☆ɛn, perhaps from OChi *ar.

163. Pulleyblank has *xiōng* 匈 < MChi ☆xuawŋ$_1$ (Pul. 346) + *nú* 奴 < MChi ☆nɔ$_1$ (Pul. 227). With the attested late MChi transcription *lo* for *nu* 奴 in *Lolad,* an Old Tibetan transcription of *Nu-la* 奴剌 (*Núlá*), q.v. Beckwith (1993: 236), which is regularly from earlier *lâ/*râ/^{n}dâ, the name would derive from HSR OChi *s^{w}awŋlâ ~ *s^{w}awŋ^{n}dâ, as the word onset *s^w directly before a vowel regularly gives the attested Middle Chinese onset h^w [χ^w]. In the Old Chinese *o + *ɣ/g dialect (Beckwith 2008) it would give *soɣlâ ← East Scythian *soɣla ~ *sugla < attested *Sugda.* Both *o* and *u* are transcriptionally attested for this word, but *u* is earlier, and <o> mostly had the phonetic value [ʊ] or [u]. The shift from the first syllable coda *ɣ/g to *ŋ before a liquid onset is a feature of the Northeast Asian linguistic area including Hsiung-nu and northern Chinese, as noted. Cf. Endnote 147.

164. Its usual form 夏, meaning 'summer', first appears as a transcription of *Ḥarya* 'the Royals (the Chinese)' in the earliest authentic historical work from the Spring and Autumn and Warring States period, the *Ch'un ch'iu* 春秋 (*Chūnqiū*) 'Spring and Autumn Annals'. See Beckwith (2016a: 231–232 and note 5).

165. *Hua* is still, today, an element—the second character—of the official names of both the first Republic of China, Chung-*hua* min-kuo 中華民國 (which continues in Taiwan) and the second, the People's Republic of China, Chung-*hua* jen-min kung-ho-kuo 中華人民共和國, and in the compound *Hua-jen* 華人 (*Huárén*) 'Chinese (people)' it is still used in formal Mandarin today.

166. The Chou had a traditional monarchy which has widely been called "feudal" (e.g., Hsu 1999: 550, 586), but as medievalists have long pointed out, that early system is technically not really feudal. China did develop a feudal hierarchical system, thanks to Ch'in Shih huang ti's thorough reshaping of government in his new Chinese Empire, which boasted the same remarkable new Scythian features found in the Achaemenid Empire in the Middle East and in its close copy the Mauryan Empire in India, as pointed out by Miyazaki (1993: 128–129).

167. In the same passage Herodotus compares the "circular" (in Godley's translation) walls of Ecbatana to "the wall that surrounds the city of Athens" (Herodotus i 98,5b), using the same word, κύκλος, translated correctly by Godley in the

Athenian case as "surrounds", since everyone knew that Athens' fortifications were not "circular", though the Themistoclean Wall was roundish in plan, like a half-deflated, well-kicked balloon. The problematic passage (i 98,5b) on the city wall of Athens and the putative colors of the other walls of Ecbatana needs specialized study; I have replaced it with ellipses.

168. The Old Persian form of the name is written 𐏃𐎥𐎶𐎫𐎠𐎴 *<hgmtan>*, i.e., *Hagamatāna* or *Hagmatāna* or *Hagamtāna*, with initial *h*, unlike all other transcriptions. Unfortunately, the name is usually spelled by scholars as some, notably Schmitt (2014: 185–186), have etymologized it, i.e., *Haŋgmatāna or *Hamgmatāna, and it has then been interpreted to mean 'gathering place', based on this reconstruction. However, the reconstruction is problematic. The putative Old Iranic base form *ham-gam- ~ *ham-gmata- *does not actually occur* in Old Persian, nor does the doubtful *hangmatā-, according to the transcriptional citations (Sch. 57), and they *cannot* occur. The actual default reading of the Old Persian cuneiform must be *Hag(a)matāna*, even if it were underlyingly *Hamgmatāna, because Old Persian speakers could not pronounce a nasal before a stop. The name occurs twice in Old Persian, both times in paragraph 32 of Darius' Behistun Inscription (DB 276–278), both with the locative singular ending *-ay* (Schmitt 2009: 61; 2014: 57, 93, 185–186). The Old Persianized forms attested with <gm> or the like (principally the Elamite and Greek transcriptions) instead of <gam> are evidently all post-Darius, no doubt due to the Persians' continued use of Ecbatana as a summer capital. Nevertheless, there is no reflection of an original *ham- prefix before the participial form *gmata-* in any of the non-Persian transcriptions of the name (the languages of which do not have a constraint preventing pronunciation of a nasal before a stop). Young Avestan also has the reconstructed verb form *ham-gmata- (Sch. 179), but all actual attested examples of it are built on a different stem, *jasa-*, and *ham has become *han-* or *hən-* when prefixed to it (Bar. 501). (When the "prefix" occurs *separated* from the verb *in Avestan* it is *hąm* or *hə̄m.*) Thus, according to all hard data, the name had the prefix *a-* and the forms with *H* onset are Old Persian folk-etymologizations. The name was thus Scytho-Median (cf. the remarks of Sch. 186), but it had time to be folk-etymologized via the Old Iranic prefix *ham-*, which is common to both Avestan (Imperial Scythian) and Old Persian. Besides, the Scythians or their Scytho-Mede successors can hardly be imagined to have given their capital city—located in a Scytho-Median speaking region far from Pārsa—a *Persian* name instead of a Scythian or Scytho-Mede one.

As noted, the non-Persian evidence for the name in all other languages is unanimous against the word onset *h* occurring *in this name*. The Ancient Near Eastern languages and scripts that have an *h* and are capable of transcribing an onset *h* lack it in this word. In particular, Imperial Aramaic—the written literary language of the Empire—has a clear, distinct consonant *h* ה [h], which frequently occurs in onset position and contrasts phonemically with other onsets. If the name had an onset *h* it should be written with one in Aramaic; but Aramaic writes an *aleph*, a glottal stop consonant followed (in this case) by the default vowel *a*.

If the original name *Ag(a)matāna* had been perceived (perhaps by Persian speakers) as an underlying or already folk-etymologized *Hamgmatāna, it was clearly missing its initial *h*, so they added it, making the theoretical name *Hamg(a)matāna. Yet, as noted, Old Persian speakers could not pronounce any nasal before another consonant in inherited words or loanwords (they never write such nasals in the Old Persian inscriptions, and they are typically omitted in Elamite too), so the putative name *Hamg(a)matāna would actually have been pronounced by them as *Hag(a)matāna, which is exactly what we have in Old Persian script, *<hgmtan>*, i.e., *Hagamatāna* or *Hagmatāna*, not *Hamgmatāna or *Haŋmatāna as has been proposed.

However, *if the name were from an Imperial Scythian dialect* (as we should expect for the capital city of the Scytho-Mede people), the speakers should not have had any trouble pronouncing it as *Hamg(a)matāna or *Hang(a)matāna, as they could pronounce both initial *h* and nasals before stops. The fact that it is *not* so transcribed in any language, including Akkadian, Aramaic, Greek, Old Persian, etc., indicates the theory is wrong. The problem is putting the theory before the data. We must explain *the attested name* of a Scytho-Mede city which has no *h* (except in the Persian form) and has no nasal before the *g*. If the reconstruction were right, the Imperial Scythian form should have retained both the *h* and the nasal. The conclusion must be that it did not have the prefix *ham* at all, but another one.

Young Avestan (Imperial Scythian), like Old Persian, has the verb *gam-* 'come' with the prefix *ā-*, making theoretical *ā-gam-* '(*heran*)*kommen* [come up, draw near]' (Sch. 94, 179, 186). Schmitt cites the putative participial form "*hangmatā*", but as noted, it actually does not exist in Old Persian; the text writes 𐏃𐎥𐎶𐎫𐎠𐎴𐎡𐎹 h-g-m-t-a-n-i-y *h(a)g(a)m(a)tānai* (Sch. 57) 'in Hag(a)m(a)tāna'. It is thus not that the Persian writing system had no letter for <m> or <n>, but that the Persian *language* did not allow a nasal in syllable coda position in contact with a following stop, as we can see in many faithful Elamite transcriptions of Old Persian forms. Imperial Scythian *ā-gam-* is actually attested in Old Avestan, specifically as *āgəmaṯ.tā* 'will reach/attain/partake of' (Bar. 497), which also confirms the pronunciation of the syllable **gam* with undeleted *a* vowel (unstressed *ă*, i.e., schwa [ə]). It thus agrees with the Akkadian transcription *Agamatana* <A-ga-ma-ta-nu> and is solidly confirmed by the Aramaeo-Sogdian transcription of the capital city name *Hsien-yang* 咸陽 (*Xiányáng*) and the Chinese transcription of the name of the capital of Chao, *Han-tan* 邯鄲 (*Hándān*), as presented and analyzed in Chapter 8. The Median city's name is thus a Scythian word for 'the capital' or 'the city' that was slightly modified in Old Persian. Under the Achaemenid rulers, who spoke Old Persian, the city continued to serve as the capital during the summer, so the Elamite and Greek transcriptions reflect the Old Persianized form *hagmatāna*, with no nasal before the *g* and deletion of the vowel *a* after the *g*. Nevertheless, the local (non-Persianized) pronunciation, without *H*, survived up until very recently; see Chapter 8.

169. Pul. 119, 70. Pulleyblank (1991a: 118–119) also gives an alternate Middle Chinese reading ☆ɣan for the first character, but a final *n in this word may be ruled out for *Old* Chinese, as the character's very well attested phonetic 甘 ☆kam (Pul. 102) has a clear coda ☆m. The motivation for the ☆n reading is undoubtedly assimilation of the coda ☆m of Middle Chinese ☆gam to the following coronal onset ☆t of Middle Chinese ☆tan in the spoken language *in this very word*, Han-tan 邯鄲 (*Hándān*), because *the characters only occur in this name*. The reverse directionality is impossible, i.e., the reading ☆ɣan cannot have become ☆ɣam, since all examples of pre–Middle Chinese coda *m canonically changed to *n* in Mandarin.

170. The strictly linguistic reconstruction of Old Chinese is currently in a state of flux, with several major discoveries in recent publications, especially Shimunek (2017a), Beckwith and Kiyose (2018), and other recent works in the References. The rules at the time of writing that are relevant to the topic under discussion here are: 1. a morpheme-initial *unstressed* open syllable vowel spirantizes a following voiced velar stop onset (i.e., making a *g into a *ɣ), or in other dialects nasalizes it (making a *g into an *ŋ) and the initial unstressed vowel is later deleted itself; 2. an *unstressed* vowel V̆ in the intersyllabic position in a string such as (C)VCV̆CV(C) is canonically deleted sometime *before* the Late Old Chinese period; 3. a final unstressed vowel V̆ in Late Old Chinese is deleted during the shift to Proto-Mandarin/pre–Middle Chinese (Beckwith 2017; Shimunek 2017a, 2017b, 2021: 66, note 3; Beckwith and Kiyose 2018). Note in addition that the symbol (*)*â* represents the Old Chinese /a/ vowel which became rounded to *ɔ or *o in Early Middle Chinese, and then, usually, became *u* in Mandarin, as long recognized in Chinese reconstruction.

171. The crucially important state of Chao, though often noted for being the first to adopt steppe people's innovations, remains largely unstudied, as does the historical significance of Ch'in Shih huang ti's birth and early life in Chao. See Chapter 7.

172. Each of these arguments aims to support one or another extra-philosophical agenda. In addition, all of the philosophers have been argued to be purely later *inventions*. It must be recognized that even absolutely rock-solid historical people of our own time (today), including both good and evil ones, have been mythologized to the point of divinization while still alive. For these four ancient individuals we have no concrete historical accounts, but only later mythologized ones. In both cases it is invalid to conclude that they did not exist. Modern scholars are rarely aware of the striking commonalities among our four philosophers' teachings, or of their other highly distinctive but shared features, which amount to history telling us to pay attention.

173. Many have contended that Anacharsis is purely legendary, and that his legend was shaped mainly by the Cynics, but Martin (1996) makes three important points which counter that view. He notes, "it is hard to believe that the

Herodotean Anacharsis bears no relation to the later figure of Cynic propaganda whom we see most clearly in the *Letters of Anacharsis*. Either there was an Anacharsis legend before Herodotus or not; if it existed before, he either ignored it and made up his own, modified the inherited version, or passed it down unchanged; if he did change it, of course, we cannot now on our evidence tell, but unless Herodotus himself was a Cynic—a possibility never imagined—we can be sure the Herodotean Anacharsis picture is not Cynic. And yet the odd thing is, there do not appear to be many shifts in the subsequent depiction of the Scythian." However, Herodotus himself tells us that one thing he wanted to find out about in Scythia was the truth about Anacharsis, so he did of course know at least one story about him. Because Cynicism did not exist until after Herodotus' time, the ideas of that school are irrelevant to Herodotus' picture of the philosopher. Martin's second important point is that Diogenes Laertius' "account does not make any overt claims for an affiliation between the Scythian and the Cynics (one would expect to see such claims in Book 6), nor does it give any hints that the Cynics wrote about him." Another important point Martin makes is that one striking, unique feature of the accounts of Anacharsis (particularly in *Epistle 1* of the *Letters*) is language, both his characteristic use of it and reference to his foreign accent. As Martin says, Anacharsis "problematizes" foreign speech. Martin also notes that Diogenes Laertius (1.101) says Anacharsis' way of speaking gave rise to the proverb, "Speech from the Scythians", because Anacharsis was outspoken. All this could of course have developed on its own based on a stock "foreigner" or "outsider" figure, for which many prototypes have been noted, including Homer's Odysseus, as Martin dutifully points out. Nevertheless, the bits of data on the language of Anacharsis agree with the man's remarkable, *unique* epithet (for a Greek philosopher), "the Scythian", and no other Greek philosopher is accused of not speaking like a Greek. Martin (like many others) states that Herodotus could not find any evidence of Anacharsis in Scythia, but he then notes that Herodotus (iv 76,6) actually says he did finally meet someone who knew about Anacharsis ("Tymnes, the deputy of Ariapeithes") and relates what he was told.

In general it would seem that in this case there is a cardinal rule to follow: when dealing with immigrants such as the Scythians living among peoples in different parts of Eurasia, it is necessary to examine what the different native peoples say about the immigrants to see if it is at all similar. In the case of the very early Scythian immigrants discussed here, what is shared is a distinctive philosophical viewpoint and characteristic way of analysis: Scythian philosophy.

174. Kingsley (1990), citing the 1923 work of Robin (1948: 37) on "Greek philosophy's indebtedness to the East" being "already clearly implied or overtly stated by Herodotus, Plato, Isocrates and Aristotle." Reluctance to accept that indebtedness still affects studies of Classical philosophy and history. Kingsley (1995: 188) notes further, "The fact is that almost all our knowledge of events in classical antiquity has been filtered through the medium of pro-Hellenic authors,

resulting in a massive Athenocentrism which has biased our surviving information about the ancient world on such a vast scale that even today it is scarcely ever questioned."

175. It is of course theoretically possible that the Sanskrit epithet *Śākyamuni* was inherited from his parents or ancestors who moved to some unknown location before he was born (in yet another unknown location), but that sort of speculation violates Ockham's Razor (the Principle of Economy) and is based on the absence of data. The traditional late story that he was born in or near Lumbini (in modern Nepal) has been disproven by Bareau (1987); cf. Beckwith (2015: 12–13).
176. The name Li Erh 李耳 (*Lǐ Ěr*) means 'Ear(s) Li'. It is obviously based on folk etymology and Sinification of Lao-tan 老聃 (*Lǎo Dān*), which is variously written but usually explained by folk etymology, based on the literal sense of the transcriptional characters, as meaning 'Old Long-ears'. Lao-tan occurs frequently in the *Chuangtzu* 莊子 (*Zhuāngzǐ*) and the *Han Fei-tzu* 韓非子 (*Hán Fēizǐ*). Therefore the bureaucrat *Li Erh*—both name and story—must be later than these two works.
177. The modern Mandarin readings are some two millennia younger than the Old Chinese readings. The transcription and reading of the name was corrected several times by Chinese scholars, both in Antiquity and again in the early medieval T'ang Dynasty, to give (in modern pronunciation) *K'ao-tan*. The reverse writing of the characters is noted by Mair (1990: 26). See Beckwith (2015: 118–121) for full details and references to the scholarly literature.
178. Cf. Starostin (1989: 590), with the alternate writing *tan* 耽 (*dān*) < OChi *təm—given by him with a long vowel, but as noted by Pulleyblank, Starostin reversed vowel length in his Old Chinese reconstructions, so his long vowels should (mostly) be short, and vice versa, thus *təm, i.e., with final short *ă: *tămă. Gāndhārī was the Prakrit (Middle Indic) dialect spoken in northwestern India on the frontier with Central Asia.
179. The recent discovery of the site of Shih-mao 石峁 (*Shímǎo*) in the Ordos (the northern part of the region inside the great northern bend of the Yellow River in Inner Mongolia), dated to ca. 2000 BC (Li et al. 2018), invalidates the traditional isolationist view of the development of East Asian civilization.
180. Unfortunately, text philologists are a rare breed today. Yet it is clear that all major literary works transmitted from Classical Antiquity have been affected by the long transmission process, so that virtually all of them have undergone deletion or loss of passages, incorporation of marginal annotations into the text, corruption of preserved passages, interpolations (passages added by later writers), and so on, as noted above.
181. It is often argued that the *Tao te ching* is a compilation of heterogenous origins, not originally a sole-authored work. One recent conclusion is that "the nature of Tao and the application of Taoist insight to ethics and governance probably formed the twin foci in collections of Laotzu sayings from the start" (Chan

2018). The insightful survey of Shaughnessy (2005) concludes that scepticism is perhaps the best choice, while the current consensus denies that there was ever an original, coherent core work (Goldin 2020: 128).

However, the analyses have always assumed that the text was a *substantial* work from the very beginning. If that assumption were correct, it would no doubt raise the noted insurmountable problems concerning authorship. We have no reason to make such an assumption. Looking at what we do have, it would seem that a philosophical theory on "the nature of Tao" would necessarily have *preceded* any application of its "Taoist insight" to "governance", and that is how the received text actually starts out. Nevertheless, the most striking passages in the entire book are actually about ethical antilogies and their logical analysis. They are hardly mentioned by most scholars today, who (like the ancient Chinese) are mainly interested in the political topics, yet the reverse directionality—from government to epistemology to logic—is unlikely in the extreme. In view of the work's clear Western connections, discussed in the Epilogue, it appears that whatever authorship model is accepted, the heart of the work is its timeless logical-epistemological chapters, which focus on ethics, certainly not the chapters on 4th century BC Chinese politics, which apply the logical-epistemological-ethical chapters' teachings to government. It is notable that the preserved works of Anacharsis, Zoroaster, and Gautama Buddha also have no *internal* anchors in time or space. They are timeless works, and any political ramifications of their teachings developed long after their appearance. Some accounts, including Chan (2018), conclude in reference to the universal logical-epistemological-ethical chapters of the *Tao te ching*, "The emphasis on naturalness translates into a way of life characterized by simplicity, calmness, and freedom from the tyranny of desire (e.g., Liu Xiaogan 1997)." (N.B.: quotations from Chan are reformatted to fit the style of this book.) That famous Taoist message, the core of the book, is *precisely* the message of the Buddha.

Our received *Tao te ching* as a whole (like the recently discovered early manuscript versions) is to be sure undoubtedly an accretional "growth text", not the work of a single author, and many writers contributed to it over the period of its formation and transmission. Yet without an original kernel, an actual text, however short, there would not have been anything to which any potential additions could accrete. Moreover, the authors would perforce have shared such closely similar ideas and viewpoints that they would have belonged to the same school of thought anyway. That would require Laotzu to have existed first, taught a number of people his very unusual and difficult to understand ideas, and disappeared. His students would then have written the short, foundational school text that they wanted or needed (the eventual *Tao te ching*), by writing down the wise oral teachings of their master to the best of their abilities. They and their own students, as well as later Taoists, gradually contributed more to the original core work. Yet it is proverbial that the students of great philosophical and religious teachers do not understand their master, so we would expect there to be many misunderstood misrememberings, followed by confusion and increasingly religious mystical developments, which is to a great extent exactly what we do have. In any case, Laotzu the person would still be needed.

Another possibility is that some early sages invented Laotzu and made up the *Tao te ching* for fun or profit. It is easy to imagine some old geezers who called themselves "Taoists" sitting under a picturesquely twisted Chinese pine tree, drinking themselves silly and laughing as they came up with sagely maxim after sagely maxim. It is also somehow a very Taoist idea that Laotzu, the author of the *Tao te ching* and founder of Taoism, did not even exist: *Poof!* We like such conspiracy theories because they sound truly human and believable, and a little magical, too.

Nevertheless, the multi-author theories contrast with the equally human and even more realistic theory that there was one unique, unusually perceptive person, a genius who stood out from all other people of his time and place. Let us call him "Laotzu". He established the philosophical tradition in an original core text, which was no doubt *very* short, as is the core teaching of the Buddha quoted in the Epilogue, as well as the one accepted genuine teaching of Anacharsis, also quoted. *Short* means *easily memorized* and *accurately transmitted*. So Laotzu's students, and many others later on, added to this core teaching, eventually creating the *Tao te ching*, an unprecedented, unique, stunning work, difficult to understand. It has been famous since Antiquity and is still, today, unprecedented, unique, stunning, and difficult to understand, whether in Chinese or in translation. Yet it is the single most famous Chinese book.

Is it really conceivable that a random assortment of writers who *did not know each other* contributed to an anonymous compilation of contributions, like a modern collective volume of scholars' articles, and unexpectedly produced an unprecedented work of genius? Or that a group of writers, effectively a committee, composed an anonymous work which turned out to be an unprecedented work of genius? I think there is not a single instance in world history of a work of genius being written by a committee or a random collection of authors, and no matter how important some collections of articles may be, none of them are works of genius. Rather, all works of genius are written, or at least begun, by individual geniuses. And in fact, not one of the other early Chinese philosophers or the works attributed to them have achieved such great fame or attracted any following among non-scholars in China, not to speak of other parts of the world. Only Laotzu has done so. The age-old Chinese governmental support for Confucius and the government-fixated Confucians is no exception, at least at the level of Philosophy.

But by no means is the received *Tao-te Ching* full of brilliant, insightful thinking throughout. Most of it is highly derivative, and like other Classical philosophical works, much of it is about politics. So the book has grown by accretion of anonymous additions to a core work of genius, and probably only a very small part of the original work has survived. (The originals of many Chinese—and Greek—philosophical works are mostly or completely lost.) Since the accretions are the contributions of many other writers, and most writers are very far from being literary or philosophical geniuses, it is not surprising that many passages even in the *Tao-te Ching* seem to be rather poorly thought through. But again, those passages are as a whole completely different in character and topic from what is proposed here as the small original core or kernel of the work. The same is true for the other great Taoist work from the following generation, the *Chuangtzu*, a work that has been formed by accretion to a brilliant core.

Moreover, we cannot forget Ockham's Razor, which tells us to choose the theory that is the most economical solution for a problem. We should also not forget Sturgeon's Law, which tells us that the vast majority of authors are not very good, so that a longer list of authors only means a deeper deposit of sludge. It is unquestionable that the text—like all ancient and medieval texts, whether sole-authored or not—has changed over time and transmission, thus accounting for much of the variation of every kind seen in the book, certainly including many questionable additions.

Returning to the issue of whether the text *started out* that way—without any original core—as some would claim, such a conjecture is not supportable by the text itself. It is unlikely, even unimaginable, that the author of the logical-epistemological core of the work is responsible for the political (governmental-bureaucratic) parts too. The logical-epistemological chapters focus on ethical concepts, so not surprisingly the ethical concerns inspired those who wrote the political chapters. The reverse directionality makes no sense.

Like all other ancient Chinese works, changes were made to the original text or texts very early. It was famous in the Classical period, so during its transmission by hand from manuscript copy to manuscript copy around ancient China it was much altered, even if unintentionally, before one copy was buried in a tomb at Guodian dated archaeologically and historically to ca. 300 BC, while other copies continued to circulate, some of them were buried in later tombs (such as the ones dated ca. 200 BC found at Mawangdui), and so on. There may well be even earlier copies that have not yet been discovered. Between the many excavated or "discovered" (not continuously transmitted) manuscripts of the book, as well as the transmitted versions, there are substantial differences. They are, no doubt, what has given rise to the doubtful idea of "multiple authorship".

That idea certainly did not appear as a result of critical edition of the Chinese text, since (as far as I know) there is still not a single scientific critical edition of a Chinese text of any kind, there is not even an established word for "critical edition" in Chinese, and most Sinologists do not know what an actual "critical edition" is. As ancient Chinese scholars would say, these are 三可憂 'three worrisome points'. (However, the *Tao te ching* would frankly be a daunting choice for a first critical edition; a better choice would be a T'ang Dynasty work or another medieval work that is well attested in early manuscripts and xylographs. There are many deserving candidates.) The Classical period was a time of change in all aspects of Chinese civilization, so that even the earliest Laotzu manuscript so far known, from Guodian, is already composite in nature; but that does not mean the original text had no foundational core.

182. Most translations—e.g., the scholarly variant translations quoted in Nivison (1999: 803)—treat all the nouns as if they were equally verbs, and vice versa. Certainly one can find famous examples that seem to do just that, but there are two parallel lines here, and the grammatical functions are clear. They also suggest greater care in the use of English articles. In *Tao te ching* Chapter 1 and Chapter 2A (Guodian *Laotzu* Chapter A:9) quoted below, the inferences that are drawn from these statements seem to have the mystical character that is typical of much of the book, but the logic is primary, and study of comparative philosophy suggests that the mystical character is a normal, *later*, development.

183. It would seem to confirm the often proposed Indian influence in early China at the time of Laotzu, presumably to be expected based on his Indic or Iranic name *Gudama ~ *Gautama, as discussed above. However, though it is usually assumed that such meditation is native Indian in origin, there is not the slightest indication of anything meditational or yoga-like in the Rig-Veda. That suggests such practices are late and could have been introduced to India from another culture, in which case it is quite possible that the Buddha practiced a form of meditation he had already learned in Scythia, or from Scythians.

184. Did "weak" and "innocent" Chinese, Romans, etc. conquer huge empires by accident, or by kindness? There is no excuse for the continuing demonization of early Central Eurasian peoples as "barbarians" rather than as people (with the good and the bad) like everyone else. For a thorough critique see Beckwith (2009: 320–362). Some dislike that chapter and the chapters on Modernism (with examples taken from the arts) too, not surprisingly because both deal with cruel realities and contemporary historians' (and others') determination to perpetuate them.

185. Many modern historians do not want wide-ranging history that explains things beyond (or even including) their own narrow specializations. However, the world is not simple. It is complex on many levels, not only the close-up level of institutional or "bureaucratic" history, the field of most academic historians today. Yet their studies are hardly meaningful without being placed in a broader context, and it is doubtful that one can do so by attempting to base it solely on bureaucratic-level materials.

The field of history needs to understand things at all significant discernible levels, from the finest to the broadest. Scholars who have shouted down the old Axial Age theory of Karl Jaspers for the past half century or so have done it at the deepest bureaucratic level: the bureaucrat railing at the philosopher. But Jaspers' theory was not and is not a bureaucratic-level theory. It is a "world" or "global" type of theory. We therefore need to respect the early scholars who noticed that something important happened on a Eurasian *continental* scale, even though they themselves could not explain it because they did not have enough of the poor data then available, and because they did not in any case have the requisite historical, philological, and linguistic skills to treat the subject properly. We do not have a tremendous amount of new data today, but we do have some, plus some good scholarship on many related topics.

186. Claims that the "Japan rule" falsifies this principle are erroneous. In the mid-19th century Japan "modernized" and became European in many cultural respects, including warfare, clothing style, state organization, and to a great extent, language. Modern Japanese is full of European loanwords, mainly from English; it is often said that essentially the entire lexicon of English became an open book available for use by Japanese. But this did not happen in isolation or because the Japanese had read Dutch books *about* European culture or about English. It happened because American warships blasted their way into Tokyo Bay and forcibly opened the country to the outside world. The Americans were followed immediately by many other people from European or Europeanized countries, and they dominated Japan directly, in person, for a full generation, long enough for cultural creolization to take place. The same Europeanization, or modernization, happened (if not as dramatically) all along the littoral of Asia, where Europeans and their offspring dominated the local peoples, and in many places ruled over them.

The key event can be characterized as "Europeanization" in recognition of its source and the means of transmission—direct European rule or domination by Europeans and European-Americans in Asia over the peoples of the Asian littoral. That event coincided with the first and most powerful blow of Modernism, a radical European movement that first took shape in Europe in the mid-18th century, with the American and French revolutions. Modernism struck traditional European (and European-American) civilization full force only at the end of the 19th century and beginning of the 20th. It was most obviously signaled by the destruction or sidelining of all traditional elite art traditions and their replacement by non-elite or anti-elite forms of non-art or anti-art, as pointed out previously (Beckwith 2009: 263–319). The thoroughness of the radical changes, as well as their localization at that time only to regions under European rule or domination, is significant.

In short, the changes that took place in Japan in the mid-19th century exactly paralleled the changes that took place in regions under Scythian rule or domination: both affected warfare, clothing style, state organization, and language. The changes in both places and times happened for the same reason. The "Japan rule" is a principle that does not conform to the data.

187. Schmitt (2002a) says, "The only point universally agreed upon is that the second element is Av. *uštra-* 'camel' (it is found in other anthroponyms also)." In a linguistic milieu where languages and dialects interacted rather intensely, these arguments (including the parenthetical one) are not convincing. They do not explain one of the chief morphophonological obstacles to his and other proposals: the phone θ (th), or the syllable θu, in the middle of the name *Zarathushtra*. However, names, like other words, tend to be folk-etymologized and reshaped

to agree with more frequent similar words, so that loanwords, including names, better fit speakers' native language. In view of the problems with his chosen etymology, Schmitt suggests, "It is more reasonable to regard the name as reflecting a dialectal origin of not genuine Avestan form."

188. Skjærvø (2006) continues, "The Old Avestan text exhibits a few morphological features that have led scholars to assume that the two Avestan languages are separate dialects descended from proto-Avestan. The evidence is scarce, however, and not compelling; it is quite possible that these special features belong to the transmission, rather than the composition, stage of the texts." However, he also remarks, "On the other hand, Young Avestan and Old Persian have features in common (e.g., the 3rd person pronominal stem *di-* and the use of the augmented optative as past narrative tense), which give the impression of being common innovations." It is perhaps more likely that they are evidence of mutual influence via extensive borrowing, as is clear in the case of Middle Persian.

189. We can only assume that while the Greeks no doubt sometimes made conscious attempts to transcribe the foreign words in question according to their Greek perceptions of them, at other times they partly translated them into Greek, or they converted the foreign words to similar-sounding Greek words (as Schmitt has shown), with the apparent goal of making them more accessible to Greek readers, or they used already created "Greek" forms of the words. We simply cannot expect pervasive regularity. When the identity of the things or people or semantics in question is clear, and the forms are close (for Greek), we assume that they do in fact transcribe the same underlying words, no matter how poorly they sometimes do it. The Old Persian transcriptions are often not much better than the Greek ones.

190. Cunliffe (2020) compares them to artistic portrayals from the Pontic Steppe (West Scythian). The book provides excellent photographs, many in color, showing the great variety of materials and methods of workmanship, as well as the high quality and tailored character of the Pazyryk finds, many of which are still brightly colored and in general extraordinarily well preserved.

REFERENCES

Abdi, Kamyar. 2001. Malyan 1999. *Iran* 39: 73–98.

Adams, Douglas Q. 1999. *A Dictionary of Tokharian B*. Amsterdam: Rodopi.

Alekseyev, A. Yu. 2005. Scythian Kings and 'Royal' Burial-Mounds of the Fifth and Fourth Centuries BC. In: David Braund, ed. *Scythians and Greeks: Cultural Interactions in Scythia, Athens and the Early Roman Empire*. Exeter: University of Exeter Press, 39–55.

Allsen, Thomas T. 1997. Ever Closer Encounters: The Appropriation of Culture and the Apportionment of Peoples in the Mongol Empire. *Journal of Early Modern History* 1.1: 2–23.

———. 2002. *Commodity and Exchange in the Mongol Empire*. Cambridge: Cambridge University Press.

———. 2006. *The Royal Hunt in Eurasian History*. Philadelphia: University of Pennsylvania Press.

Álvarez-Món, Javier. 2009. Notes on the 'Elamite' Garment of Cyrus the Great. *The Antiquities Journal* 89: 21–33.

Arnason, J. P. and S. N. Eisenstadt, B. Wittrock. 2005. *Axial Civilizations and World History*. Leiden: Brill.

Apte, Vaman Shivaram. 1978. *The Practical Sanskrit-English Dictionary*. Revised and enlarged edition. Kyoto: Rinsen. (Original edition: Poona, 1890.) Online.

Bäbler, Balbina. 2005. Bobbies or Boobies? The Scythian Police Force in Classical Athens. In: D. Braund, ed. *Scythians and Greeks. Cultural Interactions in Scythia, Athens and the Early Roman Empire*. Exeter: University of Exeter Press, 114–122.

Bachrach, Bernard S. 1973. *A History of the Alans in the West; from Their First Appearance in the Sources of Classical Antiquity through the Early Middle Ages*. Minneapolis: University of Minnesota Press.

Bailey, Harold W. 1967. *Indo-Scythian Studies*. Vol. 6. Cambridge: Cambridge University Press.

———. 1985. *Indo-Scythian Studies*. Vol. 7. Cambridge: Cambridge University Press.

Bang, W. and G. R. Rachmati. 1932. Die Legende von Oγuz Qaγan. *Sitzungsberichte der Preussischen Akademie der Wissenschaften. Philosophisch-Historische Klasse* 15: 683–724.

Bareau, André. 1987. Lumbinī et la naissance du futur Buddha. *Bulletin de l'École Française d'Extrême-Orient* 76: 69–81.

Barnes, Jonathan, ed. 1984. *The Complete Works of Aristotle*. 2 Vols. Princeton: Princeton University Press.

Bartholomae, Christian. 1904. *Altiranisches Wörterbuch*. Photomechanically reprinted. Berlin: Walter de Gruyter, 1961. (= Bar.)

Baumann, Brian. 2012. Whither the Ocean? The Talu Dalai in Sultan Öljeitü's 1305 Letter to Philip the Fair of France. *Archivum Eurasiae Medii Aevi* 19: 59–80.

Baums, Stefan and Andrew Glass. 2020. *A Dictionary of Gāndhārī*. https://gandhari.org/dictionary.

Baxter, William H. 1992. *A Handbook of Old Chinese Phonology*. Berlin: Mouton de Gruyter.

Beaulieu, Paul-Alain, trans. 2007/2020. Nabonidus Cylinder from Sippar. Livius.org. https://www.livius.org/sources/content/nabonidus-cylinder-from-sippar/.

Beck, Ulrike and Mayke Wagner, Xiao Li, Desmond Durkin-Meisterernst, Pavel E. Tarasov. 2014. The Invention of Trousers and Its Likely Affiliation with Horseback Riding and Mobility: A Case Study of Late 2nd Millennium BC Finds from Turfan in Eastern Central Asia. *Quaternary International* 348 (October 20): 224–235.

Beckwith, Christopher I. 1984a. Aspects of the Early History of the Central Asian Guard Corps in Islam. *Archivum Eurasiae Medii Aevi* 4: 29–43. Reprinted in C. Edmund Bosworth, ed. *The Turks in the Early Islamic World*. Aldershot: Ashgate, 2007, 275–289.

———. 1984b. The Plan of the City of Peace: Central Asian Iranian Factors in Early 'Abbâsid Design. *Acta Orientalia Academiae Scientiarum Hungaricae* 38: 128–147.

———. 1993. *The Tibetan Empire in Central Asia: A History of the Struggle for Great Power among Tibetans, Turks, Arabs, and Chinese during the Early Middle Ages*. Princeton: Princeton University Press, revised edition (first edition, 1987).

———. 1996. The Morphological Argument for the Existence of Sino-Tibetan. *Pan-Asiatic Linguistics: Proceedings of the Fourth International Symposium on Languages and Linguistics, January 8–10, 1996*. Bangkok: Mahidol University at Salaya, Vol. 3: 812–826.

———. 2005. On the Chinese Names for Tibet, Tabghatch, and the Turks. *Archivum Eurasiae Medii Aevi* 14: 5–20.

———. 2006. The Sonority Sequencing Principle and Old Tibetan Syllable Margins. In: C. I. Beckwith, ed. *Medieval Tibeto-Burman Languages II*. Leiden: Brill, 45–55.

———. 2007a. *Koguryo, the Language of Japan's Continental Relatives: An Introduction to the Historical-Comparative Study of the Japanese-Koguryoic Languages, with a Preliminary Description of Archaic Northeastern Middle Chinese*. Leiden: Brill, 2nd ed. (first edition, 2004).

———. 2007b. On the Proto-Indo-European Obstruent System. *Historische Sprachforschung* 120: 1–19.

———. 2007c. *Phoronyms: Classifiers, Class Nouns, and the Pseudopartitive Construction*. New York: Peter Lang.

———. 2008. Old Chinese Loanwords in Tibetan and the Non-uniqueness of 'Sino-Tibetan'. In: C. I. Beckwith, ed. *Medieval Tibeto-Burman Languages III*. Halle: IITBS GmbH, 161–201.

———. 2009. *Empires of the Silk Road: A History of Central Eurasia from the Bronze Age to the Present*. Princeton: Princeton University Press.

———. 2010. A Note on the Heavenly Kings of Ancient Central Eurasia. *Archivum Eurasiae Medii Aevi* 17: 7–10.

———. 2012a. *Warriors of the Cloisters: The Central Asian Origins of Science in the Medieval World*. Princeton: Princeton University Press.

———. 2012b. On Zhangzhung and Bon. In: H. Blezer, ed. *Emerging Bon*. Halle: IITBS GmbH, 164–184.

———. 2014. The Aramaic Source of the East Asian Word for 'Buddhist Monastery': On the Spread of Central Asian Monasticism in the Kushan Period. *Journal Asiatique* 302.1: 111–138.

———. 2015. *Greek Buddha: Pyrrho's Encounter with Early Buddhism in Central Asia*. Princeton: Princeton University Press.

———. 2016a. The Earliest Chinese Words for 'the Chinese': The Phonology, Meaning, and Origin of the Epithet *Ḥarya ~ Ārya* in East Asia. *Journal Asiatique* 304.2: 231–248.

———. 2016b. The Pronunciation, Origin, and Meaning of *A-shih-na* in Early Old Turkic. In: István Zimonyi and Osman Karatay, eds. *Central Eurasia in the Middle Ages: Studies in Honour of Peter B. Golden*. Turcologica 104. Wiesbaden: Harrassowitz, 39–46.

———. 2017. Once Again on the Aramaic Word for 'Monastery' in East Asia. *Journal Asiatique* 2017.2: 211–227.

———. 2018. On the Ethnolinguistic Identity of the Hsiung-nu. In: Zsuzsanna Gulacsi, ed. *Language, Government, and Religion in the World of the Turks: Festschrift for Larry Clark at Seventy-Five*. Brepols: Turnhout, 33–55.

———. 2020. Vihāras in the Kushan Empire. In: Richard E. Payne and Rhyne King, eds. *The Limits of Empire in Ancient Afghanistan: Rule and Resistance in the Hindu Kush, circa 600 BCE–600 CE*. Classica et Orientalia 24. Wiesbaden: Harrassowitz, 157–167.

———. Forthcoming-a. On *gtsug-lag khang* 'monastery, *vihāra*'. In: Kurtis Schaeffer, William McGrath, and Jue Liang, eds. *Festschrift for Leonard W. J. van der Kuijp*.

———. Forthcoming-b. *Biblical Imperial Aramaic: An Introduction Based on Authentic Texts*. Wiesbaden: Harrassowitz.

Beckwith, Christopher I. and Gisaburo N. Kiyose†. 2018. Apocope of Late Old Chinese Short *ă: Early Central Asian Loanword and Old Japanese Evidence for Old Chinese Disyllabic Morphemes. *Acta Orientalia Academiae Scientiarum Hungaricae* 71.2: 145–160.

Beckwith, Christopher I. and Öner Özçelik, Andrew E. Shimunek. The Sons of Attila and the Hunnish Language: Analysis of the Earliest Turkic Language Data (under review).

Beckwith, Christopher I. and Michael L. Walter. 2010. On the Meaning of Old Tibetan *rje-blon* during the Tibetan Empire Period. *Journal Asiatique* 298.2: 535–548.

Beekes, Robert S. P. 2011. *Comparative Indo-European Linguistics: An Introduction*. Amsterdam: John Benjamins.

Behr, Wolfgang. 2007. Xià: Etymologisches zur Herkunft des ältesten chinesischen Staatsnamens. *Asiatische Studien/Etudes asiatiques* 60.3: 727–754.

Bellah, Robert N. and Hans Joas, eds. 2012. *The Axial Age and Its Consequences*. Cambridge, MA: Harvard University Press.

Benveniste, Émile. 1958. Les données iraniennes. *Journal Asiatique* 246: 36–48.

———. 1966. *Titres et noms propres en iranien ancien*. Paris: C. Klincksieck.

Bielmeier, R. 1989. Sarmatisch, Alanisch, Jassisch und Altossetisch. In: R. Schmitt, ed. *Compendium Linguarum Iranicarum*. Wiesbaden: Reichert, 236–245.

Boardman, John, et al. 1988. Preface. In: John Boardman et al., eds. *The Cambridge Ancient History*, 2nd ed. Vol. 4. Cambridge: Cambridge University Press, xvii–xxi.

Bodde, Derk. 1986. The State and Empire of Ch'in. In: Denis Twitchett and Michael Loewe, eds. *The Cambridge History of China*. Cambridge: Cambridge University Press, 1: 52–72.

Boucharlat, Rémy. 2001. The Palace and the Royal Achaemenid City: Two Case Studies—Pasargadae and Susa. In: Inge Nielsen, ed. *The Royal Palace Institution in the First Millennium BC: Regional Development and Cultural Interchange between East and West.* Athens: The Danish Institute at Athens, 113–123.

———. 2013. Other Works of Darius and His Successors. In: J. Perrot, ed. *The Palace of Darius at Susa: The Great Royal Residence of Achaemenid Persia.* London: I. B. Tauris, 359–408.

Boyce, Mary. 1984. Ahura Mazdā. *Encyclopædia Iranica,* online, revised 2011.

———. 2000. Fravaši. *Encyclopædia Iranica,* online, revised 2012.

———. 2003. Haoma ii. The Rituals. *Encyclopædia Iranica,* online, revised 2012.

Boyce, Mary and M. L. Chaumont, C. Bier. 1989. Anāhīd. *Encyclopædia Iranica,* online, revised 2011.

Boyce, Mary. 1975. *A History of Zoroastrianism.* Vol. 1. *The Early Period.* Leiden: Brill.

———. 1982. *A History of Zoroastrianism.* Vol. 2. *Under the Achaemenians.* Leiden: Brill.

Boyce, Mary and Frantz Grenet. 1991. *A History of Zoroastrianism.* Vol. 3. *Zoroastrianism under Macedonian and Roman Rule.* Leiden: Brill.

Bracey, Robert. 2017. The Date of Kanishka since 1960. *Indian Historical Review* 44.1: 1–41.

Brentjes, Burchard. 2006. Anahita. *Brill's New Pauly,* online.

Briant, Pierre. 2002. *From Cyrus to Alexander: A History of the Persian Empire.* Winona Lake, IN: Eisenbrauns. Translation of *Histoire de l'Empire perse: De Cyrus à Alexandre.* Paris: Fayard, 1996.

Brooks, E. Bruce and A. Taeko Brooks. 1998. *The Original Analects.* New York: Columbia University Press.

———. 2015. *The Emergence of China: From Confucius to the Empire.* Amherst: Warring States Project.

Brosius, M. 2007. New out of Old? Court and Court Ceremonies in Achaemenid Persia. In: A. J. S. Spawforth, ed. *The Court and Court Society in Ancient Monarchies.* Cambridge: Cambridge University Press, 17–57.

Brosseder, Ursula B. 2018. Hiongnu and Huns: Archaeological Perspectives on a Centuries-Old Debate about Identity and Migration. In: Nicola Di Cosmo and Michael Maas, eds. *Empires and Exchanges in Eurasian Late Antiquity.* Cambridge: Cambridge University Press, 176–187.

Brown, Stuart S. 2011. Ecbatana. *Encyclopædia Iranica,* online.

Bukharin, M. D. 2013. К дискуссии о языке скифов: переход др.ир. *xš- > *s- и его отражение в древнегреческом. [Transition of Old Iranian *xš- > *s- and Its Reflection in Ancient Greek as an Issue of Debate on Scythian Language.] Проблемы Истории, Филологии, Культуры = *Journal of Historical, Philological and Cultural Studies* 40.2: 263–285.

Bywater, J., ed. 1894. *Aristotle's Ethica Nicomachea.* Oxford: Clarendon Press, online.

Calmeyer, Peter. 1982–1983. Zur Genese altiranischer Motive: VIII—Die 'Statistische Landcharte des Perserreiches'. *Archaeologische Mitteilungen aus Iran* 15: 105–187; 16: 141–222.

Campbell, Lyle. 2013. *Historical Linguistics: An Introduction.* 3rd ed. Edinburgh: Edinburgh University Press.

Caspari, Gino and Timur Sadykov, Jegor Blochin, Irka Hajdas. 2018. Tunnug 1 (Arzhan 0)—An Early Scythian Kurgan in Tuva Republic, Russia. *Archaeological Research in Asia* 15: 82–87.

Chan, Alan. 2018. Laozi. *The Stanford Encyclopedia of Philosophy,* online.

Chang, Kwang-chih. 1999. China on the Eve of the Historical Period. In: Michael Loewe and Edward L. Shaughnessy, eds. *The Cambridge History of Ancient China: From the Origins of Civilization to 221 B.C.* Cambridge: Cambridge University Press, 37–73.

Chavannes, Edouard, trans. Ssŭma Ch'ien. 1897. *Les Mémoires Historiques*. 2, Chapitres V–XII. Paris: Leroux.

Chugunov, K. and H. Parzinger, A. Nagler. 2010. *Der skythenzeitliche Fürstenkurgan Aržan 2 in Tuva*. Archäologie in Eurasien, Bd. 26. Mainz: Verlag Philipp von Zabern.

Clauson, Gerard. 1972. *An Etymological Dictionary of Pre-Thirteenth-Century Turkish*. Oxford: Clarendon.

Cornillot, François. 1981. Origine du nom des Scythes. *Indo-Iranian Journal* 23.1: 29–39.

Cunliffe, Barry. 2020. *The Scythians: Nomad Warriors of the Steppe*. Oxford: Oxford University Press.

Curtis, John and St John Simpson, eds. 2010. *The World of Achaemenid Persia*. London: I. B. Tauris.

Curtis, Vesta Sarkhosh and Sarah Stewart, eds. 2005. *Birth of the Persian Empire*. London: I. B. Tauris.

Dandamaev (Dandamayev), M. A. 1989. *A Political History of the Achaemenid Empire*. Tr. W. J. Vogelsang. Leiden: Brill.

Dandamayev, M. A. 2012. Magi. *Encyclopædia Iranica*, online.

Dandamayev, M. A. and È. Grantovskiĭ. 2012. ASSYRIA i. The Kingdom of Assyria and Its Relations with Iran. *Encyclopædia Iranica*, online.

Dandamayev, M. A. and I. Medvedskaya. 2006. Media. *Encyclopædia Iranica*, online.

Davis, Stuart. 1998. Syllable Contact in Optimality Theory. *Korea Journal of Linguistics* 23: 181–211.

de Jong, Albert. 2010. Ahura Mazdā the Creator. In: John Curtis and St John Simpson, eds. *The World of Achaemenid Persia*. London: I. B. Tauris, 85–89.

Diachenko, Aleksandr 2023. Cultural Diversity, Convergence and Transmission Scales. ARWA North Pontic & Southeast Balkans Lecture Series, online lecture.

Diakonoff, Igor. 1956. История Мидии от древнейших времен до конца 4 в. до н.э. [History of Media from earliest times to the late 4th c. BC.] Moscow & Leningrad.

———. 1981. The Cimmerians. *Monumentum Georg Morgenstierne* I, Acta Iranica 21. Leiden: Brill, 103–140.

———. 1985. Media. In: Ilya Gershevitch, ed. *The Cambridge History of Iran*. Vol. 2. *The Median and Achaemenian Periods*. Cambridge: Cambridge University Press, 36–148.

Di Cosmo, Nicola. 1999. The Northern Frontier in Pre-imperial China. In: Michael Loewe and Edward L. Shaughnessy, eds. *The Cambridge History of Ancient China: From the Origins of Civilization to 221 B.C.* Cambridge: Cambridge University Press, 885–966.

———. 2002. *Ancient China and Its Enemies: The Rise of Nomadic Power in East Asian History*. Cambridge: Cambridge University Press.

———. 2018. Maligned Exchanges: The Uyghur-Tang Trade in the Light of Climate Data. In: Haun Saussy, ed. *Texts and Transformations: Essays in Honor of the 75th Birthday of Victor H. Mair*. Amherst, NY: Cambria Press, 117–132.

Doerfer, Gerhard. 1967. *Türkische und Mongolische Elemente im Neupersischen*. Wiesbaden: Franz Steiner Verlag.

Drews, Robert. 1973. *The Greek Accounts of Eastern History*. Washington, DC: Center for Hellenic Studies.

———. 2004. *Early Riders: The Beginnings of Mounted Warfare in Asia and Europe*. London: Routledge.

Drompp, Michael. 2005. *Tang China and the Collapse of the Uighur Empire: A Documentary History*. Leiden: Brill.

Eisenstadt, S. N., ed. 1986. *The Origins and Diversity of Axial Age Civilizations*. Albany: State University of New York Press.

Fakour, Mehrdad. 2012. Garden i. Achaemenid Period. *Encyclopædia Iranica*, online.

Finkelstein, Israel and Neil Asher Silberman. 2001. *The Bible Unearthed: Archaeology's New Vision of Ancient Israel and the Origin of Its Sacred Texts*. New York: The Free Press.

Frye, Richard N. 2010. Cyrus the Mede and Darius the Achaemenid? In: John Curtis and St John Simpson, eds. *The World of Achaemenid Persia*. London: I. B. Tauris, 17–19.

Garrett, Andrew. 1999. A New Model of Indo-European Subgrouping and Dispersal. In Steve S. Chang, Lily Liaw, and Josef Ruppenhofer, eds. *Proceedings of the Twenty-Fifth Annual Meeting of the Berkeley Linguistics Society, February 12–15, 1999*, 146–156.

Georg, Stefan. 2007. *A Descriptive Grammar of Ket (Yenisei-Ostyak)*. Vol. 1. Introduction, Phonology, Morphology. Folkestone: Global Oriental.

Gershevitch, Ilya. 1964. Dialect Variation in Early Persian. *Transactions of the Philological Society* 63.1: 1–29.

Gethin, Rupert. 1998. *The Foundations of Buddhism*. Oxford: Oxford University Press.

Gharib, B. 1995. *Sogdian Dictionary: Sogdian-Persian-English*. Tehran: Ferhangan. (= Gharib)

Giele, Enno. 2010. The Hsiung-nu, Memoir 50. In: William H. Nienhauser Jr., ed. *The Grand Scribe's Records, Vol. IX: The Memoirs of Han China*. Part II. Bloomington: Indiana University Press, 237–310.

Gnoli, Gherardo. 2003. Agathias and the Date of Zoroaster. In: *Ērān ud Anērān: Webfestschrift Marshak*. http://www.transoxiana.org/Eran/Articles/gnoli.html.

Godley, A. D. 1920. *Herodotus, with an English translation*. Cambridge, MA: Harvard University Press. Perseus Digital Library, online.

Goldin, Paul R. 2020. *The Art of Chinese Philosophy: Eight Classical Texts and How to Read Them*. Princeton: Princeton University Press.

Gómez, Luis O. 1976. Proto-Mādhyamika in the Pāli Canon. *Philosophy East and West* 26.2: 137–165.

Gouskova, Maria. 2004. Relational Hierarchies in Optimality Theory: The Case of Syllable Contact. *Phonology* 21.2: 201–250.

Grant, Edward. 1996. *The Foundations of Modern Science in the Middle Ages*. Cambridge: Cambridge University Press.

———. 2007. *A History of Natural Philosophy: From the Ancient World to the Nineteenth Century*. Cambridge: Cambridge University Press.

Grantovskij, Èdvin A. 1970. Ранняя история иранских племен Передней Азии. 2nd ed. Moscow: Izdatel'skaja firma "Vostočnaja literatura" RAN, 2007.

Grenet, Frantz. 2003. *La geste d'Ardashir fils de Pâbag*. Die: Editions A Die.

Griffith, Mark. 2013. *Aristophanes' Frogs*. Oxford: Oxford University Press.

Gunter, Ann. 1982. Representations of Urartian and Western Iranian Fortress Architecture in the Assyrian Reliefs. *Iran* 20: 103–112.

Harmatta, János. 1994a. Languages and Scripts in Graeco-Bactria and the Saka Kingdoms. In: János Harmatta, G. F. Etemadi, and Baij Nath Puri, eds. *History of Civilizations of Central Asia*. Vol. 2. *The Development of Sedentary and Nomadic Civilizations: 700 B.C. to A.D. 250*. Paris: UNESCO, 397–416.

———. 1994b. Conclusion. In: János Harmatta, G. F. Etemadi, and Baij Nath Puri, eds. *History of Civilizations of Central Asia*. Vol. 2. *The Development of Sedentary and Nomadic Civilizations: 700 B.C. to A.D. 250*. Paris: UNESCO, 485–492.

Harper, Donald. 1999. Warring States Natural Philosophy and Occult Thought. In: Michael Loewe and Edward L. Shaughnessy, eds. *The Cambridge History of Ancient China: From the Origins of Civilization to 221 B.C.* Cambridge: Cambridge University Press, 813–884.

Henderson, Jeffrey. 2002. *Aristophanes: Frogs, Assemblywomen, Wealth*. Cambridge, MA: Harvard University Press.

Henkelman, Wouter F. M. 2003. Parthians, Medes and Elamites: Acculturation in the Neo-Elamite Period. In: G. B. Lanfranchi, Michael Roaf, and Robert Rollinger, eds. *Continuity of Empire (?). Assyria, Media, Persia. Proceedings of the International Meeting in Padua, 26th–28th April 2001*. History of the Ancient Near East Monographs V. Padova: S.a.r.g.o.n. editrice e libreria, 181–231 + pls. 9–15.

———. 2011. Cyrus the Persian and Darius the Elamite: A Case of Mistaken Identity. In: Robert Rollinger, Brigitte Truschnegg, and Reinhold Bichler, eds. *Herodot und das Persische Weltreich—Herodotus and the Persian Empire*. Wiesbaden: Harrassowitz, 577–634.

———. 2012. The Achaemenid Heartland: An Archaeological-Historical Perspective. In: D. T. Potts, ed. *A Companion to the Archaeology of the Ancient Near East*. 1st ed. Malden, MA: Wiley-Blackwell, 931–962.

Henkelman, Wouter F. M. and Matthew W. Stolper. 2009. Ethnic Identity and Ethnic Labelling at Persepolis: The Case of the Skudrians. In: *Organisation des pouvoirs et contacts culturels dans les pays de l'empire achéménide*. Actes du colloque organisé au Collège de France par la 'Chaire d'histoire et civilisation du monde achéménide et de l'empire d'Alexandre' et le 'Réseau international d'études et de recherches achéménides' (GDR 2538 CNRS), 9–10 novembre 2007, sous la direction de Pierre Briant et Michel Chauveau. Paris: De Boccard, 271–329.

Henricks, Robert G. 2000. *Lao Tzu's Tao Te Ching: A Translation of the Startling New Documents Found at Guodian*. New York: Columbia University Press.

Hicks, R. D. 1925. *Diogenes Laertius, Lives of Eminent Philosophers*. Cambridge, MA: Harvard University Press.

Hill, Nathan. 2009. Tibetan <ḥ> as a Plain Initial and Its Place in Old Tibetan Phonology. *Linguistics of the Tibeto-Burman Area* 32.1: 115–140.

Hintze, Almut. 2009. Avestan Literature. In: R. E. Emmerick and M. Macuch, eds. *The Literature of Pre-Islamic Iran*. (Companion Volume 1 to *A History of Persian Literature*.) London: I. B. Tauris, 1–71.

———. 2015. Zarathustra's Time and Homeland: Linguistic Perspectives. In: M. Stausberg et al., eds. *The Wiley Blackwell Companion to Zoroastrianism*. Oxford: John Wiley & Sons, 31–38.

Hinz, Walther. 1969. *Altiranische Funde und Forschungen*. Berlin: Walter de Gruyter.

Hinz, Walther and Heidemarie Koch. 1987. *Elamisches Wörterbuch*, 2 Teilen. Berlin: Dietrich Reimer Verlag.

Hoffmann, Karl. 1975–1976. *Aufsätze zur Indoiranistik*. 3 Vols. Wiesbaden: Reichert.

———. 1987. Avestan Language i–iii. *Encyclopædia Iranica*, online, revised 2011.

Horky, Phillip Sidney. 2009. Persian Cosmos and Greek Philosophy: Plato's Associates and the Zoroastrian Magoi. *Oxford Studies in Ancient Philosophy* 37: 47–103.

Hsu Cho-yun. 1999. The Spring and Autumn Period. In: Michael Loewe and Edward L. Shaughnessy, eds. *The Cambridge History of Ancient China: From the Origins of Civilization to 221* B.C. Cambridge: Cambridge University Press, 545–586.

Humbach, Helmut and Pallan Ichaporia. 1994. *The Heritage of Zarathushtra: A New Translation of His Gāthās*. Heidelberg: Universitätsverlag C. Winter.

Hung, Wu. 1999. The Art and Architecture of the Warring States Period. In: Michael Loewe and Edward L. Shaughnessy, eds. *The Cambridge History of Ancient China: From the Origins of Civilization to 221* B.C. Cambridge: Cambridge University Press, 651–744.

Ivantchik, Askold. 2018. Scythians. *Encyclopædia Iranica*, online.

Jacobs, Bruno. 1982. Persepolisdelegationen und Satrapienordnung. *Acta Praehistorica et Archaeologica* 13/14: 75–84.

———. 2006. Achaemenid Satrapies: The Administrative Units of the Achaemenid Empire. *Encyclopædia Iranica*, online, revised 2011.

Jaspers, Karl. 1949a. *Vom Ursprung und Ziel der Geschichte*. Zürich: Artemis Verlag. Tr. Michael Bullock 1953. *On the Origin and Goal of History*. New Haven: Yale University Press.

———. 1949b. Die Achsenzeit der Weltgeschichte. *Der Monat* 2.6: 3–9.

Justi, Ferdinand. 1895. *Iranisches Namenbuch*. Marburg: N. G. Elwert.

Justinus, tr. J. S. Watson. 1853. Epitome of Pompeius Trogus' *Philippic Histories*. Books 1 and 2. See Watson (1853).

Kanga, M. F. 1988. Barsom. *Encyclopædia Iranica*, online.

Karlgren, Bernhard. 1957. *Grammata Serica Recensa*. Stockholm: Museum of Far Eastern Antiquities. (= Kar.)

Kaufman, Stephen A. and Joseph Fitzmyer, et al. 2005 et seq. *The Comprehensive Aramaic Lexicon*. Cincinnati: Hebrew Union College, online. (= *CAL*)

Keightley, David N. 1999. The Shang: China's First Historical Dynasty. In: Michael Loewe and Edward L. Shaughnessy, eds. *The Cambridge History of Ancient China: From the Origins of Civilization to 221* B.C. Cambridge: Cambridge University Press, 232–291.

Kellens, Jean. 1989. Avestique. In: R. Schmitt, ed. *Compendium Linguarum Iranicarum*. Wiesbaden: Reichert, 32–55.

———. 1998. Considérations sur l'histoire de l'Avesta. *Journal Asiatique* 286.2: 451–519.

———. 2012. Avesta i. Survey of the History and Contents of the Book. *Encyclopædia Iranica*, online.

———. 2015. The *Gāthās*, Said to Be of Zarathustra. In: Michael Stausberg and Yuhan Sohrab-Dinshaw Vevaina, eds. *The Wiley Blackwell Companion to Zoroastrianism*. Chichester: John Wiley & Sons, 44–50.

Kent, Roland G. 1950. *Old Persian: Grammar, Texts, Lexicon*. New Haven: American Oriental Society.

Kern, Martin. 2000. *The Stele Inscriptions of Ch'in shih-huang: Text and Ritual in Early Chinese Imperial Representation*. New Haven: American Oriental Society.

———. 2007. Imperial Tours and Mountain Inscriptions. In: Jane Portal and Hiromi Kinoshita, eds. *The First Emperor: China's Terracotta Army*. London: British Museum, 104–113.

Khazanov, Anatoly M. 2014. The Scythians and Their Neighbors. In: Reuven Amitai et al., eds. *Nomads as Agents of Cultural Change: The Mongols and Their Eurasian Predecessors*. Honolulu: University of Hawaii Press, 32–49.

———. 2016. Notes on the Scythian Political Culture. In: István Zimonyi and Osman Karatay, eds. *Central Eurasia in the Middle Ages: Studies in Honour of Peter B. Golden*. Wiesbaden: Harrassowitz, 171–188.

———. 2019. Steppe Nomads in the Eurasian Trade. *Chungara Revista de Antropología Chilena* 51.1: 85–93.

Kindstrand, Jan Fredrik. 1981. *Anacharsis, the Legend and the Apophthegmata*. Uppsala: Acta Universitatis Upsaliensis.

Kingsley, Peter. 1990. The Greek Origin of the Sixth-Century Dating of Zoroaster. *Bulletin of the School of Oriental and African Studies* 53.2: 245–265.

———. 1995. Meetings with Magi: Iranian Themes among the Greeks, from Xanthus of Lydia to Plato's Academy. *Journal of the Royal Asiatic Society*, 3rd ser., 5.2: 173–209.

Kiyose, Gisaburo N. and Christopher I. Beckwith. 2008. The Origin of the Old Japanese Twelve Animal Cycle. *Arutaigo kenkyû—Altaistic Studies* 2: 1–18.

Kōno, Rokurō (河野六郎). 1987. 百済語の二重語性 [Kudarago no nijūgosei]. In: Nakagiri sensei no kiju o kinen suru kai, ed. *Chōsen no kobunka ronsan: Nakagiri sensei no kiju kinen ronshū*. Tokyo: Kokusho Kankōkai, 81–94. English translation, 1987: The Bilingualism of the Paekche Language. *Memoirs of the Research Department of the Toyo Bunko* 45: 75–86.

Kuhrt, Amélie. 2007. *The Persian Empire*. 2 Vols. London: Routledge.

Kuzmina, E. E. 2007. *The Origin of the Indo-Iranians*. Leiden: Brill.

Lanfranchi, G. B. and Michael Roaf, Robert Rollinger, eds. 2003. *Continuity of Empire (?). Assyria, Media, Persia. Proceedings of the International Meeting in Padua, 26th–28th April 2001*. History of the Ancient Near East Monographs V. Padova: S.a.r.g.o.n. editrice e libreria.

Lecoq, Pierre. 1987. Le mot *farnah-* et les Scythes. *Comptes rendus des séances de l'Académie des Inscriptions et Belles-Lettres* 131.4: 671–682.

———. 1997. *Les inscriptions de la Perse achéménide*. Paris: Gallimard.

Legge, James. 1893/1985. *The Chinese Classics*. Vol. 5. *The Ch'un ts'ew with the Tso chuen*. Taipei: Southern Materials Center (reprint of the Shanghai 1935 revised edition).

Legrand, Philippe-Ernest, ed. and trans. 1932–1954. *Hérodote: Histoires*. Paris: Les Belles Lettres.

Lenfant, Dominique, ed. and trans. 2004. *Ctesias. La Perse: l'Inde; autres fragments. Collection des universités de France. Série grecque*, v. 435. Paris: Les Belles Lettres.

Leongue, Vitor. 2018. Structural Evolution of the Tibetan Syllable: A Cross-Dialectal Study. Ph.D. dissertation, Indiana University, Bloomington.

Lewis, Mark Edward. 1999. Warring States Political History. In: Michael Loewe and Edward L. Shaughnessy, eds. *The Cambridge History of Ancient China: From the Origins of Civilization to 221 B.C.* Cambridge: Cambridge University Press, 587–650.

Li, Jaang and Zhouyong Sun, Jing Shao, Min Li. 2018. When Peripheries Were Centres: A Preliminary Study of the Shimao-Centred Polity in the Loess Highland, China. *Antiquity* 92.364: 1008–1022.

Liddell, H. and R. Scott, H. Jones. 1968. *Greek-English Lexicon*. 9th ed. Oxford: Clarendon. (=*LSJ*)

Ligeti, L. 1950. Mots de civilisation de Haute Asie en transcription. *Acta Orientalia Academiae Scientiarum Hungaricae* 1: 141–188.

Lincoln, Bruce. 1991. *Death, War, and Sacrifice: Studies in Ideology and Practice*. Chicago: University of Chicago Press.

———. 2012. *'Happiness for Mankind': Achaemenian Religion and the Imperial Project*. Leuven: Peeters.

Liu, Xiaogan (劉笑敢). 1997. 老子 [*Lao-tzu*]. Taipei: Tung-ta t'u-shu kung-si. 2nd rev. ed. 2005.

Loewe, Michael. 1999. The Heritage Left to the Empires. In: Michael Loewe and Edward L. Shaughnessy, eds. *The Cambridge History of Ancient China: From the Origins of Civilization to 221 B.C.* Cambridge: Cambridge University Press, 967–1032.

Lubotsky, Alexander. 2002. Scythian Elements in Old Iranian. In: Nicholas Sims-Williams, ed. *Indo-Iranian Languages and Peoples*. Oxford: Oxford University Press. *Proceedings of the British Academy* 116: 189–202.

Mair, Victor. 1990. *Tao te ching: The Classic Book of Integrity and the Way, by Lao Tzu*. New York: Bantam.

———. 2013. *Was There a Xia Dynasty?* Sino-Platonic Papers 238. Philadelphia: University of Pennsylvania.

Malandra, W. W. 2009. Zoroaster ii. General Survey. *Encyclopædia Iranica*, online.

Mallory, J. P. and D. Q. Adams, eds. 1997. *Encyclopedia of Indo-European Culture*. London: Fitzroy Dearborn.

Martin, R. P. 1996. The Scythian Accent: Anacharsis and the Cynics. In: R. Bracht-Branham and Marie-Odile Goulet-Cazé, eds. *The Cynics: The Cynic Movement in Antiquity and Its Legacy*. Berkeley: University of California Press, 136–155.

Martin, Samuel. 1987. *The Japanese Language through Time*. New Haven: Yale University Press.

May, Walter, trans. John Colarusso and Tamirlan Salbiev, eds. 2016. *Tales of the Narts: Ancient Myths and Legends of the Ossetians*. Princeton: Princeton University Press.

Mayrhofer, Manfred. 1968. Die Rekonstruktion des Medischen. *Anzeiger der Österreichische Akademie der Wissenschaften, Philosophisch-Historische Klasse* 105.1: 1–22.

———. 1992. *Etymologisches Wörterbuch des Altindoarischen*. 1 Band. Heidelberg: Carl Winter Universitätsverlag.

———. 2006. *Einiges zu den Skythen, ihrer Sprache, ihrem Nachleben*. Österreichische Akademie der Wissenschaften, Philosophisch-historische Klasse, Sitzungsberichte, 742. Band. Wien: Verlag der Österreichischen Akademie der Wissenschaften.

Meillet, Antoine. 1925. *La méthode comparative en linguistique historique*. Oslo: Aschehoug, reprinted Paris: Champion, 1984; tr. Gordon B. Ford Jr. 1967. *The Comparative Method in Historical Linguistics*. Paris: Champion.

Meillet, Antoine and Émile Benveniste. 1931. *Grammaire du vieux-perse*. 2nd ed. Paris: Champion.

Mertens, Matthias. 2019. Did Richthofen Really Coin "the Silk Road"? *The Silk Road* 17: 1–9.

Miller, Margaret Christina. 2004. *Athens and Persia in the Fifth Century BC: A Study in Cultural Receptivity*. Revised edition. Cambridge: Cambridge University Press.

Miyazaki, Ichisada (宮崎市定). 1977–1978. 中国史 [*Chūgoku-shi*]. Reprinted 1993, 2 Vols. Tokyo: Iwanami.

Molè, Gabriella. 1970. *The T'u-yü-hun from the Northern Wei to the Time of the Five Dynasties*. Rome: Istituto Italiano per il medio ed estremo oriente.

Monier-Williams, Monier. 1899. *A Sanskrit-English Dictionary, Etymologically and Philologically Arranged, with Special Reference to Cognate Indo-European Languages*. New edition. Oxford: Clarendon. Reprinted: Delhi: Motilal Banarsidass, 1988. Online edition.

Murray, Oswyn. 2001. Herodotus and Oral History. In: Nino Luraghi, ed. *The Historian's Craft in the Age of Herodotus*. Oxford: Oxford University Press.

Naveh, Joseph and Shaul Shaked. 2012. *Aramaic Documents from Ancient Bactria (Fourth Century B.C.E.): From the Khalili Collections*. London: The Khalili Family Trust.

Nichols, Johanna. 1997a. The Epicentre of the Indo-European Linguistic Spread. In: Roger Blench and Matthew Spriggs, eds. *Archaeology and Language I: Theoretical and Methodological Orientations*. London: Routledge, 122–148.

———. 1997b. Modeling Ancient Population Structures and Movement in Linguistics. *Annual Review of Anthropology* 26: 359–384.

Nickel, Lukas. 2013. The First Emperor and Sculpture in China. *Bulletin of the School of Oriental and African Studies, University of London* 76.3: 413–447.

Nivison, David Shepherd. 1999. The Classical Philosophical Writings. In: Michael Loewe and Edward L. Shaughnessy, eds. *The Cambridge History of Ancient China: From the Origins of Civilization to 221 B.C.* Cambridge: Cambridge University Press.

Ollapally, Deepa. 2021. The Fallacy of a Taliban Strong State. *Rising Power Initiative Policy Commentary*. August 27, online.

Omodaka, Hisataka (澤瀉久孝), et al. 1967. 時代別国語大辞典, 上代編 [*Jidaibetsu kokugo daijiten, jōdaihen*]. Tokyo: Sanseido. (= *JDB*)

Oppenheim, A. Leo and Erica Reiner, et al. 1964–2006. *The Assyrian Dictionary of the Oriental Institute of the University of Chicago*. Chicago: Oriental Institute. (= *CAD*)

Özçelik, Öner. Forthcoming. Kazakh Phonology. In: Lars Johanson, ed. *Encyclopedia of Turkic Languages*. Leiden: Brill.

Özçelik, Öner and Rex Sprouse. 2017. Emergent Knowledge of a Universal Phonological Principle in the L2 Acquisition of Vowel Harmony in Turkish: A 'Four'-fold Poverty of the Stimulus in L2 Acquisition. *Second Language Research* 33: 179–206.

Parpola, Simo. 2003. Sakas, India, Gobyras, and the Median Royal Court: Xenophon's Cyropaedia through the Eyes of an Assyriologist. In: G. B. Lanfranchi, Michael Roaf, and Robert Rollinger, eds. *Continuity of Empire (?). Assyria, Media, Persia. Proceedings of the International Meeting in Padua, 26th–28th April 2001*. History of the Ancient Near East Monographs V. Padova: S.a.r.g.o.n. editrice e libreria, 339–350.

Pelliot, Paul. 1912. Les noms tibétains des T'ou-yu-houen et des Ouigours. *Journal Asiatique* sér. 10, tome 20: 520–523.

———. 1934. Tokharien et Koutchéen. *Journal Asiatique* 224.1: 23–106.

Perry, John R. 1998. A Review of the 'Encyclopaedia Iranica'. *Iranian Studies* 31.3/4: 517–525.

Pollock, Sheldon. 2006. *The Language of the Gods in the World of Men: Sanskrit, Culture, and Power in Premodern India*. Berkeley: University of California Press.

Potts, D. T. 2005. Cyrus the Great and the Kingdom of Anshan. In: Vesta Sarkhosh Curtis and Sarah Stewart, eds. *Birth of the Persian Empire*. Vol. 1. London: I. B. Tauris, 7–28.

Pulleyblank, Edwin G. 1984. *Middle Chinese: A Study in Historical Phonology*. Vancouver: University of British Columbia Press.

———. 1991a. *Lexicon of Reconstructed Pronunciation in Early Middle Chinese, Late Middle Chinese, and Early Mandarin*. Vancouver: University of British Columbia Press. (= Pul.)

———. 1991b. Ch'ien Han Shu. *Encyclopædia Iranica*, online.

———. 1999. The Peoples of the Steppe Frontier in Early Chinese Sources. *Migracijske teme* 15.1–2: 35–61.

Rackham, H. 1934. *Aristotle in 23 Volumes*. Vol. 19. Cambridge, MA: Harvard University Press.

Razmjou, Shahrokh. 2005. Religion and Burial Customs. In: J. E. Curtis and N. Tallis, eds. *Forgotten Empire: The World of Ancient Persia*. London: The British Museum Press, 150–180.

Reade, Julian. 2003. Why Did the Medes Invade Assyria? In: G. B. Lanfranchi, Michael Roaf, and Robert Rollinger, eds. 2003. *Continuity of Empire (?). Assyria, Media, Persia. Proceedings of the International Meeting in Padua, 26th–28th April 2001*. History of the Ancient Near East Monographs V. Padova: S.a.r.g.o.n. editrice e libreria, 149–156.

Robin, Léon. 1948. *La pensée grecque et les origines de l'esprit scientifique*. Éd. rev. Paris: A. Michel.

Rolle, Renate. 1989. *The World of the Scythians*. Berkeley: University of California Press (translation of *Die Welt der Skythen*. Luzern: C. J. Bucher, 1980).

Rosenthal, Franz. 2006. *A Grammar of Biblical Aramaic*. 7th ed. Wiesbaden: Harrassowitz.

Rossi, Adriano V. 2010. Elusive Identities in Pre-Achaemenid Iran: The Medes and the Median Language. In: Carlo G. Cereti et al., eds. *Iranian Identity in the Course of History: Proceedings of the Conference Held in Rome, 21–24 September 2005*. Serie Orientale Roma CV, Orientalia Romana IX. Rome: Istituto Italiano per l'Africa e l'Oriente, 289–329.

Schafer, Edward H. 1963. *The Golden Peaches of Samarkand: A Study of T'ang Exotics*. Berkeley: University of California Press.

Schmid, Stephan G. 2013. Foucault and the Nabataeans: Or What Space Has to Do with It. In: M. Mouton and Stephan G. Schmid, eds. *Men on the Rocks: The Formation of Nabataean Petra. Proceedings of a Conference Held in Berlin, 2–4 December 2011*. Berlin: Logos, 251–269.

Schmidt, Erich F. 1953. *Persepolis*. Vol. 1. Chicago: University of Chicago Press.

———. 1970. *Persepolis III: The Royal Tombs and Other Monuments*. Oriental Institute Publications. Vol. 70. Chicago: University of Chicago Press.

Schmidt, Hanns-Peter. 2006. "Mithra." *Encyclopædia Iranica*, online.

Schmitt, Rüdiger. 1967. Medisches und persisches Sprachgut bei Herodot. *Zeitschrift der Deutschen Morgenländischen Gesellschaft* 117.1: 119–145.

———. 1976. Der Titel 'Satrap'. In: A. Morpurgo Davies and W. Meid, eds. *Studies in Greek, Italic and Indo-European Linguistics Offered to Leonard R. Palmer on the Occasion of His Seventieth Birthday, June 5, 1976*. Innsbruck: Innsbrucker Beiträge zur Sprachwissenschaft Bd. 16: 373–390.

———. 1984. Perser und Persisches in der alten attischen Komödie. In: *Orientalia J. Duchesne-Guillemin Emerito Oblata*. Leiden: *Acta Iranica* 23: 459–472.

———. 1989. Altiranische Sprachen im Überblick. In: R. Schmitt, ed. *Compendium Linguarum Iranicarum*. Wiesbaden: Reichert, 25–31.

———. 1990. Candys. *Encyclopædia Iranica,* online.

———. 1997. Onomastica Iranica Symmicta. In: R. Ambrosini et al., eds. *Scríbthair a ainm n-ogaim*. Vol. 2. Pisa: Pacini Editore, 921–927.

———. 2002. Zoroaster i. The Name. *Encyclopædia Iranica,* online.

———. 2003. Die skythischen Personennamen bei Herodot. *Annali, Università degli Studi di Napoli "L'Orientale"* 63: 1–31.

———. 2004. Haumavargā. *Encyclopædia Iranica,* online.

———. 2009. *Die altpersischen Inschriften der Achaimeniden*. Wiesbaden: Reichert.

———. 2010. Review of Grantovskij 2007 (second, expanded edition of Grantovskij 1970). *Abstracta Iranica,* online.

———. 2011a. Aryan. *Encyclopædia Iranica,* online.

———. 2011b. Astyages. *Encyclopædia Iranica,* online.

———. 2011c. Deioces. *Encyclopædia Iranica,* online.

———. 2011d. Achaemenid Dynasty. *Encyclopædia Iranica,* online.

———. 2012a. Aria. *Encyclopædia Iranica,* online.

———. 2012b. Hesiod. *Encyclopædia Iranica,* online.

———. 2012c. Greece xii. Persian Loanwords and Names in Greek. *Encyclopædia Iranica,* online.

———. 2012d. Protothyes. *Encyclopædia Iranica,* online.

———. 2014. *Wörterbuch der altpersischen Königsinschriften*. Wiesbaden: Reichert. (= Sch.)

———. 2015. Herodotus as Practitioner of Iranian Anthroponomastics? *Glotta* 91: 250–263.

———. 2018. Scythian Language. *Encyclopædia Iranica,* online.

Sextus Empiricus. 2005. *Adversus mathematicos*. Tr. Richard Bett, *Sextus Empiricus: Against the Logicians*. Cambridge: Cambridge University Press.

Shahbazi, Shapur. 1992. Clothing ii. In the Median and Achaemenid Periods. *Encyclopædia Iranica,* online, revised 2011.

———. 1994. Darius iii. Darius the Great. *Encyclopædia Iranica,* online, revised 2012.

Shaughnessy, Edward L. 2005. The Guodian Manuscripts and Their Place in Twentieth-Century Historiography on the "Laozi". *Harvard Journal of Asiatic Studies* 65.2: 417–457.

Shen, Yüeh (沈約). 1974. 宋書 [*Sung Shu*]. Peking: Chung-hua shu-chü.

Shimunek, Andrew E. 2017a. *Languages of Ancient Southern Mongolia and North China: A Historical-Comparative Study of the Serbi or Xianbei Branch of the Serbi-Mongolic Language Family, with an Analysis of Northeastern Frontier Chinese and Old Tibetan Phonology*. Wiesbaden: Harrassowitz.

———. 2017b. An Old Chinese Word for 'Silk' in Mongolic, Turkic, Tungusic, and Persian. *Eurasian Studies* 15.1: 142–151.

———. 2021. Loanwords from the Puyo-Koguryoic Languages of Early Korea and Manchuria in Jurchen-Manchu. *Altai Hakpo* 31: 65–84.

Shimunek, Andrew E. and Christopher I. Beckwith. Forthcoming. *Mūga* (*al-Mūjah*) and *Mānk*: Variants of the Pre-Imperial Mongol Ethnonym in a 9th Century Passage in the 10th Century *Akhbār al-Ṣīn wa al-Hind* and Parallel Texts. (under review)

Shimunek, Andrew E. and Christopher I. Beckwith, Jonathan North Washington, Nicholas Kontovas, Kurban Niyaz. 2015. The Earliest Attested Turkic Language: The Chieh 羯 (*Kɨr) Language of the Fourth Century A.D. *Journal Asiatique* 303.1: 143–151.

Shiratori, Kurakichi. 1929. On the Territory of the Hsiung-nu Prince Hsiu-Tu-Wang and His Metal Statues for Heaven Worship. *Memoirs of the Research Department of the Toyo Bunko* 36.4–8: 1–77.

Sims-Williams, Nicholas. 1988. Bactrian Language. *Encyclopædia Iranica*, online, revised 2011.

———. 1997. New Findings in Ancient Afghanistan—The Bactrian Documents Discovered from the Northern Hindu-Kush. www.gengo.l.u-tokyo.ac.jp/~hkum/bactrian.html.

———. 1999–2012. *Bactrian Documents from Northern Afghanistan*. 3 Vols. Oxford: Oxford University Press.

———. 2001. The Sogdian Ancient Letter II. In: *Philologica et linguistica: Historia, pluralitas, universitas: Festschrift für Helmut Humbach zum 80. Geburtstag am 4. Dezember 2001*. Trier: Wissenschaftlicher Verlag Trier, 267–280.

———. 2004. The Bactrian Inscription of Rabatak: A New Reading. *Bulletin of the Asia Institute*, new ser., 18: 53–68.

Sinor, Denis. 1990. The Hun Period. In: Denis Sinor, ed. *The Cambridge History of Early Inner Asia*. Cambridge: Cambridge University Press, 177–205.

Skjærvø, Prods Oktor. 1983. Farnah: mot mède en vieux-perse? *Bulletin de la Société linguistique de Paris* 78: 241–259.

———. 1995. Aramaic in Iran. *Aram* 7: 283–318.

———. 1999. Avestan Quotations in Old Persian? Literary Sources of the Old Persian Inscriptions. In: *Irano-Judaica IV: Studies Relating to Jewish Contacts with Persian Culture throughout the Ages*. Jerusalem: Ben-Zvi Institute, 1–64.

———. 2005. The Achaemenids and the Avesta. In: Vesta Sarkhosh Curtis and Sarah Stewart, eds. *Birth of the Persian Empire*. London: I. B. Tauris, 52–84.

———. 2006. Iran vi. Iranian Languages and Scripts (1) Earliest Evidence. *Encyclopædia Iranica*, online.

———. 2014. Achaemenid Religion. *Religion Compass* 8/6: 175–187.

Soudavar, Abolala. 2010. The Formation of Achaemenid Imperial Ideology and Its Impact on the Avesta. In: John Curtis and St John Simpson, eds. 2010. *The World of Achaemenid Persia*. London: I. B. Tauris, 111–138.

Ssu-ma Ch'ien (司馬遷). 1959. 史記 [*Shih chi*]. Peking: Chung-hua shu-chü.

Ssu-ma Ch'ien, trans. and ed. William H. Nienhauser Jr. 2010. *The Grand Scribe's Records*. Vol. 9. *The Memoirs of Han China, Part II*. Bloomington: Indiana University Press.

Starostin, Sergei A. 1989. Реконструкция древнекитайской фонологической системы [Rekonstrukcija drevnekitajskoj fonologičeskoj sistemy]. Moscow: Nauka. (= Sta.)

Starr, Ivan, et al. 1990. *Queries to the Sungod: Divination and Politics in Sargonid Assyria*. State Archives of Assyria. Vol. 4. Helsinki: Helsinki University Press.

Stronk, Jan P. 2010. *Ctesias' Persian History*. Part 1. Düsseldorf: Wellem.

Struve, V. V., et al. 1965. *Corpus inscriptionum Regni Bosporani*. Moscow: Nauka.

Stuttard, David. 2018. *Nemesis: Alcibiades and the Fall of Athens*. Cambridge, MA: Harvard University Press.

Szemerényi, Oswald J. L. 1980. *Four Old Iranian Ethnic Names: Scythian—Skudra—Sogdian—Saka*. Österreichischen Akademie der Wissenschaften, Philosophisch-Historische Klasse, Sitzungsberichte, 371 Band. Vienna: Verlag der Österreichischen Akademie der Wissenschaften.

———. 1991. *Scripta Minora: Selected Essays in Indo-European, Greek, and Latin*. Vol. 4. *Indo-European Languages Other than Latin and Greek*. Innsbruck: Innsbrucker Beiträge zur Sprachwissenschaft.

Taillieu, Dieter. 2003. Haoma i. Botany. *Encyclopædia Iranica*, online, revised 2012.

Takata, Tokio (高田時雄). 1988. 敦煌資料による中国語史の研究 [Tonkō shiryō ni yoru Chūgokugoshi no kenkyū]. *A Historical Study of the Chinese Language Based on Dunhuang Materials*. Tokyo: Sobunsha. (= Tak.)

———. 2000. Multilingualism in Tun-huang. *Acta Asiatica, Bulletin of the Institute of Eastern Culture* 78: 49–70.

———. 2010. *Khumdan* 的對音. In: 張廣達先生八十華誕祝壽論文集 [Chang Kuang-ta hsien-sheng pa-shih hua-tan chu-shou lun-wen-chi]. Taipei: Hsin wen-feng ch'u-pan kung-ssu, 965–973.

Tavernier, J. 2007. *Iranica in the Achaemenid Period (ca. 550–330 B.C.): Lexicon of Old Iranian Proper Names and Loanwords, Attested in Non-Iranian Texts*. Orientalia Lovaniensia analecta 158. Leuven: Peeters. (= Tav.)

Taylor, Timothy. 2021. The Arrogation of Slavery: Prehistory, Archaeology, and Pre-Theoretical Commitments Concerning People as Property. In: Felix Biermann and Marek Jankowiak, eds. *The Archaeology of Slavery in Early Medieval Northern Europe: The Invisible Commodity*. Themes in Contemporary Archaeology. Cham: Springer, 7–19.

Taylor, Timothy and Christine M. Havlicek, Christopher I. Beckwith. 2020. The Scythian Empire: Reassessing Steppe Power from Western and Eastern Perspectives. In: St John Simpson and Svetlana Pankova, eds. *Masters of the Steppe: The Impact of the Scythians and Later Nomad Societies of Eurasia. Proceedings of a Conference Held at the British Museum, 27–29 October 2017*. Oxford: Archaeopress, 616–626.

Tekin, Talat. 1968. *A Grammar of Orkhon Turkic*. Uralic and Altaic Series Vol. 69. Bloomington: Indiana University.

Thompson, G. 1965. Iranian Dress in the Achaemenian Period: Problems Concerning the *Kandys* and Other Garments. *Iran* 3: 121–126.

Tokhtas'ev, Sergei R. 2012. Cimmerians. *Encyclopædia Iranica*, online.

Tuplin, Christopher J. 2005. Medes in Media, Mesopotamia and Anatolia: Empire, Hegemony, Devolved Domination or Illusion? *Ancient West and East* 3: 223–251.

Turchin, Peter. 2012. Religion and Empire in the Axial Age. *Religion, Brain & Behavior* 2.3: 256–260.

Vallat, François. 2013. Darius the Great King. In Jean Perrot, ed. *The Palace of Darius at Susa: The Great Royal Residence of Achaemenid Persia*. London: I. B. Tauris, 29–48.

Vasmer, Max. 1923. *Untersuchungen über die ältesten Wohnsitze der Slaven: Die Iranier in Südrußland*. Leipzig: Markert & Petters.

Vladimirtsov, Boris Jakovlevič. 1934. Общественный строй монголов: Монгольский кочевой феодализм. Leningrad: Akademija Nauk SSSR. Tr. Michel Carsow, 1948: *Le régime social des Mongols: Le féodalisme nomade*. Paris: Maisonneuve.

Vogelsang, Willem J. 1992. *The Rise and Organization of the Achaemenid Empire: The Eastern Iranian Evidence*. Leiden: Brill.

———. 1998. Medes, Scythians and Persians: The Rise of Darius in a North-South Perspective. *Iranica Antiqua* 33: 195–224.

von Bredow, Iris. 2006. Borysthenes. *Brill's New Pauly*, online.

Wagensonner, Klaus. 2017. *Sargon's Birth Legend*. University of Oxford: A Library of Knowledge of the Cuneiform Digital Library Initiative. http://cdli.ox.ac.uk/wiki/doku.php?id=sargon_birth_legend.

Walser, G. 1966. *Die Völkerschaften auf den Reliefs von Persepolis: Historische Studien über den sogenannten Tributzug an der Apadanatreppe*. Berlin: Mann.

Walter, Michael L. 2013. "All That Glitters *Is* Gold": The Place of the Yellow Metal in the Brahmanic, Scythian, and Early Buddhist Traditions. In: Franz-Karl Ehrhard and Petra Maurer, eds. *Nepalica-Tibetica: Festgabe for Christoph Cüppers*. Vol. 2. Andiast: International Institute for Tibetan and Buddhist Studies, 283–298.

Waters, Matthew W. 1999. The Earliest Persians in Southwestern Iran: The Textual Evidence. *Iranian Studies* 32.1: 99–107.

———. 2004. Cyrus and the Achaemenids. *Iran* 42: 91–102.

Watkins, Calvert. 1995. *How to Kill a Dragon: Aspects of Indo-European Poetics*. New York: Oxford University Press.

———. 2011. *The American Heritage Dictionary of Indo-European Roots*. 3rd ed. Boston: Houghton Mifflin.

Watson, Burton. 1961. *Records of the Grand Historian of China*. Translated from the *Shih chi* of Ssu-ma Ch'ien by Burton Watson. 2 Vols. New York: Columbia University Press.

———. 1968. *The Complete Works of Chuang Tzu*. New York: Columbia University Press.

Watson, J. S., trans. 1853. Justinus, Epitome of Pompeius Trogus' *Philippic Histories*. Books 1 and 2. http://www.attalus.org/translate/justin8.html#1.1.

Weissbach, F. H. 1911. *Die Keilinschriften der Achämeniden*. Leipzig: J. C. Hinrichs'sche Buchhandlung.

Whitman, John. 1990. A Rule of Medial *-r- Loss in Pre–Old Japanese. In: Philip Baldi, ed. *Linguistic Change and Reconstruction Methodology*. Berlin: Mouton de Gruyter, 511–545.

Widengren, Geo. 1956. Some Remarks on Riding Costume and Articles of Dress among Iranian Peoples in Antiquity. *Arctica. Studia Ethnographica Upsaliensia* 11: 228–276.

———. 1969. *Der Feudalismus im alten Iran*. Köln-Opladen: Westdeutscher Verlag.

Wittrock, Björn. 2005. The Meaning of the Axial Age. In: Johann P. Arnason, S. N. Eisenstadt, and Björn Wittrock, eds. *Axial Civilizations and World History*. Leiden: Brill, 51–85.

Witzel, Michael. 2011. Gandhāra and the Formation of the Vedic and Zoroastrian Canons. In *Travaux de Symposium international: Le livre. La Roumanie. L'Europe: Troisième édition—20 à 24 Septembre 2010*. Bucharest: Éditeur Bibliothèque de Bucarest, 490–532.

———. 2014. Mitanni Indo-Aryan Mazda and the date of the Ṛgveda. In DN Jha, ed. *The Complex Heritage of Early India. Essays in memory of R. S. Sharma*. New Delhi: Manohar, 73–96.

Wu, Fu-chu (吳福助). 1994. 秦始皇刻石考 [Ch'in shih huang k'e shih k'ao]. Taipei: Wen-shih-che ch'u-pan-she.

Young, T. Cuyler. 1988. The Early History of the Medes and the Persians and the Achaemenid Empire to the Death of Cambyses. In J. Boardman et al., eds. *The Cambridge Ancient History*. 2nd ed. Vol. 4. *Persia, Greece and the Western Mediterranean c. 525 to 479* B.C. Cambridge: Cambridge University Press, 1–52.

Zawadzki, Stefan. 1988. *The Fall of Assyria and Median-Babylonian Relations in Light of the Nabopolassar Chronicle*. Poznan: Adam Mickiewicz University Press.

Zhengzhang, Shangfang. 1991. Decipherment of Yue-Ren-Ge (Song of the Yue Boatman). *Cahiers de linguistique Asie Orientale* 2: 159–168.

Zlotnick-Sivan, H. 2004. Moses the Persian? Exodus 2, the 'Other' and Biblical 'Mnemohistory'. *Zeitschrift für die alttestamentliche Wissenschaft* 116.2: 189–205.

Zürcher, Edmond. 2007. *The Buddhist Conquest of China: The Spread and Adaptation of Buddhism in Early Medieval China*. 3rd ed. Leiden: Brill.

ILLUSTRATION CREDITS

1. Western Steppe Scythian stringing the Cimmerian bow. Kul-Oba bowl. Hermitage. Photograph by Joanbanjo, 2011.
2. Western Steppe Scythian scene of medical treatment showing the Cimmerian bow and *gorytos*. © The State Hermitage Museum, St. Petersburg.
3. Mede in *bashlyq* headgear with *akinakes* short sword, holding *barsom*. Oxus Treasure. British Museum. Photograph by MarisaLR, 2010.
4. Scythian *sagaris* battle-axe, detail from a Greek vase by Euphronios. Louvre G106. © Campana Collection 1861. Photo by Bibi Saint-Pol.
5. Scythian archer. Louvre F126. Campana Collection, 1861. Photo by Bibi Saint-Pol, 2008.
6. Pointed-cap Scythians bearing tribute of footies and *candys*. Persepolis, Audience Hall of Darius I, E. Stairs. ART73188. Photo credit: © Bridgeman-Giraudon/Art Resource, NY.
7. Medes in Scytho-Mede court outfit and weapons and Persians in Perso-Elamite court outfit and weapons. Persepolis, Apadana N. Stairs. © Livius.org. Photo by Jona Lendering, detail.
8. Late Achaemenid man in Mede riding dress. Detail of Alexander Sarcophagus (showing Alexander in the Battle of Issus, 333 BC). Photograph by Ronald Slabke, 2012.
9. Neo-Assyrian period Median tribute bearer to Sargon II. Detail of a relief in Room 10 of Sargon's palace at Dur-Šarruken, Louvre AO 19887. Photo by Karen Radner. https://www.ucl.ac.uk/sargon/essentials/countries/themedes/
10. Neo-Assyrian period Assyrian archers attacking an enemy town, reign of Tiglath Pileser III (730–727 BC). British Museum. Photo by Mary Harrsch.
11. Scytho-Medes in *candys* with weapons and Persians in Perso-Elamite outfits (Persepolis, Apadana E. Stairs). Photo by Bontenbal, 2011.
12. Achaemenid period Magi in *candys* and *bashlyq* with *barsoms* before a sacrificial sheep and bull, from Dascylium, ca. 520–330 BC. Istanbul, Arkeoloji Müzesi. © Livius.org. Photograph by Jona Lendering. https://www.livius.org/pictures/turkey/ergili-dascylium/dascylium-magians/

13. Early Han Dynasty period mounted archer in footies and *bashlyq* (tomb figurine). Photo: Anthony Deprez, © The Avantiques Collection.
14. Darius III wearing Late Achaemenid royal *bashlyq*. Alexander Mosaic, Pompeii. Naples National Archaeological Museum. Photo by Berthold Werner, 2013.
15. The Persian Empire's throne-bearers in their national costumes. Naqš-i Rustam. Drawing © G. Walser (1966), detail.

INDEX

Note: Unspecified common nouns refer to Scythian or Creole Scythian cultures.

A NOTE ON THE TYPE

This book has been composed in Arno, an Old-style serif typeface in the classic Venetian tradition, designed by Robert Slimbach at Adobe.